C000244401

Geoff Lambert

THE CORN SUPPLY OF ANCIENT ROME

THE CORN SUPPLY OF ANCIENT ROME

GEOFFREY RICKMAN

CLARENDON PRESS · OXFORD

Oxford University Press, Walton Street, Oxford OX2 6DP
Oxford New York
Athens Auckland Bangkok Bogota Bombay
Buenos Aires Calcutta Cape Town Dar es Salaam
Delhi Florence Hong Kong Istanbul Karachi
Kuala Lumpur Madras Madrid Melbourne
Mexico City Nairobi Paris Singapore
Taipei Tokyo Toronto
and associated companies in
Berlin Ibadan

Oxford is a trade mark of Oxford University Press

© G. E. Rickman 1980

First published by Oxford University Press 1980
Special edition for Sandpiper Books Ltd, 1996

All rights reserved. No part of this publication may be reproduced, stored in a retrieval system, or transmitted, in any form or by any means, without the prior permission in writing of Oxford University Press. Within the UK, exceptions are allowed in respect of any fair dealing for the purpose of research or private study, or criticism or review, as permitted under the Copyright, Designs and Patents Act, 1988, or in the case of reprographic reproduction in accordance with the terms of the licences issued by the Copyright Licensing Agency. Enquiries concerning reproduction outside these terms and in other countries should be sent to the Rights Department, Oxford University Press, at the address above

British Library Cataloguing in Publication Data
Rickman, Geoffrey
The corn supply of ancient Rome.
1. Wheat trade—Rome 2. Food supply—Rome
I. Title
339.4'8'633110937 HF377 79-42924
ISBN 0-19-814838-0

Printed in Great Britain by
Bookcraft Ltd.,
Midsomer Norton, Somerset

For E.R.M.R., E.J.R., and D.E.R.

PREFACE

This book is a history of the corn supply of ancient Rome. The subject has interested me ever since I was an undergraduate, when I often felt impatient with the traditional topics on which I was asked by kindly tutors to write essays. It was an undeniable exhilaration, in the words of Louis MacNeice, 'to draw the cork out of an old conundrum and watch the paradoxes fizz', but what I wanted to know was how the ancient world really worked. A quarter of a century later I have learned from experience how difficult that aim is to achieve but the desire is still in me. My work on *Roman Granaries and Store Buildings*, published in 1971, led naturally to this attempt at a wider survey of Rome's corn supply, just as Professor Pavis D'Escurac's recent book, *La Préfecture de l'annone d'Auguste à Constantin* grew out of her earlier unpublished thesis on the storebuildings of Rome, Ostia and Portus. Friends will bear witness that I am no farmer's boy; on the contrary I am rather an urban type. But I have always been intensely aware of the pattern of services and support which have allowed me to lead the kind of urban life I prefer. To understand how Rome worked as a great city in antiquity one of the vital threads is to see how she fed herself, yet there has been no full-scale study of this topic in English.

The shape of this book has undergone several changes. An original spare outline became unevenly swollen with learned discussion. Critical readers and kind friends gave encouragement and urged reorganization and the relegation of knotty problems, for which there is often no certain solution, to a series of appendices. I have tried therefore to produce a readable narrative, unclogged by too much scholarship, but setting out a large selection of the evidence available, and drawing attention to the problems which seem to me particularly important and worth discussion. I have been greatly helped in various ways by E. Bowie, M. H. Crawford, D. J. Crawford, Professor R. Crawford, R. Duncan-Jones, M. Frederiksen, Professor J. K. B. Nicholas, J. R. Rea, J. S. Richardson, J. G. Schovánek, D. L. Stockton, R. J. Talbert, Professor J. M. Toynbee, and

Professor G. W. Williams. I owe a special debt to Professor P. A. Brunt for reading and criticizing the whole text, and to Mrs. Mary Bennett, née Fisher, for allowing me to use the notes she made in the 1930s when she started to collect evidence for a study of the Roman corn supply which was never completed. It was Russell Meiggs who passed these notes on to me, and he above all others has taken time and trouble with this book. I wish that it was more worthy of him. The British Academy made a generous grant which allowed me to take my family to Italy for three months during the period of Study Leave granted by the University of St. Andrews when the bulk of the work was written up at the British School at Rome. My wife has typed it in many drafts, and the Oxford University Press has improved it. To all these and to others who, by accident or design, have had to live with the making of this book, I am deeply grateful. It is dedicated to my mother, and to my children.

In the *De Brevitate Vitae* Seneca addressed some salutary advice to his father-in-law Pompeius Paulinus, who was apparently reluctant to retire from being prefect of the corn supply at Rome: 'Reflect that you were not aiming from your earliest years, in all your training in liberal studies, at this, that it might be safe to entrust many thousands of *modii* of corn to your charge.' Enough said.

St. Andrews, March 1979 G.E.R.

CONTENTS

Preface vii

page

I The Governing Factors 1
II The Republic 26
III Transition: Pompey, Caesar, and Augustus 55
IV The Early Empire 67
V The Corn Lands 94
VI Transport, Storage, and Prices 120
VII The Corn Distributions 156
VIII The Late Empire 198
Epilogue 210

APPENDICES

1. The Senate, the Emperor, and the Distributions 213
2. The *Praefectus Annonae* and *Annona* Officials under the Empire 218
3. *Corpora Naviculariorum* 226
4. Africa and Egypt 231
5. Warehouse Leases in Puteoli 236
6. Flour Prices and the Price of Grain at Rome 239
7. The Table of Heraclea 241
8. *Tesserae frumentariae* 244
9. Porticus Minucia 250
10. *Curatores Aquarum et Miniciae* 253
11. Corn and Coins 257
Bibliography 268
Index of Classical Authors 277
Index of Papyri 280
Index of Inscriptions 281
General Index 283

ABBREVIATIONS

AEpigr.	*L'Année épigraphique*
AHR	*American Historical Review*
AJ	*Archaeological Journal*
AJA	*American Journal of Archaeology*
AJP	*American Journal of Philology*
Annales	*Annales: économies, sociétés, civilisations*
APF	*Archiv für Papyrusforschung*
ArchCl	*Archeologia Classica*
BASP	*Bulletin of the American Society of Papyrologists*
BIFAO	*Bulletin de l'Institut Français d'Archéologie Orientale*
Broughton, *MRR*	T. R. S. Broughton, *The Magistrates of the Roman Republic* (American Philological Association Monographs No. 15) Lancaster, Pa.; (Oxford, 1951–2)
BSAA	*Bulletin de la Société d'Archéologie d'Alexandrie*
BullComm	*Bullettino della Commissione Archeologica Comunale di Roma*
Cardinali, *Frumentatio*	*Dizionario epigrafico di antichità romane* (de Ruggiero), s.v. *frumentatio*
CE	*Chronique d'Égypte*
CEHE	*Cambridge Economic History of Europe*
CIL	*Corpus Inscriptionum Latinarum*
CP	*Classical Philology*
CR	*Classical Review*
CRAI	*Comptes Rendus de l'Académie des Inscriptions et Belles-Lettres*
Diz.Epig.	*Dizionario epigrafico di antichità romane di de Ruggiero*
Duncan-Jones, *ERE*	R. P. Duncan-Jones, *The Economy of The Roman Empire* (Cambridge, 1974)
EcHR	*Economic History Review*
EtPap	*Études papyrologiques*
FIRA	*Fontes Iuris Romani AnteJustiniani* (S. Riccobono and others)
Frank, *ESAR*	Tenney Frank, *An Economic Survey of Ancient Rome*, 5 vols. (Baltimore, 1933–40)
HSCP	*Harvard Studies in Classical Philology*
HThR	*Harvard Theological Review*
ILS	*Inscriptiones Latinae Selectae*
JRS	*Journal of Roman Studies*
MEFR	*Mélanges d'archéologie et d'histoire de l'École Française de Rome*
MemAcInscr	*Mémoires présentés par divers savants à l'Académie des Inscriptions et Belles-Lettres*
MemLinc	*Memorie della R. Accademia Nazionale dei Lincei*

NSc	*Notizie degli scavi di antichità*
OCD	*Oxford Classical Dictionary*
PBSR	*Papers of the British School at Rome*
RA	*Revue archéologique*
RE	Pauly–Wissowa, *Real-Encyclopädie der Classischen Altertumswissenschaft*
REA	*Revue des études anciennes*
REL	*Revue des études latines*
RendNap	*Rendiconti della R. Accademia di Archeologia, Lettere ed Arti, Naples*
RivFC	*Rivista di filologia e d'istruzione classica*
Rostovtzeff, *SEHRE*²	M. Rostovtzeff, *The Social and Economic History of the Roman Empire* (2nd edition, by P. M. Fraser), 2 vols. (Oxford, 1957)
Rostovtzeff, *Frumentum*	Pauly–Wissowa, *Real-Encyclopädie der Classischen Altertumswissenschaft*, s.v. *frumentum*
SCO	*Studi classici e orientali*
SDHI	*Studia et Documenta Historiae et Iuris*
TAPA	*Transactions of the American Philological Association*
ZPE	*Zeitschrift für Papyrologie und Epigraphik*
ZSavignyStift	*Zeitschrift der Savigny Stiftung für Rechtsgeschichte, Romanistische Abteilung*

A TABLE OF MEASURES AND WEIGHTS

1 *modius*, the principal Roman dry measure = approx. 9 litres = $\frac{1}{4}$ bushel, i.e. 1 peck.
1 *medimnus*, the principal Greek dry measure = approx. 54 litres = $1\frac{1}{2}$ bushels, i.e. 6 Roman *modii*.
1 *artaba*, the principal Egyptian dry measure, varied in size from approx. 39 litres in the early Empire to 29 litres in later Empire.
1 *iugerum*, the principal Roman measurement of area = 2,517 square metres, i.e. approx. $\frac{5}{8}$ acre.
1 *aroura*, the principal Egyptian measurement of area = 2,756 square metres, i.e. approx. $\frac{2}{3}$ acre.

Weights *per modius* of wheat after threshing (Pliny, *N.H.* 18·66):
Light—20 *librae* = 14·4 lb = 6·55 kg.
Medium—$20\frac{5}{6}$ *librae* = 15·03 lb = 6·82 kg.
Heavy—$21\frac{3}{4}$ *librae* = 15·7 lb = 7·12 kg.
Therefore 1 ton of wheat on average = approx. 150 *modii* or 25 *medimnoi*.

I

THE GOVERNING FACTORS

I

The city of Rome grew up at a point on the Tiber some 15 miles (24 km) inland from the sea. It was located in an area which, if adequately drained, was of sufficient fertility to ensure the survival of its early inhabitants. From the start, however, Rome like every other community in the ancient world was doomed to hunger if her harvests of grain were poor or her crops were destroyed by her enemies. Fortunately her position on a navigable river allowed food to be sought, and to be imported by water, from neighbouring areas, either coastal or inland, at moments of crisis. Increasing in military and political importance, Rome came to dominate first Latium and then the whole of Italy. By the second century B.C. the Romans were the greatest power in the Mediterranean. The city itself increased in size, outstripping all others, and it came to depend more and more for its food supply on regular but precarious shipments from Roman possessions overseas. The citizen inhabitants of Rome were in a position of privilege superior to the Italians and provincials abroad. They came to expect as a right a guaranteed supply of food, and they could not be allowed to go hungry without unpleasant political consequences for those whom they held responsible. They were certainly from the period of the late Republic onwards in a position to bring pressure to bear in the most directly personal way. For example, in the year 75 B.C. the consuls, L. Octavius and C. Aurelius Cotta, were chased in the Forum by an angry crowd at the time of an acute grain shortage.[1] A century later the Emperor Claudius himself was waylaid in the Forum by a furious starving mob, who screamed abuses, and pelted him with pieces of

[1] Sallust, *Hist.* Fr. 3 (Kurfess).

bread, before he managed to slip through a back door into his palace on the Palatine.[2]

From the beginning of the Republic, however, if not earlier, the magistrates and government of the state had regarded it as a duty to organize emergency supplies if necessary. During the middle and late Republic the beginnings of a regular system were created. With the change from Republic to Principate the system was reorganized and elaborated by the new *principes*. The burden of feeding Rome was one which they could not shirk and which with their ever increasing paternalism they dealt with more and more openly as the Empire developed. As early as A.D. 22 the Emperor Tiberius in a letter to the senate wrote sombrely about the gravity of the problem and the Emperors' ultimate responsibility for it: 'Hanc, patres conscripti, curam sustinet princeps; haec omissa funditus rem publicam trahet.' 'This duty, senators, devolves upon the *princeps*; if it is neglected, the utter ruin of the state will follow.'[3]

Rome was not peculiar in having to face such a problem. Famine, or the threat of famine, was a permanent fact of life for most people in the ancient world, not least in the cities. It was brought about largely by a combination of the low level of technology, the difficulties of transport, and the limited ability to preserve foodstuffs. Powerful communities, like Athens, had already tried to take steps to secure continuous and adequate supplies of food.[4] But the city of Rome was peculiar in the sheer size of the population and therefore the scale of the problem, and in the intense political importance, at least from the time of Gaius Gracchus, which surrounded the whole issue. We have, as a result, more evidence for the corn supply of Rome than for that of any other single community in the ancient world. Varied though the evidence is, however, it falls far short of being comprehensive. Because of their direct political importance the corn distributions which started in 123 B.C. have monopolized the attention of modern scholars.[5] The larger problem of the organization of the corn supply in general,

[2] Suet. *Claud.* 18.

[3] Tac. *Ann.* 3. 54. 6–8.

[4] M. I. Finley, *The Ancient Economy* (London, 1973), pp. 169–70; R. MacMullen, *Enemies of the Roman Order* (Cambridge, Mass., 1967), Appendix A.

[5] e.g. D. Van Berchem, *Les distributions de blé et d'argent à la plèbe romaine sous l'empire* (Geneva, 1939).

the guaranteeing of adequate amounts and stable prices has until recently been relatively neglected.[6] It is not difficult to see why. Statistical data on topics such as population, production, and prices in the Roman world are often so inadequate as to forbid any modern-style approach to the problems.[7] The answers cannot be set out in neat charts with absolute accuracy like a document from a modern government department. Nor is there, as in the case of the water supply of Rome, any single archaeological reminder of potent visual force, such as the aqueducts which stride across the landscape near the city to focus our attention. The supply of corn to the city was equally vital, but it demanded the co-ordination of many individual efforts diffused all over the Mediterranean. Only, therefore, by the slow and patient unravelling of the organization which developed can we begin to appreciate both the problem and the methods adopted to try to solve it.

Certain factors determined the nature and extent of the problem: the importance of grain, particularly wheat but also barley, in the diet of the ancient world, and the difficulties of growing it; the rapid expansion and enormous size of the population of Rome during the late Republic and early Empire; the difficulty and cost of transporting heavy or bulky goods in general, including grain; and the special conditions for the storage of grain to keep it both safe and sound, yet available when needed throughout the year between one harvest and the next. An outline of these governing factors now will make it easier to understand the difficulties Rome faced and the options open to her, but many questions will be explored in greater depth later.

2

The importance of grain in the diet of the ancient world was a result of the geology and climate of the Mediterranean area. The light soils of the region watered by winter rains and parched by long summer droughts could, by the use of so-called 'dry-farming' methods, grow adequate supplies of cereal

[6] See now H. Pavis D'Escurac, *La Préfecture de l'annone, service administratif impérial d'Auguste à Constantin* (Rome, 1976).

[7] See however the important work of R. P. Duncan-Jones now collected together in *The Economy of the Roman Empire* (Cambridge, 1974).

crops, vegetables, and fruits, especially grapes and olives.[8] The main growing period had to be during the rainy winter season with the crops planted in the autumn, although in some areas it might be possible to add a quick-growing crop planted in the spring. There was some grazing suitable for small animals such as goats, sheep, and pigs, but very little pasture for cattle. The eating of meat, therefore, on a scale typical of the diet of most people in northern Europe or America in the modern world was simply not possible for, and perhaps not desired by, large numbers of Mediterranean people in ancient times. As the diet of modern Africa and Asia shows, however, cereals can be an important and cheap source of calories, capable of supporting large populations. The modern theoretical ideal for the daily intake of calories by an adult male is about 3,300. In Rome in the late Republic the monthly ration of wheat for an adult male, 5 *modii*, had a calorific value equivalent to between 3,000 and 3,500 calories a day.[9] While such a ration may well not always have been consumed by only one person, the correlation is instructive. It was this value of grain as fuel for humans that led to the pre-eminent importance of cereal agriculture throughout the Mediterranean in antiquity, to the special position of cereals in the diet of most people, and therefore to the problem of keeping the population, not least that of the city of Rome, supplied with grain.

There are basically eight grains which are of major importance as human food in the world today and six of them were either unknown or not grown in any quantity in antiquity.[10] Maize (American corn) was unknown in Europe before the discovery of America. Sorghum and rice were exotic and rare, and not grown plentifully in southern Europe until the arrival of the Arabs. Oats, rye, and the millets, although all grown for economic reasons in districts with less favourable climates, never fully established themselves as main crops in the Mediterranean area itself. The fields were therefore in general left open to two grain crops, barley and wheat, which were in competition with one another.

[8] See below, p. 96.

[9] Duncan-Jones, *ERE*, p. 147.

[10] N. Jasny, 'Competition among grains in classical antiquity', *AHR* 47 (1941–2), 747–64; J. André, *L'Alimentation et la cuisine à Rome* (Paris, 1961), pp. 52–74.

Barley was a crop supremely well suited to the climate and soil conditions of much of the Mediterranean.[11] It could make do with less rainfall than wheat and ripened early anyway, so as to avoid the summer drought. It also flourished on poor-quality alkaline soil, of which the Mediterranean with its extensive areas of decomposed limestone had much. Particularly, therefore, in the southern and eastern parts of the Mediterranean basin, even in an area like Attica in the south-east, barley was the natural cereal crop. But not all the Mediterranean is so short of rainfall, and there are areas where because of volcanic activity the earth is richer and blacker, better suited to the growing of wheat rather than barley. This was particularly true of certain areas on the west coast of Italy, such as Campania, Latium, and southern Etruria. Barley was more prolific than wheat and could yield anything from 10 to 50 per cent more than wheat in terms of weight, depending on the climatic and soil conditions favouring it. Wheat however had a distinct advantage over barley in that it had 10 per cent more nutritive value than barley in terms of equivalent weight and 35 per cent more nutritive value than barley in terms of equivalent volume. Barley was a very bulky commodity to move around, even in comparison with other grains, a factor which was not in its favour in the international grain trade.

Although barley continued to be grown in quantity as animal fodder and food for the poor, wheat became the preferred food for humans. The crucial factor was the development of bread-making by the fifth century B.C. which demanded a grain that could be easily freed from its husk and had a high gluten content. Barley grain was extremely difficult to free from its husk and the ancient world knew of no other really effective way of doing it apart from roasting, which destroyed the gluten needed in making leavened bread. Barley kernels therefore had to be ground into a coarse meal and then moulded into a paste, and consumed either as a toasted cake or a porridge. It was true that some of the early forms of wheat also were 'hulled' and therefore equally difficult to free from their husks and had to be consumed as porridge. Early Rome had not only *polenta*, barley porridge, but also and more commonly *puls*, a porridge made

[11] L. Moritz, *Grain Mills and Flour in Classical Antiquity* (Oxford, 1958), Introduction.

from *far*, a hulled form of wheat. There were, however, also 'naked' wheats whose grain could be freed from the husk on the threshing floor, a fact which was highly advantageous for the making of bread.

The varieties of wheat which were grown in the ancient Mediterranean from primitive times were many and the terms used to describe them, sometimes vaguely, sometimes with accuracy, in classical authors have been a source of great confusion to modern classicists and students of ancient history.[12] There were in fact three main groups of wheat grown in the Mediterranean area; the Einkorn group, the Emmer group, and the Spelt group.

The first, Einkorn, group was certainly the least significant for the Greeks and Romans. It was the original wild wheat, *triticum monococcum*, of poor quality grains with a poor yield. The two latter groups were far more important and each had sub-species of both hulled and 'naked' varieties. It was a hulled variety of the Emmer group, *triticum dicoccum*, which was the original Roman *far*. Because of the difficulties of freeing that grain from its husk, and its unsuitability for bread-making, certain naked sub-species of the same Emmer group gained in importance. Two were pre-eminent, *triticum durum* (macaroni wheat), from which modern pasta dishes are made, and *triticum turgidum* (rivet or poulard wheat). These two sub-species of the Emmer group were the main autumn-sown cereal crops of the Mediterranean in ancient times. *Triticum durum* was widely grown in Sardinia, Sicily, Africa, Spain, and southern Italy, while both *triticum durum* and *triticum turgidum* were grown in Egypt. Roman imports from these areas therefore belonged predominantly to the naked varieties of the second group of wheats.

It was however a naked variety of the third group, the Spelt group, which came to be the most favoured of all the wheats by connoisseurs in the Roman world. This was *triticum vulgare*, the ancestor of modern wheat. In the fifth and fourth centuries B.C.

[12] The Einkorn group was diploid wheat with 14 chromosomes as its distinguishing characteristic; the Emmer group tetraploid wheat with 28 chromosomes; the Spelt group hexaploid wheat with 42 chromosomes. N. Jasny, *The Wheats of Classical Antiquity*, Johns Hopkins Univ. Studies, lxii (Baltimore, 1944), 19; J. M. Renfrew, *Palaeoethnobotany. The Prehistoric Food Plants of the Near East and Europe* (London, 1973), Chs. 4–6.

the main autumn-sown crops in both Greece and Italy belonged to the Emmer group while only the 'three-month' wheat sown in the spring was of the softer *triticum vulgare* type. Later, and perhaps first in Italy, the greater popularity of the fine flour, *siligo*, derived from it led to an increase in the cultivation of *triticum vulgare* at the expense of wheats of the Emmer group. They, it is true, continued to be thought of as 'wheat' *par excellence*, *triticum* in the strict sense, but *triticum vulgare* by Roman imperial times comprised not just spring wheat but a large part of the main autumn-sown crop, particularly in Campania and Etruria. While all three kinds of naked wheat were used for bread, *triticum vulgare*, easier for milling than *durum* in particular, alone produced *siligo* from which the perfectly white loaf preferred by the favoured few could be made.

Highly nutritious though they are, wheats, whatever their species, also have their limitations. Their protein content is by no means so valuable as that of milk, eggs, cheese, fish, and meat, and that protein content is still further reduced by the cooking which is essential to make the cereal digestible for human beings. Their calcium content is low and largely unavailable to man, as is their iron content which happens to be high. More significant still with the exception of thiamine and vitamin E, they are almost totally deficient in vitamin content. The lack of vitamins A, C, and D is a serious drawback in any diet of which 60 per cent or more is composed of cereals.[13] People in Rome therefore needed fish, vegetables, fruits, and other foods as well as barley or wheat to keep them fit and healthy. It is no surprise that rickets, which is brought about by starchy food deficient in vitamin D, and by lack of sunshine and is therefore typical of an urban situation, was common among the children of the city of Rome according to Soranus of Ephesus, who gives the first recognizable account of the disease in the early second century A.D.[14] But whatever its deficiencies it was grain which was the mainstay of life, and which had to be eaten in quantity throughout the year by the majority of people to provide the greater part of their calorific needs.

[13] V. H. Mottram and G. Graham, *Hutchison's Food and the Principles of Dietetics*, 11th edn. (London, 1956), p. 264.

[14] D. and P. Brothwell, *Food in Antiquity* (London, 1969), p. 182.

3

The population of the city of Rome therefore had to be fed predominantly with wheat. It can be established beyond doubt that the size of the population grew enormously during the course of the Republic, but to quantify that growth with precision is another matter. Attempts to compute the total population at various periods have invoked numbers of dwellings, the area within the walls available for habitation, and various other data. It has been shown that no confidence can be placed in the results.[15] In arguments from area we have to assume what we most want to know, namely the density of habitation. In arguments about housing there is not only that same problem but also the uncertainty about the meaning of the terms describing the various forms of habitation. The only approach which allows any hope of indicating at least the right order of magnitude for the total has to be based on the numbers of corn-recipients in the distributions of the late Republic and Augustan periods. It is possible to infer particularly from the numbers given by Augustus himself in his *Res Gestae* at least a minimum figure for the population of Rome at that time although guesses have to be made about the size of families and the numbers of slaves.

In *Res Gestae* 15.2 Augustus recorded that in 5 B.C. he made distributions to 320,000 members of the urban plebs. This figure is the only basis, in default of a better one, upon which to start a calculation for the population of Rome at this time. These 320,000 were by definition 'adult' males, that is, fourteen years of age or above. How many women, children, resident aliens, and slaves there were in addition to them, we do not know. There are reasons for believing that the number of women, the rate of marriage, and the incidence of childbirth among the urban plebs might have been restricted.[16] How

[15] F. G. Maier, 'Römische Bevölkerungsgeschichte und Inscriftenstatistik', *Historia* 2 (1953–4), 318–51; E. S. Gruen, *The Last Generation of the Roman Republic* (California, 1974), pp. 358–9; K. Hopkins, *Conquerors and Slaves* (Cambridge, 1978), pp. 96–8. See in general Duncan-Jones, *ERE*, Ch. VI, 'The size of cities'.

[16] P. A. Brunt, *Italian Manpower* (Oxford, 1971), pp. 382–3. A ratio often assumed in interpreting population figures is that adult males = $\frac{2}{7}$ (28·6 per cent) of the free population (Duncan-Jones, *ERE*, p. 264 n. 4) but special factors distorted the situation in Rome. For age of eligibility see Suet. *Aug.* 41, but cf. *Oxyrhynchus Papyri* xl. 13 (Rea).

restricted is a matter for guesswork. It has been suggested that we should merely double the numbers of the corn recipients in order to allow for both their wives and their children, bringing the free population to 640,000. But that seems too low. If it were true, very large numbers of the urban plebs must have remained unmarried, or, if married, completely childless. I should prefer to guess that the living conditions in Rome did not have quite such an inhibiting effect, and that there were at least 400,000 women and children, so as to allow for perhaps a higher rate of marriage or the existence of more families with two or more children.[17] This would mean that there was a free population of three-quarters of a million people or more.

Estimates for the numbers of slaves in Rome are even more difficult to arrive at than any of the figures suggested so far. A recent estimate puts the number of slaves in Rome at this period at 100,000–200,000.[18] The lower end of that scale seems to me again too low. Slave numbers of course must have varied considerably according to where there were concentrations of wealth sufficient to afford slaves. Random figures preserved for certain places in the provinces show a proportion of slaves to the total population no higher than one-tenth; in Italy it was certainly higher, perhaps a quarter, if not more.[19] In a city such as Rome with a high concentration of wealth a high proportion of slaves might be expected, but for the fact that the rate of manumission in the late Republic was so rapid and so generous that Augustus was obliged to put a brake on it. We do not know what allowance we should make for that fact. My guess is that given, for example, the numbers needed in the docks and the building operations in the Campus Martius the higher figure of 200,000 is nearer the truth for the slave population of Rome at this time.

The limitations of this calculation hardly need stressing. But the figure of 320,000 recipients at the distributions in 5 B.C.

[17] Cf. B. Rawson, 'Family life among the lower classes at Rome in the first two centuries of the Empire', *CP* (1966), 71–83.

[18] Brunt, *Italian Manpower*, p. 383; estimates have ranged from 100,000 to 300,000, see W. L. Westermann, *The Slave Systems of Greek and Roman Antiquity* (Philadelphia, 1955), pp. 63–9.

[19] Duncan-Jones, *ERE*, pp. 272–3; R. MacMullen, *Roman Social Relations* (New Haven, 1974), p. 92 and p. 185 n. 7; L. Casson, 'Unemployment: the Building Trade and Suetonius *Vesp.* 18', *BASP* 15 (1978) 43–51, is more controversial.

does make it clear that at a minimum there must have been at least three-quarters of a million inhabitants in Rome. A slightly more generous, and in my view more natural, set of assumptions would bring the size of the population near to 1,000,000.

The amount of grain needed to feed such numbers of people was gigantic. The only size of ration known to us in the distributions at Rome was 5 *modii* a month, that is 60 *modii* a year, for each recipient. This was more than enough for one man, but insufficient for a family. We can deduce this from various pieces of evidence, the most specific of which is the elder Cato's rations for his slaves in the second century B.C.[20] They were allowed oil, salt, olives, and wine as well as bread or grain in their subsistence diet. Unchained field slaves were given 4–4½ *modii* of wheat a month according to the time of year. Those with lighter work received only 3 *modii* a month, while the chain gang with the heaviest work of all, who apparently could not grind their own grain, were given an allowance in bread which was roughly equivalent to 4·8–6 *modii* of wheat a month. This range of size of corn rations agrees with evidence we have for other periods, and with figures for average cereal consumption in the Mediterranean in the nineteenth century.[21] In the light of this evidence it seems not unreasonable to guess, as Beloch did, that the average consumption of grain in Rome was perhaps about 40 *modii* per person per year.[22] From the time of Augustus, therefore, Rome needed not the mere 12 million *modii* to cope with up to 200,000 recipients of the corn distributions but something nearer 40 million *modii* for the population of the capital as a whole.

Of course that had not always been the case nor was it necessarily to remain so throughout the history of the Empire. There are some reasons for thinking that during the later second century A.D. the plagues from the time of Marcus Aurelius may have led to a shrinkage of population in Rome back towards three-quarters of a million or below.[23] Similarly the precise

[20] Cato, *De Agri cultura*, 56–8.

[21] For a convenient discussion of the comparative figures see D. Crawford, *Kerkeosiris* (Cambridge, 1971), pp. 129–30.

[22] Brunt, *Italian Manpower*, pp. 124, 382; cf. the classic study by K. J. Beloch, *Die Bevölkerung der griechischrömischen Welt* (Leipzig, 1886), esp. pp. 392–412.

[23] J. F. Gilliam, 'The plague under Marcus Aurelius', *AJP* 82 (1961), 225–51, but cf. F. G. B. Millar, *A Study of Cassius Dio* (Oxford, 1964), p. 13 n. 4.

rate of the population growth during the Republic is irrecoverable. We do not have any means of guessing the urban population of early Rome. But the record of frequent famines and of imports of grain into early Rome should not be interpreted as showing that from the beginning of the Republic the population had outstripped local resources. We are told that they were caused specifically by droughts, or because enemies had prevented the farmers either from sowing their fields or reaping their harvests.[24] The real growth of the city population seems to have started in the third century B.C. and accelerated rapidly in the second century B.C. The growing wealth of the upper classes, the import of slaves to swell their households, the increase of craftsmen, shopkeepers, and labourers to cater for their needs and the increasing drift of the rural poor into the city all contributed to the enormous size of the city in the late Republic. We can gain some tentative indicators of the rate of this growth from the increasing number of public buildings of utilitarian purpose, porticoes, markets, and docks which were constructed from the end of the Hannibalic war, and from the increasing need for greater supplies of water.[25] Rome had originally been supplied with water from the Tiber and from local wells. By the end of the fourth and beginning of the third century B.C. the first efforts were made to bring water from a distance by aqueduct, a clear indication that local resources were insufficient. New efforts to improve the water supplies came in the second half of the second century B.C., in the 30s B.C. and under the Emperor Claudius in the first century A.D. The suspicion is that before each of these efforts the water supplies had become grossly insufficient for the numbers of people to be served. In no sense had the growth of the city been planned after its sack by the Gauls in 390 B.C. or really controlled since. By the time of Augustus Rome was a crowded, jerry-built muddle of house-blocks too high for their own safety, vulnerable both to fire and flood, with one or two public areas of some architectural distinction. We may guess that the population had reached at least half a million by the middle of the second century B.C.

Just as Rome gradually outstripped the local water resources,

[24] Brunt, *Italian Manpower*, p. 704; see below, p. 29.
[25] Brunt, *Italian Manpower*, p. 384.

so she also outgrew the resources of regions from which she had originally sought for corn. Traditionally when the fields surrounding the city failed, she had sought for corn from central Etruria, whence it could be brought by water down the Tiber, or from the coastal areas of southern Etruria, Latium, and Campania, whence it could be brought by sea to the Tiber mouth and then on up the river.[26] There is every reason to believe that the Val di Chiana in inland Etruria, and the Campanian plain continued even after the third century B.C. to be very fruitful and able to yield surpluses useful to Rome. But the other areas may have become less reliable. In Latium the large plain, south of Antium between the Volscian hills and the sea, which had once been very fertile, was allowed to become water-logged for lack of a proper drainage system and the area was on the way to becoming the Pomptine marshes.

Perhaps too the cultivated area of coastal Etruria was diminishing in size, or was less devoted to cereal agriculture. Tiberius Gracchus in the later second century B.C. on his way to Spain was said to have been shocked by the growth of large estates and the desertion of the fields by free men. A change in the patterns of agriculture was occurring in conjunction with other shifts in the social and economic structure of Rome. For large landowners who were no longer thinking in subsistence but purely in commercial terms olives, vines, and, where appropriate, grazing cattle all seemed to offer the prospect of better profits on land investment. Even imperial enactments could not reverse the trend, as was shown by Domitian's abortive edict in A.D. 92, prohibiting the extension of vineyards in Italy and ordering the destruction of half the vineyards in the provinces; it was rescinded by Domitian himself.[27] Even for small-holders, who were close enough to the city, it made sense to concentrate on fresh fruit and vegetables for Rome. The growing numbers of people in the city however still had an urgent need for corn, and in greater quantities than the traditional local sources in Italy could ever have yielded as regular surpluses beyond their own needs.

After the end of the Hannibalic War in 201 B.C. this corn came in ever-increasing amounts from overseas. First Sicily, in

[26] Brunt, *Italian Manpower*, p. 705; see below, p. 102.
[27] Statius, *Silvae* 4. 3. 11–12; Suet. *Domitian*, 7.2, 14.2.

which the Romans had from the early Republic prospected for corn from time to time, then Sardinia came into Roman control, and revenue was taken from these islands not in coin but in corn. Later it was Africa and then Egypt which were important for sending corn to Rome. It has sometimes been suggested that these imports had an adverse effect on the Italian grain growers, and drove Rome into dependence on overseas sources by ruining local producers. But this can be shown to be invalid by even a brief glance at the conditions for transporting grain in the ancient world.

4

One of the things which the Romans did supremely well was to plan and build roads. From the fourth century B.C. Italy and then the provinces were opened up by road systems which were often so shrewdly plotted and magnificently constructed that both the line and the structure of many Roman roads have endured till modern times. Originally many of them had a military purpose, but throughout history trade has often not been slow to follow the military flag. It might be expected that the same would be true of the Roman situation; that trade and transport generally would be greatly benefited by the road system. In fact it was only partially true. Trade did follow the military. The armies of the Republic, forts and fortresses of the Empire became magnets for trade, markets with ready money that needed service. But the road system on land did not lead to a throbbing growth of trade all along its length. It was an irremovable fact that however well made the roads were, movement along them, particularly of heavy goods, was both extremely slow and intolerably expensive.[28]

To transport goods by land in the Roman world meant putting them in a cart or on the back of some kind of pack animal, whether a donkey, a mule, or even, in Egypt, a camel. Carts were drawn by oxen, which were the main draught animals in the ancient world, before the invention of the horse-collar. Oxen move at about 2 miles (just over 3 km) per hour;

[28] Finley, *Ancient Economy*, pp. 126–7; Duncan-Jones, *ERE*, p. 1; J. G. Landels, *Engineering in the Ancient World* (London, 1978), pp. 173–9; Lynn White, *Medieval Technology and Social Change* (Oxford, 1962), pp. 57–9.

pack animals in general rather faster, but even then only at 3 to 4 miles (5–6 km) per hour, which is the walking pace of a man. The expense of transport by land is also undoubted, but the details are more speculative. It has been estimated, however, from information given in Diocletian's Edict on maximum prices in the fourth century A.D. that a wagon-load of wheat would double its price on a journey of 300–400 miles (480–640 km), the authorized charge for transportation of a wagon-load of wheat being 20 *denarii* per mile, when each *castrensis modius* of wheat was priced at 100 *denarii* and a wagon is assumed to hold 60 *modii.*[29]

When we turn to transport by water the picture is very different. The freightage rates by sea given in Diocletian's edict are very much lower particularly for long journeys. The charge for the whole journey from Alexandria to Rome, some 1,700 miles (2,720 km), given the circuitous route, was 16 *denarii*, that is, in the case of wheat, per *castrensis modius.* Since the ceiling price on the sale of wheat was set by the Edict at 100 *denarii* per *castrensis modius*, this charge and all the other rates given for the Mediterranean shipping lanes are really percentages of the selling price. In other words freightage of wheat from Alexandria to Rome only increased the price by 16 per cent (although we must remember that shippers were also allowed to retain a small percentage of the actual cargo as well). Even the highest rate quoted, from Syria to Lusitania in Spain, is only some 26 *denarii*, which means that it was cheaper to ship grain from one end of the Mediterranean to the other than to cart it by land 75–100 miles (120–60 km).

So far as speed of journey was concerned water transport was again superior. Of course there was great variation in speed depending on whether the ship was on a route where the prevailing winds were favourable or unfavourable.[30] In general it

[29] A. H. M. Jones, *The Later Roman Empire* (Oxford, 1964), pp. 821–3 and notes. Jones made his famous calculation on the assumption that the *castrensis modius* of the late Empire was equivalent to 2 Italian *modii.* This may not be correct and the calculation therefore has needed adjusting a little, see R. P. Duncan-Jones, 'The size of the *modius castrensis*', *ZPE* 21 (1976), 53. Cf. in general Duncan-Jones, *ERE*, Appendix 17, and A. M. Burford, 'Heavy Transport in Classical Antiquity', *EcHR*², 13 (1960), 1–18.

[30] L. Casson, *Ships and Seamanship in the Ancient World* (Princeton, 1971), pp. 281 ff. J. Rougé, *Recherches sur l'organisation du commerce maritime en Méditerranée sous l'empire romain* (Paris, 1966), pp. 31 ff.

would seem that under favourable wind conditions ancient vessels averaged between 4 and 6 knots over open water, but the average dropped to less than 2 to 2½ knots if they were working against the wind. What this meant in real terms, for example on the run from Italy to Egypt, was that freighters going from Ostia or Puteoli to Alexandria went direct with the wind behind them and took only about ten days to two weeks to complete the journey of over 1,000 miles (1,600 km). The voyage from Alexandria against the prevailing northerly winds necessitated less direct routes and took twice as long; indeed it might even take up to two months under really unfavourable conditions.

In addition to the problem of contrary winds, there were two other inhibiting factors, which hampered even transport by sea. The first was that during the winter months sailing was more or less completely suspended not least because cloudy conditions veiled sun and stars and made navigation very difficult. According to Vegetius the seas were closed for four months from 11 November to 10 March, and were very dangerous for eight months from 22 September to 27 May. Although we do hear of some ships which make a run for it in a spell of fine winter weather, there is no need to doubt the overall truth of what Vegetius says. It is borne out by detailed rescripts from the Emperors preserved for us in the late legal Codes and it was a truth well known to the medieval world as well.[31] The second factor which inhibited sea transport was the very real possibility of unexpected storms. Although sea transport might be relatively quick, there was a greater risk of total or partial loss of cargo. That might come in the dramatic form of an outright shipwreck, or by jettison to lighten a ship at the height of a storm, or less dramatically by spoiling with sea water from the bilges or down through the hatches.

The overall effect of these facts of life on trade in raw materials and foodstuffs is fairly clear. Wherever possible heavy or bulky goods were moved by water, and even so generally only those raw materials which were of great interest to the

[31] Vegetius 4. 39; *Cod. Theod.* 13. 9. 3. Cf. Jones, *LRE* i. 403; iii. 92; J. Rougé, 'La navigation hivernale sous l'Empire romain', *REA* 54 (1952), 316–25; F. Braudel, *The Mediterranean and the Mediterranean World in the Age of Philip II* (London, 1972), i. 248.

community or to rich individuals, who could afford to pay for them, were traded over long distances. So, for example, metals such as copper and iron, mined only in certain areas but needed universally, were worth transporting. The same was true for high-quality marbles and big timbers needed by the state or for private luxury contracts. Oil and wine, particularly special vintages, were also worth transporting, since they were profitable in relation to their bulk and there was a ready market of willing and rich buyers. But fruit and vegetables and all other perishables could not be traded far because of the slowness and vagaries of the transport systems, and had to be sought in local market gardens. Meat was of interest to the state, particularly in the later Empire, for the feeding of Rome, but in general it was transported on the hoof, and therefore could not be driven too far without losing too much weight. Only for the army was the state prepared to move meat in salted form considerable distances.

So far as grain was concerned it is quite clear that the economics of the transport system made it prohibitively costly to haul so heavy and bulky a commodity long distances over land. Grain must go by water for most of its journey if the cost was to be endurable either by the state or a private merchant. Only in the special case of the army was the state prepared on occasion to carry grain by land, and even then water transport, sea, river, or canal, had to be used wherever possible. One of the inevitable results of this fact was that civil communities away from the coasts had to rely on their local resources. Inland towns without water communication suffered both local famines and local gluts.[32] If the local harvest was bad it was virtually impossible to move in supplies from outside. If the local harvest was good the surplus was difficult to dispose of profitably. It is this which makes the hypothesis that imports of corn to Rome from overseas ruined local production in Italy implausible. Only the growers in the immediate environs of Rome could conceivably have been affected and it was more profitable for them to supply fruits and vegetables to the city anyway.

The corn trade was therefore necessarily a trade carried on

[32] Duncan-Jones, *ERE*, pp. 1, 38, 252–3; Brunt, *Italian Manpower*, pp. 703–6; Rostovtzeff, *SEHRE*², pp. 599–601; R. MacMullen, *Enemies of the Roman Order*, pp. 249–54.

mainly by sea, but even so it demanded considerable effort. Apart from the natural hazards of sea transport there was the threat of pirates, prolific in the Mediterranean particularly in the late Republic, who might interfere with supplies or cut them off altogether.[33] There was moreover a fundamental problem over who was to do the transporting of the corn and in what. Rome never possessed a state-owned merchant marine. It was largely left to private enterprise, aided and abetted by the state in different ways at different periods, to see to the carrying of the corn from overseas.[34] For much of the history of the Republic there was an *ad hoc* atmosphere to the arrangements with insufficient understanding on either side as to who was committed and for how long to making sure that corn commensurate to Rome's needs was being brought to the city. It seems that by the end of the second century A.D. the standard size of ship used for the transport of grain had to have a capacity of at least 50,000 *modii* (between 340 and 400 tons).[35] If Rome needed some 40 million *modii* of grain a year in the late Republic and early Empire, 800 such shiploads had to reach Italy during the sailing season. In fact there must have been many more. Although we know that some of the Alexandrine freighters were giants of over 1,000 tons, many of the cargo boats both earlier and later were much smaller, often a mere 10,000 *modii* (70–80 tons).[36] Allowance must be made too for shipwreck and spoiling of cargo *en route*. The numbers involved therefore must have been so great, the knowledge as to which merchants and skippers were carrying corn to Rome at a given time so confused, and the rumours as to whether all had successfully completed the crossing of the sea so many, that it is no surprise if there was often real uncertainty about whether enough grain had been brought to the city.

The transport difficulties of course did not end with the successful crossing of the open sea. Corn ships needed to find safe harbour, but Rome was not on the sea and there was no harbour at Ostia at the mouth of the river Tiber during the

[33] See below, p. 50. [34] See below, p. 126.

[35] *Dig.* 50. 5. 3 (Scaevola). Certainly a single ship had to have a capacity of not less than 50,000 *modii* if its owner was to be entitled to privileges.

[36] Lucian, *Navig.* 5, cf. L. Casson, 'The Isis and her voyage', *TAPA* 81 (1950), 43–56 and *Lucien, Le Navire ou les souhaits*, Commentary by G. Husson (Paris, 1970); Gaius, *Inst.* i. 32c.

Republic. Ostia as well as Rome itself was originally simply a river port, its docks and warehouses lying along the bank of the river as it flowed into the sea. Some ships undoubtedly docked at the riverside quays; more unloaded their goods out at sea, off the river mouth into lighters which took them ashore. The biggest sea-going merchantmen could neither dock at Ostia nor run the hazards of unloading offshore at the river mouth. They made instead for Puteoli in Campania with its fine natural harbour, and from there the corn was sent in smaller vessels up the coast to the Tiber mouth. This was clearly an unsatisfactory state of affairs but the difficulties of creating a harbour at or near Ostia were so great that, if we disregard the unfulfilled plans of Julius Caesar, it was not until the Emperor Claudius that the problem was tackled.[37] Even then there was only partial success. The site chosen for the Claudian harbour was some 2 miles (just over 3 km) north of the Tiber mouth where there may already have been a small bay. Communication with the Tiber itself was to be by canals by a short and easy route. Unfortunately the coastal current and prevailing winds in the area swept not only sand but also the considerable amounts of silt brought down by the Tiber itself northwards, so that the Claudian harbour was almost as vulnerable to silting up as if it had been constructed at the river mouth itself. Moreover the scale was perhaps too ambitious. An enormous roughly circular basin of about 200 acres (81 ha) was enclosed within two arms over half a mile apart at their maximum point. The area seems to have been too big to ensure smooth and calm conditions if a storm blew up, as was shown when in A.D. 62 almost 200 ships with grain for Rome were sunk within the harbour.[38] A new smaller inner harbour, a hexagonal basin of about 81 acres (nearly 33 ha) was excavated by Trajan in the land previously crossed by the canals linking the Claudian harbour to the Tiber, and at last proper protection was afforded to big sea-going ships as they unloaded their goods for Rome. During the second century A.D. the African and Alexandrian

[37] R. Meiggs, *Roman Ostia*[2] (Oxford, 1973), Ch. IV; L. Casson, 'Harbour and river boats of ancient Rome', *JRS* 55 (1965), 31 ff.; for the effect on Puteoli, not to be exaggerated, see J. D'Arms, 'Puteoli in the second century of the Roman Empire: A Social and Economic Study', *JRS* 64 (1974), 104–24.

[38] Tac. *Ann.* 15. 18. 3.

corn fleets no longer went to Puteoli but sailed straight for the Ostia harbours. Their existence helped to change the rhythm of its life, diminishing for example the importance of the sea-going lighters ready to unload ships at the river mouth and increasing the importance of the tugs which organized the berthing of the ships in the new harbours. Slowly the harbours developed into a new centre, Portus, which was by the late Empire to be independent of Ostia itself.

Even when the grain was safely brought to harbour at either Ostia or Portus there was still the problem of dispatching it upstream to the river port at Rome, the so-called Emporium district, which had started to develop in the early second century B.C. just downstream from the Pons Sublicius, the first of the city bridges. The Tiber was certainly navigable between Ostia and Rome, perhaps even for quite large ships, but its course was so winding that there was little real alternative to being towed. To be towed up the meandering 22 miles (35 km) to Rome took three days,[39] while the journey by road, either by the Via Ostiensis south of the river, or the Via Portuensis north of the river, took only two and a half to three hours. The grain and other goods for Rome were therefore reloaded into a special type of barge, the *navis codicaria*, the most common of all the various craft making their way to Rome. It was particularly suited to the needs of river transport and to towing. The mast was set well forward and may have been used for a fore-and-aft sprit sail to allow it to catch the wind; it was certainly used for attaching a tow rope. Along the towpaths on either side of the Tiber teams of men, or sometimes of oxen, dragged the barges and other craft up river to Rome. If the average capacity of the river craft used to transport goods upstream or downstream to Rome was about 68 tons, as seems likely, then the 40 million *modii* of grain alone would provide more than 4,500 boat loads. In addition to grain there were massive imports of wine and oil, building materials, and luxury items. Given the fact that it took some three days to be towed upstream it is obvious that even with the winter months being used for barging goods up the river an enormous number of river craft would have to be available. It is not without interest that in A.D. 62 when the 200

[39] Philostratus, *Vit. Apoll. Tyan.* 7. 16. Cf. J. Le Gall, *Le Tibre, fleuve de Rome, dans l'antiquité* (Paris, 1953), p. 257.

ships were sunk within the Claudian harbour by a storm a further 100 ships full of corn were burned by a chance fire at the docks in Rome itself. The congestion on the river at times must have become intense, and there must have been attempts at organization. As the ships neared the city wharves, they made for quays which handled their particular material, such as marbles or timbers, or for the landing stage nearest the warehouses for which their goods were known to be assigned. The facilities of the river port in Rome were improved and long stretches of the river bank in the Aventine area were carefully walled, especially in the early second century A.D., in a way not to be rivalled until the modern embankments.[40] In many places the wharves or the warehouses themselves had ramps and steps leading down to the river. There were plentiful mooring points made from great travertine blocks, set into the concrete brick-faced embankments, pierced by great holes for tethering ropes. But whereas in the harbours the ships could be moored with their prows to the quay, in Rome the ships must have swung broadside on to the quay because of the river current, thereby limiting the number of vessels which could be unloaded at any one time. The ships were unloaded laboriously by porters, *saccarii*, who carried individual loads down the narrow gang-planks on to the docks. If the 40 million *modii* of grain is divided into sackloads able to be carried by one man we have to think in terms of at least 6 million sacks, and that is to ignore both the other goods coming to Rome, and the other men swarming in the river port; *urinatores* who had to salvage merchandise which had fallen overboard or from ships which had sunk, *saburarii* who carried off the sand used for ballast, and the *mensores*, who had to measure carefully all the corn, and perhaps check its quality, before it was consigned to the granaries of the city. The successful transport of adequate supplies of corn to Rome was meaningless if it could not be stored in sufficient bulk and with complete security once it had arrived in the city. The proper organization of any food supply depends ultimately on the ability to store the produce of one year's harvests to satisfy all needs until the harvest of the next year is ready. The survival of the capital rested upon it.

[40] G. E. Rickman, *Roman Granaries and Store Buildings* (Cambridge, 1971), pp. 9 and 108–17.

5

Grain was, and still is, a bulky and difficult commodity to store.[41] If stored loose or in bins grain is not only heavy (for storage to a height of 6 ft, or 2 m, about 240 lb. per sq. ft, or 12,000 kgm per sq. m) but exerts considerable lateral thrust (about two-thirds of the vertical pressure). Moreover the condition of stored grain has to be carefully maintained. It must be protected both from moisture which produces mildew and attacks by weevils and other vermin. The limit of moisture permissible in stored grain is usually between 10 and 15 per cent depending upon the climate, length of storage, and type of grain. Grain must also be kept cool, if possible below 60° F (15·5° C) and free from vermin which tend to breed if grain overheats. Grain storehouses in the ancient world had not only to be able to cope with these problems, but also to take account of the difficulties of transportation at that time and the fact that every sack of grain must be manhandled into store. The warehouses had therefore to be aptly sited, if possible near the water or orientated in that direction, and easy of access, with adequate space for loading and unloading. On the other hand, given the importance of the grain, the buildings had to be absolutely secure, with only a limited number of entrances which, if necessary, could be locked, or kept under surveillance and control.

By the late Republic and early Empire it is clear both from excavations and from the Severan Marble Plan of Rome that the kind of storehouse most favoured in Ostia and Rome consisted of rows of rooms of equal size, with entrances aligned, arranged around either a central corridor or a courtyard.[42] The sizes of these buildings varied considerably from the modest to the gigantic, but the largest and best examples in Rome and Ostia had certainly more than one storey and were buildings of considerable architectural power. The rows of rooms broke up the space for storage into manageable portions, the courtyards allowed for sorting and manoeuvre, while the few main entrances offered security for the whole satisfying architectural scheme. In examples known to us at Ostia and Rome where the

[41] Rickman, *Roman Granaries*, p. 1; see below, p. 134.
[42] Rickman, *Roman Granaries*, Chs. I and II.

storage of grain was clearly the primary purpose of the building, the rooms were built in a special way so as to allow a cooling current of air to circulate beneath the floors.[43] The thresholds set high in the entrances to the rooms allowed the air to pass beneath them and between the dwarf walls which supported strongly built floors. High thresholds in fact helped the porters in setting down their sacks just as the staircases, which after the first few steps turned into sloping ramps, helped them to carry their burdens to rooms on the upper storeys.[44] Such rooms lit only by a narrow splayed slit window at the rear and a small square window above the door provided the cool and dim conditions good for grain storage. Built of the finest materials of their day, brick-faced concrete, these buildings were in no sense shoddy commercial structures but capable of standing comparison with the best in Roman architecture.

But these were sophisticated buildings of the early second century A.D. constructed at a time of major imperial concern with the corn supply. It is doubtful whether originally the state had concerned itself at all with storage. It seems to be the case that warehousing no less than merchant shipping was left to private enterprise and luck. At least it is true that the major warehouses of the late Republic and early Empire still bore the names of the wealthy private families who built them, for example the *Horrea Galbana* and *Horrea Lolliana*, built by the Sulpicii Galbae and Lollii respectively outside the Porta Trigemina in the developing river port at Rome. Originally such families appear to have owned the buildings, and even if they did not exploit them directly they enjoyed the rental revenue from them as valuable property. The same seems to have been true at Puteoli.[45] An entrepreneur would often rent the whole building from the owner and then sub-let storage space to individual merchants or depositors. In such a system corn merchants had to take their chance along with others.

The Roman state is said to have started to provide its own storage capacity, for grain at least, on the initiative of Gaius Gracchus in the late second century B.C.[46] Although we have

[43] Rickman, *Roman Granaries*, pp. 28, 51, and Appendix 1.
[44] Rickman, *Roman Granaries*, p. 22.
[45] Rickman, *Roman Granaries*, pp. 164–72; see below, p. 139.
[46] Festus, p. 392L; cf. Plut. *Gaius Gracchus* 6.

no archaeological confirmation of that yet, the fact is likely enough. At Ostia in either the late second or early first century B.C. a great area along the Tiber bank, where clearly merchantmen unloaded their cargoes, was declared by the praetor Caninius to be public property and marked as such with boundary stones.[47] The family-built warehouses of the late Republic did not survive in private ownership for long after the establishment of the Principate. One by one they seem to have been absorbed into the property of the Emperors to be used for the public weal. But the Emperors also encouraged new building for storage purposes in the early Empire. The construction of the new harbours at the river mouth by Claudius and then Trajan stimulated the construction of store rooms not only at the harbours but in Ostia itself.[48] It can hardly be a coincidence that one of the biggest granaries in Ostia, the so-called *Grandi Horrea*, with over sixty rooms on the ground floor, dates from the middle of the first century A.D. Similarly not only was the Trajanic harbour itself enclosed on all sides by ranges of store rooms placed back to back but in the major rebuilding of a whole area north-west of the Forum at Ostia at the same period many new warehouses, some undoubtedly for grain, were built. If the Trajanic harbour provided safe anchorage for eastern merchantmen including the Alexandrine grain fleet which had gone previously to Puteoli, the desperate need for more storage capacity is obvious.

Some of the Roman storehouses were enormous. The *Horrea Galbana* covered some 225,000 sq. ft (nearly 21,000 sq. m) and more than 140 rooms were available for storage on the ground floor alone. The staff who ran it in the early Empire were divided in a quasi-military way into three groups associated with its three great courtyards, while in the late Empire it was still so important to the provisioning of the capital that its administrative head with the title *curator* was directly responsible to the City Prefect himself.[49] Other storebuildings at Rome, Ostia, and Portus were individually on a smaller scale but in total the labour force involved with them must have been colossal. Porters, measurers, and custodians of one kind

[47] Meiggs, *Roman Ostia*², p. 32.
[48] Rickman, *Roman Granaries*, pp. 123–32; p. 84.
[49] Rickman, *Roman Granaries*, pp. 97–104; 176–7.

or another fetched and carried, checked and counted, locked and unlocked all the time. The effort was great but it had to be made if the corn which had so laboriously been brought from so far was to be kept safe, and, if possible, in sound condition for the people of Rome.

6

The main preoccupation of modern scholars when they have concerned themselves with the corn supply of Rome has often been with the distributions, *frumentationes*, of the late Republic and the Empire.[50] But the problems of feeding Rome were on a bigger scale, and of a more varied nature, than those posed solely by the distributions, important though they were. The history of the procurement of corn for the growing population of the whole city must first be surveyed. While detailed statistical data are not available, and not to be expected, we can follow the ordinary working of the corn trade through from Republic to Empire, we can plot changing attitudes towards the problems, and we can study the developing mechanisms for ensuring supplies. After that historical survey we shall look at the geographical sources from which Rome drew her corn supplies at the height of her power, and in more detail at the transport, storage, and price of grain. Only then will the distributions be considered as a special topic in their own right. The arrangements for the late Empire will bring the study to a close, and will also be considered separately since the system then was fundamentally different in important respects from that of the late Republic or early Empire. In order not to interrupt the main text supporting arguments for statements on certain controversial questions will be found in the appendices.

If there is a single thread which deserves to be emphasized in the story it is the slow but ever-growing involvement by the state in the wide range of activities which supported the supply of corn to Rome. In this sphere, as in so many others, the history of Rome saw a fundamental change in the relationship of the state to the individual, whether he was a farmer, a

[50] See e.g. D. Van Berchem, *Les Distributions de blé* (Geneva, 1939).

shipper,[51] a baker, or metropolitan corn recipient. The feeding of Rome was always a political as well as an economic problem and it involved much more than simply putting food into the stomachs of the inhabitants.

[51] The word 'shipper' is ambiguous in English. It has come to mean, according to the *Concise Oxford Dictionary*, 'merchant, etc., who sends or receives goods by ship, or by land or air'. I have adhered throughout this book to the traditional meaning, given by the *Oxford English Dictionary*, 'one who ships goods for transportation', that is the actual ship-owner or ship-operator.

II

THE REPUBLIC

I

Although our main concern, the feeding of Rome, naturally draws our attention to the western Mediterranean, it is a fact that in the early stages of Rome's history as a Republic, in the fifth and fourth centuries B.C., the main focus of corn trading centred on the Aegean. The Greek cities of the Aegean world faced problems in their food supply and gradually adopted patterns of behaviour which are not without interest in view of Rome's later actions.[1] One of the early aims of the Greek *polis* was self-sufficiency, but limited territory, poor-quality soil, and growth in population combined with almost continuous warfare to make the corn supply of many Greek states often inadequate and always precarious. For states of limited power and wealth, particularly those situated in inland areas, little could be done to alleviate their plight. But in states on the coast or on the islands of the Aegean it was always possible to turn to the sea and seek for supplies elsewhere which might be imported cheaply. The Black Sea area of southern Russia, Sicily, and later increasingly Egypt all proved to be areas from which Greek states of the Aegean might hope for corn imports.

The greatest amount of our evidence comes of course from fifth- and fourth-century Athens,[2] but other coastal and island states had similar solutions to their food problems. In this increasing amount of import by sea private initiative played a large part. Individual merchants, hoping for a profit, were willing to run physical and financial risks in order to bring grain from an area where there was an abundance to an area

[1] F. Heichelheim, *RE* Sup. vi (1935), s.v. *Sitos*, cols. 819–92.

[2] L. Gernet, 'L'approvisionnement d'Athènes en blé au Ve et IVe siècle', in G. Bloch, *Mélanges d'histoire ancienne* (Paris, 1909), cf. M. Austin and P. Vidal-Naquet, *Économies et sociétés en Grèce ancienne* (Paris, 1972), pp. 133 ff.

where there was a need. Xenophon in his *Economics*[3] says of these corn merchants:

So deep is their love of corn that on receiving report that it is abundant anywhere, merchants will voyage in quest of it; they will cross the Aegean, the Euxine, the Sicilian Sea; and when they have got as much as possible, they carry it over the sea, and they actually stow it in the very ship in which they sail themselves. And when they want money, they don't throw the corn away anywhere haphazardly, but they carry it to the place where they hear that corn is most valued and the people prize it most highly and deliver it to them there.

Of course more people than the individual private merchants were involved. Such merchant ventures were costly; merchants were often not rich; consequently it was common to find several men acting as a group, or raising loans elsewhere.[4]

Moreover since grain in one form or another was the staple food of the population of the Greek world the state too felt a concern. The corn supply was an obligatory subject on the regular agenda for the main meetings of the Assembly at Athens ranking in importance with matters like defence.[5] The state if it had the power sometimes tried to earmark the corn from specific areas for its own use, or by honouring individual leading men of corn growing areas, or individual important grain merchants to bind them to its interests.[6] Sometimes boards of corn buyers were set up by the state to administer specially endowed funds that were to be used at times of emergency to alleviate famine.[7] At no time did any Greek state take over a complete monopoly of its corn supply system; but at no time was it completely indifferent to it; at no time, so far as we can see, was there complete success for any length of time in ensuring corn supplies.

The pattern was mixed in the way that was to be typical of the Roman situation; private enterprise was the backbone of

[3] Xenophon, *Ec.* 20. 27–8.

[4] J. Hasebroek, *Trade and Politics in Ancient Greece* (London, 1933), pp. 84 ff. Cf. G. E. M. de Ste. Croix, 'Ancient Greek and Roman Maritime Loans', *Debits, Credits, Finance and Profits*, Essays in Honour of W. T. Baxter, ed. Harold Edey and B. S. Yamey (London, 1974), pp. 41–59.

[5] A. H. M. Jones, *Athenian Democracy* (Oxford, 1957), p. 108; cf. pp. 77–8 and 93–4.

[6] Demosthenes 20. 30–7; 34. 36–9; 25. 50–4; Tod, *GHI* 2. 167 and 200.

[7] A. R. Hands, *Charities and Social Aid in Greece and Rome* (London, 1968), pp. 94 ff.

the whole business, but the state could and did interfere at some times and in some ways. There was an important difference in that the private corn merchants of the Greek world, particularly in a place like Athens, were not citizens, but metics, resident aliens, often rich, enterprising, and contributing to the wealth of Athens, but forming a stratum in society quite distinct from the citizen body, endowed with its full political rights.[8] Although many merchants active in the Roman market in the middle Republic may have been south Italians, during the first century B.C., they had become Roman citizens.[9] Many of the merchants active in the early Empire in feeding Rome could hope for political privileges.[10] The metics of Athens were never absorbed into that political body.

It is clear, however, that the combined efforts of both private and public enterprise in the Greek world could do little to root out the basic uncertainty of variable harvests, dangers at sea, and fluctuating prices even in the most regular markets. The corn trade in Greece was originally, and to a large extent remained, highly unstable.

2

Rome originally was better placed than many of the Greek states to cope with the feeding of her population. Situated some 15 miles (24 km) inland on a plain composed of rich volcanic earth well suited to the growing of cereals, she started her life as a community of peasant farmers. Not only was this fact not forgotten, it was even idealized and the myth of the noble peasant, self-sufficient and content with simple wants, haunted Rome during the height of her power.[11]

But Rome also had a position on important lines of communication not only on the old salt-route which led from the saltpans near the mouth of the river at Ostia up to the hills inland from Rome,[12] but also on a land-route between Etruria to the north and Campania in the south. It was not likely that

[8] A. H. M. Jones, *Athenian Democracy*, pp. 10–11.
[9] Frank, *ESAR* i. 275–82.
[10] Suet. *Claud.* 18, 2–19; Gaius i. 32c.
[11] D. Dudley, *The Romans* (London, 1970), Introduction by J. H. Plumb, p. xix.
[12] Festus 437L, cf. Pliny, *N.H.* 31. 89.

even if they had wished the Romans would have been allowed to remain a totally self-absorbed agricultural community.

Already before the fall of the monarchy an Etruscan dynasty had been established in Rome, probably in the early sixth century B.C. The impact of this event on the physical structure of Rome can be seen in the archaeological evidence. The influence on architecture and planning is palpable, and has been preserved for us to see.[13] Although it is more difficult to prove, the commercial effect is likely also to have been considerable. Rome for a period even at this early moment in her history was forced into the mainstream of influences Greek and Etruscan which came through trade—of a rough and ready kind.

With the collapse of the monarchy, traditionally dated at the end of the sixth century B.C., Rome relapsed for a while more into an agricultural community out of the mainstream of events and with considerable social difficulties.

Among those difficulties were periodic famines and corn shortages, which necessitated a search for food from other sources, from the coastal lowlands of southern Etruria, from the Volscian hills and the Pomptine area, from Campania further south, and even from Sicily. In their histories of the earliest period of the Republic, Livy and Dionysius of Halicarnassus, both writing at the very end of the Republic, preserve notices of corn shortages and famines.[14]

Although there is no reason now to doubt the authenticity of these reports of corn shortages, or the fact that public action was taken by officials in response to them, there are problems in the passages of Livy and Dionysius of Halicarnassus over details. How exactly corn was procured from elsewhere, and who were the people involved, is not always entirely clear, nor is the information always reliable. In the original pontifical annals, which formed the bone structure of early Roman history, there may have been nothing more than the fact of a corn shortage with little detail on how supplementary corn was secured. There was therefore the temptation for the late Republican historians,

[13] E. Gjerstad, 'Legends and facts of early Roman history', *Scripta Minora* (Lund, 1960–1), 2, p. 33; A. Boethius and J. B. Ward-Perkins, *Etruscan and Roman Architecture* (Harmondsworth, 1970), Ch. IV.

[14] e.g. Livy 2. 9. 6(508 B.C.); 2. 34. 2–5 (492 B.C.); 4. 12. 8; Dion. Halic. 5. 26. See R. M. Ogilvie, *Commentary on Livy I–V* (Oxford, 1965), p. 256, for discussion of authenticity of this information.

or their sources, to invent fictitious details, which were anachronistic; coloured, that is, by either the family traditions of *gentes* important in later Roman history, or by political themes and slogans which dominated the struggles of the late Republic.

A good example of this kind of problem occurs in the account by Livy and Dionysius of the famine and the attempts to alleviate it in 440 and 439 B.C.[15] In Livy in particular the story is worked up into a great set piece. According to Livy, L. Minucius was created *praefectus annonae* by the people on the urging of the tribunes and with no opposition from the senate to deal with the shortage, but was not in fact very successful in procuring more corn. Meanwhile a private citizen of equestrian status, Spurius Maelius, organized things rather more successfully. At his own expense he bought grain in Etruria through the agency of friends and dependents there ('per hospitum clientiumque ministeria') and in Campania and distributed it in Rome. This gave him great popularity and encouraged great political ambitions in him. A conspiracy was formed, of which Minucius became aware through the corn merchants and others who were frequenting both his house and that of Maelius. The senate created the aged Cincinnatus dictator to deal with the situation, and he in his turn appointed C. Servilius Ahala as his Master of Horse. Maelius resisted arrest and was summarily killed by Ahala. Minucius sold the grain collected by Maelius cheaply, and thus calmed the common people, and was rewarded for his part in the whole affair by being presented with a statue outside the Porta Trigemina, the gate near the Tiber by the Aventine Hill.

Livy's moralizing about the bare-faced insolence of Maelius in supposing that he could buy the liberty of the Romans with a bag of flour must make us immediately wary of accepting an account whose political colouring is clearly affected by the conflict in the late second century B.C. between the senate and the Gracchi[16] and by the political struggles of the 70s B.C.

But a closer analysis of the passage reveals more complex difficulties.[17] The kernel of fact seems to be that Maelius took

[15] Livy 4. 13–16; Dion. Halic. 12. 1–4.

[16] Meiggs, *Roman Ostia*^{2}, pp. 481–2. Cf. Livy 4. 15. 6 and Sallust, *Oratio Macri* 17–19.

[17] Ogilvie, *Commentary on Livy I–V*, p. 550.

advantage of a corn shortage and was killed for his pains by C. Servilius Ahala. This traditional legend was integrated by the Roman historians into an annalistic framework of facts and dates, and acquired additions in the process. One of the earliest of such additions seems to have been L. Minucius and his part in the story.

By the late Republic the Minucii had fairly strong traditional connections with the corn supply of Rome, and there was a famous column and statue outside the Porta Trigemina. It seems clear now that neither of these was older than the third century B.C.[18] and it is highly unlikely that the association of the Minucii with the corn supply can go right back to the days of Maelius in the mid-fifth century B.C.

But not all the references in Livy to corn shortages in the early Republic have this elaborate treatment, and there may be more to be learned from rather sparer allusions. Some are too bald, such as the reference to the problems of 508 B.C. where it is stated that men were sent to buy corn ('ad frumentum comparandum') and that is all.[19] More details are given in the account of the famine in 492 brought about by a secession of the plebs.[20] The consuls ordered agents to be sent over a wide area to try to purchase grain. It was no easy matter. At Cumae in Campania Aristodemus, the heir of the Tarquins, the Etruscan rulers of Rome, retained the Roman ships, after supplies had been bought, in lieu of the property he ought to have inherited. From the Volscians and the people of the Pomptine area nothing could be obtained, indeed there were even attacks on the *frumentatores*.

This is more interesting since it reminds us, if we need reminding, how dangerous such 'trading' voyages could be. At the start they were a mixture of buccaneering adventures and commercial shrewdness, and in a way that was what they always remained, certainly to the end of the Republic. But the passage also raises immediately the question of whose ships were involved and who exactly these *frumentatores* and *frumentarii* were.

[18] A. Momigliano, *SDHI*², 2 (1936), 374 = *Quarto contributo*, p. 332. Cf. M. H. Crawford, *Roman Republican Coinage* (Cambridge, 1974), i. 273–5.

[19] Livy 2. 9. 6.

[20] Livy 2. 34. 2–7.

There can be no doubt, I think, that they were private corn merchants, the first of that long line of *negotiatores* or *mercatores frumentarii*, who were to play a major role in provisioning the capital throughout her history.[21] Although the Etruscan dynasty at Rome had been expelled, Rome still had interests at sea, even if only civil ones, as the treaties signed between Rome and Carthage in 348 B.C., and very likely in 509 B.C. as well show us.[22] But Rome was as yet in no sense a sea power. The evidence of Livy and Dionysius of Halicarnassus for Roman corn imports by sea in the early Republic must be accepted, but only if one understands by that the activities of private merchants, who were willing to take risks.

Rome seems to have been extremely slow to create anything like a proper navy and not persistent in keeping it up. In 338 B.C. the Volscians of Antium, after raiding the area of the Tiber mouth, were crushed and forced to surrender their fleet.[23] The ships were put on display in Rome and their beaks were used to adorn the speakers' platform in the Forum; some of the ships were destroyed. Rome had not yet decided to man a large navy. It was during the following century that the emphasis shifted. With Rome's commitment to the defence of the Campanian coastal towns came the realization that warships were necessary. In 311 *duumviri navales* were appointed 'to equip and keep in repair a fleet'.[24] More important, in 267 B.C. additional *quaestors* were appointed, and although both the number and functions of the new *quaestors* are controversial, it seems possible that they had the title *classici* and were to collect money and ships from Rome's allies for her fleet.[25] Whatever the original intention, the first Punic War which broke out with Carthage in 264 B.C. and which centred on a struggle for Sicily, dictated a build-up of Roman naval forces. The war left Rome with the greater part of Sicily under her control and with a strong navy. During the struggle with Hannibal which followed the Roman

[21] *Thes. Ling. Lat.*, s.v. *frumentarius*, col. 1407. Frank, *ESAR* i. 204–5, 354–5; v. 219.

[22] Polybius 3. 22 (509 B.C.); Livy 7. 27. 2, Diod. 16. 69. 1, Polyb. 3. 24. 9 (348 B.C.). The treaties refer to the actions of traders and not state fleets either commercial or military.

[23] Livy 8. 14.

[24] Livy 9. 30. 4.

[25] Lydus, *De Mag.* i. 27, cf. T. Mommsen, *Staatsrecht* ii (1)³ (Leipzig, 1887), 570.

navy played a less spectacular role, but it performed highly important work. Not only did it prevent reinforcements from Africa reaching Hannibal in Italy, it also played a key role in transporting provisions from Sicily and Sardinia to feed the Roman legions in Italy, and in Spain. The Roman fleets consisted not just of war galleys but also of many transports.[26] With the defeat of Carthage at the end of the third century B.C. Rome's naval power was allowed to decline. For her wars in the East in the second century B.C. she relied predominantly on the ships of her allies. She was not to maintain a large fleet of her own—a fact which had an undoubted effect in allowing the widespread flourishing of piracy in the late Republic, only feebly checked by *ad hoc* measures from time to time.[27] Augustus learned from the mistakes and created standing fleets to control waterways and safeguard Mediterranean trade.[28]

The slow growth, short heyday, and speedy decline of Roman naval power in the Republic may be contrasted with the increasing vigour of the private trade of all kinds, not least that in corn. Roman trade even in the fourth century was by no means negligible and Ostia's function was already transcending her original defence purpose by providing a river harbour for Rome, dealing with goods from Etruria, the Greek towns of southern Italy, and from Sicily.[29] These traders were not removed by the growth of Rome's navy during the third century B.C. Indeed in 215 there is a notorious example of private businessmen (*negotiatores*) coming to the aid of the state which was bankrupt.[30] There was a grave problem of supplying the Roman armies in Spain and the praetor let out contracts for supplying clothing (*vestimenta*) and grain (*frumentum*) to the soldiers in Spain. The *negotiatores* took on the provisioning of the armies on credit until the state was solvent again, and as a result claimed very special privileges. Among them was indemnity by the state for any losses they might suffer as the result of storms or enemy action. It was in part at least not unlike the special privileges granted by the Emperor Claudius to encourage winter voyages during a later crisis.[31] Unfortunately in 215 the privilege seems to have been exploited and merchants took

[26] Cf. Livy 22. 11.

[27] See below, p. 50.

[28] Suet. *Aug.* 49. 1.

[29] Meiggs, *Roman Ostia*², p. 24.

[30] Livy 23. 48. 6–49. 4.

[31] Suet. *Claud.* 18–19.

the opportunity to use their oldest hulks, and when they sank, to claim on the state.

If we take it as proven that the ships and *frumentarii* involved in the provisioning of Rome during the corn shortages of the early Republic were private, we have nevertheless to acknowledge that the stimulus to action at moments of crisis came from the state. The consuls, or praetors, ordered that corn must be sought out. This raises the question of the relationship of the state to the problem of provisioning the capital, which is one of the continuous themes in any study of the Roman corn supply.

It is absolutely typical that the officials involved in the earliest history of the Republic should be the consuls or praetors. It was not simply state shipping which Rome lacked, the actual machinery of government itself was rudimentary. The magistrates were few and dealt with whatever executive needs there might be. It was only as Rome grew in power and complexity, that various functions once all performed by the consuls were hived off and given to an increasing number of newly created officials.

In the case of corn imports into Rome the officials who came to exercise a special responsibility were the aediles.[32] Quite when and how it all began is far from clear. Originally two officers who were helpers of the plebeian tribunes, they seem to have started life as superintendents of the common temple (*aedes*) and cult of the *plebs*, which significantly enough was that of Ceres on the Aventine Hill. Ceres came to be a goddess particularly associated with corn, and her prominence on coins particularly in the early Empire was largely, although not exclusively, owed to that fact.[33] But the *aediles* came to include the corn supply only incidentally in their range of duties as their administration extended. Their care for the Temple of Ceres was expanded to include oversight of public buildings and archives in Rome generally. With the addition in 367 B.C. of two curule aediles, at first elected from the patricians but later from either order alternately, the aedileship became a magistracy of the whole people. The first undisputed example of a curule aedile taking action with regard to the *annona* is

[32] *OCD*², s.v. aediles. Cf. Mommsen, *Staatsrecht* ii (1)³. 503 n. 1.

[33] See below, p. 260.

Q. Fabius Maximus in 299 B.C.[34] Their duties came to be succinctly defined as care of the city, *cura urbis*, care of the food supply, *cura annonae*, and care of the sacred games, *cura ludorum sollemnium.*[35]

There can be little doubt that their duties in relation to *cura annonae*, the food supply, grew from their overall care for the city—its buildings, its streets, and its administration. In particular as magistrates concerned to prevent abuses in the market places of Rome they became to some extent a Roman equivalent of the Greek *agoranomoi*, who in the Hellenistic world checked weights and measures in the open market, watched prices, particularly of corn, and tried to prevent sharp practice of all kinds in commercial dealings.[36] It was in their power, as general market police, to levy fines for abuses and consequently it is no surprise to find them fining corn dealers for pushing up market prices by hoarding grain.[37] Even so it is also clear that the aediles did have responsibilities for corn in particular on the Roman market. After a campaign in Sardinia in 215 B.C. the praetor T. Manlius, according to Livy, delivered up on his return to Rome *stipendium*, cash, to the quaestors, *frumentum*, grain, to the aediles, and captives to a fellow praetor Q. Fulvius.[38] Similarly any great windfalls of corn, like the great quantity from Spain in 203 B.C., were put on the market at a low price, or distributed free, through the agency of the aediles.[39] The popularity that could be gained in this way seems to have encouraged some aediles while in office to put corn on the market through their own personal generosity.[40] Certainly it was the responsibility for corn retail and for the mounting of shows that gave the office what political attractiveness it had in the second and first centuries B.C.

What evidence there is about what the aediles actually did in relation to the corn supply seems to suggest that they were

[34] Livy 10. 11. 9, cf. 10. 13 and T. R. S. Broughton, *The Magistrates of the Roman Republic* (Lancaster, Pa.: Oxford, 1951–2) i. 173 n. 3. Pliny, *N. H.* 18. 15 (distribution by M. Marcius *c.* 440 B.C.) not reliable.

[35] Cicero, *De Leg.* 3. 3. 7.

[36] *RE* i. s.v. *agoranomos*, col. 883.

[37] Livy 38. 35. 5 (189 B.C.).

[38] Livy 23. 41. 7.

[39] Livy 30. 26. 6.

[40] Cicero, *De Off.* 2. 17. 58. Cf. Gruen, *The Last Generation of the Roman Republic*, p. 36.

more concerned with the retailing of corn on the market in Rome once it had reached the capital than with the procurement of the corn from foreign parts. Special authorization of such procurement would seem to have remained the responsibility of the senior magistrates, or more often, as the Republic evolved, of the senate as a whole, although perhaps the aediles, being the magistrates most in touch with the private corn merchants, who had actually to find the corn, got caught up in some of the administrative details of carrying out the senate's wishes.

3

The most important developments during the Republic for the procurement of corn to feed Rome came at the end of the third century and the beginning of the second century B.C. They were in different ways bound up with the long and exhausting struggle by the Romans against Hannibal. In the wake of her victory in the Second Punic War, and her other victories in the east during the early second century B.C. the population of the city of Rome seems to have increased rather rapidly, partly as a result of migration of peasants from the land, partly by the influx of foreign slaves.[41] But while the population of Rome was on the increase, the traditional sources of her grain were yielding less. Areas immediately to the north and to the south from which she had imported grain at time of need in the past were perhaps less reliable. The spacious and once fertile plain, south of Antium beside the sea, was allowed to become waterlogged, and the area was soon to become the Pomptine marshes.[42] On the other hand coastal Etruria was undergoing changes in agriculture which may have diminished the cultivated area of cereals. Tiberius Gracchus later in the second century B.C. on his way to Spain was said to have been shocked by the growth of large estates there.[43] Olives, vines, and grazing cattle all seemed to offer the prospect of better profits to land-

[41] Frank, *ESAR* i. 108–214; cf. Brunt, *Italian Manpower*, pp. 134 ff., 383 ff., and 705.

[42] Pliny, *N. H.* 3. 59; cf. Livy 6. 6. 1 and 21. 4. Brunt, *Italian Manpower*, p. 349 n. 6.

[43] Plut. *Tib. Gracch.* 8. 9; cf. A. J. Toynbee, *Hannibal's Legacy* (Oxford, 1965), ii. Ch. V.

owners who were no longer thinking in subsistence terms but in commercial ones.

In these circumstances there was bound to be a new emphasis on corn from overseas for the capital, and it came in a new way. Sicily, in which the Romans had prospected for corn since the early Republic, and Sardinia had been won from the Carthaginians during the First Punic War and its aftermath, but they had to be reconquered during the war with Hannibal. This was essential not simply for the sake of pride, but because with Roman control over these islands Hannibal could be isolated in Italy and Rome could draw from them large quantities of grain, livestock, clothing, and other war supplies needed for her armies.[44] With the latter problem in mind Rome began to revitalize Sicilian agriculture, an effort which Livy characterizes as being advantageous both to the Romans and to the natives of Sicily itself.[45]

It is not surprising therefore that the Romans did not apply the system of alliance which had been used in Italy with its obligation of providing men for Rome's armies, but instead retained the tribute system of tithes which had obtained in the island before its conquest. Sicily and Sardinia were to be the great storehouses that would supply Rome's needs, not so much in men, as in goods, and above all corn.[46]

The tithe system was a remarkable institution, which had existed both in the Carthaginian part of Sicily and in the Greek kingdom of Syracuse.[47] Hiero II had only recently systematized the organization within Syracusan territory on the basis of 10 per cent, a literal tithe, of the corn crops but with a number of humane provisions to prevent abuse and safeguard the interests of the cultivators. The Romans seem to have taken this system as their example, to have adopted its provisions, and to have applied it to the whole island and not merely the old

[44] Livy 26. 39. 1.

[45] Livy 26. 40. 15–16; cf. Livy 27. 5; cf. Toynbee, *Hannibal's Legacy* ii. 210 ff.; G. P. Verbrugghe, 'Sicily 210–70 B.C.: Livy, Cicero, and Diodorus', *TAPA* 103 (1972), 535–9.

[46] Cf. Cicero, *De Imp. Gn. Pomp.* 34.

[47] Frank, *ESAR* iii. 237 ff. (Scramuzza); cf. J. Carcopino, *La loi de Hieron et les romains* (Paris, 1914). R. T. Pritchard, 'Cicero and the *Lex Hieronica*', *Historia* 19 (1970), 352–68; R. T. Pritchard, 'Gaius Verres and the Sicilian Farmers', *Historia* 20 (1971), 224–38.

territory of Syracuse; to its advantage if the Carthaginians had taken up to a quarter of the crops.

We know quite a lot about the system and the *lex Hieronica* because of Cicero's prosecution speeches against Verres in 70 B.C. when the system was still in force and it was among Cicero's contentions that Verres contravened it both in the letter and in the spirit.

The system revealed in these speeches is that in each year the officials of each city-state, liable to the tithe, compiled a careful census of the farmers in their area, whether they were landowners, or merely renters of private or public lands. The men so listed were obliged to declare (*profiteri*) the number of *iugera* under cultivation, the kind of crop, and the amount of seed planted. These records were open to inspection by the prospective collectors of the tithe (*decumani*). In the light of the information in the records and their knowledge of the conditions in the area, weather, quality of soil, competence of the farmers, those competing for the contract to collect the tithes made their estimate of the likely crop and made a bid on the basis of the tithe that this would yield. The auction was held before the governor, and if his bid was successful, the *decumanus* then went round his district to make a contract (*pactio*) with each farmer as to the amount each should contribute. This *pactio*, once agreed, was made in triplicate and signed by both parties. One copy remained with the *decumanus*, another with the farmer, and the third was lodged with the city officials for the protection of both sides to the agreement. If, however, no agreement could be reached at that time, the amount to be taken by the *decumanus* was settled after the harvest at the threshing floor itself. There were severe penalties for both a *decumanus* who took more, and a farmer who surrendered less, than the legal due; according to an edict of Verres himself, eightfold restitution in the former case, and fourfold restitution in the latter.

The first thing to grasp about this system is that the farming of the tithes shows not merely Roman good sense in retaining and extending a local practice but also yet again the lack of any direct state machinery for such tediously detailed work. All was to be done under the aegis of the state and goods collected for the benefit of Rome, but the donkey work was to be delegated to men other than state officials.

The second point is that the system as framed by Hiero and in theory practised by the Romans was absolutely fair, above all to the farmers themselves. Come what may, whether the successful *decumanus* had bid high or bid low in securing the contract to collect the tithes, the farmer simply paid a tithe. It was in theory the *decumanus* who ran the risk of a serious shortfall, if he had bid too high or if the harvest proved disastrous, and he must make up his deficit by buying corn from other sources to fulfil his contract. But that was fair since it was also he, rather than the farmer, who stood to make a greater profit if the tithes in fact proved greater than his estimate.

In fact, of course, abuses could and did creep in. In Sicily the *decumani* were permitted by law to collect an extra three-fiftieth of the tithe (i.e. almost a tithe of the tithe) as their own perquisite to help cover their expenses. Pressure from the tithe collectors, particularly if there was collusion with the provincial governor, could lead to the farmers being forced to give more of their crops than was legally due. It was of course also true that a tithe taken from a good harvest would always leave the farmer enough to survive into the next year, but a tithe taken from a bad harvest, even if legally just and properly scaled to the size of his crop, could leave a farmer in dire straits. There was after all a level below which a farmer was not able both to keep back enough seed corn for the next year's planting and to feed his family and dependants throughout the winter.

Normally, despite the sensational nature of Cicero's speeches against Verres, Sicily was to some extent protected from the more outrageous pressures because the tithes were contracted out locally in the province. The more normal pattern for the letting of contracts of all kinds was for the censors to act in Rome.[48] Such contracts in Rome were let to companies of *publicani*, Roman business men, many of them belonging to the stratum of non-senatorial rich in Roman society which was developing fast during the late Republic and which was to be included under the honourable name of 'Equestrians' by Cicero.[49] The farming of the tithes of Asia later in the second

[48] E. Badian, *Publicans and Sinners* (Blackwell, 1973).

[49] P. A. Brunt, 'The Equites in the Late Republic', reprinted in *The Crisis of the Roman Republic*, ed. R. Seager, pp. 83–118 (authorized and revised German text in H. Schneider (ed.), *Zur Sozial- und Wirtschaftsgeschichte der späten römischen Republik* (Darmstadt, 1976), pp. 175–213).

century B.C. to such companies delivered that province into the hands of Romans.[50] In Sicily on the other hand the farming of the corn tithes was done in the province and was largely competed for by local people, including the cities themselves which might farm their own tithes. Resident Romans of course did compete, but the majority of the *decumani* known to us were Sicilians.[51] The Roman *publicani* were only permitted to collect the customs dues (*portoria*) and the grazing tax (*scriptura*) in Sicily. This was not just due to historical accident, to the fact that the Roman *publicani* may not have been so potent a force at the end of the third or the beginning of the second century B.C., when the Sicilian corn tithes were first auctioned, as they were later to become. We know that a determined effort as late as 75 B.C. by the Roman *publicani* to be allowed to bid for the Sicilian corn tithes was resisted by the Roman government.[52]

The Sicilian system was therefore unique, and we have a great deal of evidence about it. But even so it is extremely difficult to grasp exactly how it worked, from the time the wheat was grown in Sicily to the time it was eaten in Rome, how exactly the senate handled corn provided by the tithe system.

The first puzzle is whether the *decumani* in Sicily bid for the contracts in cash or in kind. If they offered a cash sum to the state and bound themselves to deliver the corn they collected to Rome and sell it there on the market, that would at first sight provide an easy mechanism for retailing state corn in Rome. But there are various insuperable objections to the idea that the Sicilian *decumani* put in their bids in cash. Although there is one passage in the Verrines which shows that it was possible to calculate a cash equivalent for the corn tithes reckoned in wheat,[53] the general impression given by the language used by Cicero is overwhelmingly in favour of the bids being made in wheat. Moreover, it is clear that the *decumani* were responsible for transporting the tithes they collected only as far as the sea (*deportatio ad aquam*);[54] they were not automatically responsible

[50] See below, p. 42.
[51] Frank, *ESAR* iii. 305 (Scramuzza).
[52] Cicero, *In Verr.* 2. 3. 18.
[53] Cicero, *In Verr.* 2. 3. 39. 90.
[54] Cicero, *In Verr.* 2. 3. 14. 36.

for transporting them over the sea. Nor, I believe, were the *decumani* automatically responsible for retailing the corn in Rome. It would have demanded resources and organization greater than most Sicilian *decumani* could command, and would have offered further sources of enrichment and profiteering at the expense of the state during the actual process of import into Rome itself, of which we should have heard some hint.

It is perhaps significant that when he refers to the transport of the tithe from Sicily to Rome Cicero calls the men responsible for organizing it not *decumani* but *mancipes*.[55] Rostovtzeff believed that they were the same men, namely, the tithe collectors.[56] It is of course possible that some of the *decumani* acted on a fairly big scale, dealing as wholesalers, buying up surpluses from the farmers' threshing floors as well as collecting the tithes, and could perhaps also have bid for the contracts to ship the corn tithe to Rome. But it seems more likely that the contracts for the shipping of the corn tithe from Sicily, unlike the collection itself, were open to the bids of other contractors from Rome and elsewhere.[57] It seems to me possible that when the government authorized the compulsory purchase of a second tithe, and even further amounts of corn, in Sicily, that the donkey work of carrying out such purchases for the governor could be carried out by *mancipes* who may not have been local.

If this is true, how was the corn provided by the original tithe from Sicily put onto the market in Rome? It would have been gathered from the threshing floors of the farmers by the *decumani* in Sicily and transported by them to the nearest convenient export centre by the sea. From there it would have been shipped to Rome by *mancipes* who had undertaken shipping contracts with the state and who would be paid for undertaking this public duty. But the wheat concerned, although handled by private intermediaries, remained public property. Despite this, and despite the fact that the aediles would have the final say about when and at what price the wheat might be sold, I believe that physically the wheat may have remained in private hands, either with representatives of the contractor who had brought the grain from Sicily or with other corn merchants

55 Cicero, *In Verr.* 2. 3. 74. 172.
56 *RE*, s.v. *frumentum*, col. 153.
57 Frank, *ESAR* iii. 312 (Scramuzza).

in the city of Rome, who would handle government grain as well as their own business.

4

There were without doubt significant differences between the tithe system in Sicily and that in another part of the developing Roman Empire where it was employed later in the second century B.C., the province of Asia.[58]

In 123 B.C. Gaius Gracchus passed a law which granted to the companies of *publicani* in Rome the right to contract for the collection of the revenues of the new province of Asia, formed some six years earlier from the lands of the old Kingdom of Pergamum. The revenues to be farmed out to such companies were not merely the taxes on pasture (*scriptura*) and customs-duties (*portoria*) as in Sicily, but also the tithes themselves on the produce (*decumae*). The three sources of revenue were each farmed by a separate organization, but the same men might be shareholders in all three, and the three companies could and did on occasion combine for a common purpose.

The representatives of the companies in Rome appeared before the censors, or failing them, the consuls, and made their bids in money for the revenues of Asia for the next five years. Not only were they bidding in Rome, and in cash, and for a period of years, they were basing their offers not on precise information as in Sicily but on what was supposed to have been a fair yield during previous periods. If the bid was successful, that amount was guaranteed to the Roman government by the company, which in this way underwrote the payment promised. Anything extra above that amount became profits of the company of *publicani* and its shareholders.

As the system evolved in Asia, during the seventy-five years of its life, the *publicani* and their agents did not deal directly with the individual tax-payers, as the *decumani* did in Sicily, but under the governor's aegis they made their sub-contracts (*pactiones*) probably yearly with the communities as a whole who became responsible for the payment of the quotas. Any lateness in payment was penalized by the imposition of interest

[58] D. Magie, *Roman Rule in Asia Minor* (Princeton, 1950), pp. 164 ff. and notes 14 ff.

at a rate fixed in the sub-contracts. It was this, together with the contracting at Rome on insufficient evidence for periods that were too long, that was most harmful in the Asian system, since the people from whom the individual farmers, or whole communities, would borrow, when they fell into arrears with their quotas, were the very *publicani* to whom they were in debt, acting in their other capacity as bankers.

The most significant aspect of the whole system for us is that if tithes or harvests were actually delivered in kind, they appear to have been immediately sold and the cash was credited to the company. The companies thus became repositories of public money as well as their own private funds. The *magister* of the company remained in Rome and was represented in the province, at Ephesus, by a deputy (*pro magistro*) aided in turn by many clerks and agents, free and slave, who performed a multiplicity of duties in collecting the taxes and acted as dispatch bearers between the capital and the province. It was the *pro magistro* who conducted negotiations both with the governor and the communities, who handled the funds of the company and ran their banks at Laodicea and Ephesus, from which could be paid to the *quaestor* the amount the company had contracted to pay to the Roman government. These banks were important and were used both by Roman state officials on the spot to deposit their ready money and by the government at home for giving bills of exchange to officials on their way to the province.

The important point is that just as public money from Asia lay in the hands of the *publicani*, so, I suspect, public corn from Sicily lay in the hands of *publicani* or private corn merchants in Rome.

What needs explaining, however, is why when Rome needed the corn tithes from Sicily so badly at the beginning of the second century B.C. she was prepared to commute the Asian corn tithe into cash at the end of the same century. The answers to that question could be many and varied. The distance from Rome, the amounts of corn grown in Asia, the local needs of the cities to feed themselves, the fact that Asia paid its taxes in cash to its previous rulers, the Attalids, and Gaius Gracchus' need for more cash in the Treasury at Rome to pay for the subsidized *frumentatio* which he started,[59] all could have

[59] Cf. E. Badian, *Roman Imperialism in the Late Republic*² (Oxford, 1968), pp. 46 and 76.

been factors. But the prime reason must have been that ways had been found of meeting the corn demands of the capital without the need to import laboriously from the eastern Mediterranean the corn tithes of Asia. What had happened during the second century B.C.?

At the start of that century the dangers of corn shortages and the need for overseas corn were both obvious. Livy records how the annual tithes of Sicily and Sardinia, even when supplemented as they were in 196 B.C. by the gift of 1,000,000 *modii* of wheat from the Sicilians in honour of C. Flaminius,[60] were not enough for the combined needs of the capital and the Roman armies that were being fielded in Greece and elsewhere. In 191 B.C. for the first time a second tithe was ordered to be purchased from Sicily for the Roman army in Greece, while a second tithe from Sardinia was to be sent to Rome itself.[61] In that same year the Numidian prince Masinissa and Carthage sent half a million *modii* of wheat, and a quarter of a million *modii* of barley to Rome.[62] Even so in 190, in 181, and in 171 B.C., a second tithe was again demanded from Sicily and Sardinia, and divided again between the army and the city.[63] It was during this tricky period in 188 B.C. that the corn dealers were heavily fined for hoarding supplies against a rise in prices.[64]

The situation seems to have eased after the middle of the century and that may be largely though unwittingly because of the destruction of Carthage and the creation of the province of Africa in 146 B.C. It was not so much the corn provided by taxation of the new province that made the difference, but rather the rich and extensive corn growing areas in the hinterland which were now opened up to the speculative purchases of private corn dealers buying for the Roman market.[65] Moreover it was Gaius Gracchus himself who introduced large numbers of Italian settlers to farm on large allotments in the territory of Carthage.[66] Despite the repeal of the law by his political opponents at Rome, much land had been assigned and the

[60] Livy 33. 42. 8.
[61] Livy 36. 2. 12.
[62] Livy 36. 4. 5.
[63] Livy 37. 2. 12; 50. 9.
[64] Livy 38. 35. 5.
[65] Cf. Meiggs, *Roman Ostia*², p. 29.
[66] Greenidge and Clay, *Sources*, pp. 38 and 43; cf. Appian, *B.C.* 1. 24; *Pun.* 136; some 6,000 settlers, whether authorized by law or not, were involved.

new owners continued to farm. If Africa which was to be so important a source of corn in the Empire was already being systematically drawn upon from 146 B.C. that might help to explain why the Asian tithes were not needed at Rome.

Even so it would not be correct to paint too rosy a picture of Rome's corn resources. The Social War in the early part of the first century B.C. suddenly put a greater premium on the corn supplies coming from Campania,[67] and at the time of the Spartacus revolt in 73 B.C. the *lex Terentia–Cassia* turned what had previously been random purchasing of a second tithe in Sicily into a regular system to be applied every year. Cicero in 70 B.C. speaks as if it were now a permanent and necessary fact of Roman life.[68]

5

The expansion of imports from overseas to Rome from the second century B.C. onward was bound to have an effect on Rome itself and Ostia at the mouth of the Tiber.[69] It was to the early second century B.C. that the first physical development of the river port in Rome itself belonged. The Forum Boarium and Forum Holitorium, the original meat and vegetable markets, in the low-lying heart of Rome between the hills, owed their names and their position no doubt to produce brought by boat. But this was essentially local produce, brought in fairly small quantities down the Tiber from the hills, even from the Val di Chiana in Etruria,[70] or up the Tiber from the farms surrounding the city. It was carried without too much danger of congestion right to the very heart of the city. But the influx of goods in the early second century B.C. made the creation of a proper river port a necessity and it was the Aventine area much further from the centre of civic life, and below the Pons Sublicius, the first city bridge, that was developed. It was in 193 B.C. according to Livy that two Aemilii, aediles of the year, built outside the Porta Trigemina a great porticus which bore

[67] Cicero, *De Imp. Gn. Pomp.* 34; *leg. agr.* 2. 80.
[68] Cicero, *In Verr.* 2. 3. 163; see below, p. 166.
[69] Meiggs, *Roman Ostia*², pp. 30 ff.
[70] Pliny, *N. H.* 18. 87.

their name.[71] Livy also says they added an *emporium* by the Tiber. In 174 B.C. the censors paved this *emporium* and fenced it round. They also did some restoration work on the Porticus Aemilia and created steps from the Tiber to the *emporium*.[72] This work seems to have been just the nucleus of a great deal of building activity for commercial purposes in this area at this time. Other porticoes were constructed; in 192 B.C. we hear of a 'porticus extra portam Trigeminam inter lignarios';[73] in 179 B.C. M. Fulvius as censor built two porticoes, one outside the Porta Trigemina and another beyond the *navalia*, buildings specifically described as being of great utility.[74]

The development of this Emporium area was obviously designed to cope with the increasing volume of goods, including corn, which flowed into Rome from overseas in the second century B.C. Most of the building activity associated with it however seems to be concentrated into the first half of that century; the domestic crises which developed in Rome during the latter part of the century may have been partly caused by a reduction of building operations by the state and may have had among other effects that of limiting the amount of new building.[75]

Granted that almost all goods for Rome had to be unloaded at the river mouth and transferred either directly or after a period of storage into river boats (*naves codicariae*) for transshipment to Rome, one might expect to find signs of similar physical development at Ostia. Unfortunately while we can say that physical expansion beyond the fourth-century walls of the original settlement did take place during the second century B.C., we cannot yet understand in detail what form it took.[76] The development may have been limited by the fact that during

[71] Livy 35. 10. 12. The view that parts of this *porticus* still survive in the area has now been questioned by L. Richardson, Jr., 'The Evolution of the Porticus Octaviae', *AJA* 80 (1976), pp. 57–64; but see P. Coarelli, 'Public building in Rome between the Second Punic War and Sulla', *PBSR* 45 (1977), 9, and p. 5 n. 23 for possible *Horrea Aemiliana*, located by the river near the temple of Portunus. Cf W. L. MacDonald, *The Architecture of the Roman Empire* (New Haven, 1965), pp. 5 ff.

[72] Livy 41. 27. 8. [73] Livy 35. 41. 10. [74] Livy 40. 51. 4–6.

[75] A. H. Boren, 'The urban side of the Gracchan economic crisis', *AHR* 63 (1957–8), pp. 890–8; but cf. M. H. Crawford, *Roman Republican Coinage* (Cambridge, 1974), ii. 636 n. 7.

[76] Meiggs, *Roman Ostia*², p. 31.

the Second Punic War the Romans had already encouraged the growth on the bay of Naples of Puteoli as their commercial harbour.

The one form of utilitarian building that may have been positively encouraged in the second half of the second century B.C. was the construction of corn storehouses. Gaius Gracchus' law guaranteeing the distribution of corn to citizens below the market price was said to have been coupled with the greater provision of storage facilities, although we know nothing about them.[77] It must also have provided a stimulus to the corn trade in general and also to state involvement in it.

At Ostia at some time between 150 and 80 B.C. a long area north of the Decumanus Maximus up to the bank of the Tiber was declared by the praetor C. Caninius to be public property of the Roman people and boundary stones were set up to define it.[78] Along this stretch of the river bank during the Republic merchantmen of all kinds must have unloaded their cargoes.

A more specific indication of the increasingly vital role that Ostia was playing not just in general trade but in the import of corn can be seen in the changing character of the duties of the quaestor based at Ostia.[79] Originally as a *quaestor classicus* he was concerned with the needs of Rome's fleet in the third century B.C., but with the decline of the fleet and the new regular import of corn from overseas it is clear that by the end of the second century B.C. his main duties concerned corn. In 104 B.C. when there was a critical corn shortage in Rome one of the measures taken by the senate was to relieve L. Appuleius Saturninus of his post as *quaestor Ostiensis* greatly to his wrath, and to replace him with no less a person than M. Aemilius Scaurus, who was *princeps senatus* at that time.[80]

The Ostian quaestor therefore was or could be important, and his duties were intimately connected with the corn supply, but what exactly those duties were is more difficult to say. Cicero later regarded it as an onerous post, involving trouble and hard work without any social or political distinction to make up for it.[81] During the late Republic the *quaestor Ostiensis*

[77] Plut. *G. Gracchus* 6. 2, cf. Rickman, *Roman Granaries*, pp. 150 and 173.
[78] *CIL* 14 Suppl. 4702.
[79] Meiggs, *Roman Ostia*², pp. 33, 299, 499.
[80] Cicero, *Pro Sestio* 39; *De har. resp.* 43; Diod. 36. 12; see below, p. 162.
[81] Cicero, *Pro Murena* 18.

seems to have supervised the reception, storage, and transshipment of corn from the provinces. This must have involved dealing with shippers, among others, with whom the state had contracts, and in order to deal properly with his duties it seems that the Ostian quaestor exercised a jurisdiction greater than that normally connected with the quaestorship. He certainly had a tribunal in the forum at Ostia and an inscription, admittedly perhaps of Augustan date, set up to a certain Pacceius by the shippers of Ostia gives the full title of his office as *quaestor pro pr(aetore)*.[82] It is probable that all Roman quaestors at Ostia came to have some, at least, of the judicial competence of a praetor. The growth in the judicial work performed by the *praefectus annonae* later under the Empire shows how natural a part of the work of a corn-supply supervisor was the hearing of a variety of civil cases which were relevant in one way or another to his duties *propter utilitatem ad annonam pertinentem.*[83]

The Ostia quaestor performed his work throughout the late Republic and into the early Empire. It is significant that at the time of the corn crisis in 23–22 B.C. when Augustus took upon himself the *cura annonae*, Tiberius the Emperor's stepson was sent to be the quaestor at Ostia, the first important step in a public career that was to take him to the imperial purple.[84] It was only under the Emperor Claudius with the building of a new harbour at Ostia that the quaestorship was replaced by new imperial officials, the *procurator annonae Ostis* and the *procurator portus*, responsible to the *praefectus annonae*, an office itself created only late in the reign of Augustus.[85]

6

Much earlier than this, with the tribunate of the younger of the two Gracchus brothers, Gaius, in 123 B.C., several new elements were introduced into the history of the corn supply. The *lex Sempronia frumentaria* established the basic right of every Roman citizen to a ration of corn at a cheap rate below the normal

[82] *CIL* 14. 3603; Bloch, 'Ostia: Iscrizioni rinvenute tra il 1930 e il 1939', *NSc* (1953), n. 32.
[83] *Dig.* 48. 2. 13 (Marcianus); see below, p. 220.
[84] *R. G.* 5; Vell. Pat. 2. 94. 3; Suet. *Tib.* 8.
[85] Suet. *Claud.* 24. 2; Dio 60. 24. 3; cf. Meiggs, *Roman Ostia*², pp. 55 and 299; see below, p. 76.

market price.[86] Without anticipating a later detailed discussion of the law, it may be said that the grain was sold monthly, probably at the rate of 5 *modii* for each person eligible. This distributed corn was not sold through ordinary shopkeepers—for the first time the state seems to have sold at least this corn at a given location, and also to have built state granaries for the first time. It is no surprise that with the institution of a cheap corn ration Gaius should have been concerned with the revising of the tax administration in the new province of Asia and with the revival of the commercial and agricultural prosperity of the old territory of Carthage where a new colony was sent.[87] In the history of the corn distributions in the late Republic changes in the amount of corn needed for distribution or in the price charged were often accompanied by annexation or rearrangements of provinces abroad.

The *lex Sempronia frumentaria* and the distributions of corn, *frumentationes*, became a hot political issue during the next sixty years, with attempts to limit or abolish them competing with attempts to extend them. The culmination of this struggle, to be analysed later, came when Clodius in his tribunate in 58 B.C. abolished all payment by the recipients of the corn ration.[88]

Despite the undoubted improvement in the amount of supplies and efficiency of organization by the end of the second century B.C. there were to be considerable and continuing difficulties in supplying Rome adequately during the ensuing century.

The corn distributions made the capital even more attractive to possible incomers and encouraged masters to manumit slaves in ever-increasing numbers, so as to transfer the expense of their upkeep from themselves to the state.[89] Greater numbers may have needed to be fed in Rome and a higher proportion of those numbers at the expense of the state. The physical ability to supply such numbers lagged behind the political decisions that they must be fed.

The situation was not aided by the large amount of military

[86] Plut. *G. Gracchus* 6; Appian, *B. C.* 1. 21; Cicero, *Tusc. Disp.* 3. 20. 48; see below, p. 158.

[87] Cf. E. Badian, *Roman Imperialism*², pp. 47–9. S. J. de Laet, *Portorium* (Bruges, 1949), pp. 71–6.

[88] Ascon. *In Pisonem*, p. 8 (ed. Clark); Schol. Bobb. p. 132; see below, p. 172.

[89] Dio 39. 24. 1; Dion. Halic. 4. 24. 5; cf. Brunt, *Italian Manpower*, p. 380.

activity which characterized the history of the last century of the Republic; military action that was not taking place in areas away from Italy, as in the second century B.C., but in Italy itself. There was the Social War and its repercussion from 90 B.C., the revolt of Spartacus in the mid-70s, civil war between Pompey and Caesar in the 40s, followed by the struggle between Octavian and Sextus Pompeius and between Octavian and Antony in the 30s. Political instability had repercussions on the never-ceasing need to feed Rome year in and year out.

No less important at the beginning of the century was the havoc being created for all normal shipping by the great growth of piracy. The signs had all been there in the late second century B.C. Even since the decline of the great Hellenistic powers the eastern Mediterranean had been a prey to piracy. Centred originally in Cilicia, the pirates had clearly been interfering increasingly with Rome's corn supply. A corn shortage in 104 B.C. was followed by a special command given to the praetor M. Antonius for 102 B.C. against the pirates.[90] In 100 B.C. it is significant that among the laws of the tribune L. Appuleius Saturninus was a measure dealing with corn distributions and at the same period a *lex de piratis* which was designed, so far as we can judge from the fragments of the inscription, to take comprehensive action against piracy.[91] It was however Mithridates who encouraged the pirates in the first century B.C. to major attacks on Roman shipping.[92] Since Rome had no navy the pirates, organized in regular fleets, very rapidly came to control a large part of the Mediterranean. The senate reacted to the danger but not very effectively. In 77 B.C. P. Servilius Vatia was sent to attack the pirate strongholds in Cilicia itself. This he did with great severity, but the taking of their lands in Cilicia exacerbated the problem rather than solved it.[93] In 74 B.C. M. Antonius with unlimited authority went to Crete which had become a new centre for pirate activity. But he

[90] Broughton, *MRR* i. 568.

[91] The authorship of this far-ranging law is disputed, with Saturninus himself a possible, but not now fashionable, candidate, see M. Hassall, M. Crawford, and J. Reynolds, 'Rome and the Eastern Provinces at the end of the second century B.C.', *JRS* 64 (1974), 195–220.

[92] Appian, *Mithr.* 63; cf. Frank, *ESAR* i. 302.

[93] Oros. 5. 23; Cicero, *In Verr.* 2. 1. 56; *leg. agr.* 2. 50. Cf. also Pirate Law of 100 B.C.

achieved little. Verres, as governor of Sicily in this period, was caught up in the pirate problem, because the shipping lanes from the south and east converged upon the straits of Messina and offered great opportunities to the pirates.[94] Based in this area on the island of Malta, they kept the eastern seaboard of Sicily in a perpetual state of nervous terror.[95] Verres' small fleet of ten Sicilian ships was captured and burned by the pirates.

After the death of Antonius, Q. Metellus was sent out in 68 B.C. to continue his work. He succeeded in subduing towns in Crete but that did little or nothing to eliminate piracy in general. If anything the situation got worse. Shortly before 67 B.C. pirates sailed into the mouth of the Tiber, destroyed a fleet under the command of a consul, and plundered Ostia itself.[96]

Consequently there is no need to suppose that it was a specifically commercial lobby that was pressing for the appointment of Pompey to deal with the pirates in 67 B.C. The very food supply of the capital was in jeopardy and the disgrace at Ostia would awaken large sections of public opinion at Rome to the idea that something drastic must be done. The tribune Gabinius passed a law, despite opposition from the senate, specifically naming Pompey to a supreme command over all the seas for a period of three years with ships up to a total of 500 if needed, an army, an immediate grant of 6,000 talents, together with the right to use any available revenue and an order to draw on Roman allies for whatever might be needed. Moreover he had the right to appoint twenty-four *legati pro praetore*. On the mere announcement of his appointment the price of goods fell in the markets of Rome.[97]

In carrying out his extraordinary command Pompey showed strategic and administrative ability of a very high order. He saw the problem as one of Mediterranean-wide extension, which demanded the co-ordination by him of the efforts of a large number of individual commanders. His plan was to clear first

[94] Cicero, *In Verr.* 2. 1. 12; *In Verr.* 2. 5 *passim.*
[95] Livy 5. 28. 2; Cicero, *In Verr.* 2. 4. 144.
[96] Cicero, *De Imp. Gn. Pomp.* 33; Dio 36. 22.
[97] Plut. *Pomp.* 25; Vell. 2. 31; Appian, *Mithr.* 94.Cf. Gruen, *The Last Generation o the Roman Republic,* p. 435.

the western seas, so as to make safe the sea lanes from the grain-producing provinces of Sicily, Sardinia, and Africa to Rome, and then to flush the pirates out of all their bases by moving eastwards to a final *coup de grâce* in the eastern Mediterranean. He started in early spring and moving rapidly round the western shores of the Mediterranean drove the pirates out of their bays and harbours, and stationed there instead strong naval units under his lieutenants. Within forty days the west was safe. After a brief visit to Rome he hurried to Brindisi where his main forces were and sailed for the east. The pirate fleets were destroyed and more than 1,300 ships were burned. Pirate settlements were also blotted out and the survivors were resettled elsewhere, well away from temptation. The second campaign was finished within forty-nine days, and the whole war had taken just on three months. There was to be no organized piracy again in the Mediterranean for several hundred years.

It was an astonishing performance by Pompey, demanding an organizational ability which was probably his greatest strength. It did not of course by itself rectify all Rome's supply problems, it merely guaranteed one of the conditions, the safety of the seas, necessary for the proper functioning of the supply system.

In 62 B.C. Cato carried a law which extended the number of recipients in the corn distributions at Rome,[98] and when he became tribune for 58 B.C. Clodius abolished all charge for the rations distributed, an act which attracted more people into the city. Clodius' law, however, if we can trust Cicero, dealt with more than just the distributions. According to Cicero, all matters concerning both public and private corn, the corn lands, the contractors, and the corn stores were put under the power of an agent of Clodius named Sextus Cloelius.[99] While it is understandable that Clodius might want to ensure as much public control as possible, and to prevent private grain speculation at the expense of both the *plebs urbana* and the treasury, if we can trust Cicero's allegations about the powers of Cloelius, this action marked an attempt at state interference in the private rights of individuals that was unprecedented. It may in fact have helped to increase the difficulties of the corn supply

[98] Plut. *Cat. Min.* 26; *Caes.* 8. 6.
[99] Cicero, *De Domo* 25.

which became increasingly acute in the next two years. Clearly there were poor harvests and other normal difficulties at this time, which the leading political figures to some extent ignored while blaming each other for the corn shortages, but there is little doubt that part of the trouble was that the corn traders themselves were for some reason not willing to bring their cargoes to Rome, or release their stocks except at exorbitant prices. The situation had reached crisis proportions by 57 B.C.[100] Pompey had shown himself extraordinarily brilliant in organizing the sweeping of the pirates out of the whole Mediterranean in three months, rather than the three years he had been granted; why should he not prove equally successful in sweeping the corn of the whole Mediterranean into the market at Rome? Whatever Cicero's private motives after his recall from exile for proposing Pompey's appointment in the senate on 7 September 57 B.C., whatever Pompey's private hopes in relation to it or his enemies' political fears, there is no doubt that Pompey after the pirate command was the man best suited to trying to solve so tangled an administrative problem.

7

The Republic had seen many changes in the procurement of corn for Rome. While the state in the fifth century B.C. had only acknowledged the need to step in at moments of crisis, from the end of the third century B.C. there was a regular system for tapping the corn resources of the overseas provinces such as Sicily. Physical improvements had been carried out in Rome from the early second century B.C. to help cope with the new imports up the Tiber. But the physical improvements had not included the provision of state granaries until perhaps the time of Gaius Gracchus and the system of supply from Sicily and other sources in no way implied state control of shipping or retail. Piracy had flourished and had been suppressed only by spasmodic efforts by the state and there were no state fleets to police the seas. Now however by the mid-first century B.C. things were on the change again. The great dynasts of the late Republic exercised more than republican wealth and power, in Rome, in Italy, and the Mediterranean. Pompey's *clientela*

[100] Cicero, *De Domo* 5. 11; Dio 39. 9. 2.

stretched in fact from one end of the Mediterranean to the other, from Spain to the East. There was a foreshadowing of imperial modes of action and of thought. It is not merely Julius Caesar who must be coupled with Augustus in considering the shift to Empire. Pompey too in his actions relating to the corn supply of Rome showed in many ways a grasp of the problem that was imperial in its breadth and subtle in its administrative insight. A period of transition had begun.

III

TRANSITION: POMPEY, CAESAR, AND AUGUSTUS

I

On 8 September 57 B.C. the consuls P. Cornelius Lentulus Spinther and Q. Caecilius Metellus Nepos carried a law by which Pompey was to be granted for five years complete command over the corn supply throughout the entire Roman world ('omnis potestas rei frumentariae toto orbe terrarum').[1] What exactly this *potestas* amounted to and how it compared with the power he was allowed to wield in the other extraordinary commission against the pirates is not entirely clear. We know that he asked for, and was granted, fifteen *legati*, among whom both Cicero and his brother Quintus were included. We may infer from the proposal of the tribune C. Messius, which was defeated, that Pompey did not have unlimited control over the treasury, nor authority to levy troops and ships, nor *maius imperium* over all provincial governors. This was to be no great military command. But money there must have been and we know of one grant made to Pompey on 5 April 56 B.C., some six months after the start of his *cura*, to the tune of 40 million sesterces.[2]

As the date of that grant already indicates, there was to be no miraculous cure within three months this time, as there had been with the pirates. Although the price of corn had sunk dramatically at the time of Pompey's nomination, we hear throughout the next year, in February, April, and August 56 B.C., of high prices, infertile fields, and poor harvests. It was to be a longer, harder struggle. But although there were to be no immediate easy solutions, Pompey was up to his task. He did not merely deploy his lieutenants in key areas, but sailed off

[1] Cicero, *Ad Att.* 4. 1. 6–7; Dio 39. 9. 3; Livy, *Epit.* 104.
[2] Cicero, *Ad Q.F.* 2. 5. 1.

himself to the three crucial sources of supply, Sardinia, Sicily, and Africa.[3] The story was told that when the captains of the ships were not eager to weigh anchor, on the return journey during a great storm, he led the way on board himself and gave the orders to sail for Rome, with the ringing phrase, 'To sail is essential, to live is not', 'Navigare necesse est, vivere non necesse.' It was a phrase that was to have a long history and to be carved over the offices of great Hanseatic trading firms in Bremen in the Middle Ages.[4]

From stray references in some of Cicero's letters and from the fragments of his speech for M. Aemilius Scaurus we can penetrate behind the public façade and can see a little of the methods that Pompey used. Quintus Cicero was sent as one of Pompey's lieutenants to Sardinia and we have six letters written by Cicero to him at this period; the first was sent in December 57 B.C. while Quintus was on his way to Sardinia, the next four in January, February, March, and April 56 B.C. while he was actually in Sardinia, and the final one in the middle of May when he was on his way back to Rome.[5] The letters are mainly full of gossip and political manoeuvrings at Rome but they do reveal how long Quintus spent in Sardinia, that he seems to have had his main residence in Olbia in the north-east of the island, and that his departure was to be just after a visit by Pompey to the island, presumably to inspect the arrangements made.

Quintus seems to have done his work well and enjoyed a good reputation in the province, but what he actually did is not stated. A clue to that comes in another letter of Cicero written in 53 B.C. to Titus Titius who was another of Pompey's lieutenants during his *cura annonae*.[6] It was a letter recommending to Titius a man named C. Avianius Flaccus and it was written by Cicero at the latter's request. It is clear from the letter that Avianius Flaccus was a corn merchant, as well as being an intimate friend of Cicero's, and Titius is urged to look after his interests, particularly to accommodate Avianius with regard to both the place and the time at which he was to deliver his

[3] Plut. *Pomp.* 50.

[4] Plut. *Pomp.* 49 and 50 (cf. apophth. Pomp. 12); cf. J. Carcopino, *Histoire romaine* (Paris, 1936), ii. 2. 731.

[5] Cicero, *Ad. Q. F.* 2. 1–6.

[6] Cicero, *Ad Fam.* 13. 75.

corn. He had enjoyed both courtesies apparently through Cicero's good offices during the previous three-year period, while Pompey was playing a leading role personally in the corn supply. In a later letter written in 46 B.C. Cicero also commends Avianius' sons Gaius and Marcus to the proconsul of Sicily.[7] Clearly we have in this family firm of corn merchants an example of the kind of men through whom the *legati* of Pompey actually did their business. The corn supply of Rome was improved by the letting of contracts to private corn merchants over a period of years—in this case a three-year contract in the first instance. One of the keys to solving the problems about continuity of supply was to plan over a long enough period rather than leave things to chance, and to year-by-year arrangements. It does not seem to have survived the period of Pompey's *cura annonae*, but it was an important idea that was to re-emerge. It was implicit not least in the Emperor Claudius' grant of privileges to those who put a ship into the service of the *annona* for at least six years.[8]

A final hint as to how Pompey may have operated in securing sufficient supplies of corn comes in the speech delivered by Cicero in 54 B.C. in defence of M. Aemilius Scaurus against charges of extortion during his governorship of Sardinia in 55 B.C. In a not very edifying oration, which includes much sneering at the Sardinians, and blackening of their character, Cicero makes certain exceptions among the unprincipled Sardinians, men such as A. Domitius Sincaius 'and others who have received the citizenship from Cn. Pompeius.'[9] Although it may be impossible to prove it, there is the strongest suspicion that these men owed their citizenship to the help that they rendered to Pompey during his *cura annonae* in some capacity or other, as corn merchants or as shippers. If that is so, we have another example of Pompey anticipating in his actions for the corn supply something that was to be characteristic of the attitude of the Emperors; privileges up to and including the citizenship were to be available to those who helped the state sufficiently in its problems of keeping Rome fed.

[7] Cicero, *Ad Fam.* 13. 79. C. Nicolet, *Rome et la conquête du monde méditerranéen*, i: *Les Structures de l'Italie romaine* (Paris, 1977), 203. Cf. also J. D'Arms, 'CIL X. 1792: A municipal notable of the Augustan age', *HSCP* 76 (1972), 207–16.

[8] Suet. *Claud.* 18–19.

[9] Cicero, *Pro Scauro* 43; cf. Gaius I. 32c.

Although it is not the major concern in this chapter it is worth noting that Pompey's responsibilities seem to have gone beyond the provision of corn and to have extended to the distribution of it as well. It seems that Pompey may have tried to introduce some order and system into the *frumentationes*, which had become increasingly chaotic, perhaps by reorganizing lists of those eligible to receive free corn since Clodius' legislation.[10] If he was responsible, then here again he was helping to lay the foundations of an administrative framework that was to continue into the Empire.

Pompey's work was successful at the time, and set an example for the future, but for all that it belonged to the Republican tradition of occasional extraordinary commissions. Pompey's special *cura* was not renewed, and there was no permanent system created under a permanent head.

2

During the civil war which ensued after Caesar had crossed the Rubicon in 49 B.C. both he and Pompey showed a shrewd awareness of the importance of supplies. Pompey was perhaps the more successful in organizing the supply system for his army;[11] his administrative experience in these matters, together no doubt with the contacts that he had made while exercising his *cura annonae* saw to that. Caesar by comparison lived rather from hand to mouth on what his army could forage or his agents could seize. But in relation to the problems of supplying Rome itself, both Pompey and Caesar showed that they knew well the basic principles. When Pompey retreated to Greece he gathered a great fleet from the east to cut the supplies to Italy and take the *provinciae frumentariae*; Caesar in his turn, before starting on his campaign in Spain, made sure of both Sicily and Sardinia. The senatorial governor of Sardinia was forced to retire to Africa.[12] Indeed with Africa in Pompeian hands and Egypt within Pompey's eastern sphere of influence, the control of the two islands was vital, if Rome was not to starve. The majority of Caesar's warships was used to guard the approaches

[10] Dio 39. 24. 1–2; see below, p. 174.
[11] Appian, *B. C.* 2. 10. 66; cf. 2. 8. 54, 2. 9. 61.
[12] *Ad Att.* 9. 9; Caesar, *B. C.* 1. 30; Dio 41. 18.

of Sicily and Sardinia, not always successfully, and Caesar was rather embarrassed for ships in his pursuit of Pompey to Greece.[13] But Rome had to be fed even if civil war raged.

Caesar's activities in relation to the corn supply during the short period of his dictatorship showed in general the same bold grasp of essentials as in his other administrative reforms.

First, there was the problem of numbers to be fed in the capital. The number of recipients of the corn distributions which we are told had crept up to 320,000 was reduced to a fixed limit of 150,000.[14] Certainly now, if not before, there were lists for the corn distributions. But the problem of numbers hoping to benefit from corn distributions was part of a larger overall problem of increase in the size of the capital's population, all of whom needed corn. Caesar attempted to drain population away from Rome altogether by colonization on a massive scale.[15]

Secondly, instead of expecting the ordinary aediles to couple a watching brief over the corn supply with all their other duties, two special aediles were created, the *aediles Cereales*, specifically for corn problems whether to do with the *frumentationes* or the general market.[16] This was a sensible move and reflected the need for multiplication of officials as the duties created by a growing capital city became too complicated for the original numbers of officials in each magistracy.

Thirdly, Caesar gave thought to the major practical problem besetting the import of corn, namely the lack of proper harbour facilities at Ostia, which was still simply a river mouth. There were schemes for cutting a canal direct from the Tiber southwestwards to the sea at Terracina to allow ships approaching from the south a more direct access to Rome itself, and also to build a harbour at Ostia.

Nothing in fact was started, but Caesar's intentions were a major inspiration to the Emperor Claudius who did create a harbour at Ostia, and to Nero who started work on a similar canal from Lake Avernus to Ostia.[17]

Caesar, in fact, achieved little that was to be permanent in

[13] Appian, *B. C.* 2. 54.
[14] Suet. *Caesar* 41. 3; Dio 43. 21. 4.
[15] Suet. *Caesar* 42. 1; cf. Brunt, *Italian Manpower*, pp. 255 ff.
[16] Dio 43. 51. 3, cf. Broughton, *MRR* 2. 306.
[17] Plut. *Caesar* 58. 10; Suet. *Claud.* 20. 1; Suet. *Nero* 31. 3.

his direct arrangements for the corn supply, but he pointed the way to the imperial future where strong central government might successfully control numbers, create a more effective administrative machinery, and harness sufficient resources to undertake major building schemes. Augustus during his much longer period of power in Rome seems, so far as the corn supply was concerned, to have put most of his effort into the first two of these desirable aims, but the latter was also possible, as Caesar had believed.

Perhaps more striking in their effect on the supply system, although more concealed in the sources, were the changes that Julius Caesar started to make in the taxation methods in some of the corn-producing provinces. There is no doubt that in Asia the tithe system farmed out to *publicani* from Rome was changed to one where a lump sum was paid over to the Roman government directly by the communities.[18] But Rome had always drawn cash rather than goods from Asia, so that whatever the improvement, if any, for the Asian communities, the result was much the same for the government. It is, however, possible that Julius Caesar made a start towards a similar kind of tax reform in Sicily from which the Romans had drawn corn revenues.[19] The evidence is tenuous and, it has been argued, is tied up with the equally baffling evidence about the granting of political privileges to Sicily. It is likely anyway that the new Sicilian privileges and the new tax system for Sicily did not become finally settled until the reign of Augustus, who showed a considerable interest in the area.

3

Whatever Caesar's long-term plans may have been, with his murder the political situation was back in the melting pot. In the tangled events of the ensuing ten years the importance of the feeding of the capital was not, indeed could not be, lost sight of. Immediately after the assassination of Caesar, Brutus and Cassius, unable to remain in Rome, were given special corn commissionerships, and purchases were made in both Sicily

[18] Plut. *Caesar* 48; Dio 42. 6. 3; Appian, *B. C.* 5. 4.

[19] Frank, *ESAR* iii. 344 (Scramuzza); Rostovtzeff, *SEHRE*² i. 208–9, ii. 629 n. 20; but see below, n. 37.

and Asia. Cicero was scandalized and exclaimed that no state office could be more contemptible.[20] But it was significant that the senate in April 43 B.C., in passing measures by which it thought to prevent the emergence of rule by one man in the future, included among them the provision that no one man should be chosen to control the corn supply.[21] It was no less significant that Sextus Pompeius by controlling Sicily created such a threat of famine in Rome in 40–39 B.C. that Octavian and Antony under public pressure were forced to agree to the so-called treaty of Misenum with Sextus.[22] In 36 B.C. there was a final show-down when Octavian organized the invasion and capture of Sicily to the greater ease of the supply problems of Rome.

But within six years Octavian had within his hands an even more important source of corn, Egypt. Its capture in 30 B.C. helped to alleviate many of Octavian's pressing financial problems and put into Roman control an area on which covetous eyes had been cast throughout the last century of the Republic. Although Egypt was added to the possessions of the senate and Roman people, it was to be governed not by a senator but by an equestrian *praefectus*, appointed by the Emperor himself. The country remained particularly closely tied to the Emperor and somewhat cut off from the rest of the Roman world. Its highly developed centralized bureaucracy remained and was harnessed to imperial purposes. Egypt was to be a source of both cash and corn. Improvements in the agricultural system of the country were to be set in hand—for the benefit of the corn supply of Rome.[23] A very late source claims that Egypt sent annually to Rome in the time of Augustus 20 million *modii* of grain. How far we can trust this precise figure is difficult to judge, but it seems clear that Egyptian corn regularly met up to a third of Rome's needs in the early Empire and could by itself cover the 12 million *modii* needed annually for the free distributions to up to the 200,000 recipients fixed by Augustus in 2 B.C.[24] Yet no permanent security seems to have been achieved.

[20] Cicero, *Ad Att.* 14. 3; 15. 9; 15.10; *Phil.* 2. 31.
[21] Dio 46. 39. 3.
[22] Suet. *Aug.* 16. 1; Vell. Pat. 2. 77. 1; Appian, *B. C.* 5. 18, 66–9, 71–2.
[23] Suet. *Aug.* 18. 2.
[24] *Epit. de Caesaribus* i. 6; Josephus, *Bell. Iud.* 2. 383–5; see below, Appendix 4.

In 23 and 22 B.C. a critical situation in the feeding of Rome occurred. The Tiber burst its banks and flooded Rome; there was plague in Italy and, if Dio is right, elsewhere too; fields were untilled and people were starving.[25] In 23, according to his own boast, Augustus at his own expense provided the corn for twelve *frumentationes*.[26] In 22 the crisis continued and among the many honours and offices pressed upon him including the dictatorship Augustus accepted only, and apparently reluctantly, the *cura annonae* which allowed him to alleviate the crisis 'within a few days'.[27] It was at this time that the Emperor's stepson, Tiberius himself, was acting as the *quaestor Ostiensis*. In the same year Augustus hived off the work associated with the distributions into a separate organization run by two ex-praetors annually appointed and later to have the title *praefecti frumenti dandi*.[28] There can be no doubt that this led to greater efficiency in the organization of the distributions and the use of *tesserae*, tickets, for the corn ration. But at least at this stage in his career Augustus did nothing to upset the previous arrangements whereby the *aediles Cereales* exercised some sort of supervision over other aspects of the corn supply.

It seems very probable that Augustus' acceptance of the *cura annonae* was not for a limited period, but permanent at least in the sense that from this time the princeps acknowledged, if not too openly, a continuous ultimate responsibility for the supply of Rome.[29]

In 18 B.C. there was further private generosity from Augustus in that he distributed corn and money from his own stores and purse to 100,000 people or more. There was also a further adjustment on the appointment of the officials supervising the *frumentationes*, who were now raised to four in number.[30]

In 2 B.C. came even more important work in relation to the *frumentationes* with a complete *recensus* of the *plebs frumentaria*, and the reduction of the numbers, which had risen again, to some 200,000 recipients. Another administrative reform was considered whereby the grain would have been issued once

[25] Dio 54. 1. [26] *R. G.* 15. 1. 10–12.
[27] *R. G.* 5. 1–2; Dio 54. 1. 4.
[28] Suet. *Aug.* 37; Dio 54. 1. 4.; Front. *De Aqu.* 100; see below, p. 180.
[29] Cf. Tiberius' remarks in A.D. 22. Tac. *Ann.* 3. 54. 6–8, 'Hanc curam sustinet princeps . . .' Cf. Pavis D'Escurac, *Préfecture*, pp. 17–19. But see below, p. 179.
[30] *R. G.* 18; Dio 54. 17.

every four months rather than monthly, but this idea was too unpopular with the recipients.[31]

All these measures however were concerned with distribution not with supply. That appears to have become a major problem again during the last decade of Augustus' reign, which was beset by many difficulties. In A.D. 5 there was flood and famine in Rome. The situation did not improve and in the following year drastic measures were taken to try to reduce the number of mouths that had to be fed in Rome.[32] Gladiators and slaves for sale were banished to 100 miles; all foreigners, except doctors and teachers, were expelled; large parts of the households of Augustus and other officials were dispersed; the courts were recessed and even senators were permitted to leave the city. The implication was that while there might be corn enough for them in Italy there was none in Rome, and it was easier to send the men to the corn than bring the corn by land to the men. Two ex-consuls were appointed by Augustus to oversee the whole corn supply and to ensure that only a fixed amount was sold to each person. But Augustus himself also distributed apparently from his own supplies, or at least at his own expense, to the *plebs frumentaria* free supplementary rations equal to those they were already receiving.

It looks very much as if it is from this time and as a result of the crisis from A.D. 5 that Augustus and his advisers began to take stock of the whole question of supplying Rome, and trying to improve the system in some permanent way that would look to the interests no less of the farmers and grain merchants than of the populace itself.[33] He is said to have contemplated abolishing the whole system of *frumentationes* at this time, because of the possible deleterious effect they were having on cereal agriculture in Italy, a theme that Tiberius was to take up later.[34] He rejected the idea, because he felt sure that even if he did they would one day be renewed through the desire to curry popular favour.

Two ex-consuls were again appointed to look after the corn supply in A.D. 7,[35] and at some point between A.D. 8 and 14 the first equestrian *praefectus annonae*, possibly C. Turranius, was

[31] Suet. *Aug.* 40. 2; Aug. *R. G.* 15. 4.
[32] Dio 55. 22. 3, 26. 1–3, 28. 1; Suet. *Aug.* 42. 3.
[33] Suet. *Aug.* 42. 3. [34] Tac. *Ann.* 3. 54. 4. [35] Dio 55. 31. 4.

appointed.[36] At last at the very end of Augustus' life there was a special permanent official of non-senatorial status whose sole task it was to watch over the procurement of corn for Rome and who was responsible to the Emperor personally. This man, not a proper magistrate in his own right but specifically a deputy of the Emperor, was to carry out the sort of *cura* which Augustus had undertaken in 22 B.C. and Pompey in the 50s B.C. There was still to be no state monopoly or even state control of the corn trade, but the Emperor through his deputy made himself ultimately responsible for the proper functioning of the corn supply at all times. Without direct powers of control the prefects had the peculiarly difficult job of maintaining a steady flow of supplies and a fair market price for all.

4

In this unadorned account of what Augustus did in relation to the feeding of the capital two things stand out.

The first is that despite the addition of Egypt to the traditional Republican mainstays of Rome's supply, Sardinia, Sicily, and Africa, there were at least two periods in Augustus' reign when Rome was frighteningly short of corn—in 22 B.C. and in A.D. 6. Why was that? Obviously there were special circumstances at work in both these periods such as crop failure which helped to knock the system awry. But what was the system, and what made it vulnerable to such crises?

A clue may perhaps be given by Sicily. The system in Sicily had apparently been changed from that which was current at the time of Cicero. There seems to have been both a reform of the method of taxation and an extension of political privileges throughout Sicily. The effect of these two things on the export of corn to Rome is not clear.[37] It appears that the tithe system had been abolished and a fixed levy (*stipendium*) imposed instead. It is an irritation that we do not know for certain whether the new fixed tax was paid in cash or in kind, but it seems most

[36] Tac. *Ann.* 1. 7; Pavis D'Escurac, *Préfecture*, pp. 317–19; see below, p. 218.

[37] Strabo 265 c ff.; Pliny, *N. H.* 3. 88–91; M. I. Finley, *Ancient Sicily* (London, 1968), p. 153; S. Calderone, 'Il problema delle città censorie e la storia agraria della Sicilia romana', *Kokalos* 6 (1960), 3–25; cf. Rostovtzeff, *SEHRE*² i. 208–9, ii. 629 n. 20; Frank, *ESAR* iii. 345 (but Scramuzza believes, wrongly in my opinion, that tax exemption accompanied the grant of political privileges).

likely that it was paid in cash.[38] The grant of political privileges may not have significantly diminished the number of tax payers if it was divorced from a grant of tax immunity. But Rome was officially taking cash not corn from Sicily from this time. Since I do not believe in a great fall in Sicilian corn production at this time,[39] I am forced to conclude that considerably more corn than formerly was available for private speculators and corn merchants to buy up.

How much of the corn coming from other provinces, such as Africa and Egypt, was also bought up by private traders, who brought it to Rome, is not known. Perhaps not much of the Egyptian corn import, apart from the revenues of estates of the Emperor or certain other great private landlords,[40] could be regarded as private, but it is not impossible that the greater proportion of corn from Africa was being brought in by private corn merchants.

If these speculations have any truth in them, it was still the case during the reign of Augustus, even after the annexation of Egypt, that a high proportion of the corn being brought to Rome was being handled privately. That can only have made the co-ordination of the corn supply an extremely difficult task. If conditions remained favourable the multiplicity of different traders involved was not of particular importance. Once something went wrong, the attempt to put the pieces back together again might be very complicated.

This brings me to the second striking feature of Augustus' activity in the corn supply.

It is right to stress how Augustus marks a new beginning of imperial ways, but it is equally, if not more, important to remember that he also belonged to the late Republic and was keen for political purposes to stress that it still continued. For the greater part of his reign his acts in relation to the corn supply had Republican precedents, and if anything looked backwards rather than forward. The distributions at his own expense, even if on a bigger scale, were not unlike what the aediles had done from time to time for hundreds of years. The

[38] This depends on the meaning of *frumentum mancipale* in *CIL* 3. 14195. 5, see below, p. 84.

[39] Frank, *ESAR* iii. 349–50 (Scramuzza).

[40] M. Rostovtzeff, *SEHRE*² ii. 670–2 n. 45; see below, p. 117.

adjustments in the administration of the *frumentationes* made no change of importance in the attitude to or organizational system for procuring corn. The *cura annonae*, acknowledged as the Emperor's responsibility from 22 B.C., seems not to have led to the kind of vigorous activity, involving state officials making contracts with corn merchants, that characterized the work of Pompey and his *legati*.

Only towards the very end of Augustus' life do we get a change of attitude. The appointment of two consulars to supervise the corn supply in A.D. 6 and 7 marked a beginning, although even that action might be regarded as no more than the usual Republican response to a crisis by creating a temporary and extraordinary commission to look into a problem. So far as the procurement of corn is concerned, it was the creation of the prefectship of the *annona*, as a permanent post, to be held by a man of equestrian status, and that alone, which marked the beginning of anything that might be called an imperial system. The irony is that it came when the Emperor was over seventy years old and arrangements were being made to try to ensure no major breakdown occurred at the time of his death. Modern scholars have concentrated on the political and military aspects of these arrangements, but the social and economic problems were just as great. It was the imminent threat of Augustus' death that made the beginning of an imperial system in the corn supply necessary. The feeding of the capital, no less than the control of the armies, had to be so arranged that it could survive the shock of the death of the *princeps*.

IV

THE EARLY EMPIRE

I

The year A.D. 69 was thought by Tacitus to have been very revealing about the realities of the early Empire. The secret was out—that the Emperor could be made elsewhere than at Rome. The eventual winner in the struggle by the four contenders for the imperial throne, Vespasian, launched his bid for power from the East, and his control of those rich resources, particularly the corn from Egypt, (the *claustra annonae*, 'the keys to the corn supply') seemed significant in gaining political control of the capital Rome.[1] But important though Vespasian's control of Egypt was, it is misleading if we assume that Egypt was at this time the most important source of Rome's corn. Africa sent greater amounts of corn to Rome, a fact which Vespasian himself well knew.

From the time of Hannibal's defeat at the end of the third century B.C. African corn had found its way on to the Roman market no less than that of Sicily and Spain.[2] After the destruction of Carthage and the creation of an African province in the late second century B.C. matters were regularized, and the growth in African corn exports has been invoked to explain why Rome felt no need of the actual crops from the Asia tax tithes. In the first century B.C. Cicero in his speech *Pro lege Manilia* about the work of Pompey, where Egypt is remarkable by its absence, clearly specifies Africa as one of the three great props to the corn supply of Rome along with Sardinia and Sicily.[3] By the time of Augustus even the Sicilian tithes do not seem so necessary to Rome, and the suggestion has been made that it is not merely the addition of Egypt to the Empire but a

[1] Tac. *Hist.* 2. 82; 3. 8.
[2] Livy 31. 50, 36. 3; cf. 30. 26, 33. 42.
[3] Cicero, *Pro lege Manilia* 12. 9; cf. Plutarch, *Pompey* 50.

continuing expansion of African corn surpluses which made this possible. The uncertainties in all this are to some extent removed when we come to the first century A.D. and the Jewish author Josephus. In an important passage of the *Bellum Iudaicum*, discussed in detail elsewhere, he states categorically that by the time of Nero Egypt was a major source of financial revenue to Rome and in addition sent enough corn to feed Rome for a third of the year, while Africa fed Rome for two-thirds of the year.[4] Even allowing for a rhetorical and over-schematic presentation of the facts, the passage supports what had already been suspected, that by the late first century A.D. corn from Africa was quantitatively more important to the Roman market than that from Egypt and by a considerable margin.

Whatever the passage in Josephus means in real terms, in numbers of *modii* exported, and that is a matter of some difficulty, the greater importance of Africa in the early Empire is borne out by Tacitus himself, who mourns the reliance of Rome on Africa and Egypt, in that order.[5] It is easy to forget when we concentrate only on Vespasian dominating Egypt and the eastern Mediterranean in A.D. 69, that the governor in Africa had it in his power to starve Rome, a fact which Vespasian himself did not forget as he was also preparing an invasion of Africa for just this purpose.[6] Only one year later in A.D. 70 bad weather held the African grain ships in port and the populace in Rome jumped to the alarmed conclusion that the proconsul of Africa had revolted, a popular error which cost that unfortunate man his head.[7] Vespasian could take no chances with Africa any more than a century later Septimius Severus could afford to allow his rival Niger to seize Africa and cut off the grain supply.[8] The importance of the African supplies to Rome at this time, made explicit only shortly before this by the organization of an African corn fleet under Commodus because of increased uncertainty about Egyptian corn, was shown again and again in the ensuing third and fourth centuries A.D.[9] But by then of course Rome was reduced

[4] Josephus, *Bell. Iud.* 2. 383–5; see below, Appendix 4.
[5] Tac. *Ann.* 12. 43.
[6] Tac. *Hist.* 1. 73; 3. 48.
[7] Tac. *Hist.* 4. 38.
[8] SHA *Septimius Severus* 8.
[9] SHA *Commodus* 17. 7.

specifically to the resources of the western Mediterranean while Constantinople tapped those of Egypt and the east.[10]

A piece of archaeological evidence reinforces the impression drawn from the literary authors. The Piazzale delle Corporazioni at Ostia, the portico behind the theatre, constructed and reconstructed during the early Empire, is dominated by traders from African towns.[11] Of course Africa had valuable exports, for example in olive oil, as well as corn, but most of the African towns represented in the portico were concerned with corn. It is an important fact that Africa of all the Roman provinces had the closest association with Ostia, the port of Rome, whose harbour facilities were to be extensively developed in the first two centuries A.D., and of those African towns represented most were corn exporting centres.

If all this is true, and I believe it to be indisputable, however we quantify the exact figures, why Egypt looms so large in discussions of the Roman corn supply both ancient and modern needs to be explained.

First, Egypt was peculiar in that its corn grew in the relatively restricted area which was either flooded by, or could be irrigated from, the river Nile.[12] The perennial refreshment of the soil in this area, despite some variation, seemed little short of miraculous. The Nile moreover provided the main communication whereby the grain could be assembled and passed downstream to a single outlet at Alexandria. The organization inherited from the Ptolemies of the grain collection from village threshing floors to storehouses, and then on to boats which carried it, as ordered, down the Nile was highly bureaucratic and centralized. Because of the many papyri preserved we have documentary evidence for an elaborate administration of the Egyptian corn supply based in the Neapolis district in Alexandria and supervised by a Roman *procurator*. Given the compactness of the area, the closely knit homogeneity of the organization and the outlet through Alexandria alone, it is

[10] Cf. *De Bell. Gild.* 62; Symmachus, *Ep.* 3. 82, 4. 54, 7. 63. See in general E. Tengström, *Bread for the People: Studies of the Corn Supply of Rome during the late Empire* (Stockholm, 1974).

[11] Meiggs, *Roman Ostia*², pp. 283 and 286.

[12] Frank, *ESAR* ii (Johnson), esp. pp. 1 ff., 7 ff., 481 ff.; N. Hohlwein, 'Le blé d'Égypte', *Et Pap* 4 (1938), 33–120; Rickman, *Roman Granaries*, Appendix 2; see below, p. 114.

little wonder that the Emperors from the beginning treated Egypt as a special case. There was to be no senatorial governor, only an equestrian prefect, and special permission had to be given to visit the country even for a member of the imperial house. In the winter of A.D. 18–19 Germanicus set out on an unauthorized journey to Egypt and relieved a food shortage in Alexandria by opening granaries and lowering prices.[13] Although this act was almost certainly not responsible for the food shortage in Rome during the following winter, the Emperor Tiberius made an acid speech in the senate about Germanicus' visit which was contrary to Augustus' regulations. The political danger of the domination of this single most valuable source of cash and corn by a potential rival set the Emperor's nerves tingling. By contrast Africa was a sprawling, less easily grasped, area, more like the rest of the Mediterranean region in its farming methods, and exporting through a series of harbours along its coasts.

Secondly, Egypt was undoubtedly an important source of corn not simply for Rome but for the eastern Mediterranean in general. There is no reason to suppose that with the Roman capture of Egypt from Cleopatra, traditional customers for Egyptian corn lost out completely. We know that Helena of Adiabene purchased Egyptian corn in the late 40s A.D. in the reign of Claudius just as Herod the Great had bought from Egypt in the late 20s B.C. under Augustus.[14] Less exalted customers were less likely to be mentioned in the literary sources. The difference lay in the fact that permission had now to be sought from Roman authorities to export Egyptian corn elsewhere than to Rome. But there is no reason to suppose that that permission was not given whenever possible. Epictetus records for us the standard form of the petition to take grain from Egypt, which implies that it was no uncommon practice.[15]

Thirdly, the length of the journey from Egypt to Rome both in distance and in time made the arrival of the corn freighters from Alexandria something special.[16] The Alexandrian corn

[13] Tac. *Ann.* 2. 59.

[14] Josephus, *Ant. Iud.* 20. 51 and 101; 15. 304–16.

[15] Epict. 1. 10. 10. Cf. M. Wörrle, 'Ägyptisches Getreide für Ephesos', *Chiron* 1 (1971), 325–40; see below, Appendix 4.

[16] Casson, *Ships and Seamanship*, p. 297; see below, p. 128.

fleet made for Rome in the teeth of the prevailing winds and had to sail up to 1,700 miles (2,720 km) by circuitous routes along southern Turkey or along the North African coast. Those journeys could take as much as seventy days, if the weather was bad. It is hardly surprising therefore that the sighting of the forerunners of the fleet, the *naves tabellariae*, at Puteoli in the mid-first century A.D. which indicated the start of the safe arrival of Egyptian corn, was greeted with excitement and relief.[17] Until an African corn fleet was organized under Commodus the haphazard arrivals of its ships after their shorter journeys of some 270 miles (432 km) which need take only two or three days were much less striking to ordinary observers.

The fascination and importance of Egypt and her corn production are therefore not in doubt, but during the Empire it was Africa even more than Egypt that was vital for the procurement of Rome's corn, and transport by sea dominated its organization.

2

One of the causes, and one of the signs, of the returning stability of the Roman world under Augustus was the creation by him of a series of naval fleets. The most obvious were the Italian-based naval contingents at Misenum and Ravenna,[18] but there were other important naval contingents elsewhere in the Mediterranean, as at Alexandria. The seas, only sporadically controlled by the Romans during the Republic, were now to be permanently policed; piracy which had reasserted itself during the triumviral period was to be no more; the seas should be safe for peaceful traffic.[19]

In this way one of the essential conditions was created for the flourishing of commerce during the early Empire. But although Augustus took the step, which the Romans seem to have been reluctant to take before him, of creating a permanent navy, there was still no national merchant marine. The fleets of Misenum and Ravenna were warships, and not cargo vessels for carrying goods, and a sharp distinction has to be drawn in

[17] Seneca, *Ep.* 77.
[18] Tac. *Ann.* 4. 5.
[19] Horace, *Odes* iv. 5. 19; Suet. *Aug.* 98. 2.

the case of Alexandria between the fully organized military *classis Augusta Alexandrina* under its *praefectus*, and the rather more amorphous group of commercial shippers from Alexandria, whose vessels came to be regarded as the fleet for conveying the corn of Egypt to Rome.[20]

Hence the importance of the private shipper, *navicularius*, already stressed in the chapter on the procurement of corn under the Republic continued into the Empire. That was necessarily so, because the state had no commercial shipping of its own. But it seems to me also to be true that many of these men involved in the corn trade at least in the first century of the Empire were not merely shippers but also corn merchants, that is, not merely *navicularii* but *negotiatores* and *mercatores* too. This is clear not least in the literary sources. When Tiberius came to the rescue during the corn shortage of A.D. 19 by fixing the price to be paid by the ordinary buyer in Rome at two sesterces a *modius* less than the prices asked, he promised to make good the difference, according to Tacitus, to *negotiatores*.[21] Similarly when Claudius tried to encourage unwilling merchants to make dangerous winter journeys by promising compensation for any loss incurred through storm, he was, in Suetonius' account, clearly dealing with *negotiatores*, that is, those who both bought and sold, and not those who simply conveyed corn.[22]

Why this should be so is not so clear, but it may be connected with the changes which were taking place in the late Republic and early Empire in methods of taxation and which have already been mentioned. Fixed taxes in cash had taken the place of tithes in both Sicily and Asia. If there was less paying of taxes in kind than previously, except in Egypt, and yet the need in Rome for corn to eat was certainly no less than before, the important role that private corn merchants could play is obvious. They were ready to seek out corn, buy it, transport it and sell it again, on the Roman market.

But although the role of the *navicularii*, and even more of the private *negotiatores*, was as great, if not greater, than ever before,

[20] *Classis Augusta Alexandrina, CIL* 16. 32, *CIL* 2. 1970 = *ILS* 1341, P. Oxy. 1451; commercial shippers of Alexandria, Kaibel, *IG Italiae* 918 and 919 = *CIG* 5889, 5973. Seneca, *Ep.* 77. 1; see below, p. 129.

[21] Tac. *Ann.* 2. 87.

[22] Suet. *Claud.* 18.

there was from the latter part of the reign of Augustus the permanent imperial official the *praefectus annonae*, who in some way was meant to preside over the whole business.[23] The problem immediately therefore becomes what the relationship was to be between them all. It is a problem for us in the sense that we find it difficult to grasp exactly how the *praefectus* and his officials dealt with the shippers and merchants. But it was, I suspect, a problem at the time as well since there were few precedents to guide the actions and reactions of the various parties. It was of course made even more difficult by the fact that all the participants were, in the first century A.D. in particular, caught up in a situation that was constantly evolving politically and economically around them.

The final result of that evolution by the beginning of the fourth century A.D. was that shipping in general and the corn supply in particular became to the highest degree state-controlled.[24] Hereditary *navicularii*, under permanent contract as members of a corporation chartered and supervised by the state, were unable either to retire or to alienate their wealth from the exercise of their designated profession. Shippers who served the supply system of the city, like other groups in the state, found themselves imprisoned, in theory at least, in one of the closed departments of the Empire.

By what stages exactly that evolution came about has always been difficult to establish with certainty, but the early stages of the evolution have been made more muddled and more difficult, I suspect, by a rather bogus controversy over who controlled, and took credit for, the corn distributions and the corn supply of Rome under the early Empire—the senate or the Emperor?

3

The traditional approach by modern scholars to the corn supply in the first century A.D. has tended to stress the technical role of the senate up to the reign of Claudius, who in a major upheaval transferred the cost of the corn supply from the *aerarium* to the *fiscus*. From his reign onward it was the imperial

[23] *RE* 22. 2, s.v. *praefectus*, cols. 1263–78; H. Pavis D'Escurac, *Préfecture*.
[24] *Cod. Theod.* 13. 5 *De Naviculariis* (from A.D. 314), cf. 7. 4. 11 (A.D. 364).

administration which bore the burden and monopolized the credit for the corn supply although later individual Emperors, such as Nerva, again allowed the senate an apparent share in the running of the system.[25]

I find this thesis thin and unconvincing. There is a tendency to generalize about Claudius' work on the corn supply, and to repeat without question conclusions about the administrative structure of the early Empire reached almost a century ago which perhaps need to be reframed.[26] There is certainly a need to restate the facts.

Whatever the role of the senate in the 'restored republic' of Augustus it is a fact that from the end of his reign the *praefectus annonae*, an imperial official of equestrian status, represented the Emperor's permanent concern for the feeding of Rome. The *cura* which he exercised was no secret and its connection with the Emperor was patent, as is shown by Tiberius' words to the senate in A.D. 22, which were literally 'The Emperor sustains this *cura*.' He had already intervened quite openly in the corn market three years earlier to reduce prices.[27]

It is a fact that among the many difficulties which Claudius faced on his sudden and surprising elevation to the imperial throne in A.D. 41 was a severe shortage of grain in the capital.[28] As a result of Gaius' eccentricities and perhaps because of his use of valuable shipping to build a bridge of boats at Baiae there was supposedly only corn for eight days left in the capital.

It is not surprising therefore to find in the copious issue of coinage which marked the first year of Claudius' reign, there should appear legends and symbols on some of the bronze coins destined to reassure people about the corn supply. There were two main types. One, with the head of Claudius on the obverse, had on the reverse the figure of Ceres seated and veiled, holding two corn ears in her right hand, surrounded

[25] A. Momigliano, *Claudius: the Emperor and his Achievement* (reprint, Cambridge, 1961), pp. 49 and 107; D. Van Berchem, *Les Distributions de blé et d'argent à la plèbe romaine sous l'empire* (Geneva, 1939), p. 172; Frank, *ESAR* V (1940), 41.

[26] See e.g. the interesting but over-systematic treatment, relying heavily on secondary sources, by T. F. Carney, 'The Emperor Claudius and the Grain Trade', *Pro Munere Grates*, Studies presented to H. L. Gonin (Pretoria, 1971), pp. 39–57.

[27] Tac. *Ann.* 3. 54. 6–8 'Hanc curam sustinet princeps'; 2. 87 for price fixing in A.D. 19; 15. 36 for fears about the corn supply whenever the *princeps* was absent from Rome.

[28] Seneca, *De Brevit. Vitae* 18. 5, cf. Suet. *Calig.* 19.

by the legend 'Ceres Augusta SC'. The other had on its obverse a *modius* standing on three legs surrounded by the Emperor's names, while on the reverse, the large letters 'S C' were encircled by the Emperor's titles and offices.[29] Parallels for the seated figure of Ceres can be found on the coinage of Augustus and Tiberius, and she was often equated with the reigning empress, but the emphasis on the smallest bronze coins of the corn *modius* is new. Even so we must not exaggerate its importance, since it was simply one of some twelve types issued by Claudius at this critical point in his life, many of which were of greater importance, such as his acknowledgement of his debt to the Praetorian Guard.[30]

It is a rather more surprising fact that, despite opposition, Claudius managed in A.D. 42 to get work started on a completely new harbour at Ostia some 2 miles (just over 3 km) north of the Tiber mouth, a work that Julius Caesar had once envisaged.[31] There was no doubt that it was necessary, and that it might help to prevent a recurrence of the crisis at the end of Gaius' reign, but in view of the size and cost of the undertaking it is remarkable that the new Emperor was able to get the project under way so quickly. It was not in fact to transform the situation overnight, as perhaps Claudius had hoped, since the Alexandrian corn ships still seem to have gone to Puteoli in the reign of Nero and later in the first century A.D.[32] But it was a great improvement on the unloading of goods into lighters at the mouth of the river. The inner basin created by Trajan was to combine with the Claudian work to make a safe and commodious series of harbours for the biggest merchantmen afloat and to accommodate even the Egyptian grain ships.

Sea transport was clearly much in the Emperor's mind and although his inducements to shippers are undated, it seems very likely that at least the offer to indemnify merchants for storm damage during winter journeys was an emergency measure that should be associated with the beginning of his reign.[33] It

[29] Mattingly, *BMCEmp* i, Pl. 35 n. 1 and n. 12 and 14.

[30] C. H. V. Sutherland, *Coinage in Roman Imperial Policy, 31 B.C.–A.D. 68* (London, 1951), p. 130.

[31] Dio 60. 11. 3; Meiggs, *Roman Ostia*², pp. 54 ff. O. Testaguzza, *Portus* (Rome, 1970).

[32] Sen. *Ep.* 77. 1; cf. Meiggs, *Roman Ostia*², pp. 56–7.

[33] Suet. *Claud.* 18, cf. Livy 23. 48. 6–49. 4.

was an act which was not without a Republican precedent, of which perhaps this antiquarian Emperor was aware. But whether it is to be dated at the beginning of his reign or to the year A.D. 51[34] when he was pelted with scraps of bread by an angry mob in the Forum, it seems to have been a purely temporary arrangement to meet a sudden crisis, because there is no trace of it in later juristic writings.

But some of the inducements to shippers and merchants were permanent; the offer of privileges for those who put ships of not less than 10,000 *modii* capacity into the corn trade and kept them in the service for six years.[35] Romans were to gain exemption from the Lex Papia Poppaea, Latins were to get the *ius Quiritum*, and women the *ius quattuor liberorum*. Nero later in A.D. 58 added that the ship of a *negotiator* serving Rome should not be rated with the rest of his taxable property but be exempt from *tributum*.[36]

In the light of all this the withdrawal of the senatorial quaestor from Ostia and his replacement by an imperial procurator in A.D. 44 was only to be expected.[37] The Ostian quaestorship had long been regarded as a tedious post by senators and with imperial commitment to an Ostian harbour came a natural substitution of an imperial official subordinate to the *praefectus annonae* at Rome.

Certainly from the time of the fire of Rome in A.D. 64 Nero too gave serious attention to the problems of the corn supply although they are misrepresented in our sources. So far as Ostia was concerned there was a scheme for digging a canal direct to Rome, a serious project that would greatly have eased the shipment of grain and other cargoes from Africa and the western provinces to the city by eliminating the bends of the river Tiber and its strong current. To ease the shipment of the cargoes from the eastern Mediterranean which still arrived at Puteoli there was a project to dig a canal from Lake Avernus to Ostia, actually begun in A.D. 64. It would have reduced considerably the dangers of the stormy passage up the west coast of Italy.[38] Most significant of all, it was from A.D. 64 that Nero

[34] Tac. *Ann.* 12. 43. 2.
[35] Cf. Gaius, *Inst.* i. 32c; Ulpian, 3. 6.
[36] Tac. *Ann.* 13. 51 (A.D. 58).
[37] Dio 60. 24. 3.
[38] Suet. *Nero* 16. 1; Tac. *Ann.* 15. 42. Cf. Meiggs, *Roman Ostia*[2], pp. 57 and 63.

issued the great bronze *sestertii* with the legend 'Annona Augusti Ceres S C'.[39] On the obverse was the head of Nero. On the reverse Annona standing right with a cornucopia in her left hand faced Ceres who was veiled and seated holding corn ears in her right hand and a torch in her left. Between them was a garlanded altar on which stood a *modius* with corn ears, while in the background the stern of a ship, garlanded, could be seen. It was one of the most beautiful coin types the Romans ever issued, much more successful than the well-known representation of Claudius' harbour that Nero issued at the same time. It was copied and repeated in whole or in part by later Emperors and was more than worthy of an Emperor with artistic pretensions.

Apart from these facts there is some indirect evidence that the machinery of the corn distributions was centralized at the Porticus Minucia at an unknown date which is likely to have been in the first century A.D. and possibly during the reigns of Claudius or Nero.[40]

What needs to be stressed is that there is no direct evidence for any sudden transfer of the cost of the corn supply from the *aerarium* to the *fiscus* at a given moment or for any aggressive imperial takeover of an erstwhile senatorial prerogative. The senate and senators may have had a long tradition of association with the corn supply and corn distributions, but it is equally clear that the Emperors from the beginning felt peculiarly and personally responsible for the corn supply of Rome.[41] We should therefore think not so much of the transference of revenues from one pocket to another, or the weight of some expenditure transferred from this back to that, but of a gradual blurring between the accounts of senate and Emperor, a tendency that was no doubt encouraged, once the *rationes imperii* ceased to be published.[42] The Emperor's finance clerks availing themselves of the ubiquitous *procurators* of the Emperor, who were in every province of the Empire, either looking after the Emperor's private property, or his public revenues, came to have the best

[39] Mattingly, *BMCEmp.* i. Plate 41 n. 6; see below, p. 260.

[40] See below, p. 192.

[41] H. Kloft, *Liberalitas Principis*, Kölner Historische Abhandlungen Bd. 18 (Cologne, 1970), 96 and n. 54; see now Pavis D'Escurac, *Préfecture*, pp. 14–17, 21–6.

[42] P. A. Brunt, 'The Fiscus and its Development', *JRS* 56 (1966), 75–91.

overall grasp of the total financial picture of the Empire. This was achieved by a process of evolution, not by any single decision or transference of power. By the time of Claudius, Pallas, then freedman *a rationibus*, was a man whose office could be regarded as in account with the *aerarium* on all sorts of matters.[43] The *fiscus*, in the sense of an imperial treasury office, was a concept that was formed by degrees, but which was well advanced by the middle of the first century A.D.

Once it existed, of course there was nothing to stop the spawning of other *fisci*, specialized offices of accounts, which would keep together all the financial paper-work associated with a particular sphere of administration. This may have led to the emergence, among others, of a *fiscus frumentarius*—the first clear evidence for which is Flavian.[44] As the central office of account in Rome for the corn supply under the *praefectus annonae*, it was large, staffed by various *tabularii* in charge of its records, *a libellis* who dealt with claims and *dispensatores*, pay clerks, all of whom have left inscriptional record. As one might expect there was also a branch office at Ostia.[45]

But all this would seem to be part of the natural development of *aerarium* and *fiscus* in the first century of the Empire, which perhaps accelerated in the middle of that century, but was not the result of any sweeping single decision by the Emperor Claudius. Claudius seems to have displayed his usual administrative skills in relation to the corn supply. The senate may ultimately have lost ground as a result, but almost inadvertently. I think it is impossible to prove, in the light of our evidence, that Claudius specifically transferred the corn supply from *aerarium* to *fiscus*. But more important than that is the fact that there is no need to believe in any such single measure which would have affronted the senate. In the overall co-operation between senate and Emperor in the first century A.D. the balance was tilting more and more sharply towards the Emperor all the time. This evolutionary view may be less neat and tidy than the belief in a single Claudian measure, but it is

[43] Tac. *Ann.* 13. 14.1.

[44] *CIL* 6. 544, 634 = *ILS* 1540, 1540^{a}; *CIL* 6. 8474–7 = *ILS* 1541–4. A *fiscus frumentarius*, in the sense of a chest holding actual cash for corn purposes, may have existed during the Republic, but there is no evidence.

[45] *CIL* 14. 2045 = *ILS* 1534, cf. Meiggs, *Roman Ostia*^{2}, p. 300.

more like the muddled and largely concealed development of the early principate.

The real question, so far as the corn supply of Rome is concerned, is not the relationship of the Emperor to the senate, but that of the state (whether Emperor or senate, or both combined) to the individual. For the purposes of the corn supply during at least the first two centuries of the Empire the state was represented by the person of the *praefectus annonae*, the individual in particular by the private corn merchants or shippers. The two parts of the equation must be examined separately.

4

The *praefectus annonae* was the most important new element in the situation, and was to remain so for some 200 years or more, until his Empire-wide powers were gradually absorbed by the *praefectus praetorio*.

Dio writing in the early third century A.D. makes Maecenas in a fictitious speech urge Augustus to appoint important equestrians to look after the corn supply of Rome for a fixed period of between three and five years.[46] Whether Maecenas said any such thing is more than doubtful, but as a reflection of Dio's views and perhaps of the actual practice that had grown up by the time that Dio was writing, it is interesting. The *praefecti* were never in fact appointed for a fixed period, but in practice, during the second century A.D. at least, the longest tenure known to us was seven years and many were considerably shorter. It was clearly not the practice to leave any particular *praefectus* in office for a considerable time.[47] We know that at that time the appointment was formalized by the dispatch of a letter from the Emperor to the new prefect, who could apparently accumulate considerable property and wealth.[48] At least from the time of Septimius Severus the title that went with the office was *vir perfectissimus*, but what the salary was we do not

[46] Dio 52. 24. 6, cf. Pavis D'Escurac, *Préfecture*, pp. 50–4.

[47] Volusius Maecianus A.D. 152–9 (Pflaum, no. 141); cf. Pavis D'Escurac, *Préfecture*, Appendice Prosopographique, for an up-to-date list of the *praefecti annonae* with full discussion.

[48] Epictetus i. 10. 2–5.

know. Since however the *a rationibus* from the time of Marcus Aurelius had 300,000 sesterces a year, it is likely that from the mid-second century A.D. the *praefectus annonae* enjoyed an annual salary greater than that.[49]

The first *praefectus annonae* known to us, in A.D. 14, C. Turranius, was moved from the Prefectship of Egypt to hold the new post, an office to which he clung tenaciously until after A.D. 48 when he seems to have been finally forced to retire when he was ninety years old.[50] It might have seemed at first that the Prefectship of Egypt and that of the *annona* were to be the two crowning posts of an equestrian career, and that it was not clear which represented the final promotion. But during the course of Tiberius' reign the ambitions of Sejanus had the permanent effect of elevating the Prefectship of the Praetorian Guard at Rome above the *annona* prefectship. The *praefectus annonae* settled into third place. The appointment of an Egyptian prefect to the *annona* office in Rome was not to be repeated, nor the length or influence of Turranius' tenure of the post; instead there developed by the end of the first century A.D. an almost regular pattern of promotion if there was to be any promotion at all, from the prefectship of the *annona* to the prefectship of Egypt, and if that was achieved early enough, even on to the praetorian guard.[51] Before this in the first century A.D. it was possible for Faenius Rufus, *praefectus annonae* from A.D. 55, to be promoted immediately *praefectus praetorio* in A.D. 62 because of the popularity he had gained with the mob through his handling of the corn supply.[52] Moreover there were exceptions to the later pattern, as when L. Iulius Vehilius Gratus Iulianus, *praefectus annonae* about A.D. 186 but who had previously held many military posts, was suddenly made praetorian prefect by Commodus on the downfall of Cleander.[53]

Although the pattern of promotion from the *annona* prefect-

[49] O. Hirschfeld, *Die kaiserlichen Verwaltungsbeamten*[2] (Berlin, 1905), p. 451; *RE* 23 s.v. *procurator* col. 1253 (H. Pflaum); cf. Pavis D'Escurac, *Préfecture*, pp. 66 and 68.

[50] Tac. *Ann.* 1. 7; 11. 31; Seneca, *De Brevit. Vit.* 20. 3.

[51] H. G. Pflaum, *Les Procurateurs équestres sous le haut-empire romain* (Paris, 1950), p. 257. Cf. P. A. Brunt, 'The administrators of Roman Egypt', *JRS* 65 (1975), 124–47, esp. 131.

[52] Tac. *Ann.* 13. 22; 14. 57.

[53] H. G. Pflaum, *Les Carrières procuratoriennes équestres sous le haut-empire romain* (Paris, 1960), no. 180.

ship was established fairly early, the careers that led up to it could be much more varied. The one thing they tended to have in common was the lack of any contact with, or experience of, corn-supply problems in some lesser capacity. Clearly general administrative experience was rated more highly than specialist training.[54]

But what exactly did the *praefectus annonae* do and what staff did he have to help him?

Whatever else may be uncertain it seems clear that the *praefectus annonae* did not himself move around from province to province. He stayed continuously at the centre maintaining an overall watch on the market in Rome. His primary concern may have been corn, but his care extended to the import of oil and other foodstuffs and to the maintenance of law and order throughout the markets of Rome.[55] That there was an office of the *praefectus* in Rome is proved by an inscription of a 'Festus Caes n. tabellarius ex officio annonae'.[56] Where exactly the head office of the *praefectus annonae* was in Rome is not known with certainty for the early Empire. The so-called *Statio Annonae* whose columns are now part of the structure of the church of S. Maria in Cosmedin in the old Forum Boarium was an open-sided loggia constructed in the fourth century A.D.[57] Its identification as the *annona* office of the period depends on the fact that a dedication to a *praefectus annonae* of Constantinian period was placed just outside it and other inscriptions found near it. However, it is a fact that this loggia was simply an addition to the old temple of Ceres, Liber, and Libera. Given the association of the aediles with Ceres, the location of this temple on the banks of the Tiber, and the Roman habit of depositing records in temples, it is not impossible that the headquarters of the *praefectus annonae* may have been located here even earlier in the Empire.

As the careers of many of the *praefecti* show, they were experts in the keeping of accounts and that must have been their primary personal duty. It is significant that the Younger

[54] See Appendix 2.

[55] Dio 52. 24. 6; Seneca, *De Brevit. Vit.* 18. 3 and 19. 1.

[56] *CIL* 6. 8473 = *ILS* 1705.

[57] E. Nash, *A Pictorial Dictionary of Ancient Rome* (London, 1961–2), s.v. *Statio Annonae* with full bibliography.

Seneca in the *De Brevitate Vitae* opens his description of the work of his father-in-law Pompeius Paulinus, almost certainly *praefectus annonae* with the words 'tu quidem orbis terrarum rationes administras' (18.3). When it is realized that even in the case of corn the sources of supply could range from taxes in imperial or senatorial provinces, produce and rents of imperial possessions, to private purchases by the state or by individuals, it is obvious that the system of accounts for which the prefect was responsible must have been both complicated and sophisticated. At his desk in Rome the prefect was the one man who was supposed to have a complete picture in his files of what was going on around the Mediterranean.

But in order to be able to sit at the centre of the web the prefect had to be fed with a stream of intelligence by subordinates, agents or at least informants, in all the key corn-producing areas. It would seem, however, that the number of actual agents he might use varied considerably from area to area.

For example, it is difficult to find any clear signs of agents of the *praefectus annonae* active in Egypt, an area where at first sight one might have expected them, unless we can regard the *procurator Neaspoleos* and the *procurator ad Mercurium* in Alexandria in that light which is doubtful; they would have been independently appointed by the Emperor. Instead what one finds is an organization involving the whole province from local farmers and village granary keepers up to the *procurator Neaspoleos* at Alexandria, all tightly under the surveillance of the Prefect of Egypt, and devoted to collecting the corn and clearing it down the Nile systematically.[58] Even the Alexandrine shippers, who carried the corn onwards to Rome, seem a distinct and more cohesive body than the transporters from other parts of the Mediterranean. They were to be in the charge of a separate procurator under Septimius Severus.[59] We do not even know whether they were paid for their transport services by the Prefect of Egypt or by the *praefectus annonae* like other transporters.

The Egyptian operation seems quite independent of the *praefectus annonae*, and that perhaps is not surprising. Prefects of

[58] Rickman, *Roman Granaries*, App. 2; Pavis D'Escurac, *Préfecture*, pp. 134–9.
[59] *CIG* 5973 = Kaibel, *IG Italiae* 919.

Egypt, themselves the deputy of the Emperor, may often have been promoted from the *annona* post. But for all that it is inconceivable that the *praefectus annonae* in Rome was not kept fully informed either directly by the Egyptian prefect or through the *procurator Neaspoleos* as to the state of affairs in Egypt, if not in detail about the height of the Nile flood, difficulties in harvesting, or transport problems, at least about the total tonnage likely to be shipped to Rome and estimated times of arrival. His attempt to keep full accounts could not have survived the lack of the Egyptian information.

The other imperial provinces were not of course so idiosyncratic in their organization nor so jealously guarded by the Emperors, but nor on the other hand were they generally areas which produced corn regularly for the Roman market. They might well, like Britain after A.D. 43, grow corn but that corn would be needed above all for the military garrisons that were so often stationed in them.[60]

Of the three ancient props of the Roman corn market, Sicily, Sardinia, and Africa, Sardinia alone was generally an imperial province in the early Empire. It almost certainly continued to send grain to the Roman market. There were at least two groups of Sardinian shippers represented in the Piazzale delle Corporazioni, of whom the men of Carales used corn measures to illustrate their business,[61] and Pliny the Elder includes Sardinian in his discussion of wheat types.[62] But we know of no special agent of the *praefectus annonae* involved in the island, and it may have been the case that the officials at Ostia together with the imperial governor of the island dealt with the matter.

The dispatch of corn to Rome by the governor of the imperial province of Moesia Ti. Plautius Silvanus Aelianus in the middle of the first century A.D. was a very special case.[63] Although Moesia, covering the lower reaches of the Danube, was good corn-growing land with easy export facilities on the Black Sea, it is stated in the inscription of Plautius Aelianus that he was the first to send corn in large quantities from that province to relieve the corn supply of the city. It is possible that this was a

[60] Tac. *Agric.* 19.
[61] Meiggs, *Roman Ostia*², p. 286.
[62] Pliny, *N. H.* 18. 66.
[63] *CIL* 14. 3608 = *ILS* 986.

special effort made after the great fire of Rome in A.D. 64 when the need to alleviate the suffering of the urban plebs after the destruction of a large part of the city demanded unusual efforts.

The situation seems rather different in senatorial provinces, although whether that was because they were senatorial, or because they were in general more important for the corn supply of Rome, is not obvious.

In general it appears, as has been said, that the old system of tithes in kind gave way under the Empire to a system of fixed *stipendia*, paid in cash. Yet it was still the case that companies of *publicani* could contract to collect taxes. Their activities are recorded in the reign of Tiberius by Tacitus, and that it was not just indirect taxes, such as *portoria*, that they collected, is shown not only by the passage in Tacitus but by an inscription which records the existence of 'mancup(es) stipend(iorum) ex Africa', who seem to have worked closely with the quaestor.[64] How can we reconcile these two apparently contradictory facts, and where does the *praefectus annonae* and his staff fit into the structure?

There is the strongest suspicion that in three of the great sources of corn for the Roman market in the western Mediterranean, Africa, Sicily, and Spain, the main body of whose taxes under the early Empire were to be *stipendia* paid in cash, the only corn revenues as such were from *ager publicus*, which existed in all three areas and the growing imperial estates. These were the corn revenues which were farmed by the *publicani* or *mancupes* and which consequently came to be called *frumentum mancipale*.[65] We have several bilingual inscriptions from Ephesus concerning a man named C. Vibius Salutaris who is described as having been *pro magistro* (*archones*) of the *frumentum mancipale* (*sitos demou Romaion*) in the Domitianic period in Sicily.[66] This makes him sound like the head of a firm of *publicani*, but he appears to have been also at some time an official of equestrian status and certainly later at least had a career in the imperial service. We also know of imperial slaves who are called 'dispensatores frumenti mancipalis' on inscriptions, one from Rome

[64] Tac. *Ann.* 4. 6; *CIL* 6. 31713 = *ILS* 901.

[65] Rostovtzeff, *Frumentum*, cols. 153–4; Hirschfeld, *KVB*², p. 140; Pavis D'Escurac, *Préfecture*, pp. 183–5; see above, p. 65.

[66] *CIL* 3. 14195/9 = *ILS* 7193–5.

and one from Hispalis in Spain.[67] More recently an inscription has appeared of a man who is described as 'praefectus fabrum et frumenti mancipalis provinciae Africae'.[68]

The late first century A.D. was perhaps a moment of transition when *ager publicus* in various provinces was being increasingly absorbed into imperial holdings and there was a shift under way from *ager publicus* farmed by *publicani* to imperial estates run by imperial officials. Such officials, if not subordinate to the *praefectus annonae*, and there is no evidence of any relationship, must at least have rendered their accounts in such a way as to keep him informed about the likely revenues from this source in any given year.

If it is correct that the *frumentum mancipale* was merely the revenue from *ager publicus* and imperial estates in the provinces, considerably more corn must have been grown on all kinds of other land, some of which would be available for purchase either by the government or by individual speculators.

We do not know whether the freedman procurator with a special commission to buy corn in Paphlagonia, who is mentioned in a letter of the younger Pliny from Bithynia, was collecting grain for the capital or for some other purpose.[69] But we do know that T. Flavius Macer was used by Trajan to act as a 'curator frumenti comparandi in annonam urbis' specifically to buy corn for the city of Rome, almost certainly in his native Numidia.[70] This is interesting for a number of reasons. It foreshadows the official post which we know to have existed at the beginning of the third century A.D., entitled *procurator tractus Numidiae a frumentis*[71] and is a living example not just of that general care which the younger Pliny claimed was shown by Trajan for the corn supply, but of the sentence in the Panegyricus about the state purchases which ease the *annona*: 'The imperial exchequer (*fiscus*) pays openly for its

[67] *CIL* 6. 8853 = *ILS* 1536; *CIL* 2. 1197.

[68] *Æpigr.* (1952), 225. For Flavian systematization of land administration see D. Crawford, 'Imperial Estates' in M. Finley (ed.), *Studies in Roman Property* (Cambridge, 1976), p. 53; but cf. F. G. B. Millar, *The Emperor in the Roman World* (London, 1977), Appendix I.

[69] Pliny, *Ep.* 10. 27, 28.

[70] *CIL* 8. 5351 = *ILS* 1435, cf. Pflaum ii, no. 98, pp. 229 ff.

[71] *Æpigr.* (1942), 105, cf. Pflaum, no. 275; *CIL* 8. 18909 = *ILS* 9017, cf. Pflaum, no. 274.

purchases; hence these provisions and the corn supply, with prices agreed between the buyer and the seller.'[72] It is significant too that Macer followed his special corn-purchasing commission by becoming *procurator Aug. praediorum saltuum Hipponensis et Thevestini*, in short, running one of the great estates owned by the Emperor which had become a feature of African agriculture after Nero.[73]

But of course it was not only the Emperor and his officials who could buy corn in this way. Private merchants and speculators were at liberty to bid for surpluses wherever they occurred, and to make a living by the buying and selling of grain or of other goods which were of interest to the *annona*.

It would be natural if the *annona* office had officials stationed in likely areas of export. It may well have been so, and it is often asserted that it was so, but the evidence is very slender, and needs separate discussion.[74] It is customary to stress the lack of state machinery under the Republic, but it seems also that the *annona* department in itself was relatively small under the Empire. For the system to have worked at all the constant activity of hundreds of other people from the governors of the provinces downwards has to be assumed. It was one of the prime duties of the *praefectus annonae* that corn was neither spoiled through negligence nor diverted through fraud.[75] Hence at all points upon its journey, but particularly on arrival at Ostia or Puteoli, it must be carefully measured and weighed to assess both quantity and quality. The *mensores frumentarii* at Ostia formed one of the most important guilds, with large and handsome premises of their own.[76] Mosaics at Ostia, one from the hall of the measurers itself and another from the Piazzale delle Corporazioni, show how the measurers there supervised the filling of the *modius*, the measure of volume, levelling off the corn in it with a ruler (*rutellum*), while another official kept count with a kind of *abacus*.[77] We know of 'mensores machinarii frumenti publici', who seem to have weighed the corn with

[72] Pliny, *Paneg.* 29. 4–5.
[73] Pliny, *N. H.* 18. 35, cf. Frank, *ESAR* iv (Haywood), 84; see below, p. 111.
[74] See below, Appendix 2, p. 223.
[75] Seneca, *De Brevit. Vit.* 19. 1.
[76] Meiggs, *Roman Ostia*², p. 282.
[77] *Scavi di Ostia IV: I mosaici* (G. Becatti), pp. 33–4 and Tav. 58; Meiggs, *Roman Ostia*², Pl. XXVc.

great balances, only in three inscriptions from Rome itself.[78] The corn in store was in the charge of a multiplicity of *horrearii*; it was handled over land by vast numbers of porters, *saccarii*, and was barged up the river by the *codicarii*.[79] Before these men even touched it, it had been transported over the sea by the all-important *navicularii*, *mercatores*, and *negotiatores*. Without these men the system could not have worked.

5

It is time now to examine the organization of the shippers and merchants, and to see how the needs and attitudes both of them and of the *praefectus annonae* could have shaped the development of the *collegia* into which they came to be grouped, and in which they were ultimately to be imprisoned.

The beginning and the end of the process we are to examine are quite clear. During the Republic the problem of transport had been left in general either to independent traders or to such shippers as companies of *publicani*, or individual speculators, might hire to carry corn for them. By the beginning of the fourth century A.D. by contrast there were fixed *corpora* of hereditary *navicularii* who were under permanent control by the state. What is in doubt is the process by which this final development was reached; the rate, the extent and the nature of public organization of shipping and commerce during the intervening centuries.

The questions raised are many, the evidence is complicated, and the answers given by historians have varied. But basically the answers have fallen into one or other of two groups.

On the one hand there is the orthodox view, which was scrupulously worked out in elaborate detail by Waltzing and which has largely been followed by scholars such as Tenney Frank.[80] This view in its simplest form is that during the early Empire the state still relied on the free enterprise of individuals, placing its contracts with any shippers who might present

[78] *CIL* 6. 85 = *ILS* 3399; *CIL* 6. 33883 = *ILS* 7268; *CIL* 6. 9626.

[79] Rickman, *Roman Granaries*, Introduction; Meiggs, *Roman Ostia*², pp. 293–6; Pavis D'Escurac, *Préfecture*, pp. 225–39.

[80] J. P. Waltzing, *Étude historique sur les corporations professionnelles chez les romains*, 4 vols. (Louvain, 1895–1900); Tenney Frank, 'Notes on Roman Commerce', *JRS* 27 (1937), 72 ff. Cf. *An Economic History*² (New York, 1962), pp. 298 ff.

themselves. In time the state came to offer inducements, in the form of privileges or immunities, to encourage some men to persist in the corn-carrying trade and to attract others into it. All this was done without regard to such men being members of any college. But these shippers themselves tended, for their own ends, to form colleges. These were at first unofficially permitted, then officially chartered, and finally fostered by the state. The state thus came by degrees to appreciate the advantages of negotiating through an established and united body of known size rather than with an unknown, unconnected and ever-changing aggregate of individuals. This process of state recognition took place in the course of the second century and reached its completion at about the time of Septimius Severus, and only needed to be frozen into permanence by the provisions about heredity and inalienability of funds during the social and political crises of the third century A.D.

On the other hand there is the heterodox view put forward by Calza originally in relation to Ostia, and vigorously taken up and defended by Rostovtzeff.[81] According to this view the earliest Emperors, perhaps even Augustus himself, already saw the potential merits of the collegiate system in relation to the shippers and traders, and so had the various *corpora* licensed and recognized as permanent bodies within the state with permanent functions to perform. Thus the framework was there from the beginning of the Empire, and although there might be modifications, the framework itself had no need of structural alteration throughout the first three centuries of the Empire.

It is not too much, I think, to say that this alternative view, fashionable in the twenties and thirties, is now largely exploded. The evidence on which it was based was largely archaeological and in the interpretation of that evidence the balance of argument has turned against it.[82]

It seems better to see the development of the organization of shipping in the early Empire evolving over three phases. In the first period from Augustus to the mid-first century A.D. there was no single state policy for the corn supply, which involved *collegia*. The river mouth at Ostia was crowded with ships from

[81] G. Calza, 'Il piazzale delle corporazioni e la funzione commerciale di Ostia', *BullComm* 43 (1915), 178–206; M. Rostovtzeff, *SEHRE*², p. 159 and p. 607 n. 22.

[82] Meiggs, *Roman Ostia*², p. 283; see below, Appendix 3.

the western provinces and Puteoli was the main Italian end of the eastern trade, which now included the corn from Egypt. So far as importation of supplies was concerned, the duties of the *praefectus annonae* were confined to the payment of those *navicularii*,[83] shippers, who had been chartered to carry corn for the state; to the purchase of additional supplies as needed by the state for the *frumentationes* or other purposes, from independent *negotiatores*; and to keeping an overall watch on the amount of corn brought in by independent *negotiatores* and the extent to which it corresponded to the overall needs of the capital. In this period, therefore, official control and supervision of shipping was of the slightest and it was the independent traders, the *negotiatores* and *mercatores*, who came to sell in the open market that were of predominant importance.

In the second period from the mid-first century A.D. to Trajan, however, there was a conscious effort not just to avert or diminish crises as they occurred, but to try to ensure future security as well. This took the form of certain measures by Claudius and Nero, which affected both *navicularii* and *negotiatores*, and which were aimed at increasing their numbers and securing their services by contract in the supply of Rome for a given period of years.[84] In principle anyone who put shipping of a certain tonnage into commission and used it to bring corn to the city for a certain period of years was entitled to certain privileges; in practice registration with the authorities must have been a necessary condition of securing them. A new element of complication had thus been introduced into the problems of the central administration. Henceforward the *praefectus annonae* was obliged to keep lists of all regular importers of corn. The keeping of such lists in an accurate and up-to-date form can have been no easy task.

With the construction of the Claudian harbour Ostia became an increasingly important commercial centre, thronged by traders and shippers using it more and more as the port for the Roman market. Associations of members of the same profession had long existed for mutual society and protection both in Italy and the provinces. The possible role that they might play in the new situation for those serving the *annona* might not

[83] Cf. *CIL* 2. 1180.
[84] See above, p. 76.

have been obvious to all concerned from the start, but it was very real. On the one side, while the unattached trader might have difficulty in bringing himself to official notice in order to qualify for his rightful privileges, the *corporatus*, the member of a *collegium*, could be more sure that his services would not be allowed to go unrecognized. On the other side the *praefectus annonae* might welcome any help there might be in assessing those qualified for the new privileges. He might well have recourse to consulting the *collegia* since whatever else a college might lack it at least had a list of its members and might have knowledge about their activities. The advantages of corporatization for both sides are obvious, and the conditions for the growth in importance of the *collegia* and the growth of the judicial work the *praefectus annonae* undertook were I believe both inherent in the measures concerning privileges.

In the third period from the time of Trajan it may not therefore be a pure coincidence that our first indisputable evidence that the state was beginning to think in terms of colleges when dealing with certain activities is concerned with a grant of privileges. Trajan was said by the jurists to have extended privileges to those 'who are in the college of bakers' provided that they baked 100 *modii* daily throughout a period of three years.[85] Trajan was also said by Aurelius Victor to have been the Emperor who licensed the bakers' college.[86] The connection may be significant.

It is perhaps doubtful whether we can say with certainty that it was Trajan, the first Emperor after Claudius to give particular and systematic attention to the problems of Rome's food supply, who was the first to realize the potentialities of the collegiate organization, and therefore the first to license the *corpora* of *navicularii*.[87] But the recognition must have come at about this time, because later in the second century A.D. service of the *annona* in any form had come to be regarded as a public duty (*munus publicum*) giving the right to exemption from all lesser duties (*munera*),[88] and the role of the colleges of *navicularii*,

[85] Frag. Vat. 233 (Ulpian) and Gaius *Inst.* i. 28. 34—measures only applicable to bakers in Rome.

[86] Aur. Vict. *De Caes.* 13. 5.

[87] Cf. *Dig.* 27. 1. 17. 6 for a rather cryptic rescript of Trajan about the privileges of shippers.

[88] *Dig.* 50. 6. 6. 3 (Callistratus).

pistores, and *mercatores frumentarii* and *olearii* in securing these privileges was well established.[89]

In this third period from the turn of the first and second centuries A.D. it is significant that a shift of emphasis seems to have taken place which laid greater stress on the importance of the *navicularii*, the shippers, and less on the *negotiatores* and *mercatores*, the independent traders.

The independent trader was certainly not eliminated from the Roman corn market. One has only to look at the dedication made to M. Junius Faustus, *mercator frumentarius*, by the shippers of Africa and Sardinia in A.D. 173,[90] or read the long inscribed poem in honour of T. Caesius Primus who bought corn in Umbria and Tuscany and sold it in Rome in the first half of the second century A.D.,[91] to realize the wealth and importance of such independent traders. The independent *negotiator* was still worthy of official encouragement by the state in the reign of Alexander Severus.[92] But he features less prominently in the evidence of the jurists, perhaps because more of the corn was coming from state-owned sources and was now simply being transported to Rome by hired shippers under contract to perform that limited task.

Perhaps the most vivid evidence of how the system of relationships might work has been preserved for us in a bronze inscription discovered near Beirut, which contains a copy of a letter written by the *praefectus annonae*, Claudius Julianus, at the very beginning of the third century A.D., to a local *procurator* in Narbonensis in response to complaints made by the *navicularii marini* of Arles.[93] The details are not all entirely clear, particularly about the abuses which the shippers had suffered in serving the city of Rome and what was to be done to put them right. But what is clear is that the five *corpora* of shippers had stood together and sent a complaint to the *praefectus annonae*. He passed back to the local *procurator* an account of the complaint, what he had done in response to it and what the *procurator* was to do. But the *praefectus* also communicated all this directly to the *corpora* of the *navicularii* as well. What is of paramount

[89] *Dig.* 50. 6. 6. 6 (Callistratus).
[90] *CIL* 14. 4142.
[91] *CIL* 14. 2852 = *ILS* 3696.
[92] SHA *Alex. Sev.* 33.
[93] *CIL* 3. 14165/8 = *ILS* 6987, cf. Waltzing, *Corporations* iv. 616–23.

importance is that the Arles shippers had threatened, if the abuses were not stopped, to withdraw their services. These colleges were not by any means enslaved to the state but had used their corporate status to bring something they wanted done to the attention of the authorities.

The collegiate system appeared even then to have been happily devised to advance the interests of *corporatus* and *praefectus*, to promote efficiency without destroying enterprise, and to assure both profit to the provinces and security to Rome. At the end of the second century A.D. and perhaps even in the early third century A.D. there was still no reason to suppose that it might prove otherwise.

6

The role of the *praefectus annonae* was therefore from the beginning a difficult and complex one, and not easy to define; purely local in its aims and yet empire-wide in attempting to satisfy those aims. His was not even a proper magistracy; he was precisely the delegate of the Emperor from whose *imperium* his powers were drawn and appeal could always be made to the Emperor from a decision of the *praefectus*.[94] The job of the Emperor through his deputy the *praefectus* was, as the sources state, that of exercising a *cura* over a free market, attempting to co-ordinate supplies and plan ahead to avoid famines. If there was success, the Emperor took the credit; if there was failure the *praefectus* might receive the blame.[95]

Originally the sources of corn were many; the methods of bringing it to Rome various; no long-term contracts existed; the harbour facilities at Ostia were minimal. Gradually a system was forged; incentives were created, harbours built, and order emerged out of the random muddle.

One of the developments which may have helped to simplify the *praefectus annonae*'s task was the increasing concentration of land particularly in Africa and Egypt in the hands of the Emperors. Increasingly the Emperors themselves may have come to own on their vast personal estates some of the richest sources of the corn supply. If that is true then the *praefectus annonae*

[94] *Dig.* 1. 2. 33 (Pomponius).

[95] Tac. *Ann.* 3. 54. 6–8; Seneca, *De Brevit. Vit.* 18. 3.

became increasingly merely the steward of his master's own property, run by imperial slaves and freedmen, whose produce was shipped to Rome by hired *navicularii.*[96]

But what conduces to simplicity may also be conducive to routine administration, and ultimately to lack of importance. If the system was beginning to become automatic and just a part of the imperial bureaucracy, then it is not surprising that the legal aspects of the *praefectus*'s work, based originally on the hearing of civil cases concerned with the food market, might come to be developed as they were from the mid-second century A.D. The supply system might of course break down, given a combination of unfortunate circumstances, but basically by this time it ran itself, and the attention of the *praefectus annonae* himself was free to be given to the increasing number of legal cases to be heard in Rome.

Ultimately, after the crises of the third century A.D. and by the time of the rescripts in the Theodosian Code, as we shall see the *praefectus annonae* and his office was merely of local significance, subordinate in Rome to the *Praefectus Urbi*, and in Ostia and Portus to the *Praefectus Praetorio*, and cut off to a large extent from the affairs of Africa and Egypt by the existence of the *praefectus annonae Africae* and the *praefectus annonae Alexandrinae.*[97] Although the post of *praefectus annonae* was to last into the sixth century A.D.,[98] one of the key figures in the economic administration of the early Empire had become largely redundant.

[96] Cf. Rickman, *Roman Granaries*, p. 311.
[97] *Cod. Theod.* 11. 14. 1 (A.D. 365); *Cod. Theod.* 14. 23. 1 (A.D. 400); 14. 4. 9 (A.D. 417). *Not. Dign.* s.v.; see below, Ch. VIII.
[98] Cassiod. *Var.* 12. 9.

V

THE CORN LANDS

There is a need, before discussing the individual corn lands from which Rome drew her supplies, to sketch the geographical and climatic conditions which dictated where and how grain might be grown around the ancient Mediterranean.

The French historian Fernand Braudel in the first volume of his work on the Mediterranean in the sixteenth century has shown how complex and subtle a study of the environment can and should be.[1] It has certainly never been done on such a scale and with such penetration for the Mediterranean in the Ancient World. The nearest attempt was perhaps that of the geographer Ellen C. Semple published after a lifetime's journeys in the Mediterranean area in the early 1930s.[2] But rich though that work is in facts and insights it is not as subtle in analysis as Braudel's work, and perhaps by the very nature of the evidence that has been preserved from the ancient world, it could never have been so. In his agrarian history of Western Europe from A.D. 500 the Dutch historian Van Bath has stressed the importance in any economic history of the interplay of four major 'external factors': Environment, Population, Exploited Area, and Farming Technique.[3] The limitations of our knowledge about two of these factors for the ancient world, namely, population and its distribution, and the size of the exploited areas in many provinces, prevent us from carrying out a proper analysis. We do however have considerable knowledge about

[1] F. Braudel, *The Mediterranean and the Mediterranean World in the Age of Philip II* (London, 1972), Vol. i; for an even more searching account of a particular environment see P. Toubert, *Les Structures du Latium médiéval*, i, Bib. des Écoles Franç. d'Ath. et de Rome, 221 (Rome, 1973), Chs. II and III.

[2] E. C. Semple, *The Geography of the Mediterranean Region in relation to Ancient History* (London, 1932); cf. also M. Cary, *Geographic Background of Greek and Roman History* (Oxford, 1949).

[3] B. H. Slicher Van Bath, *The Agrarian History of Western Europe A.D. 500–1850* (London, 1963), Ch. 2.

the geography, geology, and climate of the Mediterranean environment, and about farming techniques adopted there in antiquity.

I

The geographic unity of the Mediterranean area is not in doubt. Geologically the Mediterranean countries are the product of a great volcanic upheaval in the Tertiary period, which framed a deeply sunken trench with heavily folded mountains.[4] It is true that these relatively recent earth movements did not completely destroy or cover with their limestone or sandstone caps the older geological strata of granite. Massive blocks of this older granite remain in the great Spanish plateau, Sardinia, Corsica, part of Tuscany, the toe of Italy, part of the Balkans, and central Lydia. But in general the younger strata prevail and the volcanic nature of the area is still apparent today.

Despite, however, the tangled mass of mountains that was created in this way, the repeated raising and lowering of the land led to the formation of deposits from the sea floor caught in the valleys between the mountains, and between the mountains and the sea. These deposits created areas of cultivable soil which were and still are of enormous significance, not least in Italy, for human occupation.[5] As natural terraces up against the steep rock of mountain folds, they eased the transition from highland areas to lowland plains, which were increased in size and depth of soil by the flow of rivers bearing rich alluvial deposits. This facilitated intercourse between highland and lowland areas. Consequently the geography of the Mediterranean is full of paradoxes. Although the Mediterranean may be a geographic unity, in any given area will be found a great variety of different types of countryside necessarily used in different ways; sea coast, plain land, scrub upland, mountain valleys, and high mountains.[6] However, although each of these may have peculiarities of its own and can be studied separately, to do so is to risk losing sight of the way in which so often they interlock in a composite way of life. Perhaps the best example of

[4] Semple, *Geography*, Chs. II and III; Cary, *Geographic Background*, p. 7.
[5] K. D. White, *Roman Farming* (London, 1970), p. 54. Cf. pp. 77–85.
[6] Semple, *Geography*, p. 376.

this was the system of pastoral husbandry with transhumance from winter to summer pastures. In winter the sheep stayed down on the lowland pastures, but with the drying heat of summer parching the ground and burning off the vegetation, they moved high to mountain areas, where pasture was still available, along age-old tracks and drove roads.[7] Particularly after the unification of Italy during the Republic the transhumance system was a regular practice in which each part of the countryside had its part to play.

So far as the growing of cereal crops is concerned the result of these geological factors is that, except in very special areas known to the peoples of the Mediterranean such as southern Russia, the cultivation of grain could not be carried out intensively on vast level plains. Even the coastal flats were not always used for grain, being sometimes put down to meadow and used for cattle pasture. The areas of level ground used for grain were restricted and these crops might well have to share mountain valleys and hill slopes with olives and orchard trees in a system of intercultivation. This system of intercultivation was in fact well suited to the demands of soil and climate in the Mediterranean but it seems so alien to our notions as to how corn should be grown that it was once fashionable for modern chair-bound scholars to castigate the ancient farmers for their methods of cultivation. With the exception of the rich volcanic soil of areas like Campania, eastern Sicily, the plains of southern Russia, certain areas in North Africa, and the permanently renewed valley of the Nile in Egypt, the soil on which many of the grain crops had to be grown was very largely decomposed limestone. Such soil was light and was unlikely to produce the large yields which we expect from the heavier loams of northern Europe. Moreover in such soil there was a very real problem about water retention, which was made worse by the nature of the Mediterranean climate.

2

The pre-eminent importance of the climate as opposed to the geology of the area for cultivation (except perhaps in Egypt)

[7] White, *Roman Farming*, p. 199.

was recognized by the ancients themselves. 'The year bears the crops, not the earth' was a saying, old even in the time of Theophrastus,[8] which enshrined a profound truth. It was the weather and the winds which dictated what could and could not be grown, and this weather varied from season to season in a way that made farming continually hazardous and unpredictable.[9]

Basically, although there are exceptions and local differences which must be mentioned later, the Mediterranean area forms a climatic unit. It is quite simply an area with winter rains and summer droughts. The reason is that the Mediterranean basin lies in a transition zone between two regions of distinctly different precipitation, the Atlantic and the Sahara, which compete for possession of this inland sea.[10]

With the advance of summer, the sun's rays, vertical at the equator at the time of the spring equinox, move northwards. The rain-bearing westerly winds of the Atlantic are pushed into middle Europe and a heat belt from the Sahara spreads over most of the Mediterranean. The whole region becomes an area of low barometric pressure, over which the hot air rises, and draws in winds from the high pressure area of Middle Europe. These winds from the north are characteristic of the Mediterranean summer and although they become warmer as they reach the Mediterranean, they still have a tempering effect on the Saharan heat. The crucial point, however, is that they absorb moisture and shed almost none, thus increasing the drought of the summer.

After the autumn equinox the sun moves south fiom the equator and the heat belt moves into southern Africa. The prevailing westerly winds of the Atlantic move into the Mediterranean and cover it like a wet blanket. The warm air over the sea still forms a low pressure area and draws in the winds from the high pressure areas of the Atlantic and the surrounding continents. These warm moisture-laden winds shed rain over the lands which are colder than the surrounding sea.

The effects of the summer drought are fairly easy to catalogue and comprehend. This by definition could not be the main

[8] Theophrast. *Plants* viii. 7. 6; cf. *C.P.* 3. 23. 4.
[9] Semple, *Geography*, p. 93.
[10] Semple, *Geography*, pp. 85 ff.; cf. Braudel, *The Mediterranean*, Part I, Ch. IV.

growing season for crops. The drought in fact is hard upon all vegetation because it occurs in summer when there is in general low atmospheric humidity, evaporation is increased by heat, and there are strong drying winds prevailing for anything from two to six months. The consequence was that only vegetation specially adapted to resist desiccation, such as the olive, stood much chance of survival, or there had to be some means of artificial irrigation.

Winter with its rain had to be the main growing season for most sown crops. But the complexities of the climatic variations of the winter season need careful analysis. Although there are dramatic differences in the temperatures experienced in winter, depending on whether you are in the mountains or down near the sea, it is not temperature which is the crucial factor for the growing of crops, but the pattern of precipitation of rain. Granted that the winter winds are from the west and northwest, it is not surprising that there should be considerable differences in the amount of rainfall received by the west and east sides of the various countries in the Mediterranean area. While Genoa may receive 50 inches (1,270 mm) a year, Venice receives only 30 inches (762 mm). Similarly the rainfall diminishes from north to south. While Genoa may receive 50 inches a year, Palermo receives only 34 inches (864 mm), Venice 30 inches (762 mm) a year, and Catania only 20 inches (508 mm).[11]

The problem of the winter rains is however more complex than that. These figures for annual rainfall are virtually meaningless. An annual rainfall of only 23 inches (585 mm), fairly evenly distributed throughout the year, maintains fresh vegetation in southern England because of the mild moist summers. But it is quite inadequate at Palermo for a vineyard, because of the summer drought. The concentration of the rainfall within a few months causes real problems in the Mediterranean. Moreover the rainfall in the Mediterranean can vary very considerably from year to year, so that average annual figures are misleading. Within a decade rainfall in a given area can fluctuate between 34 inches (864 mm) in some years and 5 inches (127 mm) in others, with the subnormal predominating

[11] Semple, *Geography*, p. 90.

in that short period.[12] The importance of all this lies in the fact that a rainfall of between 16 and 20 inches (400 and 500 mm) in a particular year is essential for the growth of cereal crops.[13] If the precipitation falls below that level the crops may fail, and the fact that the rainfall of the next year may be more than adequate cannot compensate for the failure. Indeed a sudden rainfall very much above average may be worse than useless, since it may cause 'run off' whereby fertile soil is eroded and carried away.

Variations in the amount of rainfall in winter are of the most acute importance at the beginning and end of the growing season. The early onset of autumn showers and the continuation of showery rain into the spring were both vital for a full harvest. But in the Mediterranean showers may fall as early as the beginning of September or be delayed until almost the end of October. Similarly the rains may cease at the beginning of April or continue off and on until the end of May.[14] Ideally grain seed should be sown early while the ground is still warm and then be gently watered to allow a proper germination; at the end of the main growing season the spring showers should continue long enough to allow a full growth of the crop before it is scorched by summer heat. The ancient farmers sowed their crops in the autumn when they judged the moment right and then prayed for rain within a few days before the seed died in the dry soil. In the spring they prayed that the rains would not stop too early; it was a factor in Sicily, as important as the presence of Mt. Etna with its fertilizing lava deposits, that there the spring rains could be relied upon, with consequent heavy yields of cereals.[15] The persistence into modern times of even the very dates of ploughing and sowing, together with the virtual identity of the crops and vegetation grown, apart from a few historically documented introductions by the Arabs, all point to a basic continuity of climate and environment in the area.[16]

[12] Semple, *Geography*, p. 92.
[13] Semple, *Geography*, p. 92; cf. N. Barbour, ed., *A Survey of North-West Africa*[2] (London, 1962), p. 201.
[14] Semple, *Geography*, p. 93.
[15] Cary, *Geographic Background*, p. 144.
[16] Semple, *Geography*, pp. 99–100; Cary, *Geographic Background*, pp. 2–3. Cf. C. Vita-Finzi, *The Mediterranean Valleys, Geological Changes in Historical Times* (Cambridge, 1969), pp. 116 ff.

3

Certainly the influence of these geographic and climatic conditions on the methods of farming, particularly of cereal crops, was, and still is, very powerful. The farmer had to struggle to develop techniques to get the best out of his by no means rich, or necessarily level ground; to cope with too much winter rain, too little summer rain, and too little manuring of the soil. The techniques that emerged are called those of 'dry farming' by modern exponents, who have been forced into similar methods by climatic conditions in other parts of the world.[17]

The essence of 'dry-farming' methods is the constant working of the ground even if, as was often the case in the ancient world, only one crop was taken in alternate years with a year of fallow intervening. By working of the ground was meant constant ploughing, hoeing, and pulverizing of the surface. It was quite normal to plough land three times a year and it is known that some land was ploughed up to nine times. The object of the ploughing was not as now in northern Europe, to cut a deep slice of soil, move it to one side, and turn it over, so that in the end the whole area ploughed produced a pattern of stripes. It was on the contrary simply to break the top soil and to do it so often from so many different directions that it would be impossible to tell in which direction the area had been ploughed.

The point of this constant and regular working of the soil throughout the year, even if a year of fallow, was above all to deal with the problem of rainfall. In the torrential downpours of winter a well-pulverized soil stood more chance of being able to absorb the sudden deluge of water, and of avoiding erosion and run off of the top soil. It helped too to prevent puddles of cold water forming in the fields, chilling the young seedlings. But the real need was for the conservation of water in the ground during the spring and summer months, and in this regular working of the soil played a key part. The elimination of weeds either among growing crops or in fallow was a vital factor in preventing loss of moisture. It prevented their competing with the crops or trees for water resources, and prevented

[17] Semple, *Geography*, pp. 385–8; White, *Roman Farming*, pp. 173 ff.; C. E. Stevens, 'Agriculture and rural life in the later Roman Empire' in *CEHE*[2] (Cambridge, 1966), i. 92–124.

also loss by transpiration through their leaves. Ploughing and hoeing helped in summer to increase root range and depth of the water catchment area, while also insulating the water in lower soils from the danger of evaporation by the sun. The ploughing in of the burned stubble after the harvest also helped to restore potash, phosphorus and other nutrients to the soil.

It was the need to work the soil constantly that led also to another characteristic feature of Mediterranean agriculture, that of intercultivation of sown and planted crops.[18] The olive, although it could not stand sharp frosts and cold, was well adapted to the non-mountainous areas of the Mediterranean. Its narrow leaves lost little moisture by transpiration and its long widely spread roots caught water over a large area. But even so water conservation by hoeing and ploughing among the trees was advisable and what more natural, since the ground had to be worked anyway, than to plant a crop on it. The crop in its turn was shaded and protected by the trees above it, in a manner much approved of by modern 'dry-farming' experts. Olives were better adapted to hillsides than to rich plain land, where they tended to run to wood, and thus there came about the extension of cereal farming over areas of slope that would at first sight seem inappropriate for corn. Since there was far more broken or hilly country than level plain land, the system was to the advantage of all concerned.

4

The sources from which Rome drew corn for both her civilian population and her armies could and did change during the course of her history as we have already seen. It is now time to look a little more closely at some of these corn lands, particularly at problems relating to their productivity and the availability of their produce to Rome.

(a) *Italy*

The corn-growing areas of Italy were many, but not all of them were equally important for Rome.[19] It is difficult to prove any regular benefit derived from the rich grain crops of the Po

[18] White, *Roman Farming*, p. 48. Duncan-Jones, *ERE*, pp. 34–6.
[19] White, *Roman Farming*, pp. 77–84.

valley. Similarly although wheat from the great lowland plain of Tavoliere di Puglie around Foggia in Apulia was acknowledged in the first century B.C. as being superb in quality,[20] it is hard to find traces of any regular import to Rome. Much more useful were the products of Etruria, Latium, and Campania. The fertility and good farming of Campania were legendary from the beginning to the end of antiquity. The area produced high-quality emmer particularly *durum*, or macaroni wheat, from the earliest times and although originally it was controlled by Greeks, it could be tapped at need for the Roman market. The rich coastal plains later grew the much-favoured *triticum vulgare*, which produced the finest white flour, *siligo*, and never suffered the fate of those plains further to the north of becoming waterlogged and pestilential. The old Volscian territory to the north partly suffered this fate, and the coastal plain of Latium, south of Antium, which had once been a fertile source of corn, had become the notorious Pomptine marshes by the time of the elder Pliny in the first century A.D.[21] The corn of Etruria, both *durum* and *triticum vulgare*, came from two quite distinct areas, not simply the coastal plains around Pisa and Caere, from which it might be shipped to Rome by sea, but also from the elevated basins of the interior, which contained rich deposits of alluvium. Wheat of quite exceptional quality was produced from the most important of these, the Val di Chiana, a trough which stretches from Arezzo to Chiusi.[22] The valuable produce of these inland basins was available to Rome by the two major rivers, the Tiber and the Arno, which were navigable for considerable stretches. The productivity in cereals of the Chiusi area seems to have remained high, even though Pliny the Younger records that the Etruscan coast had become 'gravis et pestilens'.[23]

Quite apart from these specific areas going out of production, there has been some modern controversy over the growing of corn in Italy generally. The certain fact that Rome came to depend increasingly on corn supplies from overseas has been used to suggest that there was a collapse of cereal cultivation in Italy in general and even that there was a severe decline in

[20] Varro, *R. R.* 1. 2. 6.
[21] Pliny, *N. H.* 3. 59.
[22] Pliny, *N. H.* 18. 86 and 87; Varro, *R. R.* 1. 9. 6.
[23] Pliny, *Ep.* 5. 6. 1.

Italian productivity perhaps because of soil exhaustion. A close study of the evidence does not support either of these claims.[24] It must have been the case that the Italian cities continued always to be supported by Italian grown corn and not by imported corn. The very transport costs that for example prevented the rich produce of the Po valley being of much use to the Roman market meant that the dispersal of Roman imported corn far inland was not an economic proposition. It was only areas in the immediate hinterland of importing harbours that were likely to be much affected by the provincial corn imports. Even if in Latium there was an increase in mixed farming, it may have been not so much imposed upon the landowners by the influx of imported corn as deliberately adopted by them from the early second century B.C. onwards to provide themselves with more valuable cash crops that could be sold at good prices in the expanding city and that imported corn spread over the area in order partly to fill the already existing vacuum.

As for the productivity of the soil, we have very little evidence and that little has often been used arbitrarily. A passage of Columella,[25] written about the middle of the first century A.D., seems to suggest that the average maximum yield on cereals in Italy in his day was fourfold. This obviously compares badly with the yield figures given by Varro in 37 B.C. for certain parts of Etruria in Italy, where the same seed could yield tenfold in one place and fifteenfold in another.[26] Cicero, too, in 70 B.C. said that for the area around Leontini in Sicily the yield was eightfold in ordinary years and tenfold in exceptional years.[27] But both these references were to regions of outstanding fertility; Etruria was used by Varro specifically as an example of an area where the land was exceptionally good, and Leontini was the *caput rei frumentariae* of Sicily. They do not provide a proper yardstick for comparison. It is an unfortunate fact that we have no other contemporary average figure with which to compare the information of Columella who was concerned to

[24] A. Toynbee, *Hannibal's Legacy*, ii. Chs. V and VI; Frank, *ESAR* i. 97 ff. and 283 ff.; v. 139 ff.; K. D. White, 'Wheat farming in Roman times', *Antiquity* 37 (1963), 207 ff.; P. A. Brunt, *Italian Manpower*, pp. 271 ff.

[25] Columella, *De Re Rust.* 3. 3. 4.

[26] Varro, *R. R.* 1. 44; cf. 1. 9. 6.

[27] Cicero, *In Verr.* 2. 3. 112.

denigrate alternatives to viticulture in that particular passage. We know only that yields of four-, five-, and sixfold are recorded in sixteenth- and seventeenth-century Italy, and these seem likely to have been the levels within which the ancient yields may also have fluctuated.[28] The fact is that we really have no knowledge of how big 'typical' wheat yields in ancient Italy were but also no reason to use Columella's figure to suggest there had been any sort of decline in productivity.

It would be wrong therefore to conclude from the small part played by Italy in supplying the Roman market from the third century B.C. either that Italy as a whole grew little corn or that the soil of Italy was somehow peculiarly impoverished. It is interesting that in the fourth century A.D. Campania, from which goods could easily be transported to Rome by sea, was still referred to as 'cellarium regnanti Romae', and Cassiodorus stressed how Rome depended on corn supplies from southern Italy.[29]

(b) *Sicily*

For Sicily we have not only the usual general references in the ancient sources to its fertility and its importance to Rome, but also some precise figures, particularly for the late Republic, about its productivity and the availability of its produce for export.[30]

Sicily played her role as exporter of corn right from the early days of the Greek colonization of Sicily, down through the Roman period and was still in the sixteenth and seventeenth centuries A.D. acting as the granary of the Spanish Empire.[31] Yet the geography of Sicily was not particularly conducive to the growing of corn as we understand it in northern Europe, or on the prairies of North America or the steppe lands of the Ukraine. There were no large expanses of low and level ground except for the plain of Catania below Mt. Etna in south-east Sicily with the fabulously productive area of Leontini. A chain

[28] Duncan-Jones, *ERE*, p. 48 n. 4 and p. 52 n. 1; for a different view see K. D. White, 'Wheat farming', *Antiquity* 37 (1963), 207 ff.

[29] *Expositio totius mundi et gentium*, ed. J. Rougé (Paris, 1966), § 54; Cassiodorus, *Var.* 4. 5.

[30] There is a discussion of these figures, not always reliable, by V. Scramuzza in Frank, *ESAR* iii. 253 ff.

[31] A. Toynbee, *Hannibal's Legacy* ii. 210 ff.

of mountains up to 6,000 ft (1,830 m) high stretched along the north coast, broken mountain country dominated the west, while the centre and south-west coast consisted of a high plateau, which was nevertheless sharply undulating. The corn was largely grown on hill and mountain sides, as it has been ever since.

The sporadic demands by Rome on Sicily's corn, mainly *durum*, were turned into a steady and continuous monopolizing of her exportable surplus from the end of the third century B.C. Initially there was a period at the end of the third century B.C. when Rome controlled directly all Sicily except the Kingdom of Hiero of Syracuse who was simply her ally. But after Hiero's death Rome annexed all Sicily, and did much to stimulate wheat production. Sicily's produce was thenceforward reserved for Rome. Rhodes in a well-known incident in 169 B.C. had to get special permission to take 100,000 *medimnoi* of corn from Sicily.[32]

The detailed information, which gives some sophistication but no overall precision to our knowledge of Sicilian corn comes, of course, from Cicero's third Verrine oration, dating from 70 B.C. It can be deduced from a famous passage in this speech that the taxation tithe was some 3 million *modii*, that Verres was ordered to purchase an additional tithe of 3 million *modii* and a further 800,000 *modii* at certain prices.[33] If 3 million *modii* was a tithe we can estimate that the total produce of Sicily was expected to be somewhere between 30 and 40 million *modii*, perhaps nearer the latter figure once we have allowed for tax-collectors' profits and the produce of those cities untaxed. Even when Rome drew nearly 7 million *modii* from Sicily it appears that there was still a considerable amount for private export.[34] It has been guessed that perhaps as much as 5 million *modii* extra were available for private export to Rome and elsewhere.[35] If that is true Rome may at times have taken up to a quarter of Sicily's total corn produce.

Sicily's richness in corn and importance to Rome in the second and first centuries B.C. have never been in doubt, but

[32] Polyb. 28. 2.
[33] Cic. *In Verr.* 2. 3. 163. See above, p. 38.
[34] Cf. Cicero, *De Domo* 11.
[35] Frank, *ESAR* iii (Scramuzza), 263.

it has been suggested that the first three centuries A.D. saw Sicily suffering from a decline either because of competition from African and Egyptian corn going to Rome, or because of the growth of *latifundia* and pasturage in Sicily itself at the expense of wheat production.[36] But we may well question whether Sicily was much less productive in the Empire than in the late Republic. Strabo stresses Sicily's corn and its importance to Rome at the time of Augustus and Aelius Aristides does the same in the second half of the second century.[37] Pliny in the mid-first century A.D. actually lists Sicilian among the imported wheats and rates it highly for its quality and yield.[38] Archaeological evidence, in the form of coins, sarcophagi reliefs, and a mosaic at Ostia reinforce the literary statements about Sicily's continued role in the supply of Rome.[39] It was diminished, if at all, not by any lack of productivity in Sicily but only by the comparison with the greater resources of Africa and Egypt.

In the late Empire Sicily's importance is again not in doubt. The testimony of the *Expositio totius mundi*, Prudentius, Procopius, and Salvian is unanimous about Sicily's wheat being essential for the sustenance of Rome.[40]

(c) *Sardinia*

This island also came under direct Rome control by the end of the third century B.C. as a result of the Punic Wars no less than Sicily itself. But despite the fact that the island was as large as Sicily and also produced a valuable corn surplus for the Roman market, Sardinia tends to get scant attention in modern or indeed in ancient sources. It may be that Rome stimulated cereal production in Sardinia no less than in Sicily.[41] But the best corn-growing areas in Sardinia lay on the plain to the south-west of the island and the best port for export to Rome, apart from Carales in the south, lay at Olbia over the mountain in the north-east of the island, and although Sardinia was fruitful, it had a pestilential climate as a result of the lagoons

[36] Frank, *ESAR* iii (Scramuzza), 349.
[37] Strabo 6. 273; Aelius Aristides, *To Rome* 12.
[38] Pliny, *N. H.* 18. 66.
[39] *ESAR* iii (Scramuzza), 350.
[40] *Expositio totius mundi* (ed. J. Rougé, 1966), § 65; Prudentius, *Contra Symm.* 2. 939–44; Procopius, *Bell. Goth.* 3. 16; Salvian 6. 68.
[41] Frank, *ESAR* iii (Scramuzza), 240. Cf. E. S. Bouchier, *Sardinia in Ancient Times* (Oxford, 1917).

and swamps near the many river mouths and its wild mountains were occupied by unruly tribesmen. Consequently Sardinia never became so heavily studded with Roman settlements nor so Romanized as Sicily, but its corn production was prolific and important, particularly in the second and first centuries B.C. and again in the late Empire. Pompey regarded it as important in his efforts to supply Rome in the 50s B.C. and may even have rewarded Sardinian shippers with the citizenship.[42] At Ostia in the Piazzale delle Corporazioni the Sardinian port towns of Carales and Turris are represented in the mosaics around the portico and the shippers of Carales added corn measures to the picture of a ship to illustrate their business.[43] We have no precise figures for its productivity but the fact that Sardinia, Sicily, and Africa can be referred to by Cicero in one breath as 'tria frumentaria subsidia reipublicae'[44] suggests that Sardinia's corn production was not negligible for the Roman market. Certainly the elder Pliny still included Sardinian among his wheat types in the first century A.D.[45]

(d) *Spain*

Spain is the other major area which fell to the Romans at the end of the third century B.C., whose mines and whose natural resources in grain were immediately exploited by the Romans.[46] Wheat is invariably mentioned as one of the gifts of Spanish soil and there can be no doubt that there were areas of cultivation down the east coast of Spain which satisfied local needs and could even feed whole Roman armies during their campaigns in Spain. But it also seems clear that it was only in the valley of the river Baetis in south-west Spain that there was a constant and regular surplus of grain produced to guarantee an export trade.[47] It seems that the Spanish communities during the Republic paid their taxes to the Roman government direct in cash, but raised the money by a levy of a *vicesima*, one-twentieth, on corn grown.[48] The corn which actually came from

[42] Plut. *Pomp.* 50; Cic. *Pro Scauro* 43; cf. Gaius i. 32c; see above, p. 57.

[43] Meiggs, *Roman Ostia*², p. 286.

[44] Cicero, *De Imp. Gn. Pomp.* 34. Cf. Varro, *R. R.* 2. 3, Val Max. 7. 6. 1.

[45] Pliny, *N. H.* 18. 66.

[46] Frank, *ESAR* iii (Van Nostrand), 175.

[47] Strabo 3. 144; Dio 60. 24. 5; Pliny, *N. H.* 18. 66; cf. Claudian, *In Eutrop.* 1. 405.

[48] Cic. *In Verr.* 2. 3. 12; *Pro Balbo* 41; Livy, 43. 2. 12.

Spain to Rome therefore must either have been bought up on orders of the Roman state, or have come from public domains, or have been prospected for by private corn merchants. It seems that Spain was not to be ranked with Sicily and Africa or even perhaps with Sardinia, but rather with Gaul as a subsidiary source of good quality supplies in the west for the Roman market.

(e) *Africa*

With the destruction of Carthage itself in 146 B.C. the African lands of the old Carthaginian empire were turned into a Roman province.[49] This original province was not very large (some 5,000 square miles, or nearly 13,000 sq. km) but as in other territories once controlled by Carthage in Sicily, Sardinia and Spain, the Romans took over a sophisticated agricultural tradition. The areas round the coastal Punic cities and the valleys of the river Bagradas and river Miliana were not only very fertile but had been systematically farmed for generations. It seems too that Carthaginian influence had been at work in the neighbouring kingdom of Numidia, and Carthaginian agricultural techniques had increased the productivity of that area by the time Julius Caesar annexed it to the original province.[50] Despite the fact that the ground of Carthage itself had been cursed, Gaius Gracchus made a determined attempt to launch a colony in its territory in 123 B.C., supposedly the first such venture overseas.[51] It was not to be for defence or the settlement of veteran soldiers but a colony with serious social and economic purpose, drawn from the most respectable citizens, each allocated generous allotments up to 200 *iugera*. Gracchus took with him some 6,000 settlers, perhaps more than was permitted by the law concerned. Although the law was revoked, the settlers up to the number permitted by the law were not deprived of the lands assigned to them. Their descendants were probably incorporated in the new colony established by Julius Caesar,

[49] Frank, *ESAR* iv (R. M. Haywood), 3, 15 ff., and 19 ff.; T. S. R. Broughton, *The Romanization of Africa Proconsularis* (Baltimore, 1929); P. G. Walsh, 'Massinissa', *JRS* 55 (1965), 151–5. See now P. D. A. Garnsey and C. R. Whittaker (eds.), *Imperialism in the Ancient World* (Cambridge, 1978), Ch. 11, 'Rome's African Empire under the Principate' (P. Garnsey).

[50] Plutarch, *Caesar* 55. Cf. Frank, *ESAR* iv (Haywood), 21.

[51] Velleius 1. 15. 4; Cic. *Leg. Ag.* 1. 5.

who returned to the idea of colonies of this kind. Whether there were any large scale settlements of Roman veterans in Africa by Marius in the intervening period remains doubtful, but Roman interest, for various reasons, in African resources is obvious.[52]

During the early Empire the area under direct Roman control quickly expanded both westwards through the two Mauretanias towards the Atlantic and southwards towards the Sahara. But the vastly increased area that this expansion brought may have made less difference to the amount of grain available for the Roman market than we might think.

Cereals will not grow properly if the average rainfall is less than 16 inches (400 mm) per year.[53] A quick glance at a modern map giving the distribution of rainfall in North Africa defines the southern limit of possible cereal culture. Even if the distribution of rainfall has changed somewhat with the loss of forests in the area, it is clear that the southward march of the boundaries of the Roman province could not increase significantly the area of cereal cultivation. It is no surprise that the expansion southwards should be linked not with the increase of cereals but of olive cultivation.[54] This was to make Africa and particularly the eastern parts of it in Tripolitania and Libya one of the richest sources of olive oil for Rome. The olives with their deep roots could find the little water that was available and the stability created by Roman control gave the confidence to plant trees and wait for them to mature.

The areas for the growth of cereals therefore remained essentially in the northern strip of Africa. Cyrene and its hinterland between the provinces of Egypt and Africa was important. There was a small area on the east coast of Byzacium around Horrea Caelia and Hadrumetum, which was unlikely to have stretched any further south than Thysdrus, and an area on the Cap Bon peninsula itself around Clupea, Misua, and Curubis (the last two of which are represented in the Piazzale delle Corporazioni in Ostia).[55] But the main area for cereal growing

[52] Brunt, *Italian Manpower*, pp. 577–80.

[53] N. Barbour, ed., *A Survey of North-West Africa*², p. 201; cf. p. 5, map showing distribution of annual rainfall in North Africa.

[54] Frank, *ESAR* iv (Haywood), 45 ff.

[55] R. Meiggs, *Roman Ostia*², pp. 286–7; cf. Frank, *ESAR* iv (Haywood), 63; Tod, *GHI* ii. 196.

lay in the valleys of the Bagradas and Miliana rivers in the hinterland of Carthage itself. It was here that the ground was most intensively cultivated and here the great imperial estates clustered most closely. Hippo Diarrhytus, as well as Carthage, is a port whose shippers had an office at Ostia, and which would have been a natural outlet for the products of this area.

There were however important cereal-growing areas which lay to the west of the original lands of Carthage. The upper valley of the Bagradas formed the first part of this stretch of land, but it extended from as far east as Veneria Sicca to as far west as Sitifis and a little beyond.[56] It was a relatively narrow belt cut off from the sea to the north by a range of forest-covered mountains which precluded cultivation, while to the south lay the high plateaux stretching to the foot of the Aures range, too dry for cereals and more suited to olives. The northern limit of this cereal country lay at Calama while the southern limit was roughly a line from Sitifis to Madauros. Most important was that there were ways through the mountains northwards to the sea, and at these points export centres for the Roman market seem to have developed, for example at Hippo Regius, Rusicade, and perhaps Saldae.[57]

Further west still there were many areas in what is now modern Algeria, especially the region of Sidi-bel-Abbes, and above all on the plateaux of Morocco, where the rainfall was much heavier, and where grain was grown abundantly in Roman times and has been grown successfully ever since.

But the effect of westward expansion by itself may not have been dramatic. Some of the areas in Algeria although officially outside Roman territory during the Republic had, we may suspect, been yielding their products to the Roman market even in the second century B.C. Certainly an area like that of Cirta in Numidia had had many Roman and Italian businessmen active there in the late second century B.C. and some of them may, despite its distance from the coast, have been tapping the corn resources which would find so ready a market at Rome.[58] The Moroccan grain growing, although important

[56] B. H. Warmington, *The North African Provinces from Diocletian to the Vandal Conquest* (Cambridge, 1954), pp. 55–6.
[57] Frank, *ESAR* iv (Haywood), 42; cf. Rickman, *Roman Granaries*, pp. 184, 321–2.
[58] Frank, *ESAR* iv (Haywood), 17 ff.

for the local towns, was perhaps less significant for Rome because of the transport difficulties over the greater distances involved.

More important than the expansion may have been the pacification and increased security of life and property in the African area which allowed the rapid development of prosperity there. This took the form not only of increasing cultivation of olives but an intensification of the cereal growing that had existed before.

This developing prosperity in Africa took a particular form. It was already apparent under the Republic that land was being held often in the form of large estates by great senatorial landowners. This trend continued under the early Empire but with the Emperor himself as a possible rival owner of land.[59] The concentration of land in the hands of the Emperor was given a sudden impetus by Nero when he confiscated the holdings of six African landlords who, according to Pliny in an exaggerated phrase, owned half Africa.[60] That may have been an over-statement but the increase in imperial land-holdings in Africa is beyond doubt. A Hadrianic inscription from Ain-el-Djemala (*CIL* viii. 25943) in the hinterland of Carthage mentions a 'saltus Neronianus' which seems to have swallowed up earlier estates named after their original owners, the 'saltus Blandianus', the 'saltus Udensis' and parts of the 'saltus Lamianus' and 'Domitianus'. Other elaborate inscriptions have also been preserved, spelling out the details of the way the land was managed.

From these inscriptions it seems that there was a common system of renting off a proportion of the land to tenants who not only paid a proportion of their crops as rent for their own holdings but provided a certain number of days' labour (five days' labour a year) for the land of the chief lessee (*conductor*), the whole arrangement being under the eyes of a series of imperial procurators.[61] Large though these estates were, in

[59] Frank, *ESAR* iv (Haywood), 83; D. Crawford, 'Imperial Estates' in M. I. Finley (ed.), *Studies in Roman Property*, pp. 35–70; cf. Broughton, *Romanization*, p. 157.

[60] Pliny, *N. H.* 18. 35. Cf. *CIL* 8. 25902 (Henchir Mettich), 25943 (Ain el Djemala), 26416 (Ain Wassel), 10570 + 14464 (Suk el Khmis).

[61] J. Kolendo, 'La hiérarchie des procurateurs dans l'inscription d'Aïn-el-Djemala (*CIL* viii. 25943)', *REL* 46 (1968), 319–29. Cf. Crawford, 'Imperial Estates', pp. 47–9.

their actual farming they seem to have been made up of small separate lots, but despite the inscriptions we cannot map the boundaries of any of these estates with precision.

The imperial ownership of the land, the rent payment of about a third of the crops, and the supervision by an imperial agent, all meant that Africa produced more and more corn that was directly owned by, or was directly under the eye of, the state and its agents. Besides Carthage, regional offices for the administration of Africa were centred at Hadrumetum, Theveste, Thamugadi Thugga, and Hippo Regius probably from the time of Vespasian. The Emperor came to own many of the major sources of the corn supply in Africa and his deputy the *praefectus annonae* therefore knew more clearly where he stood, when making his estimates and plans. A famous passage in Josephus makes it clear that even by the Flavian period Africa was quantitatively more important than Egypt in supplying Rome with corn[62] and Commodus organized an African corn fleet in the late second century A.D. when supplies from Egypt seemed uncertain.[63] By the fourth century A.D. specific instructions for the *exactio* (or *conlatio*), the delivery of grain and other goods at the municipal granaries, and the *transmissio*, the transport of them to the *horrea fiscalia*, were carefully laid down for Africa in the constitutions of the Emperors. But by this time so important were the African supplies for Rome there was a special official, the *praefectus annonae Africae*, subordinate directly to the *praefectus praetorio* himself who was responsible for the gathering of the supplies and their dispatch to Rome.[64] Africa became Rome's greatest single granary and provided *durum* wheat of the finest quality.[65]

(f) *Gaul*

The natural fertility of Gaul was realized at least from the time of Caesar's conquests, if not before.[66] The abundance of its cereal crops supported Caesar's armies, living off the

[62] Josephus, *Bell. Iud.* 2. 383–5; see below, Appendix 4.

[63] SHA *Commodus* 17. 7.

[64] *Cod. Theod.* 11. 1. 2; 7. 4; 11. 30. 4. Cf. E. Tengström, *Bread for the People: Studies of the Corn Supply of Rome during the late Empire*. See below, Ch. VIII.

[65] Pliny, *N. H.* 18. 66.

[66] Frank, *ESAR* iii (Grenier), 578. O. Brogan, *Roman Gaul* (London, 1953), pp. 130 ff.

country, with ease and it seems clear that the Gauls even before the arrival of the Romans were interested in farming well.

The areas of greatest importance for corn were two. First, the area in south-west and southern France, the plains of Gascony, the lands of the Upper Garonne, and the Rhône Valley; secondly, the plains further to the north around the Loire and the Seine. It was the first area in the south and south-west Gaul that was most obviously connected with the exporting centres of Narbonne and Arles. The second area was most naturally connected with the supplies for the Rhine armies, but it was certainly not impossible for the products of this region to find their way up the Loire and then down the Rhône valley to Arles. The shippers of both Arles and Narbonne had offices in the Piazzale delle Corporazioni at Ostia, and there was a *procurator annonae* in residence at Arles possibly to co-ordinate supplies for the Roman market.[67] Unfortunately we have no figures for the amounts of corn Rome derived from Gaul, but it should perhaps be thought of in the same terms as Spain, although it produced a lighter wheat;[68] it was certainly not as vital to the Roman market as Sicily, Africa, or Egypt but a subsidiary supply of possible importance.

(g) *Egypt*

In relation to Egypt we have a great abundance of evidence of all kinds, mainly preserved in papyri, concerning agriculture and the export of corn, but the evidence is so complicated that it is difficult to build up a single comprehensive picture.[69]

Egypt, agriculturally speaking, is and always has been the gift of the Nile. In the Ptolemaic period before Roman control Egypt's rulers had exerted a tight central control over the agricultural and commercial life of the whole Delta and Nile valley. The country taken over by the Romans therefore had a tradition of detailed organization, but was also by the political

[67] Meiggs, *Roman Ostia*², p. 286; *CIL* 12. 672; see below, p. 223.

[68] Pliny, *N. H.* 18. 66.

[69] Frank, *ESAR* ii (A. C. Johnson), particularly pp. 1 ff., 7 ff., 481 ff. M. Rostovtzeff, 'Kornerheburg und transport im griechisch-römischen Ägypten', *APF* 3 (1906), 201–24. A. Segrè, 'Note sull'economia dell' Egitto ellenistico nell' età tolemaica', *BSAA* 29 (1934), 257–305; cf. D. J. Crawford, *Kerkeosiris*, pp. 112–17. N. Hohlwein, 'Le blé d'Égypte', *EtPap* 4 (1938), 33–120.

standards of other countries around the Mediterranean rather backward; an area of villages and worker peasants.[70]

When Augustus annexed Egypt after the death of Cleopatra, although it clearly became one of the Roman state's provinces, it was peculiar in that the Emperors kept a close personal watch upon it and made special regulations for its administration, and in that, so far as the inhabitants of Egypt were concerned, the Emperors personally took the place of the deposed Ptolemies. Egypt, therefore, historically and administratively remained peculiarly distinct and unlike any other area of the Roman Empire.

So far as corn growing and the supplying of corn to Rome is concerned, the Nile was clearly the dominating factor in Egypt.[71] From Upper Egypt down to the Delta it was the Nile which created the cultivable strip of land beset on either side by desert. In fact it was the strip of land rather than the delta itself which was so important for cultivation, since in the delta area there were considerable marshes and swamps, which seemed beyond the ancients' ability to control. A great deal of the country's corn thus came from Upper Egypt.

The most important fact about the Nile was the annual flood caused by rainfall in the Ethiopian highlands, which was channelled via the Blue Nile down into Egypt. The flood reached its height in early August and provided the necessary irrigation of the land before planting of seed could begin. Two kinds of irrigation could be used, either perennial irrigation or inundation basins. Perennial irrigation was the use of systems of small ditches to draw water from the Nile and criss-crossing an area to make it cultivable. How far the Egyptians and Romans used this system is not really known, but the chances are that while it was fairly common as a supplementary form of watering (and is now especially important in the Delta), it was not the key to fertility. Much more common throughout the Nile Valley both in Roman times and even in the nineteenth century was the system of basin inundation whereby whole areas on

[70] J. G. Milne, *A History of Egypt under Roman Rule*[3] (London, 1924), Ch. VII.

[71] D. Bonneau, *Le Fisc et le Nil. Incidences des irregularités de la crue du Nil sur la fiscalité foncière dans l'Égypte grecque et romaine* (Paris, 1972). D. Crawford, *Kerkeosiris*, Ch. 7. N. Hohlwein, 'Le Blé', Ch. 3, 'Le Nil'. Cf. also D. Crawford, 'The Opium Poppy: a study in Ptolemaic Agriculture', *Problèmes de la terre en Grèce ancienne, sous la direction de M. I. Finley* (Paris, 1973), pp. 223–51.

either side of the river were flooded to a certain depth for forty days and then after the swollen Nile had subsided the water was drained back into the river. The basins would thus be emptied in October, but only after the ground was thoroughly soaked and a deposit of silt, rich in nitrogenous material and phosphoric acid, had covered the land.

The land was in this way reinvigorated year after year and never became exhausted. A crop of wheat could be grown each year, with a rest crop planted only every third year, instead of the system of fallowing in alternate years followed elsewhere in the Mediterranean. But the fertility depended on there being a good flood, neither too little to flood the basins, nor so much that whole areas were drowned, and on an efficient central administration of the country that would see that the dykes and canals, needed to control the flood, were properly maintained. So even Egypt was vulnerable and her crop yields could fall sharply at times. Probably the most famous occasion was when as a result of the poor flood of A.D. 99 there was a famine in Egypt so severe that Trajan ordered the grain fleet to return from Rome to Egypt in order to relieve the suffering of the Egyptians.[72] The occasion gave the younger Pliny the opportunity to deliver a small sermon on the subject in his *Panegyric* of Trajan, which is worth quoting:

> For long it was generally believed that Rome could only be fed and maintained with Egyptian aid, so that this vain and presumptuous nation used to boast that they must still feed their conquerors, that their river and their ships ensured our plenty or our want. Now we have returned the Nile its riches, sent back the corn we received; it has had to take home the harvests it used to dispatch across the sea. Let this be a lesson to Egypt; let her learn by experience that her business is not to allow us food but to pay a proper tribute; let her realize that she is not indispensable to the people of Rome though she is their servant. Henceforth, if it wishes, the Nile can stick to its bed and content itself with a river's proper form—it will make no difference to Rome, nor to Egypt either, except that ships will leave her country cargoless and empty as once they used to return, while from Rome they will sail filled with the cargo they once brought us.

The norm for a good flood was given by Pliny and Strabo as either 16 cubits or 14 cubits, but Strabo is quick to point out that Augustus' good work on having the canals cleaned turned

[72] *P. Oxy.* 2958 (2 Dec. A.D. 99); Pliny, *Paneg.* 31.

a flood of only 12 cubits into a success.[73] The rise of the river was carefully observed at the nilometers, of which we have a description of the one at Elephantine in Upper Egypt, and it was on these readings that the Prefect of Egypt determined the amount of tribute to be exacted from the farms and estates in the Nile Valley.[74] The flooding sometimes changed landmarks or altered the configuration of the land in some way, so there was a need for regular surveys. Moreover every year at the time of the flood there was a need for regular inspections to fix the taxation in the light of which fields were under a deposit of sand, which had been properly flooded, and which had not been touched by the water at all.

However, not only was the Nile the source of the fertility of Egypt, it was also the main artery which allowed bulky agricultural produce to be moved with relative ease and cheapness to Alexandria, from which by another journey by water the goods could be got to Rome itself.[75] It was a fortunate fact that not only was Egypt bisected by a great river, but that while the current of this river flowed downstream to the Mediterranean, the prevailing wind was from the north, and easy passage was possible for boats both up and down the Nile. The corn was moved from the village storehouses by camel or donkey train the short distance to the harbours on the Nile, and that was the only part of the journey that had to be undertaken by land.[76]

Despite the common pattern of agriculture dictated by the dominant Nile flood, the categories of land tenure in Egypt were many and varied. We know for example of a distinction between public or crown land on the one hand and domain land on the other.[77] The first was the crown land of the Ptolemies taken over by Augustus as the public land of the province of Egypt. Some of it was sold off and became private property, but most of it was leased to farmers who were tenants of the crown. It was the taxes and rents paid by these tenants of public land which formed the main revenue in grain to the

[73] Pliny, *N. H.* 5. 58; Strabo 17. 788.
[74] Strabo, 17. 817.
[75] J. Schwartz, 'Le Nil et le ravitaillement de Rome', *BIFAO* 47 (1948), 179.
[76] Frank, *ESAR* ii (Johnson), 400.
[77] S. L. Wallace, *Taxation in Egypt from Augustus to Diocletian* (Princeton, 1938), p. 3.

state. The second, domain land, were the private estates (*ousiai*) owned mostly by members of the imperial family but also by others who enjoyed imperial favour such as the younger Seneca, which by the end of the first century A.D. had mostly been inherited or confiscated by the Emperors themselves.[78] It quickly therefore became simply part of the *patrimonium* of the Emperor. It was most often leased out like public land, but the administration of the two accounts was kept quite distinct.

Such distinctions, however, are not really important for our purposes. The real difference which mattered was that between corn-land and orchard-land, whatever the administrative grade of the land concerned.[79] Orchard-land, not least because it produced perishable goods, paid its rents and taxes in money. Such land moreover appears to have been farmed by Egyptians perhaps of a superior social level, many of whose names show Roman elements. Corn-land, perhaps two-thirds of the land under cultivation in any given year, on the other hand paid its rents and taxes in grain, and the rate, where we know it in for example the North Fayum area in the mid-second century A.D., appears to be much the same, namely just less than 5 *artabas* an *aroura*, whether on public land or on domain land.[80] The pattern of working the corn-land was also common to both divisions; short-term direct leases were the regular practice, and the plots of corn-land were individually small—the average size of holding being some seven and a half *arouras*.[81] The farmers of the corn-land were a peasantry with either the most common Greek names, hellenized Egyptian, or completely Egyptian names, and they were all tightly controlled by the Egyptian system, which left them with less freedom than many tenants in other parts of the Roman Empire.

The tightness of the grip can be seen not least in the great variety of documents that have been preserved relating to grain in Egypt.[82] There are documents about the survey and inspection of the land, leases, sales, and mortgages of land, farm accounts, loans of seed, and receipts of all kinds written by

78 M. Rostovtzeff, *SEHRE*² ii. 670–2 n. 45; D. Crawford, 'Imperial Estates', *Studies in Roman Property* (ed. M. I. Finley), pp. 35–70.

79 D. Crawford, 'Imperial Estates', p. 45.

80 e.g. *P. Bouriant* 42 (A.D. 167).

81 *BGU* 31, 104, 105, 160, 172 etc.—*sitologos* receipts from Karanis (A.D. 158/9).

82 See e.g. Frank, *ESAR* ii (A. C. Johnson), *passim.*

tax-collectors, granary keepers, and ships' captains. Responsibility weighed heavily on each link in the chain of the grain administration, and each sought protection from liability by securing receipts in several copies from those to whom they surrendered the corn.

But despite the massiveness of this documentation, the papyri are often relevant only to a particular farm, or to a particular group of people at a particular time.[83] There are no Egyptian documents giving us any overall statistical data for the total productivity of Egypt. As for Egypt's contribution to the feeding of Rome, we know only that it was a source of major importance from the time of Augustus. We have an unsupported figure of 20 million *modii* (assumed) from a late source as Egypt's annual export to Rome under Augustus.[84] We know of the excitement and anxiety which was felt in the mid-first century A.D. over the arrival of Alexandrian grain ships at Puteoli,[85] and that besides its cash contribution to Roman wealth it sent corn cargoes enough to feed Rome for four months in the year by the time of the Flavians, when Rome was already drawing twice as heavily on Africa as on Egypt.[86] The organization of an African corn fleet by Commodus was said to have been caused by anxiety over the regularity of the supplies from Egypt which reminds us of its continuing importance.[87] But with the founding of Constantinople Egyptian surpluses were devoted to the new capital and Rome had to look to the west.

(h) *The Eastern Provinces*

The situation from the fifth century B.C. to the Hellenistic period in the eastern Mediterranean[88] was that Athens and certain other areas in Greece, the islands in the Aegean and many of the large coastal cities of Asia Minor, were obliged regularly to import corn. The sources from which they derived it were Sicily, the Black Sea area, and Egypt together with her later Ptolemaic dependencies Cyrene and Cyprus. Other areas

[83] Cf. Hanna Geremek, *Karanis communauté rurale de l'Égypte Romaine au IIe–IIIe siècle de notre ère* (Warsaw, 1969) (Komitet Nauk O Kulturze Antyczney Polskiej Akademii Nauk).

[84] *Epit. de Caes.* 1. 6; see below, Appendix 4.

[85] Seneca, *Ep.* 77.

[86] Josephus, *Bell. Iud.* 2. 383–5.

[87] SHA *Commod.* 17. 7.

[88] L. Casson, 'The grain trade of the Hellenistic world', *TAPA* 85 (1954), 182–7.

produced a surplus from time to time which was disposed of by export, such as Syria, Phoenicia, Pergamum, Macedonia, and even Thessaly. The middleman in much of this trade appears to have been the island of Rhodes which provided an excellent harbour well positioned between the exporters and the customers, and a splendid merchant marine to carry the goods to and fro.

The position may have been rather altered once part of the flow of Egyptian corn was directed towards Rome, and permission had to be obtained to send it elsewhere.[89] Moreover, the areas on the north of the Black Sea seem to have suffered a steady decline in production because of barbarian raids and disruption during the Hellenistic period. It is possible that one of Augustus' reasons for interest in the Bosporus and Thracian Chersonese was that from there came the supplies for the eastern Mediterranean to fill the gap left by diverted Egyptian corn.[90] Whether that was so or not, there can be no doubt that in general the eastern Mediterranean was concerned rather with the problems of feeding itself than with exporting regularly to Rome. Once that has been said, it must also be acknowledged that Asia was a rich province with good corn-bearing lands around Pergamum where Brutus and Cassius could buy corn and the extension of Roman control into the interior of Asia Minor must have put into their hands great corn lands in areas such as Phrygia, Galatia, and Pisidia.[91]

Whether these areas ever produced a regular amount for the Roman market as opposed to the great towns in the East is not known, but it is interesting that one of the regular routes for the Alexandrian corn freighters on their way to Rome took them to the ports in southern Asia Minor.[92] It was at Myra on the southern coast of Asia Minor that the centurion escorting St. Paul found an Alexandrian freighter bound for Italy, and at both Myra and its neighbour, Patara, great granaries were erected under Hadrian.[93] It seems more likely that they were to house supplies for the imperial *annona* rather than for the local communities of the district.

[89] See below, Appendix 4.
[90] Meiggs, *Roman Ostia*², p. 472–3.
[91] Frank, *ESAR* iv (Broughton), 599 ff.
[92] L. Casson, 'The Isis and her voyage', *TAPA* 81 (1950), 51.
[93] Acts of the Apostles, 27: 1–28: 13; Rickman, *Roman Granaries*, pp. 137–40.

VI

TRANSPORT, STORAGE, AND PRICES

(a) *Transport*

I

The difficulty of transporting heavy or bulky goods over long distances in the ancient world has already been stressed. It was one of the key factors governing the problem of keeping the population of Rome fed.[1] Grain had to be moved wherever possible by water rather than by land. Whatever the risks it could be easier, quicker, and cheaper to transport corn by sea from one end of the Mediterranean to the other than to cart it 100 miles by land. In these circumstances the corn surpluses of overseas provinces such as Sicily, Africa, and Egypt were more naturally within Rome's grasp than might at first be imagined. Even so the gathering and carrying of the corn to Rome demanded considerable effort which must now be explored in greater detail.

We have virtually no evidence of how the corn was collected and got to the harbours in Sicily, only a little evidence for Africa, and that little mainly from the late Empire, but a large and detailed variety of evidence for Egypt. In Sicily we know only that the tithe-collectors of the late Republic were responsible for transporting the grain they had collected as far as the sea, but not how they did it.[2] In Africa in the late Empire it seems to have been managed by a wagon post, the *cursus clabularius*.[3] The heavy four-wheeled wagons, provided and kept in repair by the state, were each drawn by two pairs of oxen, provided by the landholders but fed at the public expense. A wagon of standard size seems to have carried between 50 and

[1] See above, p. 13.

[2] Cic. *2 Verr.* 3. 14. 36. See now G. P. Verbrugghe, *Itinera Romana 2, Sicilia* (Berne, 1976), esp. pp. 24–5, 48–53.

[3] Jones, *LRE*, p. 841; Tengström, *Bread for the People*, pp. 30–1; *Cod. Theod.* 8. 5.

75 *modii* of African wheat, and since it progressed at a stately average of 2 miles an hour along the main roads from changing post to changing post, or overnight lodging, the gathering of the supplies for Rome at the African ports must have demanded an enormous number of such wagons. In Egypt, as soon as the grain was harvested from the beginning of April to the end of May or early June depending upon the district, it was brought to the village threshing floors by whatever means possible, mainly by pack animals.[4] After threshing and winnowing the corn was then removed to the local granary to be received by the *sitologoi* and from there in turn to larger granaries of the *metropoleis*, where the grain could either be stored for seed, or sent on to the harbours on the Nile for transhipment down to Alexandria. An organized system of clearing the granaries seems to have been used, and donkey trains or even camel caravans transported the corn to the harbours, where it was carried in sacks on to the lighters, which ferried goods to the bigger ships in mid-stream. The cultivators paid a tax to cover the cost of the transport of grain to the harbours and possibly down river to Alexandria, but not the cost of the transport from Alexandria to Rome. Although transport of grain down the Nile could continue throughout the year, it is clear that the real pressure came in May and June. At Alexandria the grain was stored in great granaries, particularly in the Neapolis and Mercurium districts of the city, under the control of Roman procurators, awaiting shipment to Rome.

Every part of the organization in Egypt issued and demanded receipts to protect themselves from liability and to prevent fraud. We have therefore among the papyri from Egypt receipts issued by, and received by, the shippers on the Nile which are full of precise detail. A receipt issued in A.D. 211–12 may be taken as typical of the developed form:[5]

Given to Didymus, *strategos* of the Oxyrhynchite nome, by Posidonius also called Triadelphus, master of eight boats carrying 40,000 *artabae* in the

[4] Rickman, *Roman Granaries*, Appendix 2; E. Börner, *Der staatliche Korntransport im griechisch-römischen Aegypten* (Hamburg, 1939); cf. W. L. Westermann and C. W. Keyes, *Tax Lists and Transportation Receipts from Theadelphia* (New York, 1932); for a list of procurators *ad Mercurium* and procurators *Neaspoleos* see Pavis D'Escurac, *Préfecture*, pp. 134–9 and 431–46.

[5] *P. Oxy.* 1259; cf. *P. Lond.* 948.

Neapolis administration, I have received and had measured out to me the amount ordered by you the *strategos* [named] and by the *basilicogrammateus* [named] of the same nome, from the *sitologoi* [named] of the Psobthis district, in accordance with the order of his excellency the *procurator Neaspoleos*, from public granaries of the said village at river Tomis, [a specified amount of] wheat, produce of the year [specified], unadulterated, with no admixture of earth or barley, untrodden and sifted, which I will carry to Alexandria and deliver to the officials of the administration safely, free of all risk, and damage by ship. This receipt is valid, there being three copies of it, of which I have issued two to you the *strategos* and one to the *sitologoi*. Date.

That little was left to chance, or possible trickery by the shippers on the Nile during the course of the journey is proved by the practice common in Egypt from at least the third century B.C. to the third century A.D. of sending sealed samples of the grain cargoes, often in the charge of the soldiers who acted as guards, along with the boats.[6] These so-called *digmata*, sometimes in the form of small pots and sometimes leather wallets, contained a sample of the type and quality of the cargo, and were carefully sealed and labelled. Sometimes the details given on the label were so full as to form almost a duplicate receipt for the cargo as a whole. A pot used for a *digma* in 2 B.C. had written on the side of it not only the name of the two skippers, the emblem of their boats, the name, rank, and unit of the soldiers acting as guards on board, but also the statement that this pot is a *digma* of cargo of grain of a specified kind of a certain year, measured to them by the granary officials of a certain district, and which formed the tax payable for a certain period. The statement ends with the declaration that the cargo had been sealed with the seals of both men and the date. A second hand recorded the sealing of the *digmata* and the date. They could be useful in revealing a fraud, as we know from a papyrus of A.D. 188 when a cargo of wheat was found to be adulterated with earth and barley.[7] We know that similar *digmata* were in use in the fifth century A.D. to prevent frauds at Portus at the mouth of the Tiber[8] and it seems possible that such samples were used to prevent deception on the long overseas haul from the exporting countries to Rome.

[6] Rickman, *Roman Granaries*, pp. 189–90.
[7] *P. Oxy*. 708.
[8] *Cod. Theod.* 14. 4. 9 (A.D. 417).

2

Much work has been done recently on the size of ancient sailing ships[9] and it appears that the capacity of seagoing freighters has been seriously underestimated in the past. The smallest cargo boat that was considered suitable for overseas shipping was about 70 to 80 tons burden. In the port regulations of Thasos[10] dating from the late third century B.C., it was implied that the smallest ship allowed to use the port facilities was 3,000 talents burden (80 tons). Similarly when the Emperor Claudius was trying to encourage the building of corn ships in the first century A.D. the lower limit he set was a capacity of 10,000 *modii* of grain (68 tons).[11] Clearly a 70-tonner was at that time the smallest corn freighter that the state considered useful.

Most merchant ships, and in particular corn freighters, were bigger than that. By the end of the second century A.D. although a lower limit of 10,000 *modii* was still acceptable the standard size of ship used for the transport of grain had to have a capacity of at least 50,000 *modii*[12] (some 340 tons). The Roman jurist Scaevola wrote that those shipowners were exempt from compulsory public services who 'have had built and furnish for the *annona* of Rome a seagoing vessel no smaller than 50,000 *modii*, or a number of vessels no smaller than 10,000 *modii*'. It is likely that some of the great freighters from Alexandria dwarfed that standard to a remarkable degree. The *Isis*, a large grain ship used on the run from Alexandria to Rome in the second century A.D. and blown off her course until she docked at the Peiraeus, was visited there by Lucian who wrote an account of his experience and gave the ship's dimensions: 180 ft (54·86 m) long, 45 ft (13·72 m) in the beam, and with a hold 44 ft (13·41 m) deep.[13] From this it has been reliably computed that her carrying capacity was between 1,200 and 1,300 tons, and

[9] Casson, *Ships and Seamanship*, p. 170 and p. 183; Rougé, *L'Organisation*, pp. 66 ff.; cf. E. Tengström, *Bread for the People*, p. 37; see now H. D. L. Viereck, *Die römische Flotte* (Herford, 1975), pp. 121–56, 'Frachter und Transporter'.

[10] *IG* 12. Suppl. p. 151 no. 348 as emended in *SEG* 17. 417.

[11] Gaius, *Inst.* i. 32c.

[12] *Dig.* 50. 5. 3 (Scaevola).

[13] Lucian, *Navig.* 5, cf. L. Casson, 'The Isis and her voyage', *TAPA* 81 (1950), 43–56; also *Lucien, Le Navire ou les souhaits* with commentary by G. Husson (Paris, 1970).

the implication is that she was not unique. Such corn freighters could and regularly did take passengers in addition to cargo, as many as 600 at a time.[14] The Emperor Gaius advised the Jewish prince Herod Agrippa on his way to Palestine not to make the journey in tiring short hops from Brindisi to Syria, but to go directly from Puteoli to Alexandria,[15] since in this way he could cross on one of the superb Puteoli–Alexandria freighters whose captains 'drive them like race-horses'.

The hierarchy on such a merchant ship[16] carrying grain was headed by the owner or the charterer. The words *naukleros* or *navicularius* seem to be used indiscriminately of the man who had the use of the ship, and its exploitation whether by ownership or charter. If he actually owned it he could also be called in Greek *despotes* or *kurios*, in Latin *dominus*. In Roman legal texts the useful term *exercitor navis* is employed, meaning the ship operator, and leaving open the question of whether he was actually the owner.[17]

The *navicularius*, or his representative, was often on his ship when he was carrying cargo for his own account, and he might even act as his own captain. More often he hired a professional captain, particularly if the ship were large, and entrusted to this man the running of the ship and command of the crew. Such a captain was called in Greek *kubernetes* and popularly in Latin *gubernator*, although in Roman legal texts he was defined as *magister navis*, and *gubernator* was only the helmsman and sailing master.[18] Under this captain there were two key figures, the *proreus*, the first mate, who would assume command if need be, and the *toicharchos*, a purser-like figure, but who took care of both passengers and cargo. Beneath each of these men were groups of assistants, right down to the common sailors. Some or all of these men might presumably be laid off during the winter season, while others were retained.

It was possible for *navicularii* to be private merchants themselves, *negotiatores*, specializing in corn or some other goods.[19] It

[14] Josephus, *Vita* 15. [15] Philo, *In Flaccum* 26.

[16] L. Casson, *Ships and Seamanship*, p. 314; J. Rougé, *L'Organisation*, p. 229 ff.

[17] *Dig.* 14. 1. 1. 15.

[18] Plaut. *Rud.* 1014; cf. *Dig.* 19. 2. 13. 2; but see Rougé, *L'Organisation*, p. 235 and the criticism by L. Casson, *AJP* 89 (1966), 359–64. Cf. E. Tengström, *Bread for the People*, p. 42.

[19] Frank, *ESAR* v. 271 ff. Cf. Frank, *ESAR* i. 356 ff.

seems likely that under the Republic most *navicularii* were in this category and that in, for example, Cicero's day they were mostly independent ship-owners who were also merchants in their own right. Originally such independent merchant/ship-owners had simply tramped from port to port with whatever cargo seemed to offer prospect of a sale. They personally bought and sold their cargoes at various ports and tried to get to their home port before winter. This age-old pattern of sea commerce in the Mediterranean still persisted but beside it had grown up a commerce for profit. In this the ship-owner/merchant put some of his own capital into a venture but also borrowed money at the high interest rates for maritime loans.[20] In this way financial risk for the merchant was spread, and on the other hand it was possible for others than actual traders to put money into trading ventures. Ship-owners who were also merchants therefore continued but were not limited to small-scale tramping from port to port. Sextus Fadius Musa, whose name was on a number of the jars which made up Monte Testaccio in Rome and about whom we have a notable inscription, was an example of a prosperous *navicularius*, who was also a *negotiator*, involved in the trade from Spain in the early second century A.D.[21]

Some *navicularii* on the other hand were not themselves merchants but were simply shippers under contract to private *negotiatores* to carry their goods from one specified place to another. This seems to have been a commercial practice which grew, and it led to a more complex situation where *navicularii* regularly 'rented space' to importers and exporters.[22] A more flexible pattern therefore evolved where a *navicularius* might have within his ship perhaps cargo belonging to himself, but also goods belonging to a variety of other people to whom he was responsible for their shipment. This raised important questions in law concerning liability and it is no surprise that Roman legal texts are full of discussion of such cases.[23]

[20] Rougé, pp. 437–59; G. E. M. de Ste. Croix, 'Ancient Greek and Roman Maritime Loans', *Debts, Credits, Finance and Profits*, Essays in Honour of W. T. Baxter, ed. Harold Edey and B. S. Yamey (London, 1974), pp. 41–59.

[21] *CIL* 12. 4393. Cf. Rougé, *L'Organisation*, p. 250.

[22] *Dig.* 19. 5. 1. 1 (Labeo), cf. *Dig.* 14. 2. 2. 1 (Paulus); 14. 1. 1. 3 (Ulpian); see below, p. 133.

[23] J. Crook, *Law and Life of Rome* (London, 1967), p. 223 n. 92, and p. 225. J. Rougé, *L'Organisation*, pp. 381–437.

Thirdly, some *navicularii* were under contract not to private *negotiatores*, but to the state. There was no publicly owned merchant marine and consequently the transport of even publicly owned goods, such as the tithes in grain yielded by the new province of Sicily, had to be done privately. It is clear from Columella[24] that there were regular auctions of the state contracts to transport provincial grain. Moreover whenever there had to be public action to alleviate special corn scarcity in Rome, the public figures involved, whoever they were, would have to see to it that not only were sources of corn located but that its shipment to Rome was catered for. Consequently it is no surprise to find both Pompey in 56 B.C.[25] and the *praefectus annonae* in the early Empire deeply involved in arranging contracts with merchants and shippers.[26]

It was natural for rich shippers who went regularly to certain ports to maintain offices there, and for shippers from a particular area to maintain a kind of joint office. So, for example, we find evidence of certain eastern shippers particularly those from Tyre maintaining offices and even whole docks and warehouses at Puteoli,[27] and the shippers of, in particular, various African towns, but not only they, had rooms around the Piazzale delle Corporazioni at Ostia.[28] This tendency, combined with a growing desire by the state to plan its shipping contracts on a long term basis and to offer privileges to a known body of men, was to lead, as we have seen, to the development of *corpora* and *collegia* in shipping, as in other affairs, and in the end to state regimentation of shipping.[29]

But during the late Republic and early Empire skippers crossing the Mediterranean who contracted to carry goods might be dealing with a whole variety of customers, private as well as governmental, and even if they carried grain for the state they would be dealing with a multiplicity of different officials rather than a centralized department. The hazards to

[24] Columella i, praef. 20.

[25] Cic. *de Fin* 2. 84; Cic. *ad Fam.* 13. 75. C. Avianius Flaccus was a private corn merchant who had been put under contract for a certain number of years by Pompey. See above, p. 56.

[26] *Dig.* 14. 1. 1. 18 (Ulpian). Cf. Pavis D'Escurac, *Préfecture*, pp. 220–5.

[27] Frank, *ESAR* v. 274.

[28] R. Meiggs, *Roman Ostia*², p. 283.

[29] See above, p. 87.

be faced were many and varied and the contracts, the *recepta nautarum*, although they must have been more complex than the receipts of the shippers on the Nile, were like them above all concerned with the problem of liability. All this is reflected in the discussions in the jurists and in the so-called Rhodian Sea Law, which is part of the 51st book of the *Basilica*, a reorganization of ancient laws by the Emperor Justinian in the sixth century.[30] There are endless problems; if a merchant hires a ship, but then does not need it; if the time limit for taking up the contract passes, but the merchant has not loaded his cargo; if the merchant does not load at the place fixed in the contract; if a cargo of wheat gets wet while on board; or if it gets wet from bilge water rather than from water down the hatches; if part or all the cargo has to be jettisoned in a storm. The possibilities are almost endless, and the wording of the contracts, and the decisions of the lawyers had to take account of them.

Apart from the normal circumstances that had to be reckoned with in the contracting of shipping, it was of course possible to make special provisions to try to cope with an extraordinary situation. This was what the Emperor Claudius did at a time of sudden emergency in the grain supply of Rome. He encouraged unwilling merchants to make dangerous winter journeys by promising full compensation by the state for any loss incurred through storm.[31] This regulation seems to have applied only to *negotiatores*, that is, shippers who also bought and sold grain (not just those *navicularii* who simply conveyed the goods of others) but they may have been still the majority at this date in the middle of the first century A.D. More important, it seems to have been a temporary arrangement designed to meet a sudden crisis; there is no trace of it in later juristic writings. The facts of Mediterranean maritime life were against it as a permanent feature, and shippers in general had to guarantee to complete contracted voyages within the season.[32]

[30] J. Crook, *Law and Life of Rome*, p. 223; J. Rougé, *L'Organisation*, pp. 381–415.
[31] Suet. *Claud.* 18.
[32] *Dig.* 45. 1. 122. 1.

3

That season, as we have seen, stretched from late May to early September, or at the outside from early March to early November. During that summer sailing season the wind blows steadily, and sometimes fiercely, from the north in the Aegean, and from the north-west in the area south of Crete, in the Ionian and Tyrrhenian seas. Only in the western Mediterranean does the summer wind blow from the south-west, or beyond the Balearic Islands from the east, and even in this part of the Mediterranean the Mistral from the north has to be reckoned with from time to time.

These facts gave a pattern to ancient sea trading.[33] Most ships sailing in a southerly direction from Italy to Africa, Asia Minor, Syria, and Egypt could generally expect to make good time on an easy journey. On the other hand ships trying to sail northwards from the eastern Mediterranean had a hard task, not made easier by the fact that their sails were predominantly square-rigged, and that therefore even when they tacked they could head no closer to the wind than seven points.

The upshot of this is that a journey from Ostia to Africa is on record as the fastest journey by sea of which we know; some 270 nautical miles in two days.[34] And it was possible to go nearly as fast in the opposite direction, from Africa to the south-east coast of Sardinia, along the east coast of that island and then across the open sea. Cato the Elder showed the senate at Rome a fig that had been picked at Carthage three days before.[35] African corn should never have been too far out of Rome's grasp, so far as the journey by sea was concerned. At worst perhaps no more than a week away. Voyages between Italy and the eastern Mediterranean were a different matter. Fast speeds are on record for the journey with the wind from Puteoli to Alexandria, nine days for a journey of 1,000 nautical miles, or from Messina to Alexandria, six or seven days for a journey of 830 nautical miles.[36] But coming back was more difficult. A man congratulated himself on his great good fortune in taking only thirty days to get from Alexandria to Marseilles,

[33] Casson, *Ships and Seamanship*, pp. 272 ff.

[34] Pliny, *N. H.* 19. 3–4. Cf. Tengström, *Bread for the People*, p. 44.

[35] Pliny, *N. H.* 15. 75; cf. Plut. *Cat. Maior* 27. 1.

[36] Pliny, *N. H.* 19. 3–4.

a distance of 1,500 nautical miles, with reason, since Lucian says that it could take as much as seventy days to go from Alexandria to Rome.[37] The trouble was that the Alexandrian freighters were having to work their way north-westwards in the teeth of the prevailing winds. Consequently they were forced to take one of two alternative routes.[38] The first went north to Cyprus and then worked along the southern coast of Turkey by Myra towards Rhodes or Cnidos, then westwards south of Crete to Malta, then up to Messina. The other, the southerly route, went westwards by way of the North African coast to Cyrene which was itself rich in corn. The result was the same, a distance of over 1,400 nautical miles to be covered and a journey of at least a month and perhaps two. Egyptian grain was thus not so easily within Rome's grasp, even after Augustus' annexation of the country.

The shipment of the grain from Alexandria to Puteoli in the first century A.D. and early second century A.D., or to Ostia thereafter was quite clearly in the hands of Alexandrians. These Alexandrine *navicularii* or *naukleroi* came to form a fleet for the conveying of the grain tribute to Rome and perhaps sailed as a group. They are referred to as a *classis* by Seneca and the word *stolos* is used in Greek inscriptions.[39] A clear distinction must be drawn between these corn ships and the *classis augusta alexandrina*, the military fleet in Egypt. The implications, however, for the organization of these Alexandrian grain shippers of the references to them forming a fleet are uncertain. We know from the inscriptions that by the time of Septimius Severus the Alexandrian merchant fleet were under the supervision of an imperial procurator. If the pattern of development was the same as elsewhere in the Empire the process of growing state interest in and control of shipping groups should have been gradual during the first two centuries A.D. But Egypt was peculiar in many respects and it may be that there had been a coherent group of shippers and tight state control from the beginning of the Empire.

Certainly in Africa there had been no such single organization of the shipping. It was not until Commodus that a *classis*

[37] Sulpicius Severus, *Dial.* 1. 1. 3; cf. Lucian, *Nav.* 9.
[38] Casson, *Ships and Seamanship*, p. 297; cf. *TAPA* 81 (1950).
[39] Seneca, *Ep.* 77. 1; Kaibel, *IG Italiae* 918 and 919 (=*CIG* 5889, 5973).

Africana was formed, at a time when Egyptian supplies seemed uncertain, to convey African grain to Rome.[40] What precise organization was involved is not stated. We know from a rescript in the *Codex Theodosianus* dealing with transportation of corn in the late Empire that a regulation (*dispositio*) existed arranging the *navicularii* in a definite order.[41] Following this order or plan they had to undertake long and short voyages by turns which were to be strictly observed so that all were equal in this respect. The ships therefore, though grouped into a *classis*, were not to sail as a single group.

The Alexandrian corn ships, however, may have travelled regularly in convoy so far as that was possible.[42] The only evidence, it is true, which might imply such a convoy system from Alexandria in the early Empire is the reference in the letter of Seneca to the appearance of ships called *tabellariae* which heralded the safe arrival at Puteoli of the *classis*. This was certainly the main spring sailing of those ships of the fleet which had wintered in Alexandria. Given the time of the harvest in Egypt, the earliest possible arrival of these Alexandrine ships would have been in May. In fact the Seneca passage implies a time of arrival in early June,[43] and in a famous letter of the late second century A.D. from a man, Eirenaios, who had sailed with the Alexandrian corn ships we know that on that occasion he only arrived on 30 June and the ship did not unload until 12 July, and even on 2 August every shipper was still awaiting a *dimissoria* to allow him to leave.[44] Presumably even though the ships set sail together they might struggle into the Italian ports over a period of days or even weeks.

Moreover we know of other sailings between Rome and Alexandria at other times of year,[45] and in some of these cases

[40] SHA *Commodus* 17. 7. Cf. F. Grosso, *La lotta politica al tempo di Commodo* (Turin, 1964), pp. 215–17.

[41] *Cod. Theod.* 13. 5. 6.

[42] Cf. Rougé, *L'Organisation*, p. 265.

[43] O. Binder, *Die Abfassungszeit von Senekas Briefen* (Diss. Tübingen, 1905), esp. pp. 4–5 and 43; E. F. Albertini, *La Composition dans les ouvrages philosophiques de Seneque* (Paris, 1923), p. 45 ff. The old notion that the main group of Alexandrine ships left Egypt in August and arrived in Italy in September is clearly wrong; Waltzing, *Corporations professionnelles*, ii. 54.

[44] A. S. Hunt and C. C. Edgar, *Select Papyri* i (New York: London, 1932), no. 113.

[45] Casson, *Ships and Seamanship*, pp. 297 ff., 'The Alexandria–Rome Sailing Schedule'.

the ships appear to be travelling singly. Clearly, therefore, the majority of ships started from Alexandria in the spring, but others having wintered in Rome started from there in March or April, and made the return voyage much later, and others again, having been caught by the end of the sailing season and the onset of bad weather, started from the point *en route* at which they had wintered. Probably no more than two complete voyages would be made during the sailing year, but as many journeys as possible were made—a fact which helps to explain why some corn was allowed to be delivered from the nomes to Alexandria as late as the end of August.[46]

That there were large grain ships sailing out with full loads from Alexandria late in the season, either because they were on a second full trip or because they had wintered in Italy and had only reached Alexandria itself in May or later, is clear from the experiences of St. Paul on his voyage to Rome in A.D. 62.[47] His story is so detailed and so revealing of what could happen that it is worth recounting in full.

Paul was taken on a coasting ship from Adramyttium to Myra which was on the northern route taken by the Alexandrine grain freighters. There he was indeed put onto an Alexandrian ship sailing to Italy, with a cargo of wheat, and 276 crew and passengers on board under the command of a *naukleros*. From Myra the ship sailed slowly west below Crete. Here both the sea captain (*kubernetes*) and the *naukleros* of the ship decided, since it was late in the season, to winter at a small harbour. However, when a favourable breeze sprang up they changed their minds and decided to try for a better harbour. They were caught by an east-north-east gale and rode for fourteen days helplessly before it without sail. The crew cut away part of the rigging, passed ropes around the hull to stop the seams of the ship opening, and in the end jettisoned the grain cargo to lighten the ship. At midnight on the fourteenth day, sensing that they were near land, they cast four anchors and waited till daylight, when they decided to cut the anchors and to try to run the ship aground. The gamble worked and although the ship broke in two, everyone was saved. The land

[46] Cf. Edict of Justinian C. 6 and 22. 2; Börner, *Der Staatliche Korntransport*, p. 31.

[47] Acts 27–8.

proved to be Malta. Here Paul waited three months until another freighter, the *Castor and Pollux*, again from Alexandria, which had wintered more prudently at Malta itself, took him on to Italy. It put in at Syracuse and spent three days there, and then sailed on to Rhegium. One day out from Rhegium a favourable wind from the south sprang up and the ship reached Puteoli in two days. From there Paul went on to Rome itself.

The whole passage in the Acts is vividly interesting for the way it exemplifies the route taken by Alexandrine corn ships, the large numbers of passengers even on a late sailing, the presence of both the owner and the captain on board, the wintering of such ships at intermediate ports along the route, the dangers of sea voyages, and the problems about liability raised when cargo is jettisoned or shipwreck occurs.

One thing which is not made clear in the passage is the actual way in which the cargo of grain was stowed in the ship.[48] This is a problem about which in general we have very little evidence indeed. Our knowledge of the construction of ancient merchant ships is not really good enough to allow detailed statements about the size, layout, and shape of the holds. Whereas wrecks which were carrying amphorae of wine or oil can allow reconstructions by modern scholars of how the containers were stacked, the same is not true of grain cargoes. Obviously the grain must not be allowed to get damp. Quite apart from the spoiling of the cargo, grain which gets wet can swell so dramatically, doubling in size, that a full load can split the plates of even a modern ship. Storage therefore had to be high enough in the ship to be well clear of bilge water, and yet well protected by hatches, which were waterproof, from any waves that might come over the sides.

But the problem is more complicated than that. Everything possible must be done when shipping grain to prevent the cargo from shifting, or ensuring that if it does shift, it does not cause the ship to list, or turn turtle. It would be possible to give the ship great stability by ballast but that would be to waste room more useful for cargo. Another possibility would be to fill a hold with loose grain right up to the brim so that little

[48] Casson, *Ships and Seamanship*, p. 200.

or no movement could take place. But this would demand absolute confidence that the hold was completely dry, and could be kept so during the voyage. It would also allow little or no inspection of the cargo *en route* and would prevent the carrying of half- or three-quarter loads instead of full cargoes. It might work well enough on a river but is unlikely to have been a regular method used on long sea journeys.

It is clear that the grain was loaded onto the ships and unloaded again by means of large numbers of porters each of whom carried a sack. The question therefore becomes: did the grain remain in sacks while on board ship, or was it emptied loose into a hold which was somehow divided into bins or compartments?

The famous wall-painting showing a boat named *Isis Giminiana* being loaded with grain for barging on the Tiber makes it clear that the *saccarii* after they have come up the gangplank on to the deck of the boat emptied their sacks into a corn measure under the supervision of a measurer.[49] In this case it was obviously possible for the corn either to be rebagged and put into the ship, or simply poured loose into the hold. The question therefore remains unresolved.

There is one piece of evidence which proves that it was possible to pour grain loose into the hold of a ship. A passage in the *Digest*[50] deals with the problem of loss 'when a number of men have poured their grain in common into a ship'. The legal problem arose because of the intermingling of different people's property, and would not have arisen in the same way 'if each man's wheat was set off by planks (*tabulis*) or partitions (*heronibus*) or each was in its own container (*cupa*)' in the ship. This would seem to imply that a more normal way of transporting grain was in a hold that was carefully subdivided with wooden partitions of some kind.

But transport of grain across the sea in sacks still seems to me not improbable. It must be confessed that there is no evidence for it, and that almost all the evidence for *saccarii*, either in inscriptions or papyri, has come from transactions on the Nile or on the Tiber, and therefore may be relevant only to inland waterways. But as a method of stacking grain in a way that

[49] Meiggs, *Roman Ostia*², pp. 294–5; Tengström, *Bread for the People*, p. 56.
[50] *Dig.* 19. 2. 31.

would protect it from damp and prevent it from shifting too easily, the use of sacks had something to recommend it.

(b) *Storage*

I

The storage of corn on ships leads naturally to the many questions about the storage of corn generally on land.[51] It has been one of the major preoccupations of man throughout his history not only to grow his crops successfully and harvest them plentifully, but so to store his produce that he can be sure of supplies in the lean period until the next harvest time.

After harvesting, grain continues to take in oxygen and to give off heat, carbon dioxide, and water by a process of respiration. In order to preserve grain for consumption later during the course of the year or beyond, it is necessary to slow down this process as much as possible. If it is not eliminated or retarded the grain begins to germinate, bacteria in the air become active leading to the growth of moulds and fungi, and the rotting of the grain. Such overheating of the grain also leads to insect infestation especially by the grain weevil (*sitophilus granarius*) and the saw-toothed grain beetle (*oryzaephilus surinamensis*), both of which were known in the ancient world. It is important therefore, if possible, to reduce the amount of oxygen available, but above all to control carefully the temperature and moisture content of stored grain. If the limit of moisture could be reduced to 8–10 per cent no growth or overheating would occur, but this cannot be achieved even in the modern world, where limits of 10–15 per cent are regarded as both necessary and practicable. Similarly if grain can be kept below 60° F (15·5° C) insect activity can be prevented, although even lower temperatures are needed to prevent the growth of moulds and fungi. The eggs of insects however can survive in these adverse conditions in cracks and crannies, and become active again when temperatures rise. The walls of granaries should therefore be well plastered and smooth and the floors free from holes or cracks. Both walls and floors must be strongly constructed to resist the considerable weight and

[51] Rickman, *Roman Granaries*; A. P. Gentry, *Roman Military Stone-built Granaries in Britain* (British Archaeological Reports 32, 1976).

bulk of massed grain (about 240 lb. per sq. ft or 12,000 kgm per sq. m) and to support an absolutely waterproof roof which will ensure a good drainage of rainwater. Indeed the drainage system in general must prevent the accumulation of surface water anywhere in the area. Finally, attacks by rodents, such as rats and mice, and injury to the grain by birds, must be reduced to a minimum by limiting access and keeping the store as dark as possible to discourage birds from flying in when the doors are open.

Roman writers on agriculture were clearly aware of the need to keep stored grain both cool and dry, and to control pests, whether weevils or rodents, but there was little unanimity of opinion as to which method of grain storage was best on ordinary farms.

Storage pits sunk into the ground were known to writers like Varro and Pliny the Elder, as being typical in various countries such as Cappadocia, Thrace, Spain, and Africa.[52] It is clear from excavation that this method of storage was commonly practised even in relatively damp countries such as Britain where the corn had to be parched before being inserted, and it is known from papyri in Egypt. The advantage of such a system was that it was easy and cheap for ordinary farmers, and provided no air was allowed to get in, the build up of carbon dioxide produced by the metabolism of the grain and anything else in the pit killed off any insects and fungi. If the storage pits were properly placed in suitable soil considerable success might be achieved by this method, but it was not really a method that could be adopted for state purposes in Rome.

We know in Egypt and in archaic Greece of small individual round storehouses shaped like beehives, some 16½ ft (5 m) high and 6½–9¾ ft (2–3 m) in diameter, filled at the top through a hatch and emptied at the bottom through a trap-door.[53] Stores of this kind seemed to have persisted throughout antiquity at least in Egypt, and there are allusions to this kind of store in Roman writers.

On the other hand there was a tradition common in Europe of constructing wooden granaries that were lifted quite clear of

[52] Pliny, *N. H.* 18. 306; cf. White, *Roman Farming*, p. 197.

[53] Rickman, *Roman Granaries*, p. 298. E. L. Smithson, 'The Grave of an Early Athenian Aristocrat', *Archaeology* 22 (1969), 18–25, esp. p. 20.

the ground so as to allow a current of air to pass under the floor on which the grain was stored, thus keeping it both dry and cool.[54]

Despite the controversies in the agricultural authors over what might be the best method of storing grain on individual farms, the developed *horrea* of the late Republic and early Empire fell basically into two categories. The first was the type used in all Roman military establishments. It consisted of a long open hangar varying in length (from 50 to 150 ft, or 15–45 m) but of a more consistent width (20–30 ft, or 6–9 m), raised above the ground and with its entrance at the end. If it was constructed of wood, as in the period up to the end of the first century A.D., the stresses in the building were taken up by the ties and trusses within the building and the floor was supported by timber posts set regularly underneath. If it was built of stone, the sides were of great thickness (rarely less than 3 ft, or nearly 1 m) at least up to the louvred windows and buttressed regularly at intervals of 7–15 ft (2–4½ m) to help carry the heavily tiled roof. The floors, perhaps originally of wood, but later of stone slabs, were supported either by piers of stone or dwarf walls.[55]

The type of *horrea* favoured in important civil contexts was distinctly different, and was not so obviously just a granary. Rome, through Puteoli and Ostia, imported a great variety of goods, all of which needed storage, and of which grain was simply one item, however important.

The excavations at Ostia have revealed some fine examples of storebuildings of the early Empire and they give vivid reality to what is known for Rome itself mainly from the Marble Plan made under Septimius Severus.[56] The buildings were strongly, sometimes massively, constructed of the finest materials current in their day. Originally of great tufa blocks as in the *Horrea Agrippiana* in Rome and the earliest phase of the *Grandi Horrea* at Ostia, they came in the first century A.D. to be built in brick-faced concrete, but always with walls of striking thickness and solidity, and even if abutting onto another build-

[54] S. Piggott, 'Timber circles: a re-examination', *AJ* 96 (1939), 220–1.

[55] Rickman, *Roman Granaries*, pp. 213–50; corrected by Gentry, *Roman Military Stone-built Granaries in Britain.*

[56] Rickman, *Roman Granaries*, Chs. I and II.

ing always completely separate in construction to reduce the dangers of fire and theft. Their plans often centred on a corridor, or courtyard, onto which the rows of regularly shaped rooms opened through doorways of standard size. Some of the courtyards were large and spacious with a surrounding portico of columns, or arcades, which sheltered the entrances to the rooms, some were small and without a portico of any kind. Sometimes, in Rome in particular, the quadrangles could be doubled and even tripled, that is, two or even three courtyards flanking each other, divided by double lines of rooms placed back to back, as in the *Horrea Galbana* in Rome and the *Grandi Horrea* at Ostia. Double lines of rooms arranged back to back in this fashion were particularly suitable for the restricted space available flanking the sides of a harbour and they were much used to provide storage capacity around Trajan's hexagonal basin at Portus.[57] The number of entrances to the entire complex was always restricted to make the control of the building easier and in Ostia at least it does not seem that carts were regularly allowed access inside the buildings. All was so built as to facilitate the carrying of goods by men. Even the staircases in the storebuildings were constructed after the first few steps in the form of ramps to help the porters carry the goods on their backs up to the first floor for storage. On the Marble Plan can be seen staircases and ramps that led up directly from the water's edge into the great warehouses which flanked the Tiber at the river port.[58]

Some of these buildings had special structural devices which made their rooms particularly suitable for the storage of corn. The floor of each room was raised upon dwarf walls 1 ft (30 cm) wide and 1 ft (30 cm) apart which ran back into the depth of the room from the entrance.[59] The flooring was generally of bipedal tiles (2 × 2 ft, or 60 × 60 cm) laid from the middle of one dwarf wall to the middle of the next, three or four layers of tiles with mortar between them making up a strong floor. This flooring normally stopped short of the doorway to allow room for the travertine threshold supported on brick piers which allowed air to pass into the tunnels under the floor. The rooms

[57] Rickman, *Roman Granaries*, pp. 123–32.
[58] Rickman, *Roman Granaries*, pp. 108 ff.
[59] Rickman, *Roman Granaries*, pp. 28, 51, and Appendix I.

had hinged doors and carefully plastered walls, and the only light came through a narrow splayed slit window at the back of the room and a small square window set above the doorway itself. The conditions thus created, dim and cool, were well suited to storing grain, but they were achieved within a general scheme for the storage of all kinds of goods. In fact we do not know how grain was stored in these rooms. Whereas in military granaries it was apparently stored loose in bins arranged laterally on either side of a central corridor which ran along the axis of the building from the main door at the end, in civil *horrea* at Ostia there seems to be no trace of any system of bins and it is possible that grain was stored in the sacks in which it was carried by the porters off the ships.[60] That would make sense in that the grain at Ostia was merely awaiting transhipment to Rome, but we cannot necessarily assume that this was the way in which grain was stored in Rome when it had come to the end of its journey. However, storage in sacks rather than in bulk, provided the sacks are not stacked too close together, helps to reduce the temperature and moisture content of the grain because of the greater ventilation, so that as a method of storage it was not only possible but attractive even in Rome itself.

2

The origins of the *horrea* types are not entirely clear and it seems possible that there were few, if any, great *horrea* in Rome at the start of the second century B.C. When the river port of Rome below the Aventine Hill was developed at the beginning of that century the area was merely paved and steps were made up to it from the Tiber. The only important building was the Porticus Aemilia, a great commercial *stoa* not unlike the stoas which had graced Greek ports. *Horrea* are only firmly attested from the time of Gaius Gracchus, towards the end of the century, but there are no physical remains of *horrea* that can be dated so early.[61]

Although the state may have built some *horrea* from the time of Gaius Gracchus in the late 120s B.C., it seems that the major

[60] Rickman, *Roman Granaries*, pp. 85–6.
[61] Rickman, *Roman Granaries*, p. 149; see above, p. 47.

horrea of the late Republic and early Empire had been built largely by wealthy private families, such as the Sulpicii Galbae, who had land-holdings in the area below the Aventine.[62] Not only in Rome but also in Puteoli, the major port in Italy in the late Republic and early Empire for the eastern trade, we have reason to believe that the granaries were privately owned and of great rental value.[63]

This fact gives a fascinating complexity to the organization of civil *horrea* involved in the feeding of Rome for most of her history. Instead of a system of state employees such as is found in the papyri in Egypt or in the Codex Theodosianus under the later Empire, there is an unregimented system of private hire (*locatio–conductio*) conducted within the ordinary limits of the law. In the state system there is a total obsession with fairly simple receipts which bind or free the individual participants in the chain of transfer. In the normal working of *locatio–conductio* there is a rich and varied pattern of conditions on which storage space will be available for rent.[64]

Most often in the late Republic and early Empire the owners of the great warehouses in Rome and Puteoli do not seem to have been personally involved in the petty and complicated business of individual lettings but they either let the whole building out to a contractor (called *horrearius* in the legal texts) or acted through a bailiff *vilicus*.

Gradually in the first century A.D. many of these great warehouses fell into the possession of the Emperor by one means or other, and in both the first century A.D. and the early second century A.D. a spate of public building activity including the construction of many warehouses in Ostia, Portus and Rome, reached its peak, so that the role of the private owner was greatly diminished. When it was revived by the policy of Alexander Severus[65] in the early third century A.D. who encouraged the

[62] Rickman, *Roman Granaries*, p. 167–8. Recent work by Coarelli and Rodriguez-Almeida suggests not only that the *Horrea Galbana* may have been much bigger than have previously been thought (the three great courtyards only being part of the whole), but that there were (*Horrea*) *Aemiliana* near the river, which were also of crucial significance for the storage of Rome's corn, revealed in Suet. *Claud.* 18; see P. Coarelli, 'Public building in Rome', *PBSR* 45 (1977), 5 n. 23.

[63] Cicero, *De Finibus* 2. 84 and 85; see below, Appendix 5.

[64] Rickman, *Roman Granaries*, Ch. VI.

[65] SHA *Alexander Severus* 39. 3.

building of *horrea* in all parts of the city of Rome, it was of a different nature and for a different purpose. These were small depositories throughout Rome where men might put their valuables in times of uncertainty and they were run for the most part by their owners, but they seem to have had little direct connection with trade.

But in the late Republic and early Empire, even when some of the great warehouses had become public or imperial property, the most common pattern was for the merchant to hire space for his goods in a convenient warehouse. He deposited his wares according to the general conditions specified in the law and according to the special conditions listed and publicly displayed in the particular *lex horreorum* of the warehouse concerned. The amount of space and facilities made available varied. We hear that within a warehouse there were for hire *horrea*, *apothecae*, *compendiaria*, *armaria*, *intercolumnia*, and *loca armaris*.[66] The exact meaning of these terms is not always clear, but they seem to range in size, as one might expect, from whole rooms or suites of rooms down to chests, and spaces within the building where items might be left. Presumably the rent varied according to the facility hired, but there is to my knowledge no evidence as to the scale of costs of renting warehouse space. It is possible however that more knowledge on these problems will be gained in the near future from some remarkable wax tablets discovered recently at Pompeii. The tablets made of wood and wax were found preserved in mud in a house near the sea. The house appears to have been that of a rich man, who is unknown, but who had business affairs in the great commercial harbour of Puteoli, including the lease of a warehouse there.[67] The information given by the documents is tantalizingly complex and incomplete. They remind us that there is more to be learned about the leasing of storage space.

The renting of space in the *horrea* of Puteoli and Rome raises important questions not only about storage but also about retail. One of the surprising things to emerge from a study of the inscriptions relating to the *Horrea Galbana*, the greatest of the warehouses in the Emporium district of Rome, and the

[66] *CIL* 6. 33860 = *ILS* 5913; *CIL* 6. 33747 = *ILS* 5914; cf. Rickman, *Roman Granaries*, pp. 197–8.

[67] See below, Appendix 5.

Horrea Agrippiana, an architecturally impressive building next to the old Forum Romanum, was that retail seemed to have taken place regularly in these warehouses. The thresholds in the ground-floor rooms of the *Horrea Agrippiana* were of a type commonly found in shops,[68] and inscriptions showed that in addition to the *horrearii* on the staff of the *Horrea Galbana* and other warehouses, there were numbers of people who sold goods of various kinds, cloaks, clothing, marble, and even fish, within them.[69]

This seems to indicate that the warehouses, instead of being mere stores and repositories, formed part of a whole pattern of retail trade in the capital. This pattern included the *macella*, the *fora* for different kinds of goods along the banks of the Tiber, areas like Trajan's Market, and the shops that are visible on the Marble Plan of Rome lining virtually every street.

So far as we can judge, much of this retail trade seems to have been on a small scale.[70] The shops were single rooms, sometimes with another room at the back, and with a staircase to a mezzanine floor, but the strong impression is that the goods for sale were produced or made up on the premises and sold direct to the customers. In other words the part played by middlemen was to our eyes surprisingly small. This was probably a basic fact of the economic life of the ancient world, and it does seem that many people went also to the wharves, warehouses, and markets along the Tiber banks to buy directly what they wanted.

But it is possible that the role of the middleman in retailing imported commodities has been obscured for us by the confusing ambiguity of the terms *negotiator* and *mercator*.[71]

Originally the Roman terms *navicularii* and *mercatores* corresponded to the old Greek terms *naukleroi* and *emporoi* for those who travelled about by sea on trading ventures. Corresponding to the Greek *kapeloi*, the small trader in a local district, were the Roman *caupones*. *Negotiator* seems to have been a term used of businessmen, often bankers, who resided at a particular place, and carried on fairly large-scale business there. But gradually in the first century B.C. and first century

[68] Rickman, *Roman Granaries*, p. 95. [69] Rickman, *Roman Granaries*, pp. 173–6.

[70] H. J. Loane, *Industry and Commerce of the City of Rome, 50 B.C.–200 A.D.* (Baltimore, 1938), Ch. III. For similar lack of any evidence of middlemen in the corn trade in Egypt see Duncan-Jones, *Chiron* 6 (1976), 250.

[71] J. Rougé, *L'Organisation*, pp. 274 ff. and 287 ff.

A.D. a shift in meaning occurred. The Latin word *caupo* came to mean an innkeeper, and the word *mercator* was therefore stretched to include small traders in a defined locale. The word *negotiator* too covered a wider range of activities. Such a man might well own ships, might become very specialized in his business interests, for example, a *negotiator frumentarius*, and might travel widely in pursuit of his aims like the *mercatores* of old. The trouble for us is that the shifts of meaning were not clear cut and consistent. There are occasions when *mercatores*, such as P. Aufidius Fortis and the *mercatores frumentarii* of Ostia[72] seem to be involved predominantly in local trade and to be the middlemen and retailers for the grain consumed in Ostia. But not all *mercatores* are to be regarded as local in interest. Similarly although many *negotiatores* worked on a bigger scale than the *mercatores*, clearly the word could be used of small-fry retailers as well. The freedwoman Abudia Megiste who plied her trade as a 'negotiatrix frumentaria et legumenaria' in Rome at the 'Scala media' (perhaps steps leading up the Aventine Hill) was surely in the retail trade.[73]

Clearly either word can conceal the existence of a middleman, who had a shop in Rome and could act as an avenue for retail trade.

All this is important because it has always been a major puzzle how grain, when it got to Rome, was actually put on the market. It is perhaps not too difficult to envisage how private shippers and corn merchants could land their cargoes at Puteoli or Ostia, and sell them either directly to the ordinary people who wanted to buy, or to other local corn merchants who would transport them to Rome. A man called M. Caerellius Iazymis is described on an inscription from Ostia as a 'codicarius, item mercator frumentarius'.[74] In other words he was involved with the *naves codicariae* used for barging goods up the Tiber as well as being a corn merchant. And for good measure he was also president of the bakers' guild at Ostia. But what were the mechanics for putting on the market state corn provided either by taxes or public purchase? Much of this, I suspect, found its way into circulation also through the efforts of

[72] Meiggs, *Roman Ostia*², p. 277. But P. Aufidius Fortis was a town-councillor in North Africa as well as at Ostia, *CIL* 14. 4620.

[73] *CIL* 6. 9683.

[74] *CIL* 14. 4234; cf. Meiggs, *Roman Ostia*², p. 277.

ordinary merchants simply because the state lacked much proper distributing machinery of its own. Even during the Republic those who won the contracts to collect tithes in kind in Sicily and elsewhere would either have to be merchants themselves or act through them in order to bring the grain to Rome and to dispose of it.[75]

It is of course conceivable that during the late Republic and early Empire the state equipped itself with an increasing number of public granaries, in which to hold reserves of corn, and from which it could from the time of Claudius or Nero issue corn for the *frumentationes* to the Porticus Minucia. But the constant stress in the literary sources of the early Empire on the importance of the corn merchants[76] makes it likely that, 'state corn' or not, both the transport and the marketing of the grain was very largely in private hands. The *negotiatores* and *mercatores frumentarii* of the early Empire were rich and important people, as inscriptions show, and not least the temple they built under the Emperor Titus.[77] A whole section of the Emporium district of Rome in Region XIII was named the *Vicus Frumentarius* perhaps because of a concentration of retail outlets clustered there.

What however cannot be denied is that whether a Roman retailer bought from a public granary, or from a shipload newly arrived at the docks, he was likely to pay at any given moment very much the same for a *modius* of wheat. The government particularly in the early Empire was concerned not only to keep the city regularly supplied but also, not least through the provision of adequate storage facilities, to keep the price level and, if possible, low.

(c) *Prices*

I

Exactly how low and how level the prices of corn were in Rome we shall probably never know with precision. It may be that we should not even ask the question, but the desire to try to find

[75] Rostovtzeff, *Frumentum*, cols. 142–3; cf. G. E. F. Chilver, 'Princeps and Frumentationes', *AJP* 70 (1949), 21.

[76] Cicero, *De Domo* 11; Suet. *Aug.* 42. 3; Tac. *Ann.* 2. 87; Suet. *Claud.* 19.

[77] *CIL* 6. 814; in general see J. P. Waltzing, *Corporations professionnelles* ii. 103–8

some sort of answer is more than just busy curiosity. The price of grain is linked essentially with the concept of 'famine'.[78] As in the modern world, so in the ancient, 'famine' is a concept with class and financial connotations. The lowly and the poor in society had no reserves either of food or money and therefore suffered immediately as a result of a rise in costs of basic essentials. The rich and upper classes on the contrary rarely experienced actual hunger during a famine because of their financial resources or even private grain reserves. If the shortage of grain persisted, the rich might suffer economically by having to use more of their wealth, or their own grain, in order to cushion themselves against the crisis, but they did not starve. The poor did, not necessarily because there was a total lack of grain available, but rather because the current price of grain had risen beyond what they could normally afford to pay, whether because of crop failure, hoarding or speculation by dealers. It is not surprising that scholars have repeatedly struggled to build up a picture of average corn prices.[79] Equally clearly the difficulties and the dangers are very great. All kinds of cautionary notes must be sounded.

First, the attempt to transpose grain prices into modern equivalents must be resisted. Differences between the ancient world and modern society make such equivalents grossly misleading, even where they are not wholly inaccurate. Moreover the modern equivalents themselves very quickly go out of date, as the pages of Tenney Frank's *Economic Survey of Ancient Rome*, published in the 1930s, bear witness.

Secondly, there is no doubt that the vast majority of our evidence for grain prices in antiquity is almost by definition untypical. The price of wheat was most often cited only when, because there was a glut or a famine, the price was unusually low, or extraordinarily high. There is very little that we can point to with any confidence as being an average price.

[78] Cf. K. S. Gapp, 'The Universal Famine under Claudius', *HThR* 28 (1935), 258–65.

[79] Rostovtzeff, *Frumentum*, cols. 143–50; Frank, *ESAR* i, Index s.v. 'grain, prices of'; *ESAR* v, Index s.v. 'grain, price regulation'; A. H. M. Jones, 'Inflation under the Roman Empire', *EcHR*² 5 (1952–3), 295–6; C. Yeo, 'Land and Sea Transportation in Imperial Italy', *TAPA* 77 (1946), Appendix, 242–4. The most important contribution is the latest by R. Duncan-Jones, *ERE*, pp. 50–1, 145–6, and Appendix 8.

Thirdly, there would seem to be as many different prices for wheat as there were different places and different periods in the history of the ancient world. It matters enormously what is the source and what is the period for any quotation of a price for grain. There were great differences between different parts of the Mediterranean, and even within one area, between fertile and infertile areas, and whether they were on the sea, or some inland waterway, or completely landlocked and cut off. Some areas exported a surplus of grain; some areas imported what they needed; the majority lived on their own local resources, and how good those resources were dictated the pattern of prices for that area. Differences of period are equally important because of the fluctuation in money values which has to be borne in mind, particularly as debasement of coinage and inflation set in during the Roman Empire.

Finally, it is important to realize that even within one area and within one year, even when there has been no disaster in weather or other abnormality, the price of grain fluctuated. The most notable swing of course came between the periods just before the harvest and just after it. A sellers' market rapidly changed to a buyers' market and the price of wheat reflected that fact.

Curiously enough, despite the difficulties, what evidence we do have about corn prices has rather greater unanimity than we might have expected, although only a summary can be given here.[80]

2

If we take the evidence of the western Mediterranean first it is clear that our best information comes from Sicily about 70 B.C. In that year Cicero was the prosecutor in the case against the governor Verres, and in one part of his indictment he examined in considerable detail Verres' handling of the Sicilian corn

[80] A much more comprehensive collection and discussion of the evidence for grain prices is given in Duncan-Jones, *ERE*, esp. pp. 145–6 and Appendix 8; but cf. for a much later period M. Bloch, 'L'histoire des prix', *Annales* i (1939), 141–51, who quotes H. Hauser: 'In times before industrial civilization became general the accidents of time and place dominate the reality of economic life. Men do not live on averages or on long-term variations; they live by actual bread, sold at such and such a price for such and such a weight at such and such an instant.'

supplies. It has been said recently[81] that we must not use the data which Cicero gives on corn prices in Sicily at this time for any general understanding of market prices because they were prices paid by the government for requisitioned grain. Although the warning is timely, it perhaps goes too far; some of the prices quoted by Cicero are market prices or purport to be. There is much to be learned from the Verres' prosecution, since Cicero clearly understands the facts of life so far as corn is concerned.

The realities of the price situation are spelled out when he says:[82]

> Year by year so much labour and so much money is definitely expended for an indefinite and variable result. Further the market price is never high unless the harvest is a failure; when an abundant crop has been gathered in, a low selling price is the consequence; so you find that in a good year you have to sell cheap, and if you can sell for a good price, you have had a bad harvest. Indeed farming is throughout a thing whose profits depend not on intelligence and industry, but on those most uncertain things, wind and weather.

Variations in the harvest yields of the years 76 and 75 B.C., and the immediate effect on the market price of corn are spelled out by Cicero.[83] 'Sextus Peducaeus . . . governed the province for two years, in one of which wheat was cheap, in the other very dear.'

The swing in price levels within the year before and after the harvest is well understood:[84]

> Sacerdos, upon reaching his province [in 74 B.C.] requisitioned wheat for his maintenance. The price of wheat before the harvest was reaped being 5 *denarii* [20 sesterces] a *modius*, the communities asked him to commute the wheat for money. The price at which he did so was considerably lower than the price current in the market: he asked only 3 *denarii* a *modius* . . . In the same period the praetor Antonius commuted at the rate of 3 *denarii*; this was after the harvest when wheat was at its cheapest and when the farmers would rather have supplied the wheat for nothing . . . The whole question of wheat values is to be regarded in relation to the seasons and the current market prices.

Yet despite all this Cicero can refer to, and think in terms of, average prices of corn in Sicily lying within the range 2–3

[81] Brunt, *Italian Manpower*, p. 376. Cf. R. T. Pritchard, 'Some aspects of first century Sicilian agriculture', *Historia* 21 (1972), 651–3.

[82] Cicero, 2 *Verr.* 3. 227. [83] Cicero, 2 *Verr.* 3. 216.

[84] Cicero, 2 *Verr.* 3. 214–15.

sesterces per *modius*. He says that a letter from Verres himself at one time quoted the Sicilian price at 2 to 3 sesterces.[85] He exaggerates slightly when he talks of a uniform price throughout the island and declares that a farmer 'might buy grain anywhere at the same price he had sold it at home',[86] since he shows in other passages that prices varied from ½ to 1 sesterce from one district to another.[87] But these normal variations in normal years are small.

Of course we cannot immediately infer from these prices the price of corn in Rome at this time, but that they were typical prices in Sicily at the period seems to me certain. The prices paid by the Roman government for compulsory purchases above the tithes, of 3 to 4 sesterces a *modius*, were if anything advantageous, since in ordinary times they were as high as the current prices and very often higher.[88] The Roman purchases, far from depressing the market and the prices, probably exerted a steadying influence on the Sicilian grain trade by guaranteeing the disposal of a definite amount of the surplus at a fair return, and even at times at a bonus rate to the farmers.

We have no other evidence from the west that is anything like as detailed and as explicit as this Sicilian evidence. Polybius writing in the middle of the second century B.C. alludes to the wealth in corn of the Po valley in northern Italy[89] and to the fact that wheat cost rather less than 2 *asses* a *modius*, which is less than a quarter of the average price in Sicily in the late 70s B.C. In a list of prices for lower Lusitania in Spain Polybius[90] also makes it clear that wheat cost 9 Alexandrine obols (just less than 1 sesterce a *modius*), that is, almost twice the cost in the Po valley, but still less than half the cost in Sicily at the time of Verres. Clearly no general conclusions can be drawn from such evidence for areas of outstanding fertility but with perhaps few opportunities for export.

After the Ciceronian evidence for Sicily there is a singular dearth of evidence for the west. The single most interesting piece of evidence is the second-century-A.D. inscription from

[85] Cicero, 2 *Verr.* 3. 189.
[86] Cicero, 2 *Verr.* 3. 192.
[87] 2½ sesterces at Lipara, Petra, Halaesa, etc. (Cicero, 2 *Verr.* 3. 84, 90, 173); 3 sesterces at Agyrium (Cicero, 2 *Verr.* 3. 72).
[88] Frank, *ESAR* iii (Scramuzza), 267.
[89] Polyb. 2. 15.
[90] Polyb. 34. 8. 7.

Forum Sempronii[91] in Italy which records the gratitude of the city to a local worthy for selling wheat in a period of shortage at 1 *denarius* a *modius*. What we don't know is whether that price of 4 sesterces is above the current market price but not exorbitantly so, or whether it was distinctly under the current market price. Duncan-Jones takes it to be a price representative of normal conditions in Italy and reconcilable with alimentary rates laid down for the support of children in Italian towns under Trajan. But he believes that the alimentary rates for the support of children at Sicca Veneria, a large inland city in Africa, suggest that the price per *modius* there would be only 2½ sesterces. That would not be surprising in view of the situation of that city on the edge of a great corn-growing area.[92]

3

There is a similar imbalance in the distribution of evidence in the eastern Mediterranean. There is some scanty evidence in Palestine and Asia that the price of wheat seems frequently to have been 2–2½ sesterces a *modius* in the early Empire.[93] By far the most interesting evidence in the East again is an inscription discovered in the early 1920s concerning Antioch in Pisidia during the reign of Domitian.[94] A severe shortage of corn in a particular year had led to profiteering and in the end the government stepped in and fixed the price of corn at 4 sesterces a *modius* until 1 August, by which time the next harvest would be gathered in. But the significant fact revealed in the inscription is that this controlled price was almost double the normal price of corn in Pisidian Antioch, which is given as 2–2¼ sesterces per *modius*.

The largest amount of evidence on corn prices anywhere in the Roman Empire comes of course from Egypt.[95] But it is

[91] *CIL* 11. 6117 and p. 1397. Cf. Duncan-Jones, *ERE*, p. 50.

[92] See above, p. 110.

[93] Frank, *ESAR* iv (Heichelheim), 181 and 183; but cf. D. Sperber, *Roman Palestine: Money and Prices* (Jerusalem, 1974), for a higher set of prices.

[94] *Æpigr.* (1925), 126b; cf. *JRS* 14 (1924), 180.

[95] R. P. Duncan-Jones, 'The price of wheat in Roman Egypt under the Principate', *Chiron* 6 (1976), 241–51 is now the definitive study, cf. *ZPE* (1976); see also list of wheat prices given in Frank, *ESAR* ii (Johnson), 310–11; cf. Duncan-Jones, *ERE*, p. 145 n. 4; J. Schwartz, *Les Archives de Sarapion* (Cairo, 1961), pp. 327 ff.

difficult to use and to correlate with other prices because there are problems not simply about the size of the *artabae* but also about the value of the Egyptian drachmas. The variety of the evidence, however, does make clear what a multiplicity of different prices there might be depending on area, year and time of year. Although it was quite possible for prices to go high in Egypt not least because of the failure of the Nile flood,[96] it also seems clear that prices particularly in the first century A.D. could go even lower than the equivalent of 2 sesterces a *modius*. This is not surprising given the wealth of corn that might be available in a particular district of Egypt at a given moment. On the whole the regular governmental need for Egyptian grain helped I suspect as in Sicily to keep the price relatively steady, and higher than if there had been no outlet for the grain.[97] An analysis of the wheat prices in Egypt by Duncan-Jones shows an increase in the average price of grain in Egypt from less than 1 sesterce a *modius* under Augustus to just over 4 sesterces a *modius* by the early third century A.D., but there were regional and seasonal variations.[98]

4

The essence of our problem of course lies at Rome and it is the price of grain on the Roman market that we would particularly like to know. A vexing unknown quantity in trying to fathom the probable cost of corn in Rome has always been how much we should allow for the cost of freightage and of storage. There is extremely little evidence on either subject, as has been explained earlier in this chapter, but it seems to me probable that the cost of freightage and storage of grain from overseas did not, or was not allowed normally to, affect the cost of it unduly when put on to the open market, at least under the Empire. It is impossible to substantiate that claim, but there are one or two pointers.

The fragments of Diocletian's Edict discovered in the late 1930s made it clear that Heichelheim's computations of

[96] *P. Oxy.* 2958 and notes; D. Bonneau, *La Crue du Nil, passim.*

[97] A. H. M. Jones, 'Inflation under the Roman Empire', *EcHR*² 5 (1952–3), 295 n. 3.

[98] Duncan-Jones, *Chiron* 6 (1976), 241–51; cf. *ERE*, Appendix 16.

freightage rates were far too high.[99] Even the commercial freightage of wheat from Alexandria at the time of Diocletian would represent only 16 per cent of the permitted maximum price after its journey of over 1,000 miles (1,600 km) to Rome. That would mean the addition of not quite 2 *asses* to the price of a *modius* of wheat at Rome which had cost 3 sesterces at the other end of the Mediterranean.

There are no figures for the cost of storage at Rome but it is difficult to see how the price of a *modius* of wheat which cost say 2 or 3 sesterces at source could normally be priced on the Roman market at more than 5 to 6 sesterces at most. Augustus was said by Suetonius[100] to have regulated the corn supply with no less regard for the interests of the farmers and grain-dealers than for those of the populace. Although it is not specific, that implies a fine adjustment between prices in the producing countries and the Roman market with fair profit by the merchants and warehouse lessors but no profiteering.

If we turn from these speculations to the few facts we have about the price of corn in Rome we find our conclusions get some support.

In 211–10 B.C. Hannibal invaded Latium and destroyed the crops. Rome was forced to buy wheat in Egypt and the famine price at Rome rose to 15 drachmas a *medimnus* ($2\frac{1}{2}$ *denarii* a *modius*).[101] On the other hand at the end of the Punic War the aediles were able to release for sale in Rome stores which had originally been gathered for military use. In 203 B.C. there was a price of 4 *asses* a *modius*.[102] In 202 B.C. the supplies coming from Sicily and Sardinia to Rome reduced prices of grain to such an extent that the merchants gave over the grain to the carriers for the freightage ('ut pro vectura frumentum nautis mercator reliqueret').[103] How low the prices went then we do not know, but they went as low as 2 *asses* a *modius* when the aediles sold off 1,000,000 *modii* of military supplies after the Second Macedonian War.[104]

Clearly at the end of the third century B.C. 4 *asses* a *modius*

[99] E. R. Graser, 'Two new fragments of the Edict of Diocletian', *TAPA* 71 (1940), 161 ff.; F. Heichelheim, *Wirtschaftliche Schwankungen* (Jena, 1930), p. 72 and 92; but see Duncan-Jones, *ERE*, Appendix 17 for cautionary notes about the reliability of these figures.

[100] Suet. *Aug*. 42. 3.
[101] Polyb. 9. 44.
[102] Livy 30. 26. 5.
[103] Livy 30. 38. 5.
[104] Livy 33. 42.

was abnormally low and 2½ *denarii* a *modius* was abnormally high as the price for wheat at Rome. Neither price is typical.

Our next precise evidence is the price at which Gaius Gracchus decided to sell the corn at the *frumentationes* which he started. This was 6⅓ *asses* (just over 1½ sesterces) a *modius*,[105] and although the *frumentationes* are not to be thought of at this time as a dole for the poor, the price was nevertheless clearly below the current market price of the time. How far below we have no means of knowing. It is not a legitimate method of argument to say as Tenney Frank does[106] that the complaints that it was a *largitio* which threw a heavy burden on the treasury allow us to suppose that it was at least a 50 per cent reduction. That merely allows him to square it with the Sicilian price of 3 sesterces a *modius* in 70 B.C. We simply do not know what the market price was. All we can say with confidence is that 6⅓ *asses* was probably lower than the usual prices in Rome and that unlike them it did not fluctuate at all.

There is no evidence at all for ordinary prices of grain at Rome in the late Republic or even of the precise limits within which they fluctuated. The situation is no better for Augustus. Hirschfeld and Kornemann[107] inferred from the coincidence between the number of *denarii* per head given in Augustus' *congiaria* of 5 and 2 B.C. and the number of *modii* given in the *frumentationes*, 60 in both cases, that corn was normally reckoned at 1 *denarius*, or 4 sesterces per *modius* in Rome at that time. It has been pointed out[108] that even if the answer is correct the reasoning is faulty, since the *congiaria* of Augustus' successors soon reached much higher levels, without there being any indication that the price of corn had risen correspondingly, or that the gifts of the Julio-Claudians were in any way geared to prices of commodities.

Nor can we follow how Augustus regulated the grain market, as he claims, in the interests of all concerned, farmers, merchants and populace. We do know that in the corn shortage of A.D. 19 Tiberius dealt with public complaints by fixing a price that the

[105] Livy, *Epit.* 60; cf. Cic. *pro Sestio* 55 and Ascon. *ad Pis.* 9.

[106] Frank, *ESAR* i. 192.

[107] E. Kornemann, 'Nochmals das Monumentum Ancyranum', *Klio* 4 (1904), 90.

[108] R. Duncan-Jones, 'An Epigraphic Survey of Costs in Roman Italy', *PBSR* N.S. 20 (1965), 221. Cf. *ERE*, p. 145 n. 6.

merchants were to sell at which was less than the current price and paying them himself two sesterces for each *modius* they sold in this way.[109] But we cannot guess from this information alone what price this additional subsidy by the Emperor was meant to achieve. Claudius was highly active in many ways for the good of the corn supply,[110] but there is no clue in the ancient sources about corn prices in Rome during his reign. Tacitus is slightly more helpful when he says that Nero forced the price of corn in Rome down to 3 sesterces per *modius*,[111] but we still do not know whether this was a forced return to what was regarded as a normal price or an artificially low price. The date of Tacitus' reference is A.D. 64 and the context is the disastrous fire in Rome, when Nero was trying to do everything to alleviate the suffering of the homeless and to divert suspicion of arson from himself.

The implications of these passages about the actual mechanism of price control in the early Empire are not clear to me. The Emperor Tiberius is said by Suetonius to have proposed that the senate should annually set the price of corn in the market.[112] But there is no evidence for such regular price fixing by the senate then or later. Even late in the reign of Tiberius when in A.D. 32 the high price of corn caused riotous demonstrations in the theatre, it was the Emperor who was blamed, not the senate.[113] I do not believe that either Emperor or senate generally intervened in the market in so obvious a way in the early Empire. When a crisis occurred it was up to the Emperor to issue *mandata* to the *praefectus annonae* to take appropriate action, if he had not already done so. The *praefectus* is likely to have tried to restore the situation to normal by indirect action. Provided his reserves of imperial or public corn were high, he could either simply release more for sale and thus help to lower prices naturally, or even deliberately sell it at an artificially low price. In either case the private sector of the market would react accordingly. There was a danger in the case of the second manoeuvre of the resulting market price bringing private corn dealers to the edge of ruin as in A.D. 19, and in that case the Emperor arranged for a subsidy. However it was done, it seems likely that in the early Empire at least there was little

[109] Tac. *Ann.* 2. 87. [110] Suet. *Claud.* 18–19. [111] Tac. *Ann.* 15. 39. 2.
[112] Suet. *Tib.* 34. [113] Tac. *Ann.* 6. 13.

recourse to compulsion or direct government interference in price regulation. There is more evidence of course later in the Empire both for the varying price of wheat and for greater government intervention but that needs to be judiciously handled and assessed in relation to the coinage,[114] and it does not throw much light on the situation in the late Republic and early Empire.

The prices given by the elder Pliny for various grades of flour towards the end of the first century A.D. 'when the prices of grain are average' have teased scholars into elaborate calculations in the hope of establishing such an average grain price at Rome.[115] But the hope has proved delusive, since assumptions have to be made about the extraction rates for flour, and the costs of milling, which predetermine the answer. Rostovtzeff calculated that Pliny's price for flour was equivalent to a price of 5 sesterces a *modius* or less for corn, Jasny that the corn price implied was 8 sesterces a *modius* or even 10 sesterces a *modius* for wheat of the best quality. Neither perhaps is right.

5

At the moment despite the unsatisfactory nature of the evidence, I am inclined to believe that for much of the classical period a price frequently found in different parts of the Mediterranean was 2–3 sesterces a *modius*. It seems to have been typical of many a domestic market, whether in Sicily, Palestine, or Asia Minor, where cost of transportation did not really enter into the reckoning. Only in an area of great productivity but poor export possibilities, such as perhaps the Po valley, were corn prices ever regularly below this level, and in Italy in general the price may have been generally as much as 4 sesterces a *modius*.

In Rome itself there were two factors which pulled in opposite directions, so far as corn prices were concerned. On the one hand transport and storage costs and city-life might be expected to boost the price in the open market; on the other

[114] A. H. M. Jones, 'Inflation under the Roman Empire', *EcHR*[2] 5 (1952–3), 299–300, 303–4; cf. Duncan-Jones, *ERE*, pp. 7–11 and *passim*; D. Sperber, *Roman Palestine: Money and Prices*.

[115] Pliny, *N. H.* 18. 89–90; see below, Appendix 6.

hand the inflow of corn from many directions, and the intervention, or possible intervention, by state authorities in the market might be expected to keep the price of corn down and good value in relation to other costs[116] and wages. Rostovtzeff believed in a range of prices between 3 and 4 sesterces for the late Republic and early Empire; prices of 3 sesterces and below being typical of centres of production; prices of 4 sesterces and above being perhaps truer of the market in Rome. While that may be correct for the late Republic, it is possible that by the end of the Republic and the early Empire, the price of grain in Rome had risen to a regular level of 5 or even 6 sesterces a *modius*.

Whatever the exact figures, the price of grain, the staple part of the ordinary diet of people in the ancient world, was vitally important throughout the Mediterranean, particularly to the less wealthy members of society. Although everyone knew that the price naturally fluctuated from year to year, and even within a year in a particular area, nevertheless they could also believe in an average or normal price for grain. That normal price could be really savagely altered in most places by the failure of the local harvest, by the cost of importing grain from another region if that was possible, and by the actions of speculators or hoarders who tried to profit from the crisis. The situation in Rome itself was rather different; the local resources were not so relevant by the period of the early Empire, the cost of importing grain from overseas was a standard charge on Rome's resources, and the action of speculators, *dardanarii*,[117] who tried to force up grain prices, was officially forbidden by law. What affected the Roman market more was first the failure of harvests in provinces overseas, Africa or Egypt, Sicily or Sardinia; secondly inadequate supplies of shipping, and the destruction of corn ships in storms at sea, or in the harbours and docks of Rome; and thirdly administrative muddle and corruption in the organization. The Emperors had to try to take account of all these dangers and cushion the Roman population against their occurrence and the effect they might have on prices. The population of Rome as a whole may have rarely starved, but it was very conscious of any alteration of

[116] Duncan-Jones, *ERE*, pp. 11–12.
[117] *Dig.* 47. 11. 6 pr. (Ulpian); 48. 19. 37 (Paulus).

what it regarded as normal conditions. The mob who assaulted the Emperor Claudius in the Forum in A.D. 51 at the time of a grain shortage had scraps of bread with which to pelt him, but that was certainly no comfort to him, and apparently not to them either.[118]

[118] Suet. *Claud.* 18.

VII

THE CORN DISTRIBUTIONS

I

It had become increasingly common in the Hellenistic period for regular public distributions of corn to take place in many of the Greek cities.[1] It might therefore seem natural to suspect that when Gaius Gracchus passed his *lex frumentaria*, in 123 B.C., establishing regular corn distributions in Rome for the first time, he was influenced by Greek practice, not least perhaps because of the Greek emphasis believed to have been characteristic of the upbringing of the Gracchan brothers.[2] But on investigation the possible influence of the Greek example dwindles in importance.

There are significant differences between Greek and Roman practice. Most of our evidence for the distributions in Greek cities comes from inscriptions, particularly from the lengthy, although still incomplete, inscription from Samos.[3] From these inscriptions it is clear that, in addition to the appointment of special officers to maintain adequate supplies of corn and control its price, the main problem for the Greeks was the establishment of a permanent fund which could produce an annual revenue to pay for corn purchases and distributions. Without wishing to minimize the cost of the Roman corn distributions to the Roman treasury, and the way in which the corn laws in the late Republic were linked with other measures that were to help pay for them,[4] this was not really Rome's problem. The revenues of Rome's overseas possessions in one way or another were to provide the corn needed.

[1] A. R. Hands, *Charities and Social Aid in Greece and Rome* (London, 1968), pp. 95–100.

[2] Plutarch, *Tib. Gracchus* 8. 4–5.

[3] Dittenberger, *Sylloge* 976; for literature and translation see Hands, *Charities*, p. 164 n. 108 and p. 178 D6.

[4] Cf. Badian, *Roman Imperialism*², pp. 46, 47, and 76.

Moreover, as we have seen in Chapter II there was a Roman tradition of state intervention in the corn supply of the capital stretching back to the earliest days of the Republic, and there had been *ad hoc* distributions by the aediles from time to time. While therefore the Greek practice was certainly there as an example of regular distributions, it is also true, and more significant for Roman acceptance of the practice, that there were elements within the Roman tradition itself on which the idea of regular *frumentationes* could be based.

2

There are good reasons for subdividing the study of the corn distributions of the Republic and early Empire into three sections; first, the period from Gaius Gracchus' tribunate in 123 to Clodius' tribunate in 58 B.C.; secondly, the period from Pompey's *cura annonae* in 57 B.C. through the dictatorship of Julius Caesar to the establishment of the principate by Augustus; thirdly, the post-Augustan period up to the Severans.

Basically the problems of the first period up to Clodius' tribunate are focused on the many corn laws which were passed with bewildering rapidity. The laws were important at the time, both in themselves and for the political manoeuvres of the day, but the evidence that has survived as to their content is often minimal or non-existent. Hence in this period there are many purely factual questions relating to each of the laws—when exactly were they passed, how much was the amount of corn distributed, what price was fixed, how many were eligible to receive the corn—besides the problem of how the laws all fit into the political history of the period. After Clodius had abolished all payment by the recipients for the distributions, the spate of corn laws dried up and the problems change in type, becoming more matters of administration: what conditions did Pompey, or Julius Caesar, or Augustus lay down in order to control eligibility for free corn? How did they prune their lists of recipients? What was the relationship between the numbers of recipients and the total population of Rome at a given moment?

The third period is marked by an increasing centralization

of organization based on the Porticus Minucia from the mid-first century A.D. which was to culminate in the amalgamation of the corn distributing machinery and the water organization by the time of Septimius Severus. The questions here focus on how this centralization was achieved, who was responsible for it, and how in detail it was managed.

For the first period from Gaius Gracchus to Clodius the evidence is so paltry and sometimes so ambiguous that the accounts of the early history of the corn distributions can be quite different. One has only to compare the accounts given by Rostovtzeff, Cardinali, Hands, and Brunt to see how different they can be.[5] Van Berchem in his major study of the distributions concentrated wisely on the Empire, and made no more than a passing comment about these Republican laws in his first chapter.[6] On the other hand the evidence for the administration of the distributions under the Empire itself is by no means full and has to be 'interpreted'. Van Berchem used it to argue an elegant thesis which necessarily went beyond the evidence and which is consequently open to challenge, as we shall see. It is important therefore throughout the history of the distributions at whatever period to distinguish between the evidence, such as it is, and the historical reconstructions, more or less plausible, which may be attempted.

(a) *The Republic*

I

There is no need to search for particular crises in the corn supply in the 130s and 120s B.C., although they can be found, to account for the passing of Gaius Gracchus' epoch-making *lex frumentaria* in early 123 B.C.[7] The general conditions of the corn trade were such that prices could always fluctuate and we know that Gaius Gracchus' intention was that this should be prevented in respect of at least some of the corn which came to Rome. The

[5] Rostovtzeff, *Frumentum*, cols. 172–4; Cardinali, *Frumentatio*, pp. 229–33; Hands, *Charities*, pp. 100–3 and nn. 118 and 120; Brunt, *Italian Manpower*, pp. 376–80.

[6] D. Van Berchem, *Les Distributions de blé et d'argent à la plèbe romaine sous l'empire* (Geneva, 1939).

[7] Broughton, *MRR* i. 514; cf. Livy, *Per.* 60, Plut. *G. Gracchus* 6. Appian, *B. C.* i. 21; D. L. Stockton, *The Gracchi* (Oxford, 1979), pp. 126–9; cf. H. Schneider, *Wirtschaft und Politik* (Erlangen, 1974), pp. 361–91.

lex Sempronia established the right of all Roman citizens in Rome to buy a ration of corn at monthly distributions and the price was to be $6\frac{1}{3}$ *asses* (about $1\frac{1}{2}$ sesterces) per *modius*. The monthly provision of corn was to take place presumably throughout the year, and presumably at places and times to be announced. There seems at this stage to have been no single permanent issuing centre (and there was not to be one until the whole operation was focused at the Porticus Minucia more than a century and a half later). In association with his corn law Gaius Gracchus was supposed to have encouraged the building of *horrea* to increase the storage capacity of the capital and it is possible that they could have fulfilled a dual role of storage and issue, although we know nothing about them.[8]

Those eligible to buy at the fixed price throughout the year were, as Appian states, 'each of the citizens' and actual physical attendance at the distribution was necessary.[9] A famous story had it that Gaius Gracchus found to his surprise the consular L. Calpurnius Piso Frugi (cos. 133 B.C.), an opponent of his corn law, attending one of the distributions. When asked to explain his action Piso replied, 'I would prefer that you were not of a mind to divide my property among the citizens individually, but seeing that you are dividing it, then I shall ask for my share.'[10] Gracchus' surprise was not because Piso was a rich man but because he had been an opponent of the bill and the point of Piso's reply was that it was part of the public wealth that was being distributed, and that was his as much as anybody else's. It was to be a standard criticism of the corn distributions that they were a serious drain on public funds.[11]

The fixed price, $6\frac{1}{3}$ *asses* per *modius*, was likely to have been below the normal market price—by a debatable margin. But how much the public funds suffered is of course quite unknowable since we know neither the margin of subsidy, nor the size of the monthly ration (later to be 5 *modii*), much less the total number of the recipients. But Gaius Gracchus' measure is not to be seen as the feckless gesture of an idealist unversed in the

[8] Plut. *G. Gracchus* 6. 2; Festus, p. 392L, cf. Rickman, *Roman Granaries*, pp. 149–150.

[9] Appian, *B. C.* i. 21.

[10] Cic. *Tusc. Disp.* 3. 20. 48.

[11] Badian, *Imperialism*², pp. 45–6; but see now M. H. Crawford, *Roman Republican Coinage* (Cambridge, 1974), ii. 636.

ways of the financial world. It should be stressed that there still was a price; the corn was certainly not to be given away under Gaius Gracchus' law. Its major virtue, so far as the citizens of Rome were concerned, was that the price for this corn remained the same and did not fluctuate with the season or the whim of the corn merchants.

Gaius Gracchus may have hoped that the burden on the treasury would not be as great as it turned out to be.[12] It was true that from this time public grain, which previously could have been sold at the market price in Rome, and thus yielded a revenue to the treasury, was now to be sold perhaps below the normal market price, and therefore to that limited extent the state revenues would be diminished. It is very possible that the taxation tithes from Sicily and elsewhere did not yield enough to cover the distributions to every citizen, and that it was known therefore that the state would have to buy extra supplies on the open market. But it may have been expected that the selling of so much state grain at a low fixed price might have stabilized the grain market and brought down grain prices in general. That seems not to have happened. In fact, it may have played into the hands of grain speculators who could keep their prices high, knowing that the state had committed itself. Whether all this is true or not, Gaius Gracchus certainly devoted efforts to the financial implications of his *lex frumentaria*. His major overhaul of the taxation system of the province of Asia was meant among other things to provide a surer long-term revenue to the treasury in Rome, from which support for the corn distribution was to be found without difficulty, despite his enemies' accusations.[13]

It is difficult to appreciate Gaius Gracchus' measure in its context without regard to the later history of the Roman Republic. We know that it was to provide a focus for political dissension, that it was to add to the magnet attraction of Rome in Italy, and that it was ultimately even to increase the rate of manumission among slaves in Rome.[14] But at the time it was simply an act calculated to make the state guarantee some food at a certain price for its citizens in Rome. As such it was not in

[12] A. H. Boren, *The Gracchi* (New York, 1968), p. 92.
[13] Badian, *Imperialism*², pp. 47–9. Cf. *G. Gracchus* 2.
[14] Appian, *B. C.* 2. 120; Sall. *Cat.* 37; Dio 39. 24. 1; Dion. Halic. 4. 24.

itself a welfare scheme; there was no special provision for the poor, or for the fathers of large families, for example. But it was a scheme which was naturally of greater value to the poor and, in so far as that was true, an act of humanity to be valued.

2

What happened to Gaius Gracchus' measure after his death in 121 B.C.? The only honest answer is that we do not know. We know that the *lex Sempronia* lasted until a certain M. Octavius (presumably as a tribune) by his authority and his eloquence secured its repeal by a large majority and substituted for it his own corn law, the *lex Octavia*.[15] That law was much approved of by Cicero because, according to him, it substituted a modest for an extravagant largesse and made distributions that were tolerable to the state and necessary to the *plebs*.[16] But we do not know the date of this law which can, and has been, placed anywhere between the *lex Sempronia* in 123 B.C. and the dictatorship of Sulla in 81 B.C. Nor do we know in what ways it altered the provisions of the *lex Sempronia*, either in reducing in some way the numbers eligible, or the amount of each ration, or in increasing the price to be charged.

The placing of the *lex Octavia* is crucial for any reconstruction of the early history of the corn distributions, because, whatever other corn laws may have been attempted, the *lex Sempronia* was valid until overthrown by the *lex Octavia*, but there is no totally conclusive evidence for a particular date. We know that Gaius Marius successfully opposed an attempted corn law during his tribunate in 119 B.C. and that this opposition displeased the people.[17] Clearly this law was not the *lex Octavia*, but there have been scholars, the latest of whom is Brunt, who have seen in the law opposed by Marius in 119 B.C. an attempted liberal reaction from the *lex Octavia*, which, it is assumed, was passed amid other anti-Gracchan laws in the immediate aftermath of Gaius Gracchus' death.[18] Against this view, however, is a strong chronological and prosopographical argument, which stems ultimately from a passage in Cicero's *Brutus*.[19] In this passage

[15] Cic. *Brut.* 62. 222.
[16] Cic. *De Off.* 2. 21. 72.
[17] Plut. *Marius* 4.
[18] Brunt, *Italian Manpower*, p. 377.
[19] Cic. *Brut.* 62. 222 (ed. A. E. Douglas, Oxford, pp. 163–4).

Cicero is discussing the merits of orators of an earlier generation, among them this M. Octavius. The context of the passage and recent prosopographical work on the Octavii make it very likely that the tribunate of M. Octavius must be placed after 100 B.C.—at the earliest in the 90s, and possibly in the 80s B.C.[20] If that is so, then M. Octavius cannot possibly have led a senatorial reaction to Gaius Gracchus' *lex frumentaria* between 121 B.C. and 119 B.C., and the *lex Sempronia* must have been in force until after 100 B.C.

The last part of the second century B.C. can be regarded as a period of crisis in many senses, but so far as the corn supply and distributions are concerned the tensions congregated in the last decade. Two major areas of supply were seriously disturbed at the time, Africa by the war with Jugurtha, and even more important Sicily by the Second Slave War.[21] Italy was in danger from attack from the north by the Cimbri and Teutones, or so it was believed. At all events, Roman armies were in the field and as much in need of supplies as the population of the capital. Piracy was rife and the Mediterranean sea unsafe.[22] Even the political tensions at home, focused not least on the mutual distrust of Marius and the Metelli, were given a particular slant towards the problems of the corn supply by the liaison which sprang up between Marius and L. Appuleius Saturninus. A critical shortage of corn in the capital developed in 104 B.C. and the senate took the unprecedented step of depriving Saturninus of his Ostian quaestorship and transferring his duties to M. Aemilius Scaurus, the *princeps senatus*.[23] It was supposedly this slight that helped to set Saturninus on a career of popular demagogy and hostility to the senate. Certainly he was tribune of the *plebs* in both 103 and 100 B.C., and his career came to a violent end after his arrest by his erstwhile associate Marius, on orders of the senate, late in 100 B.C.

In 103 or 100 B.C. Saturninus proposed a corn law, the only

[20] Hands, *Charities*, p. 102 and p. 166 n. 20; G. V. Sumner, *Orators in Cicero's Brutus: Prosopography and Chronology* (Toronto, 1973), pp. 114–16; cf. G. Niccolini, *I fasti dei tribuni della plebe* (Milan, 1934), pp. 163–4. Crawford, *Coinage* i. 73 n. 5, however, believes in a date for the *lex Octavia* shortly before 100 B.C. and that it raised the Gracchan price.

[21] Cic. *De leg. Agraria* 2. 30. 83.

[22] See above, p. 50.

[23] Cic. *De har. resp.* 43; *Pro Sest.* 39; Diod. 36. 12.

known provision of which was concerned with the price of the corn ration. In the text which has come down to us the price mentioned is five-sixths of an *as*.[24] Saturninus' *lex frumentaria* was opposed vigorously by the quaestor Q. Servilius Caepio, who used violence to break up the assembly, an act for which he was later prosecuted.[25] Together with his colleague L. Calpurnius Piso, Caepio also issued coinage bearing the legend 'Ad Fru(mentum) Emu(ndum) ex s. c.', the significance of which is disputed.[26]

The figure for the price given by the manuscripts, $\frac{5}{6}$ *as* per *modius*, can without difficulty be amended to $6\frac{1}{3}$ *asses* per *modius*, the price set by Gaius Gracchus. In the past many scholars have preferred to amend the text and assumed that Saturninus was trying to return to the Gracchan price after someone unknown had made it higher.[27] This seems implausible. It is difficult to believe that an attempt to raise the Gracchan price would have stood much chance of gaining sufficient popular support to become law anyway, and the only law which could have made such a change, the *lex Octavia*, is probably to be placed after 100 B.C. rather than before it. Indeed the placing of the *lex Octavia* after 100 B.C. should mean that Saturninus' measure never became law because we know that it was the *lex Sempronia* which M. Octavius repealed. If this is true, the corn law of Saturninus is likely to belong to the year 100 B.C. and perhaps towards the end of that year when he was resorting to more and more extreme measures to attract the urban *plebs*.[28] Certainly if the corn law is dated to the first tribunate in 103 B.C. we have to ask why, if it failed then, Saturninus did not try again in 100 B.C. when he was even more popular, and why if Caepio were quaestor in 103 B.C. and used violence, he was not prosecuted by Saturninus himself. We hear of only one attempt to get the

[24] Cic. *Ad Herenn.* 1. 12. 21. The manuscripts read *de semissibus et trientibus* which would not be difficult to emend to *de senis et trientibus*.

[25] Broughton, *MRR* i. 576; *Ad Herenn.* 1. 21; 2. 17; 4. 35; Sallust, *Hist.* 1. 62 M.

[26] Greenidge and Clay, *Sources*² (ed. E. W. Gray), p. 282 n. 4; Crawford, *Republican Coinage* i. 330 no. 330.

[27] See e.g. H. Last, *CAH* 9. 165 n. 5, and now Crawford, *Republican Coinage* i. 73 n. 5.

[28] Broughton, *MRR* i. 578 n. 5; H. B. Mattingly, 'Saturninus' corn bill and the circumstances of his fall', *CR* 19 (1969), 267–70, presses the argument too hard. For different views: A. R. Hands, 'The Date of Saturninus' Corn Bill', *CR* 22 (1972), 12; Brunt, *Italian Manpower*, pp. 377 and 378; Crawford, *Republican Coinage* i. 73.

law passed and that was disrupted by Caepio. If this occurred late in 100 B.C. it may be that time simply ran out for Saturninus. Certainly there is no further trace of the price $\frac{5}{6}$ *as* in the sources for the period after 100 B.C. The coinage issued in 100 B.C. by Caepio and his fellow quaestor on the orders of the senate probably had no direct link with the corn distributions as such, but with the procurement of corn.[29] We know that at a time of shortage in 138 B.C. a tribune of the plebs C. Curiatius forced the consuls at an informal meeting of the people to say that they would introduce a motion in the senate *de frumento emundo*, although in fact this was prevented.[30] Saturninus was probably not so directly responsible for the senate's action in 100 B.C., but in a period of stress the senate was concerned to show that it cared about the food supply of the capital and that adequate funds would be earmarked for the purpose. If Saturninus' corn law was partly designed to steal the senate's thunder on this issue, the particularly violent reaction of Caepio is even more understandable. But this is pure speculation.

So far we have merely postponed the date of the *lex Octavia* until after 100 B.C., but now we have to try to define its date and its role in the history of the corn distributions more closely. A corn law, whose content is unknown, was passed by M. Livius Drusus, tribune in 91 B.C., but it was annulled.[31] Consequently the *lex Octavia* must have been the single most important piece of corn legislation in the twenty years up to Sulla's dictatorship. It is clear that M. Octavius was to be numbered with the *boni*, the *optimates*, those men who believed in group government by the senate and that he not only secured the repeal of the law of Gaius Gracchus but that his own law restricted the scale of the distributions in some way.[32] Possible contexts for the successful passing of such a law by such a man are either in the period up to 87 B.C. or during Sulla's dictatorship. The intervening period of Marius' return to Rome and Cinna's domination is an unlikely time for legislation such as Octavius' law seems to have been. The balance of probability is that the *lex Octavia* was

[29] For the date see Crawford, *Republican Coinage* i. 73, which supersedes earlier views.

[30] Val. Max. 3. 7. 3; cf. Livy, *Per.* 55.

[31] Livy, *Per.* 71.

[32] *Cic. Brutus* (ed. Douglas), p. 162.

passed sometime during the 90s rather than at the time of Sulla's dictatorship.

The case for the latter has been argued on the grounds that Octavius was simply a 'front man' for Sulla, who did not abolish the distributions, as is commonly believed, but simply restricted them in some way in accordance with the provisions of the *lex Octavia.*[33] But the evidence that Sulla actually abolished the distributions altogether, although not as strong as one might wish, is strong enough.[34] Moreover it is doubtful on prosopographical grounds whether M. Octavius could have held the tribunate so late. Another difficulty is that if the *lex Octavia* is placed in 81 or 80 B.C. we have to assume that Drusus in 91 B.C. was attempting in some way to go beyond the law of Gaius Gracchus, which had been in force for over thirty years, and was to remain in force for nearly forty-five years.

The placing of the *lex Octavia* in the 90s B.C. has the advantage that it appears to be a natural time for Octavius to hold the tribunate and in a period of senatorial ascendancy.[35] The *lex Livia* passed later in 91 B.C. can be seen as an attempt to restore a more generous distribution without necessarily going beyond, or perhaps even as far as, the original law of Gaius Gracchus. This seems more in character for the tribune M. Livius Drusus, who was trying to carry the senate with him in his schemes. If we may place the *lex Octavia* with some confidence at the beginning of the first century B.C., we nevertheless have no means of knowing what its provisions were in detail. Since it appeared to be acceptable both to the senate and to the citizens, it may have restricted the number of recipients in some way which did not deprive the free-born poor. If this is true, then cheap grain was available for all citizens in Rome from 123 until the 90s B.C.; from then until Sulla's dictatorship the right to the *frumentationes* may have been more narrowly defined; with Sulla the right disappeared.

[33] A. E. Douglas, 'Oratorum Aetates', *AJP* 87 (1966), 298.

[34] Sallust, *Or. Lepid.* 11. (Sall. *Hist.* 1. 55. 11, ed. Maurenbrecher.)

[35] Sumner, *Orators in Cicero's Brutus*, p. 114; J. G. Schovánek, 'The date of M. Octavius and his *Lex Frumentaria*', *Historia* 21 (1972), 235–43; 'The provisions of the *Lex Octavia Frumentaria*', *Historia* 26 (1977), 378–81.

3

The attempt to reverse the actions of Sulla started with M. Aemilius Lepidus, the anti-Sullan consul of 78 B.C. In fact the evidence usually quoted for the abolition of the distributions by Sulla is a rhetorical flourish in a fragment of Sallust's *Histories* in a speech of Lepidus where he complained that the great Roman people had been left not even the rations of slaves. It was of course mere stock-in-trade of radical speech makers to denigrate the rations of the *frumentationes* and to suggest that they were no more than those of the prisoners in the gaols, as we can see from a passage in the speech which Sallust put in the mouth of the tribune C. Licinius Macer in 73 B.C., but the clear implication of Lepidus' remark is that after Sulla there were no rations at all.[36] We know from a fragment of Licinianus that Lepidus supported a law to give 5 *modii* a month to the people.[37] Even if that proposal succeeded, and we have no further information about it, it may have been undone shortly afterwards, since it was necessary for the consuls M. Terentius Varro Lucullus and C. Cassius Longinus to get a law passed in 73 B.C.[38] The *lex Terentia et Cassia frumentaria* certainly re-established a ration of 5 *modii* a month, apparently at the Gracchan price of 6⅓ *asses* a *modius*. This *lex Terentia–Cassia* was much referred to three years later by Cicero in his prosecution of Verres for his conduct in Sicily because money had been set aside by the law for the purchase of corn in Sicily for Rome. In particular Cicero stated that at this time 33,000 *medimnoi* (that is, 198,000 *modii*) of corn was more or less sufficient to provide a monthly ration for the Roman *plebs*.[39] If that is taken literally and exactly, the conclusion is that no more than 40,000 men received the corn distributions in Rome at this time. Whatever view is taken of the size of the total population of Rome in the middle of the first century B.C., the figure of 40,000, even if it results from an exaggeration on Cicero's part, is so low that it reinforces the suspicion that the number of recipients in the *frumentationes* had been limited at some time and in some way.

[36] Sallust, *Or. Macri* 19. (Sall. *Hist.* 3. 48. 19, ed. Maurenbrecher). Cf. *Or. Lepid.* 11.

[37] Licinianus, p. 34 (ed. Flemisch).

[38] Sall. *Or. Macri* 19.

[39] Cic. 2 *Verr.* 5. 21. 52; 3. 70. 163; 3. 30. 72.

What was going on in the 70s B.C. and why should two consuls involve themselves in corn legislation, presumably with the blessing of the senate? In this period there was both famine and financial stringency which came to a head in 75 B.C. with angry rioting by hungry crowds in Rome and the chasing of two consuls and a candidate for the praetorship in the forum itself.[40] Not the least of the troubles was the great growth of piracy, encouraged by Mithridates.[41] Rome's lack of a navy and the ineffective efforts by the senate at the end of the second century B.C. to control piracy were now to be severely punished. The senate, it is true, ordered P. Servilius Vatia to attack pirate bases in Cilicia in 77, but by 74 B.C. it was necessary to give a special command with unlimited authority to the praetor M. Antonius, who went to Crete which had become a new centre for pirate activity. In such a situation it is not surprising either that reforming tribunes at Rome should have used the difficulties of the corn supply as a stick to beat the government, or that the senate itself should have given serious thought to the feeding of Rome in all its aspects, the problems of piracy, finance, procurement and distribution of corn. It is significant that it was in 74 B.C. that the senate decided to exploit the Cyrene bequest and that the *lex Terentia–Cassia* should be passed in the next year.[42] We know from Cicero's speeches against Verres three years later in 70 that this law was not merely concerned with the corn distributions, but had laid down methods to be used and prices to be paid for the regular purchase of extra tithes by the governor of Sicily for the benefit of Rome in general. The senate in other words had risen to the challenge of trying to put the Sicilian supply of the Roman corn market on to a regular and equitable basis. Unfortunately Antonius proved to be not up to his task of stamping out piracy and by the late 70s B.C. the shipping lanes converging on the straits of Messina from the south and east were a constant prey to the pirates based on Malta. The eastern seaboard of Sicily was terrorized, and the small fleet of Verres the governor was

[40] Sall. *Hist.* 2. 45; 2. 47. 6–7 (Maurenbrecher); cf. Gruen, *Last Generation*, p. 385; Crawford, *Republican Coinage* ii. 638.

[41] See above, p. 50.

[42] Sall. *Hist.* 2. 43 (Maurenbrecher); Appian, *B. C.* i. 111; cf. Badian, *Imperialism*^{2}, p. 36.

captured and burned by the pirates. The efforts of the Sullan senate to show itself capable of running Rome's affairs were being discredited in a number of spheres, and were to be in this as well despite the *lex Terentia–Cassia*.

The *lex Terentia–Cassia* authorized in addition to the collection of the original tithe of 3 million *modii* the purchase of additional amounts of grain, up to 3,800,000 *modii*. It has been stressed that this Sicilian grain alone could have fed some 180,000 people at the rate of 5 *modii* a month.[43] This is true, but it does not mean that this was the number of recipients admitted to the *frumentationes*. Sicilian grain surpluses, no less than supplies from Sardinia, Africa, and elsewhere, could be put onto the open market at Rome, or used for the armies needed to quell the revolt of Spartacus in Italy. Cicero implied that the numbers actually admitted to the distributions were much lower, namely somewhere in the order of 40,000.[44] That implication is confirmed, without being made precise, by the fact that we are told that in 62 B.C. Cato managed to get a *senatus consultum* passed to extend eligibility for the distributed corn rations to, in Plutarch's words, 'the poor and landless *plebs*'.[45] This must mean that some limit on the numbers of recipients had been applied either for the first time by the *lex Terentia–Cassia* itself, or by some previous law, the *lex Octavia* or the law of Aemilius Lepidus, and carried over into the *lex Terentia–Cassia*. On what principle the limitation was worked, we do not know. Brunt speculates that the system of exclusions in the earlier part of the first century B.C. had worked to the detriment of freedmen;[46] only *proletarii*, of free birth, domiciled in Rome at a particular moment, presumably that of the passing of the relevant law, had previously benefited from the distributions. But now under Cato's provision these restrictions were to be removed and both freedmen already domiciled in Rome and new immigrants to the city were all to benefit. This view to some extent stems from evidence that in the 50s B.C. and later Roman masters liberated

[43] R. J. Rowland, Jnr., 'The Number of Grain Recipients in the late Republic', *Act. Antiq. Acad. Scient. Hung.* 13 (1965), 81.

[44] Cic. *In Verr.* 3. 30. 72; 33,000 *medimnoi* of grain were 'plebis Romanae prope menstrua cibaria', but vagueness implied by *prope* should be noticed.

[45] Plut. *Cat. Min.* 26. 1; cf. Gruen, *Last Generation*, p. 386; Crawford, *Republican Coinage* ii. 638.

[46] Brunt, *Italian Manpower*, pp. 377 and 379.

their slaves in order that they might become eligible for the corn distributions and other largesses,[47] but it also forms part of Brunt's overall thesis that the greater part of the population of Rome in the late Republic was made up of freedmen, and only a small proportion was of free birth. This may be correct, but it is not obvious in Plutarch's words.

That M. Porcius Cato, the unbending opposer of popular measures and keeper of the senate's conscience, should have promoted a measure extending the corn distributions, however it was achieved, is sufficiently surprising to demand an explanation of how it came about. The senate was still unable to put an end to the pirate threat despite sending out Q. Metellus in 68 B.C. after the death of M. Antonius.[48] Ostia itself was plundered by pirates in 67 B.C. The result was that, despite senatorial opposition, the whole problem was removed from their hands by a law in the *concilium plebis*, the *lex Gabinia* of 67 B.C., which gave supreme command to Pompey. He cleared the Mediterranean of pirates in three months. Then in 63 B.C. came the conspiracy of Catiline who exploited the very real social grievances in Rome and Italy in the furtherance of his own aims. It was vital in 62 B.C., with Catiline still in arms, for the senate to show itself effectively concerned for the welfare of the poor and the landless.[49] Cato by his measure in some way increased the number of such men to be eligible for the distribution of corn rations in Rome.

4

Plutarch adds some figures of cost for Cato's action in 62 B.C. and these together with the figures given by Cicero for the cost entailed in Clodius' abolition of all charges for corn rations in 58 B.C. add a new element of complication and temptation to our problems. The temptation lies in trying to use the figures of cost to deduce the numbers of recipients in the corn distributions. The complication lies in the fact that the evidence is ambiguous in itself, and difficult to use since we do not really know the prices of grain on the Roman market at this period. In Plutarch's

[47] Dio 39. 24; Dion. Halic. 4. 24. 5; Suet. *Aug.* 42. 2.

[48] See above, p. 51.

[49] Sall. *Cat.* 37; cf. Cicero, *De Off.* 2. 58–9; Gruen, *Last Generation*, pp. 36 and 386.

life of Cato it is stated that after Cato's proposal the annual expenditure for the distribution of grain was 1,250 T; in his life of Caesar it is said that Cato added an annual outlay of 7,500,000 drachmas to the other expenditures of the state, although there is a variant reading in the manuscripts which gives 5,500,000 drachmas.[50] In fact, 1,250 T and 7,500,000 drachmas both represent the same amount of money in Roman terms, namely, 30 million sesterces, which cannot be both the total expenditure on grain distribution, and the additional cost created by Cato's measure.

Tenney Frank takes it to be the total cost of the corn distribution after Cato's measure, and by assuming that the corn cost the state 4 sesterces a *modius* and was sold for $1\frac{1}{2}$ sesterces (the Gracchan price), comes to the conclusion that the number of recipients had grown to about 200,000.[51]

He then takes the passage in Plutarch's *Life of Pompey*[52] about Pompey's increase in the revenue of the public treasury to mean that the revenue rose from 200 million sesterces to 340 million sesterces, or a little less. This would mean that Cicero's claim that Clodius' abolition of the charge for the corn distributions cost above one-fifth of Rome's revenues,[53] if it is not mere rhetoric, could be quantified at just over 64 million sesterces, which would have fed 266,000 men a ration of 5 *modii* a month at a cost to the state of 4 sesterces a *modius*.

But there are many assumptions in all this, and perhaps some positive errors. It seems likely that Pompey increased the public revenue from 200 million sesterces to 540 million sesterces—or at least that seems to be the proper meaning of the passage in Plutarch.[54] In that case a fifth of Rome's revenue would be not some 64 million sesterces but 108 million sesterces. Moreover the 30 million sesterces in the Cato passage may be only the additional cost of his measure. It may also be wrong to assume a continuing cost to the state at the rate of 4 sesterces a *modius* in this period. The period saw severe and persistent corn shortages and the price may have fluctuated unpredictably, and averaged out at a higher rate.

The whole thing becomes a game with only one dangerous result, the delusion of certainty. But the temptation to play is

[50] Plut. *Cat. Min.* 26. 1; *Caesar* 8. 6.
[51] Frank, *ESAR* i. 329–30.
[52] Plut. *Pomp.* 45.
[53] Cic. *Pro Sestio* 55.
[54] Cf. Badian, *Imperialism*², p. 78.

irresistible, given a natural reluctance to let slip a shred of numerical evidence, and one interesting result can, I think, be established irrespective of the accuracy of the figures.

Let us assume that at this time of crisis the cost to the state was 6 sesterces for every *modius* used in the distributions, and that in the period from the *lex Terentia–Cassia* until Clodius abolished it the charge to each recipient was 1½ sesterces per *modius*, but that after that date the state received no payment to offset the cost. For the 40,000 recipients believed to have been eligible under the *lex Terentia–Cassia* the total cost would have been nearly 11 million sesterces. Cato's measure in 62 B.C. on any reckoning of the inadequate evidence cost at least 30 million sesterces. On the assumptions we are making, if that was the total cost then the number of recipients must have risen to over 100,000; if it was merely the extra cost then the number of recipients would have risen to about 150,000. So far as Clodius is concerned, if Cicero was claiming in 56 B.C. that the total cost of the corn distributions took about a fifth of Rome's revenue, and if that is accurately quantified at 108 million sesterces, then on our set of assumptions the number of recipients would have risen to 300,000.

Even if these figures are inaccurate in themselves, as they may well be, two points stand out. The first is the jump in the number of recipients in 62 B.C., and the second is the jump in 58 B.C. The latter has been often commented upon, and there is evidence in the literary sources that the numbers of corn recipients did grow after Clodius, which must be discussed later.[55] The former has not so often been emphasized. The rise in the number of recipients may have been bigger or smaller than in my hypothetical figures (depending on whether the cost to the state per *modius* was lower or higher than the 6 sesterces per *modius* which is postulated), but it is there. Even if the price to the state was 8 sesterces a *modius* and the 30 million sesterces was the cost of the total corn distribution after Cato's law, the number of recipients must have been virtually doubled by his measure. This means that Cato, perhaps surprisingly, should have a greater place in the history of the corn distributions than he is normally accorded, even if it was not so sensational as that of Clodius.

[55] See below, p. 173.

Certainly four years after Cato's law P. Clodius, shortly after entering upon office as tribune for 58 B.C., passed his *lex frumentaria*, which abolished the charge of $6\frac{1}{3}$ *asses* per *modius* for the rations issued in the distributions.[56] Despite Cicero's claim that this took one-fifth of Rome's revenues, Clodius was not recklessly adding to the burdens of the treasury without seeking compensation elsewhere. The annexation of Cyprus in 58 B.C. and the selling up of the royal property there was precisely parallel to the reorganization of the finances of Asia by Gaius Gracchus in 123/2 B.C. or the exploitation of the Cyrene bequest by the senate in 75/4 B.C. to help pay for their measures, with the added irony that the man who was deputed to go to Cyprus was none other than Cato.[57] But Clodius had changed the situation more fundamentally than anyone before him and perhaps more dramatically than he himself realized. The right of the citizens, domiciled in the capital, to a monthly ration of grain, first established by Gaius Gracchus, had survived political challenge, and was now freed from previous limitations and from all cost to the recipient. It remained to be seen whether it was a practicable proposition under the new conditions.

5

Before we investigate the practical problems which beset the later distributions of free grain, certain basic points about the corn distributions in this early period of their existence in Rome must be emphasized.

First, whatever else they may have been, they were not a dole for the poor. Even if and when there were limitations set in eligibility, the criterion does not seem to have involved poverty or special need. That of course is not to deny that it was the poor among the recipients who benefited most.

Secondly, it seems wrong to see the first fifty years of the corn distributions as simply a struggle between reforming tribunes who wished to extend the distributions and the senate and its adherents who wanted to restrict them. All elements involved in the political struggles of the late Republic became

[56] Ascon. *In Pison*, p. 8 (ed. Clark); Schol. Bobb., p. 132 (ed. Stangl).

[57] Cf. Badian, *Imperialism*², pp. 47–9; S. I. Oost, 'Cato Uticensis and the Annexation of Cyprus', *CP* 50 (1955), 98–112.

entangled in the problem of the distributions, and the line taken by each of them was likely to be governed by what was to their political advantage, and the positions being taken up by their political opponents at that moment.

Thirdly, a ration of 5 *modii*, which is the only size for which we have any evidence, compares well with other evidence we have of monthly allowances of food for an individual in the ancient world. Its dietetic value has been calculated at about 3,000–4,000 calories per day, a range which is not very different from modern ideals of about 3,300 calories per day for male adults.[58] It would certainly have helped to feed some members of a man's family, but it was never in itself the whole answer even to the feeding of an individual. A man still had to find the costs of milling and baking his ration of grain as well as the means of buying vegetables, wine and other items to go with his bread.

(b) *Pompey, Julius Caesar, and Augustus*

I

It is uncertain how far Clodius' law caused the corn crisis which led to the appointment of Pompey to a special *cura annonae* in September 57 B.C. Poor harvests and other difficulties could at any time create problems, not to be overridden by the mere taking of political decisions in Rome. But Clodius' law may itself be partly to blame, if Cicero is right in claiming that everything to do with both public and private corn, namely the corn lands, the contractors and the corn stores, was put into the hands of Clodius' agent, Sextus Cloelius.[59] The corn dealers may have been alarmed at the sweeping powers which Cloelius appeared to have to interfere in their affairs and were reluctant to bring their cargoes to Rome. For the procurement of corn Pompey had to build up patiently through his *legati* relationships of trust with corn merchants in order to give continuity and confidence to the supply of corn to Rome.

What is not in doubt however is that with the abolition of the charge for rations issued at the distributions, the drift of

[58] Duncan-Jones, *ERE*, pp. 146–7; cf. V. H. Mottram and G. Graham, *Hutchison's Food and the Principles of Dietetics*, 11th edn., pp. 48 and 53. Duncan-Jones, *Chiron* 6 (1976), 241–2.

[59] See above, p. 52.

rural poor into Rome and the rate of manumission within Rome both increased dramatically.[60] The former was of course not a new phenomenon in itself; it had been a fact of life, according to Sallust, even before 63 B.C.[61] But there can be little doubt that the process was speeded up by Clodius' law. The main bulk of the literary evidence stresses the drift from the countryside after the abolition of the charge.[62] The latter was directly linked with the distributions of free corn and was if anything to cause the greater problems.

The scholiast on a line of Persius (V. 73) remarked 'At Rome it was the custom that all who on manumission became Roman citizens should receive public grain in their number.' That this is correct for the end of the first century B.C. is proved by Dionysius of Halicarnassus who remarked from his own experience in the 20s B.C. that Roman masters liberated slaves precisely so that they would become eligible for the corn distributions and other largesses.[63] The point was that the masters could bind the slaves so freed, at the moment of manumission, still to render various services and a certain number of days' labour. In essence, by manumitting slave-craftsmen the master retained the surplus of their productivity while shifting part of the burden of their maintenance onto the state because as freedmen they could obtain free grain each month.[64] It would be surprising if this trick had not been learned earlier than the time of Dionysius of Halicarnassus, and there is proof that it went back at least to the mid-50s B.C. in a passage where Dio describes the work of Pompey during his *cura annonae* in 56 B.C.[65] It seems likely that the process had been set off two years earlier when Clodius' agent, Sextus Cloelius, had perhaps admitted claimants to public corn on a most liberal scale.[66]

What Pompey did in 56 B.C. is not exactly clear. Dio says: 'Pompey encountered some delay in the distribution of grain. For since many slaves had been freed in anticipation of the event, he wished to take a census of them in order that the

[60] P. A. Brunt, 'The Roman Mob', *Past and Present* 35 (1966), 1–27, esp. p. 17.
[61] Sallust, *Cat.* 37. 4–7.
[62] Varro, *R. R.* 2 pr. 3; Appian, *B. C.* 2. 120; Suet. *Aug.* 42. 3.
[63] Dion. Halic. *Antiq.* 4. 24. 5, cf. Suet. *Aug.* 42. 2.
[64] Brunt, *Italian Manpower*, p. 380.
[65] Dio 39. 24.
[66] Cic. *De Dom.* 25.

grain might be supplied to them with some order and system.' It has been argued that there may be some confusion here;[67] that what Pompey was concerned with was not just a list of the newly manumitted who were entitled to rations, but with a list of all recipients; in short that he anticipated the work of creating proper lists for the corn distributions first clearly attested for Julius Caesar. This seems to me still doubtful, even though Pompey so often in other areas seems to foreshadow later developments associated with Julius Caesar or the early Principate. The essence of the problem for Pompey in 56 B.C. was more limited. Among the swollen numbers at the distributions were newly manumitted men, who had been receiving public corn under Cloelius, but who would not be registered as Roman citizens until the census in 55–54 B.C. He could not refuse them admission to the distributions outright without causing an uproar, but since they were as yet unregistered there was no means of checking their eligibility. For these men registration of some kind was needed to control a situation which was otherwise in danger of getting out of hand. This registration Pompey duly organized. This of course is to assume, as seems to me likely, that the ordinary census lists had been used in some way to administer the corn distributions during the early part of their history. If limits had been set on numbers in the first century B.C., lists of some kind must already have been in use. Pompey by his action may have shown that it was possible and necessary to create *ad hoc* supplements to the lists for corn distributions, but he did not, I think, either institute the use of lists for the first time or alter the principles on which they were drawn up. Certainly he did not carry out a general *recensus*, district by district, in Rome of the special kind instituted by Julius Caesar in 46 B.C.

2

Whatever may have been achieved by Pompey, it was hardly possible that order and system should have prevailed untroubled in the following decade which saw constitutional crisis and civil war between him and Caesar. By 46 B.C. the

[67] Van Berchem, *Distributions*, p. 20. Cf. C. Nicolet, 'Le Temple des Nymphes et les distributions frumentaires à Rome', *CRAI* (1976), pp. 44–8.

number of recipients was supposed to have risen to 320,000. The number is perhaps a little suspicious in that it is exactly that of the largest number of men ever to receive donations from Augustus later. But there can be little doubt that the number had risen dramatically to a level that Julius Caesar regarded as unacceptable and which he cut down to 150,000.[68]

There are basically two questions about Julius Caesar's pruning of the *frumentationes*. The first is how was it achieved at the time in 46 B.C.; the second is how was the number to be kept at the same level in the future.

In answer to the first question there is no problem about the actual mechanics whereby Caesar constructed a new and accurate list. A *recensus*, not to be confused with the ordinary census, was conducted in a new and unusual way, district by district (*vicatim*) in Rome, through the agency of the *domini insularum*, the blocks of flats which comprised so large a part of the city area. What is more difficult to understand is the gigantic drop from 320,000 recipients to 150,000, which is guaranteed by a number of sources. In order to account for it some scholars in the past have been tempted to suggest that in addition to the basic criteria of citizen rights and domicile in Rome, a new condition, that of poverty or need, had been added. Thus, it is suggested, from the time of Julius Caesar the distributions firmly assumed the character of a dole, a welfare scheme for the poor. This idea must be rejected. Van Berchem has shown that the evidence not only reveals no trace of any means test applied to the recipients, but positively proves that there can have been none.[69] Dio seems to suggest that the real problem lay in the numbers illegitimately enrolled in the lists because of the disturbed times.[70] In that case many must have been struck off the list because they were not really both full Roman citizens and properly resident in Rome. In this way informally manumitted slaves, foreigners, and even perhaps transient citizens were all deprived of corn rations. The total size of the population was also reduced by including *proletarii* among the 80,000 sent away to overseas colonies.[71]

[68] Suet. *Caesar* 41. 3, cf. *R. G.* 15; Plut. *Caes.* 55. 3; Dio 43. 21. 4.
[69] Rostovtzeff, *Frumentum*, col. 175; cf. Van Berchem, *Distributions*, p. 22.
[70] Brunt, *Italian Manpower*, p. 381; Dio 43. 21. 4.
[71] Suet. *Caesar* 42. 1; cf. Brunt, *Italian Manpower*, pp. 255–9.

The answer to the second question seems relatively straightforward, but is in fact unsatisfactorily vague when examined in detail. Clearly the number 150,000 was to be a fixed, closed limit for the distributions. Suetonius says that each year there was to be a drawing of lots (*subsortitio*) by the praetor to replace those who had died ('in demortuum locum') from among those not on the list.[72] But this does not tell us how precisely the system of *subsortitio* actually worked, or was meant to work.

Traditionally help in illuminating the details has been sought by studying the great bronze inscription known as the Table of Heraclea.[73] Unfortunately instead of illumination there has been greater confusion. The exact nature of the document contained in the Table of Heraclea has defied analysis, and the meaning of the provisions at the beginning of it, and their relation to the action of Caesar on the *frumentationes*, has remained obscure. I have come to the view that it is irrelevant to the process of *subsortitio*, and only incidental to the ordinary working of the corn distributions under Caesar.[74]

A much more satisfactory example of the practical working of a process of *subsortitio*, admittedly at a much later period and away from Rome, has recently been discovered, at Oxyrhynchus in Egypt. Among the continuing stream of papyri from this place an archive relating to a corn dole has been isolated by Dr. J. Rea.[75] The documents reveal that corn was distributed in Oxyrhynchus in the reigns of Claudius II and Aurelian in the second half of the third century A.D. They include fragments of registers of those eligible to receive the corn, which is regarded as the gift of the Emperor, but by far the greatest number are applications from individuals for admission to the distributions.

These applications are extraordinarily vivid documents, and it is worth quoting one in full:[76]

[1st hand] To Aurelius Plution, secretary of the corn dole (*grammateus siteresiou*), from Aurelius Agathus Daemon, son of Areius, grandson of Sarapion, mother Senpsois, from the glorious city of the Oxyrhynchites. Being an Oxyrhynchite, scrutinized (*epikritheis*) in the Thoëris Street quarter and

[72] Suet. *Caes.* 41.

[73] *FIRA* i, no. 13, 1 ff. = *ILS* 6085. Cf. Cardinali, *Frumentatio*, pp. 266–8.

[74] See below, Appendix 7.

[75] *Oxyrhynchus Papyri* xl (London, 1972). Cf. J.-M. Carrié, 'Les distributions alimentaires dans les cités de l'Empire romain tardif', *MEFR* (1975), 2. 995–1101.

[76] *P. Oxy.* 2892 (A.D. 269).

twenty years old in the present second year, I enter myself as a result of the draw in place of Antiochus, son of Antiochus alias Diogenes, grandson of Antiochus, mother Theodora, of the same quarter, deceased, and I ask, having shown myself a citizen, to receive my share of the distribution of the corn dole. Year 2 of Imperator Caesar Marcus Aurelius Claudius Pius Felix Augustus. Thoth 27. [2nd hand] I, Aurelius Agathus Daemon, son of Areius submitted [the petition]. I, Aurelius Apollonius, wrote for him because he does not know letters. [3rd hand] Aurelius Serenus, scrutineer (*epikrites*): This is the person scrutinized, who also answered when his name was proclaimed.

Then follow in three more hands three more witnesses to the man's identity, and finally: '[7th hand] He has been enrolled. Second Year, Phaophi. [8th hand] Thoëris Street.'

In some of the applications a more elaborate formula is used, for example:

Being listed in the Gymnasium street quarter, scrutinized in the 11th year and twenty years old in the present second year, and in the last draw in accordance with the decrees of the most excellent council having obtained the succession to a place which had fallen vacant I enter myself in place of Theon, son of . . .[77]

There are also a series of applications addressed, not to the secretary of the corn dole, but to the *hypomnematographus*, which had unusual aspects or complications, for example:

Having reached the age of maturity and been scrutinized in the Myrobalanus quarter and having been enrolled in the individual lists submitted by the phylarch for the imperial corn dole, when I took my place at the examination I was unable to produce proofs of my descent; now necessarily producing my certificate of scrutiny and the proofs of my descent, I submit this application . . .

or 'Although I was scrutinized in the Cretan quarter in the fourth year . . . of the reign of [Severus] Alexander, because I was away from home I was also mistakenly passed over by the phylarch.'[78]

We do not know whether the system reflected in these documents was based directly on that of contemporary Rome, or on that of other Egyptian communities such as Antinoopolis a century earlier.[79] But the documents illustrate in living detail what a process of *subsortitio*, such as that introduced by Caesar,

[77] *P. Oxy.* 2894 (A.D. 270).

[78] *P. Oxy.* 2898 (A.D. 270/1); 2899.

[79] See below, Appendix 8; cf. Review of *Oxyrhynchus Papyri* xl by Cl. Préaux *Chronique d'Égypte* 48 (1973), 382–9.

entailed in real terms. What is also quite certain is that with the introduction of a fixed number of recipients, which was to remain fixed for the future by a process of *subsortitio* for the places of those who died, Caesar established a limitation once again on the numbers eligible for corn distributions at Rome. Even if 150,000 was the exact number of full Roman citizens domiciled in Rome at the time of his dictatorship, it was unlikely that this would remain true for long, in which case a distinction would have been created by the system between citizenship with *frumentum* and citizenship without it.[80]

3

What Caesar's intentions were in this field as in so many others remains in doubt because of his assassination, but his system anyway did not survive his death. The maximum number of recipients which he set was not surprisingly ignored in the turmoil. Already in 44 B.C. the young Octavian made gifts of grain and money to 250,000 or more members of the *plebs*. Private generosity on this scale remained a possibility throughout Augustus' reign. In 23 B.C. he provided grain for twelve *frumentationes*, in 18 B.C. and thereafter he distributed grain to 100,000 people and more, and in A.D. 6 he gave to the poor as much grain again as they received from the state.[81] But the constitutional settlement in 27 B.C. marked a return to the framework at least of Republican institutions, and a facade of normality. When therefore in 22 B.C. the grain crisis of 23 proved to be more than a temporary matter, and led to demands that Augustus become dictator, he refused and would accept only the *cura annonae*. For that there was a Republican precedent in the grant to Pompey in 57 B.C., and it allowed the possibility of dealing with both the procurement of corn and its distribution.[82] Augustus not only relieved the particular crisis, but used the opportunity to create new administrative machinery for the running of the distributions. Interestingly, Republican forms were followed punctiliously, and little open acknowledgement of Augustus' continuing and permanent responsibility for the corn supply of Rome was made. It was to be thirty years

[80] Van Berchem, *Distributions*, p. 26.
[81] *Res Gestae* 15; Dio 55. 26.
[82] See above, p. 55.

before the link between the Emperor and the regular procurement of Rome's corn was to be publicly advertised by the creation of the *praefectus annonae*, even though it was a well known fact. If the *cura annonae* could in some sense be regarded as an alternative to the dictatorship, it is not surprising that in 22 B.C. Augustus walked with extreme political caution.

It was thoroughly in line with Republican precedent that Augustus, in accordance with a decree of the senate, established in 22 B.C. a commission of ex-praetors, selected by lot, to supervise the distributions in the capital.[83] We know from Asconius that in 66 B.C. the praetor P. Cassius was absent from the *maiestas* court and one of the possible reasons given for his absence was that he had been called away 'propter publici frumenti curam.'[84] Even under Caesar although special *aediles Ceriales* were created, the care of the lists and organizing of the *subsortitio* was entrusted to a *praetor*.[85] Originally the Augustan scheme was that two such men were chosen annually from among those who had served as praetors not less than five years previously. Later in 18 B.C. it was enacted that for the distribution of grain, one candidate, who must have served as praetor three years previously, should be nominated each year by each of the magistrates then serving, and that from these nominees four men should be chosen by lot to serve in succession as distributors of grain.[86] What these new officials were called we do not know. Suetonius simply names among the new offices established by Augustus the 'curam . . . frumenti populo dividundi.' In a *senatus consultum* of 10 B.C. quoted in Frontinus' work on the aqueducts written at the end of the first century A.D., they are referred to in various ways, as 'ii per quos frumentum plebei datur' or as 'praefecti frumento dando' or as 'curatores frumenti'.[87] At some point during the latter part of the reign of Augustus they received the title by which they were later known, 'praefecti frumenti dandi ex s. c.'.

Whatever the new organization, the numbers attending the distributions continued to grow until in 5 B.C. they reached 320,000, and Augustus called a halt. Whether it was at this

[83] Dio 54. 1. 4. [84] Asconius 59 c.

[85] Suet. *Caes.* 41. [86] Dio 54. 17.

[87] Suet. *Aug.* 37; Fronto, *De Aqu.* 100; cf. *CIL* 6. 1460 = *ILS* 887 '*frumenti curator ex s. c.*'; *CIL* 6. 1480 = *ILS* 907 '*cur(ator) fru(menti)*'.

time that he contemplated a complete abolition of the distributions or a rearrangement whereby rations would be issued only three times in a year, both of which he ultimately rejected, we do not know. Certainly in 2 B.C., like Caesar in 46 B.C., he instituted a *recensus*, district by district, throughout Rome to construct a proper list and to prune the number of recipients.[88] Did he also revert to the idea of a fixed number of recipients and a system whereby there could be no admissions except when there were vacancies in the lists? The evidence suggests that he did. According to Dio 'Augustus closed the number of the *plebs frumentaria*, which had been unlimited, at 200,000', and Augustus himself says (*R. G.* 15), 'In my 13th consulship [2 B.C.] I gave 60 denarii apiece to the plebs who were at that time in receipt of public grain; they comprised a few more than 200,000 persons.' A numerical limit seems to have been in operation at the end of the first century A.D. when Pliny the Younger in his Panegyricus (§ 25) praised Trajan for extending his *congiarium* in A.D. 99 'to people substituted in place of those whose names had been erased, and even to those to whom it had not been promised'. What the exact limit was is not quite clear, despite Dio. Augustus' own reference to his actions in 2 B.C. is curiously guarded and imprecise ('the plebs *at that time* in receipt of public grain . . . *a few more* than 200,000') if the number 200,000 was the exact target. It may well be that he, like Caesar, was working his way towards fixing not 200,000, but 150,000, as the limit. Certainly the legacies of Augustus himself in A.D. 14 and of Tiberius in A.D. 37 were both distributed to 150,000 people.[89] If 150,000 was the total which was fixed in the early Empire, but which on occasion the Emperor by his generosity might exceed, this helps to explain how in A.D. 202 in the reign of Septimius Severus there might still be only about 200,000 recipients, despite the considerable extension of the right to public corn from the time of Nero, first to the Praetorian guard, then to the Vigiles, and possibly to the Urban cohorts and others.[90]

Van Berchem, however, in the single most influential modern study of the distributions argued against the view that

[88] *R. G.* 15; Dio 55. 10. 1. Suet. *Aug.* 40; 42. 3.
[89] Suet. *Aug.* 101; Tac. *Ann.* 1; Dio 57. 14. 2; Suet. *Tib.* 76.
[90] Dio 76. 1. 1; see below, p. 188.

Augustus set a fixed limit to the number of recipients.[91] He believed that the evidence was not strong enough to justify such a view. Control was achieved instead by Augustus tightening the conditions for admission to the distributions. Traditionally there were two basic conditions, and to them Augustus, so Van Berchem argued, added a third.

Clearly full citizenship was an absolute essential, as it always had been, although in practice and perhaps in law, senators and *equites* were excluded from the time of Augustus, if not earlier.[92] Otherwise there seems to have been no objection to any citizen even on moral grounds. Seneca in the mid-first century A.D. says:

> the thief no less than the perjurer and the adulterer and everyone, without distinction of character, whose name appears on the register (*incisus*) receives grain from the state; whatever else a man may be, he gets that, not because he is good, but because he is a citizen, and the good and the bad share alike.[93]

In practice too residence in Rome was a necessary condition of admissibility. *Frumentum publicum* was available only to Roman citizens at Rome. The careful registration on lists district by district under Caesar and Augustus had established those citizens who were domiciled in Rome at that time. *Domicilium* was a precisely defined legal notion and anyone moving to Rome, who wished to, had to establish it by registration with the public magistrates.[94] But for control of the numbers of corn recipients *domicilium* was not enough, since Roman citizens could move to Rome, and the *frumentationes* had caused many of them to do just that in the late Republic.

This led Van Berchem to develop his elegant and inventive thesis that one of the conditions for admission from the time of Augustus was not mere *domicilium* in Rome but Roman *origo*.[95] His argument ran as follows: with the development of the municipal system in Italy in the first century B.C. there developed the notion of a dual *patria*; that of one's own *municipium*, in which one was born, in which one had one's

[91] Van Berchem, *Distributions*, p. 28.

[92] Cf. the use of words like '*plebs*' in *Res Gestae*, '*homilos*' and '*ochlos*' in Dio: also *Dig*. 32. 35 pr.

[93] Seneca, *De Benef*. 4. 28. 2.

[94] Cf. Cicero, *Pro Archia* 4. 9.

[95] Van Berchem, *Distributions*, pp. 34–45.

origo, and secondly that of Rome, of which community one was a member in a rather different way. On inscriptions the *origo* of these municipal Roman citizens was indicated by the name of the town in the ablative, sometimes preceded by the word 'domo'. But in its turn too Rome could be an *origo*, since on many inscriptions the words 'domo Roma' actually appear and a passage in the Digest (50. 4. 3 pr. Ulpian) refers to those 'qui originem ab urbe Roma habent'.

It was Van Berchem's contention that Roman *origo* was much prized not least because it gave the right to *frumentum publicum*, and by this mechanism the total number of recipients was held down during the early Empire. He claimed support for his theory from a slender series of inscriptions of largely unknown date but which seem to belong to the first two centuries of the Empire and which mention the fact that the person concerned was in receipt of public corn. These inscriptions concern children, a freedman, a veteran of the praetorian guard, some members of the *vigiles*, and even a woman.[96] Van Berchem claimed that the mention of *frumentum publicum* as a right was in order to prove beyond doubt to the reader their right to Roman citizenship and Roman *origo*; that each was a *civis Romanus domo Roma* (or would have become so) when otherwise that might not be clear.

This theory has difficulties. First, it is not clear how as a mechanism it could have controlled numbers, since the second generation of people whose parents had moved to Rome would presumably become eligible for the distributions. Secondly, while it might be true that the few inscriptions are concerned to stress privileged Roman citizen status, they need not be concerned to stress Roman *origo*. In only one of the inscriptions which mention *frumentum publicum* do the words 'domo Roma' occur. It is unfortunate for Van Berchem that it is also the most peculiar and untypical of the inscriptions, concerning as it does a woman, Mallia Aemiliana, who was living at the time in Moesia in the Balkans.[97] Her desire to show her provincial neighbours that she had a Roman *origo* is both understandable and traditional; she did it by using the technical phrase 'domo Roma', not simply by reference to the *frumentum publicum*. It is

[96] *CIL* 6. 10217–28 = *ILS* 6060–6.
[97] *ILS* 9275.

just as possible that the inscriptions were concerned to stress a privilege, namely right to public corn, which was not necessarily shared by all even of the citizen body. Indeed in relation to the children it must be the latter. Normally children below the age of eleven, or possibly fourteen years, were not eligible until the time of Trajan when a specified number of boys, 5,000 of them, were first admitted as a special act of grace and favour.[98] In one of the inscriptions it is said of Q. Terentius Priscianus who only lived four years and seven months that he received *frumentum publicum* for precisely nine months. Similarly the inscription of Sextia Saturnina who only lived to her seventh year stresses a special privilege when she is described as 'inc(isa) fr(umento) publ(ico) Div(ae) Faust(inae) Iunior(is)'.[99] Antoninus Pius had created an order of 'puellae Faustinianae' in memory of his wife. Marcus Aurelius, who created orders of children of either sex who would receive corn as a celebration of the marriage of Lucius Verus and Lucilla, also set up 'novae puellae Faustinianae' in memory of Faustina the younger. Sextia Saturnina was one of the beneficiaries of this special fund.[100]

Thirdly, there is a certain circularity in Van Berchem's argument: a man had to have Roman *origo* in order to qualify for public corn, and yet to have it conferred, or confirmed, a man had to be enrolled in the *recensus* for the distributions.

In the light of all this it seems more sensible to believe that there was, from the latter part of Augustus' reign, a fixed number of recipients, whether 200,000 or 150,000, and that Van Berchem's theory about Roman *origo* as one of the conditions for enrolment should be set aside. But while that may be true, Van Berchem was right to stress that what Augustus was aiming at from 2 B.C. was not just a limitation of numbers of corn recipients, but a Roman citizen body of improved tone and quality. Possibly the first of Augustus' pieces of legislation on manumission, the *Lex Fufia Caninia*, was passed in 2 B.C. and the timing is significant.[101] The aim of the manumission laws was to limit manumission to the deserving, and they would

[98] Suet. *Aug.* 41, but see *Oxy. Pap.* xl, p. 13 (Rea); Pliny, *Paneg.* 26–8.
[99] *CIL* 6. 10227 = *ILS* 6067 (Priscianus); *CIL* 6. 10222 = *ILS* 6065 (Saturnina).
[100] SHA *Pius* 8. 1; *Marc.* 7. 8; 26. 6.
[101] A. N. Sherwin White, *The Roman Citizenship*² (Oxford, 1973), pp. 331–4.

affect not least the population of the capital itself. The *plebs frumentaria* was to be restricted in size within a citizen body which itself had acquired a new lustre.[102] Since we hear of no outcry at the unfairness of Augustus' actions, it seems possible that the number fixed may at the time have encompassed all properly qualified recipients. Perhaps, although this is speculative, only gradually did there emerge within the capital a citizenship without *frumentum* which would seem to us to be a corollary of fixing the number of recipients. Certainly Fronto in the early second century A.D. speaks in terms that suggest that by his day there was a distinction between *plebs Romana* and *plebs frumentaria.*[103] But under Augustus that stage may still have been in the future. In the food crisis in A.D. 6 it is noticeable that in the attempt to reduce the numbers to be fed, gladiators and slaves for sale were banished to 100 miles and all foreigners, except doctors and teachers, were expelled.[104] The citizen body in Rome then seems to have been the *plebs frumentaria*, and was to be protected at all costs.

4

How precisely the corn was distributed to this *plebs frumentaria* is not clear. There still seems to be no single centre for the distributions of corn under Pompey, Caesar, or Augustus. No name or location of a distributing centre is preserved in the sources and the very fact that in the Table of Heraclea the list of persons with which the first part of that document is concerned is to be posted 'at the Forum and when corn is to be given to the people, there where it is to be given' indicates that there was no single issuing source.[105] We must imagine distributions at *horrea* or perhaps at some convenient *porticus*, not consistently perhaps at the same time and in the same places, but monthly on a predetermined day, at indicated locations, and, in my opinion, to all the recipients simultaneously.[106] From the reign of

[102] Suet. *Aug.* 40, 44; Van Berchem, *Distributions*, p. 61.

[103] Fronto, 210 N. Cf. also *ILS* 6045 which seems to imply that *plebs frumentaria* and the thirty-five tribes were not coextensive under Vespasian.

[104] Dio 55. 26. 1–3.

[105] *FIRA* i, no. 13. 16. = *ILS* 6085.

[106] Cf. Philo, *Leg. ad Gaium* 23 (= 158). It must be admitted that the meaning of this passage is not wholly clear.

Augustus at least, if not earlier, there was a system of tickets called *tesserae* which entitled the holders to their rations of corn. Originally they seem to have been like the traditional tickets used in the Roman world in the distribution of gifts to the public at games, although it has been argued that they were later changed in both shape and function.[107]

But if little progress had been made towards centralizing the distributions, the period from the mid-50s B.C. to A.D. 14 had nevertheless seen many significant developments. Pompey in 56 B.C. had been perplexed by the need for accurate and up to date lists of corn recipients; Caesar in 46 B.C. and Augustus in 2 B.C. resorted to a new method of establishing accuracy in a *recensus* taken district by district throughout Rome. The rate of manumission which had increased after Clodius' law in 58 B.C., and had helped to create swollen numbers of corn recipients, was brought under control again by Augustus. The numbers themselves which had reached unacceptable proportions were controlled by fixed limits set first by Caesar and later probably by Augustus too. The administrative machinery was increased first by the creation of *aediles Ceriales* under Caesar and then by Augustus hiving off the work of the distributions under a new board of ex-praetors. Above all one man had taken permanent responsibility for all problems concerning the corn supply. Pompey's *cura annonae* in 57 B.C. had been granted for only a limited period; the appointment of an imperial *praefectus annonae* some time between A.D. 8 and 14 was to be a permanent feature of the system.[108] Political tact may have prevented Augustus from taking on the *cura annonae* permanently in 22 B.C.; it may have delayed the creation of the *praefectus annonae* until almost the last moment of his reign, but in the end the appointment by the Emperor of a deputy to be responsible for the corn supply spelled out what the population of Rome had known for more than thirty years, namely, that it was the Emperor who ensured that they were fed.[109] Nevertheless even now there was need for care. The new *praefectus* was merely to exercise a *cura*. There was new state machinery for running the distributions and there was a free private market. Imperial responsibility did not yet mean constant imperial interference.

[107] Suet. *Aug.* 40; see below, Appendix 8.

[108] See above, p. 63.

[109] Cf. H. Kloft, *Liberalitas Principis* (Cologne, 1970), p. 96 and n. 54.

(c) *The Early Empire*

I

Distributions of free grain were to remain a fact of life for the capital and part of its regular rhythm from Tiberius to Aurelian, when in the third century A.D. the distributions still continued but grain was replaced by baked bread.[110] In those two and a half centuries we know of only one occasion when the distributions were abandoned on imperial order and that was in the reign of Nero. We know little about this hiatus or the reasons for it. In the brief epitome of Dio under the year A.D. 64 we are told simply that after the fire of Rome Nero deprived the Romans themselves of the distribution of *frumentum publicum.*[111] The date and the historical context, a fire which totally destroyed three regions and severely damaged seven others, may help us to understand Nero's action. We know from Tacitus' *Annals* that Nero also energetically brought provisions into Rome from Ostia and reduced the price of corn to 3 sesterces a *modius.*[112] Van Berchem rightly suggested that this all hangs together and makes sense as a series of measures for the benefit of the whole population rather than a limited section of it, in order to overcome a very severe but temporary crisis. Van Berchem however is wrong to suggest that Nero as a matter of long-term policy was not interested in the special status of Roman citizens in the capital, but only in the population of the city as a whole.[113]

Van Berchem erected this theory on two literary passages, one in Suetonius' *Life of Nero* and the other in Tacitus' *Histories* and on a coin of Galba.[114] On Nero's death, according to Suetonius, the *plebs pilleata*, the citizens, rejoiced, while according to Tacitus the non-citizens, *plebs sordida*, mourned. Under the Flavians the *frumentationes* were working again and their revival can be traced to Galba, with his restoration of the Republic and the rights of citizens. For Galba issued a *denarius* with the legend 'Libertas P(opuli) R(omani)' and the image of the goddess was flanked by two ears of corn, the only attribution of this kind to the goddess Liberty.

[110] SHA *Aurelian* 35 and 47; Zosimus i. 61.
[111] Dio 62. 18. 5. [112] Tac. *Ann.* 15. 39.
[113] Van Berchem, *Distributions*, pp. 74–6.
[114] Suet. *Nero* 57; Tac. *Hist.* 1. 4; Mattingly and Sydenham, *RIC* i. 250.

This theory of Van Berchem's must be rejected. *Plebs sordida* is not a technical term for the non-citizen part of the population of the capital and the contrast which Tacitus is drawing in this passage is between the *clientes* of the great noble houses, and the unattached mass who mourned for Nero.[115] Similarly in Suetonius there is no contrast drawn between citizen and non-citizen; some citizens rejoiced at Nero's death, others put flowers on his grave. The coin of Galba is not to be interpreted as a narrow and cryptic message about restored *frumentationes* to which it makes no allusion, but broadly as reassurance that Liberty and Plenty will go hand in hand.[116] On the whole therefore it seems much more likely that the distributions were working again normally before Nero's death, once the initial chaos caused by the fire of A.D. 64 had been cleared up. We have inscriptional proof that they were functioning again under the Emperor Titus,[117] and there is no reason to believe that any Emperor after Augustus seriously considered abolishing them permanently.

2

The necessary conditions to qualify for admission to the distributions under the early Empire remained full citizenship, properly registered domicile in the city, and a specified age, a minimum of eleven years, or possibly fourteen years of age. Gradually during the century after Augustus' death new categories of recipient seem to have been admitted to the *frumentum publicum*, although the evidence is tenuous. The praetorian guard in Rome was apparently admitted to the right by Nero in A.D. 65 and the Vigiles, after a period of service of three years, acquired both Roman citizenship and the right to *frumentum publicum*. The only clear evidence comes from the early third century A.D. but the grant may have been extended much earlier.[118] Other bodies within the capital such as the urban cohorts, and certain colleges of public servants, *apparitores*, such as the *tibicines* (flautists) and *aeneatores* (trumpeters) also seem to

[115] Z. Yavetz, *Plebs and Princeps* (Oxford, 1969), pp. 143–8.
[116] Mattingly, *BMCEmp.* i, Intro, p. cciv.
[117] *CIL* 6. 943 = *ILS* 6045.
[118] Suet. *Nero* 10; *CIL* 6. 220 and notes = *ILS* 2163.

have acquired the right at an unknown date.[119] The evidence is clearer in relation to the admission of children. The younger Pliny praises Trajan in A.D. 100 for his benevolence in enrolling 5,000 boys as special recipients of the corn rations.[120] It is clear that from this time there was a blurring of the division between the right to *frumentum publicum* and the welfare schemes of the *alimenta* for the support of minors. The *alimenta* schemes which had been set up in parts of Italy were to be paralleled in Rome itself by philanthropic arrangements for the feeding of at least some children.[121] Trajan's example was followed by other Emperors later in the second century A.D., such as Antoninus Pius and Marcus Aurelius, who created groups of both boys and girls who would receive corn as a charitable gesture and in memory or in celebration of some event in their reigns.[122] The numbers of these new additions, however, although significant, were not disproportionate, and the new recipients, even if kept in their own groups, appear to have been enrolled on the ordinary general lists for the *frumentationes*.[123]

What exactly these ordinary lists were like and how precisely enrolment was secured is by no means obvious. The conditions listed above were necessary but certainly not sufficient to secure admission, if it is granted that there was a fixed limit on the numbers throughout the history of the Empire. In normal circumstances a new admission was only possible when a vacancy in the list, caused by death or some other reason, had been properly verified and some enrolment procedure had been carried out by clerks. We know from a *senatus consultum* of 11 B.C. concerning water supplies recorded by Frontinus that the *praefecti frumenti dandi* had at their disposal numbers of *scribae*, secretaries, *librarii*, clerks, and *accensi*, assistants.[124] It was common practice to refer to those eligible for corn rations as *incisi*, 'those engraved', which implies that the lists were on bronze, and they may have been made up of sections and subsections known as *tabulae* and *capita*.[125] On what principle

[119] *CIL* 6. 2584; *CIL* 6. 10220 and 10221; cf. Cardinali, *Frumentatio*, p. 262.

[120] Pliny, *Paneg.* 26–8.

[121] Hands, *Charities*, pp. 107 ff.

[122] SHA *Pius* 8. 1; *Marc.* 7. 8; 26. 6; cf. Duncan-Jones, *ERE*, pp. 315 ff.

[123] Cf. Cardinali, *Frumentatio*, pp. 255–7.

[124] Frontinus, *De Aqu.* 100.

[125] For *incisi* see e.g. *CIL* 6. 220, 10228; cf. Seneca, *De Benef.* 4. 28. 2; *Cod. Theod.* 14. 17. 5 (A.D. 369); *tabulae* and *capita* depend on Mommsen's suggested expansion of T. and K. in *CIL* 6. 220.

the names were ordered in the lists, apart from the special military groups or orders of children, is not known. It is likely to have been either by tribe or by *vicus*.[126] There is much evidence of the importance of the tribe in the whole system of distribution and in the receiving of legacies from the Emperors, but it is possible that this prominence is owed to the need for citizenship and therefore tribal membership as the necessary condition of eligibility. There is an almost equally large amount of evidence for extraordinary largesse in the late Republic being distributed *vicatim* and for the drawing up of the lists of corn recipients by Caesar and Augustus through the aid of *domini insularum* and *vicomagistri*, but it is possible that the sheer mechanics of drawing up the lists are no clue as to the structure of the groupings of the recipients.[127] It may be that the confusing and conflicting nature of the evidence is best explained by supposing that with Augustus and his stress on the special status and dignity of Roman citizens within the polyglot capital there came a change from *vici* to grouping by tribe, which would stress yet again the importance of citizen status.[128] It is interesting, but not necessarily relevant, that the Oxyrhynchus corn dole seems to have been organized on a tribal basis.[129]

What we should particularly like to know is how a vacancy in the lists was secured by a particular applicant. Although Caesar's system of *subsortitio* may have continued into the early Principate, there is absolutely no evidence that it did so.[130] In relation to another public facility, namely the provision of water in the capital, we know that rights to public water, vacated by death or transfer of property, were immediately entered into the state records (*commentarii*) and then offered to applicants (*petitores*).[131] In this case, it is true, what was at issue was the purchase from the state of the right to a private water

[126] For organization by tribe, T. Mommsen, *Staatsrecht* iii. 444; cf. p. 195; Cardinali, *Frumentatio*, pp. 269–71. For organization by *Vici*, O. Hirschfeld, 'Die Getreideverwaltung in der römischen Kaiserzeit', *Philologus* 29 (1870), 13. Undecided, Rostovtzeff, *Frumentum*, col. 182.

[127] The evidence is best laid out in Cardinali's discussion.

[128] But see the special emphasis on *vicorum magistri* among the legatees of Tiberius, Suet. *Tib*. 76.

[129] Rea, *Oxyrhynchus Papyri*, xl. 14.

[130] Despite Rea's attempt to use the Oxyrhynchus corn dole to prove that *subsortitio* continued at Rome (*Oxy. Pap.* xl. 8–13).

[131] Frontinus, *De Aqu.* 108.

supply. But we do in fact have puzzling evidence, both in literary authors and in the jurists, that it was also possible to buy a *tessera frumentaria*, a right to a corn ration, under the Empire.[132] In some of the literary passages it seems that what is referred to is merely the ticket for a single distribution of corn. If a *tessera frumentaria* for a single distribution changed hands, either by gift or by purchase between individuals, it was perhaps no cause for the state to worry so long as the ration was issued and checked off against the proper name on the lists. But in the legal sources it appears to be the case that it was possible by the early third century A.D. to buy a *tessera frumentaria* for life and even to leave such a thing in one's will.[133] Even if these passages do not imply, as has been argued,[134] that the *tessera frumentaria* itself had changed its function from being a token to be surrendered for a single corn ration to being a document which authenticated its holder's right to a corn ration and which he held continuously, the clear implication nevertheless is that the right to *frumentum publicum* was alienable and could be hereditary. Yet indiscriminate sale and inheritance between individuals would have caused chaos in the lists and would have made the idea of checking off names at the time of issue a farce. There seem to be two alternatives therefore. Purchase must either have been possible from the state itself in a way not unlike the purchase of water rights, except that whereas this was the general rule in relation to water, for corn it was only certain *tesserae*, forfeit to the state, which were available for sale; or, secondly, purchase and inheritance may have been permitted, if the transaction was somehow under the supervision of the state and properly recorded so as to allow the lists to be brought up to date. Of these two the latter seems to be the more likely. Whatever the answer, it is obvious that we do not yet understand either the principle or the means that came to be used to fill the vacancies in the corn distribution lists.

[132] See below, Appendix 8, for full discussion.

[133] *Dig.* 31. 49. 1 (Paul); 31. 87 pr; 5. 1. 52. 1 (Ulpian).

[134] Rostovtzeff, *Frumentum*, col. 178, cf. 'Römische Bleitesserae', *Klio* Beiheft 3 (1905); Cardinali, *Frumentatio*, pp. 271 ff.; Van Berchem, *Distributions*, pp. 85–8; for a different view, Rea, *Oxy. Pap.* xl. 101 ff.

3

The distributions right from their inception took place once a month throughout the year but, as we have seen, we know of no single issuing centre either in the late Republic or in the transitional period to the early Principate. Indeed, if, as I believe, the grain was issued simultaneously to all the recipients at a single moment in the month, and there were by the time of Caesar hundreds of thousands of recipients, there can have been no single centre for the distributions. The first evidence we have that the system had changed is the inscription of a freedman Tiberius Claudius Ianuarius.[135] He was in receipt of corn at entrance (*ostium*) 42 on day 14 at the Porticus Minucia. His names suggest, without any precision, a period about the middle of the first century A.D. at the time of either Claudius or Nero. The implication of this inscription, and of others of a later date, is that from this time the distributions were centred on the Porticus Minucia, and that instead of the *frumentationes* taking place only once a month at, presumably, many different places, they were now issued at only one place, but many times during the month, on different days, at different arcades, to different groups of recipients. So far as the recipients were concerned, the rations were still issued once a month, but so far as the state was concerned the issuing took place on many days in each month. We know that the Porticus Minucia was in the ninth region of Rome, the Campus Martius, but there is difficulty and confusion over the exact site and the lay-out of the building.[136] Greater help in understanding the role of the *ostia* comes from a very late source which says: 'Servius Tullius ruled for forty-five years. He made a vow to set up as many *ostia* for *frumentum publicum* as the years of his reign.'[137] Although the connection with Servius Tullius in the sixth century B.C. is completely bogus, this confirms the function of the *ostia* known from the inscriptions and gives their total number. Clearly there were forty-five arcades, or entrances, from which as a

[135] *CIL* 6. 10223 = *ILS* 6071, cf. *CIL* 6. 10224 = *ILS* 6069, 'received corn on day 10 at entrance 39'; *CIL* 6. 10225 = *ILS* 6070, 'received corn on day 7 at entrance 15'.

[136] A. Nordh, *Libellus de Regionibus Urbis Romae* (Gleerup, 1949), p. 86; see below, Appendix 9.

[137] *Chron. Ann. 354* (Mommsen), p. 187.

properly enrolled recipient one could receive a corn ration on any given day in a month. If this is true, and if distributions took place on the majority of days in the month, even 200,000 recipients could be dealt with in groups that were no bigger than between 150 and 200 people.

The profound practical effect of the change on the way that corn was issued is therefore obvious, but did the concentration of the distributions at the Porticus Minucia affect the overall organization established by Augustus? Was the office of *praefecti frumenti dandi ex s. c.* abolished, or suspended? Were there imperial officials responsible for running the Porticus Minucia? If so, did this mean that there was an imperial takeover, perhaps under Claudius, of a senatorial prerogative? Modern scholars have been divided on these questions, but the main view has been that Claudius did take from the senate the running of the distributions.[138] In my view there is insufficient evidence to establish that claim, and it is unnecessary to make it to account for erosion of senatorial independence or growth of imperial power in this area of administration.[139]

There is certainly no statement by any historical source that the office of *praefecti frumenti dandi*, established by *senatus consultum* under Augustus, was ever abolished. All we have are inscriptions giving the careers of individual men, who held that office, and the inferences we may legitimately make from them.[140] From these inscriptions we know that the office could be held up to the reigns of Gordian III and Philip the Arab in the third century A.D., but there are some periods when inscriptional evidence is lacking, for example, from, approximately, Claudius to Trajan and at the very beginning of the third century A.D. Many scholars have inferred from these gaps in the inscriptional record that the office was suppressed in these periods, but that may not be correct.[141] Arguments from silence

[138] Van Berchem, *Distributions*, pp. 72–4; Cardinali, *Frumentatio*, pp. 241–6; Rostovtzeff, *Frumentum*, col. 177; A. Momigliano, *Claudius: The Emperor and his Achievement* (repr. Cambridge, 1961), pp. 49 and 107.

[139] See below, Appendix 1.

[140] For lists of holders of this office see H. G. Pflaum, 'La chronologie de la carrière de L. Caesennius Sospes', *Historia* 2 (1953–4), 444–5; amplified and corrected in *Bonner Jahrbücher* 163 (1963), 234–7. See now the decisive article by R. Syme, 'The Enigmatic Sospes', *JRS* 67 (1977), 38–49.

[141] Cardinali stressed that the apparent gaps in the inscriptions might well be accidental, or illusory, see *Frumentatio*, p. 248; see further G. E. F. Chilver, '*Princeps*

are never wholly satisfactory, particularly in relation to inscriptional evidence. The same of course may be said of the fact that we know of no imperial officials at the Porticus Minucia until the early second century A.D.; that does not prove that there were none. But it is interesting that under Trajan when we have evidence for a *procurator Augusti ad Minuciam* we also have evidence for *praefecti frumenti dandi.*[142] Under that *optimus princeps* at least there must have been co-operation between senate and Emperor, and between senatorial magistrates and imperial officials in the running of the distributions. The claim that the letters 'ex s. c.' appended to the title of the *praefecti frumenti dandi* meant that the post was a special senatorial prerogative, of which the senate was proud and the Emperor jealous, is more than suspect.[143] The letters 'ex. s. c.' probably means no more than that Augustus acted punctiliously in getting a *senatus consultum* passed in order to establish the office in the first place, and the retention of the letters in the title was perhaps simply to make clear that the office was a properly constituted magistracy and that the *praefecti* were not, as the *praefectus annonae* himself was, merely deputies of the Emperor. But although it was a proper magistracy, it is difficult to see in its holders any great luminaries of the senatorial order or Roman nobility. An analysis of the inscriptions shows that it was obviously possible for a man who held the post to go on to an important career. Examples might include C. Ummidius Quadratus, the governor of Syria in the mid-first century A.D. who features in Tacitus' *Annals*, and P. Cluvius Maximus Paullinus and C. Curtius Justus, who were both governors of Upper Moesia in the middle of the second century A.D.[144] But the majority of men who held the post did not have top flight

and *Frumentationes*', *AJP* 70 (1949), 7–21; G. Vitucci, 'Note al cursus honorum di M. Julius Romulus praefectus frumenti dandi ex s.c.', *RivFC* 25 (1947), 252 ff.; R. K. Sherk, 'The Legates of Galatia from Augustus to Diocletian', Johns Hopkins Studies 69. 2 (1953), 87–9. See below, Appendix 1.

[142] Despite Momigliano *Claudius*, p. 50, there is no evidence for a handover from senatorial *praefecti frumenti dandi* to an imperial official called the *procurator de Minucia*; for the Trajanic *proc. Aug. ad Minuciam* see *CIL* 11. 5669 = *ILS* 2728 (Pflaum No. 87); *CIL* 10. 7344; *CIL* 10. 8291 = *ILS* 1041; *CIL* 8. 17891 = *ILS* 1055; *CIL* 3. 6813 = *ILS* 1038.

[143] Ensslin, *RE*, s.v. *praefectus* col. 1308.

[144] *CIL* 10. 5182 = *ILS* 972, cf. Tac. *Ann.* 12. 45. 6 (Quadratus); *Æpigr.* (1940), 99 (Paullinus); *CIL* 3. 1458 (Justus).

careers. The most striking common feature is how many of them come from an Italian background. This is true of the three examples quoted, and in the case of Q. Varius Geminus who held the post under Augustus it is proudly stated on his inscription 'is primus omnium Paelign. senator factus est et eos honores gessit'—he was the first Paelignian senator.[145] The holders in short seem to come from just those Italian families which benefited so much from the establishment of the Principate, and the personal patronage of the *princeps*. The Emperor would seem to have nothing to fear from this office and little to gain from abolishing it. The concentration of the distributions at the Porticus Minucia did not in itself demand their abolition, and imperial officials for the running of that building may well have coexisted beside the senatorial *praefecti* from the start as we know they did during the second century A.D. It is not without interest that in the administration of Rome's water supply the creation by Claudius of a new group of workmen, the *familia Caesaris*, who were imperial officials, did not bring with it the abolition of the previous group, the *publica familia*, who continued to work alongside the new administration.[146]

4

The corn distributions remained centred at the Porticus Minucia through the second century A.D. until towards the end of that century there are signs of further reorganization. The facts are relatively straightforward, their interpretation is not. From the time of Commodus there appears an official, of consular rank, entitled *curator aquarum et Miniciae* (which became the usual spelling of Minucia at this period). Also from about this time officials with the title *praefecti Miniciae*, of praetorian rank,[147] appear on inscriptions where we might have expected the title *praefecti frumenti dandi*, although the latter title appears on inscriptions during the reigns of Severus Alexander and Gordian III. Some scholars have seen in this a complicated 'power struggle' between the senate and the Emperor over the use of the Porticus Minucia and the control of the corn distri-

[145] *CIL* 9. 3306 = *ILS* 932.
[146] Frontinus, *De Aqu.* 116–18.
[147] e.g. *CIL* 6. 1408 (*curator*), *CIL* 8. 12442 (*praefectus Minuciae*).

butions in this period.[148] Much more important is whether the Porticus Minucia had ceased to be used for grain distributions at all, and was now caught up in the water administration, or whether the two public services water and grain were now amalgamated, and unified under one consular head with subordinates of praetorian standing. Of these two alternatives the first seems unlikely in view of the continuing strength of the association of the Porticus Minucia with distributions of corn, while the second seems very probable. There must have been much to have been said for combining the administration of the distribution of grain and water in the city. Both were vital to the city's very existence, and the administrative patterns of the two systems had had points of similarity from the beginning of the Empire, not least in that both senate and Emperor were involved in both.

If this is true, it is striking that it was during the latter part of the second century A.D. that the amalgamation of the grain and water distribution systems in Rome started. This period is emerging as one of major importance in the history of the corn supply of Rome. The so-called *Horrea Antoniniani* at Ostia were built, and the *Grandi Horrea* were completely reconstructed at this time.[149] These were among the largest warehouses in Ostia and were used for the storage of grain rather than of other goods. It was under Commodus that the shipping of the grain supplies from Africa was organized in such a way that he was regarded as having created an African grain fleet, and that a major conspiracy to bring down the Emperor's favourite, Cleander, involved manipulation of the corn supplies.[150] Now it can be seen to have been a time of administrative reorganization at Rome affecting grain distributions. A pattern of interest and activity in corn supply problems is discernible which makes this period comparable to that of Claudius or Trajan in its importance for the feeding of the capital.

However, neither administrative re-arrangements at the Porticus Minucia nor manipulation of titles of officials by senate or Emperor were to affect the distributions in the third century

148 See below, Appendix 10.

149 Rickman, *Roman Granaries*, pp. 41 and 50.

150 SHA *Commodus* 17. 7; C. R. Whittaker, 'The revolt of Papirius Dionysius A.D. 190', *Historia* 13 (1964), 348–69.

A.D. as much as certain fundamental changes in what was distributed. Part of the new pattern was foreshadowed when Septimius Severus added distributions of oil to those of grain, and devoted a tax in oil from Tripolitania to this purpose.[151] Distributions of oil had been made from time to time in the past, even during the Republic, and they became irregular again under the immediate successors of Septimius. Aurelian, however, not only firmly re-established oil distributions, but added distributions of pork and of wine, each with their own administrations. More important for the *frumentationes*, from this time baked bread rather than uncooked grain was issued in the corn distributions.[152] Although the *curator aquarum et Miniciae* continued in existence,[153] and may still have exercised some supervision, the Porticus Minucia itself must have lost its unique role as the single issuing centre. Bread, which had to be distributed daily rather than monthly, could not be delivered simultaneously to 100,000 people or more from one place. Distribution in the form of bread must therefore have entailed the devolution of the distributions away from the single centre established in the mid-first century A.D. It might seem that the wheel had simply come full circle back to the situation of the late Republic, but in fact the new pattern that was to be typical of the Late Empire had begun.

[151] SHA *Sept. Sev.* 18, cf. *Alex. Sev.* 22; Aur. Vict. *Caes.* 41. 19–20.

[152] Aur. Vict. *Caes.* 35. 7; *Epit. de Caes.* 35. 6; SHA *Aurel.* 35. 1–2, 48. 1–4; cf. A. Chastagnol, *La Préfecture urbaine à Rome sous le bas-empire* (Paris, 1960), p. 59. Pavis D'Escurac, *Préfecture*, pp. 188–202.

[153] The last attested holder is dated to A.D. 328, *CIL* 10. 4752 = *ILS* 1223.

VIII

THE LATE EMPIRE

The rescripts of the Emperors, collected and preserved for us in works such as the *Codex Theodosianus*, give us a mass of information for the fourth and early fifth centuries A.D. about the working of the administrative system of the Roman Empire. At least they bear witness to how the system was meant to work and how the Emperors wished or assumed that it did. Sometimes the repeated instructions hint that practice differed from theory. Despite the bulk of the evidence, the feeding of Rome in this late period can be dealt with succinctly. Rome itself was from the beginning of the fourth century A.D. merely one of the capitals of the Empire, and in Constantinople had a rival that was to outlast it. Moreover the heavily bureaucratic system was peculiar to itself, and the evidence is not to be applied outside its own sphere and chronological limits.

The earmarking of the Egyptian supplies for Constantinople meant that Rome was limited to the resources of the western Mediterranean, above all those of Africa, to supply her needs. These needs were still great, even though there may have been some diminution of the population in the city by then. It is possible to argue from the *Historia Augusta* that the *canon* of Rome in the early fourth century amounted to some 27 million *modii*. It is also possible to argue from a rescript in the *Codex Theodosianus* that even in A.D. 419 the number of recipients of the distributions in Rome still amounted to 120,000.[1] Periodic famine was still a real threat.[2] It was not just at particular

[1] SHA *Septimius Severus* 23, cf. Jones, *LRE*, p. 698. See above, p. 181 and Appendix 4; *Cod. Theod.* 14. 4. 10 (A.D. 419), cf. S. Mazzarino, *Aspetti sociali del quarto secolo. Ricerche di storia tardo-romana* (Problemi e ricerche di storia antica I), (Rome, 1951), pp. 228–30. For a careful study of the rescripts in the *Codex Theodosianus* dealing with the corn supply and with emphasis on the *Realien* of the movement of corn from African farms to Roman bakeries, see E. Tengström, *Bread for the People, Studies in the Corn Supply of Rome during the late Empire* (Stockholm, 1974).

[2] A. Piganiol, *L'Empire chrétien* (Paris, 1947), p. 8. Cf. J.-R. Palanque, 'Famines à Rome à la fin du IVe siècle', *REA* 33 (1931), 346–56.

crises such as the war of Gildo at the end of the fourth century A.D. or the struggle with Alaric at the beginning of the fifth century A.D., that the threat of starvation came. As throughout the whole of her history, the food supply of Rome was at best in a state of delicate equilibrium, able to be upset by anything from poor harvests and bad weather at sea to incompetence or corruption among officials. It was still the object of careful concern to the *praefectus annonae* and his new superior the *praefectus urbi*.[3]

I

The relationship between these two men and their respective staffs has been carefully charted by Chastagnol in his magisterial study of the urban prefecture in the late Empire.[4] It seems clear that the *praefectus annonae* remained an independent office of equestrian status right up to Constantine. The post was, as it had always been, concerned with the provisioning of the capital with grain and with oil. The distributions, whether now of bread or meat or wine, were still no part of his duties. Throughout the third and still at the beginning of the fourth century A.D. he enjoyed the title of *vir perfectissimus*. It is true that the *subpraefectus* under his orders seems to have disappeared after the middle of the third century A.D.[5] and that his competence seems under Diocletian to have shrunk largely to the two harbours of Ostia and Portus and the emporium district in Rome, but he was still an independent entity with his own *officium*. Moreover the independent accounts office for the grain supply still existed although its name seems to have been changed probably under Aurelian from *fiscus frumentarius* to *arca frumentaria*. It was perhaps housed in the greatest storehouse complex in Rome, the *Horrea Galbana*, whose *curator* was an increasingly important official in the late Empire.[6]

The moment when it was decided to change the status of the prefecture of the *annona* to senatorial rank is not known to us precisely, nor what this change really implied. It is true of

[3] Sid. *Ep.* I. 10.

[4] A. Chastagnol, *La Préfecture urbaine à Rome sous le bas-empire* (Paris, 1960), pp. 297–9; cf. also Jones, *LRE*, pp. 696–704.

[5] W. Ensslin, *RE*, s.v. '*praefectus*', 22. 2. col. 1268.

[6] Chastagnol, *Préfecture urbaine*, p. 59.

course that the *curator aquarum et Minuciae*, the ultimate authority on the distributions of bread up to this point, had always been of senatorial rank, and the senate neither lost interest entirely in corn-supply problems, nor was totally excluded even at this time by the Emperors. At all events it was some time between A.D. 312 and 328 that the *praefectus annonae* also became a senator, and Chastagnol has argued for A.D. 326 as the precise moment.[7]

Certainly the change in status was followed shortly, perhaps in A.D. 331, by a general reorganization of the supply system of Rome.[8] The *praefectus annonae* for the first time in the history of the office became responsible for the distributions at Rome as well as the procurement of supplies. Moreover his duties at Ostia and Portus were increased to include general responsibility for all public works in those two towns, of which he became a kind of local mayor or provost.[9] The price that was paid for this massive expansion of his local powers was however his subordination, natural in the circumstances, to the *praefectus urbi*.

The story is a little more complicated than that because it seems clear that at the start of this period, from A.D. 328 to about 350, the senatorial holders of the *praefectura annonae* were men of formidable power and influence.[10] Naeratius Cerealis, Furius Placidus, and Avianius Symmachus were of the great Roman nobility of the period, and in the 330s and 340s we know that the prefects possessed the *ius gladii*, the right of capital jurisdiction.[11] After the middle of the century, however, the holders came from less distinguished families, often of provincial origin, and the *ius gladii* seems to have been withdrawn. Although the prefecture enjoyed periods of revived power, for example under Valentinian I, its overall subordination to the *praefectus urbi* from this time is not in doubt. In 365 a law had spelled out the relationship:[12] the orders were to be

Relation to PPO

[7] Chastagnol, *Préfecture urbaine*, p. 262 and 298. Last known equestrian prefect is Aurelius Victorianus between A.D. 312 and 324 (*CIL* 14. 131 = *ILS* 687); the first senator Naeratius Cerealis in 328 (*Cod. Theod.* 14. 24. 1).

[8] Chastagnol, *Préfecture urbaine*, pp. 57–63.

[9] R. Meiggs, *Roman Ostia*², p. 186; the last attested examples of the old *procurator annonae* at Ostia are dated to mid-third century A.D. *CIL* 14. 160 = *ILS* 1428; *Æpigr.* (1971) 23, cf. D'Escurac, *Préfecture*, pp. 414–15.

[10] See the list of office holders in Chastagnol, *Préfecture urbaine*, pp. 465–6.

[11] *CIL* 10. 1700 (Furius Placidus); *CIL* 6. 1151 = 31248; *CIL* 8. 5348 and 14. 4449; cf. *RE* 22. 2, col. 1267 (W. Ensslin).

[12] *Cod. Theod.* 11. 14. 1.

given by the *praefectus urbi* and carried out by the *praefectus annonae* and his staff. Great care was to be taken that the staff of the city prefect should not become involved in the minutiae of the *annona* organization. The same point was made in stronger terms in a law of 376 by Gratian and the control of the *praefectus urbi* was stressed.[13] Although this might imply a long and continuing rivalry for power between the *praefectus annonae* and the *praefectus urbi* and their respective offices, it seems clear that often relations between them were cordial.[14] It was certainly to their mutual advantage for them to be so.

The prefects, whether of the *annona* or of the city, were concerned above all with the smooth running of the highly organized *canon frumentarius* for the city. But that does not mean that there was no free market in grain. The great nobles of the late Empire supplied themselves and their households not just in grain but in other goods as well from their estates and grand domains.[15] The surplus of their revenues and of local Italian grain production was put onto the market in the normal way. This free market was left to run itself and was only interfered with by the prefects in order to suppress malpractice, to ensure honest weights and measures and reasonable prices. Their control would only become pervasive at times of real famine and distress.

Their main task was the *canon frumentarius* and the distributions. The canon was state grain provided from state-owned lands and revenues, or bought as supplementary amounts from private sources with state money. Basically the source of most of the grain for the canon was Africa, although for a while in the middle of the fourth century A.D. there was also regular levy of 38,000 *modii* a year on the towns of Campania and Latium in Italy.[16] That was discontinued by Gratian, but in times of real famine corn was sought virtually wherever it might be found, Egypt (the feeder of Constantinople), Sicily, Sardinia, Macedonia, Spain, and even Gaul or Germany.[17]

[13] *Cod. Theod.* 1. 6. 7.

[14] Sid. *Ep.* 1. 10.

[15] J. A. MacGeachy, *Quintus Aurelius Symmachus* (private edn., Chicago, 1942), p. 70; Ambrose, *De Off. Minist.* 3. 7. 45; cf. *Cod. Theod.* 14. 16. 1 for free market at Constantinople in A.D. 409.

[16] Symm. *Rel.* 40. 4; cf. 37. 2.

[17] Claudian, *In Eutrop.* 1. 406–7; Prudent. *Contra Symm.* 2. 937–46; Symm. *Ep.* 3. 5.

The fixing of the size of the canon was, surprisingly, the responsibility of the Emperor himself. The prefects put in requests in the light of the information they had about the size of the city population, the size of stocks, the regularity of sea traffic, and so on, but the Emperor decided. The carrying out of the order was entrusted to the praetorian prefect of the region concerned and his subordinates, the vicars and governors. We know that in the case of Rome after A.D. 357 it was the praetorian prefect of Italy, the *vicarius urbis Romae* and the governors of the provinces.

We have much specific evidence for the organization of the *canon frumentarius* from Africa in the imperial rescripts.[18] The grain was transported to the granaries at the coastal ports, particularly Carthage, under the orders of the proconsul and vicar of Africa. Once it had been gathered at the ports of embarkation it became the special responsibility of the *praefectus annonae Africae*, whose *officium* co-ordinated the activities of the *praepositi horreorum* where the grain was stored and the gatherers of the canon, the *susceptores canonis*, that is, except for a period under Valentinian, local *curiales*. The *praefectus annonae Africae* was himself directly responsible to the *praefectus praetorio Italiae*. It was the *susceptores* who delivered the grain to the *corpora* of *navicularii*, charged with carrying the grain without deceit to Rome. The embarkation was to begin as soon as possible and a third of the canon due was to be transported the moment navigation became possible, in April.[19] Transport normally stopped by October and the state could not force the *navicularii* to sail in the closed season for navigation, which was reckoned in A.D. 380 to stretch from 15 October to the end of March.[20] Such a rule could, of course, be set aside in exceptional circumstances.

After the cargo was loaded at the port of embarkation the *navicularii* had to declare that they had received the grain from the *susceptores* in good condition. They were then bound to take the shortest route and not to stop on the way. The shipper could himself suffer death or exile, if he did so, and the authorities of the place at which he stopped ran the risk of having their

[18] Chastagnol, *Préfecture urbaine*, pp. 302–5.
[19] *Cod. Theod.* 13. 5. 27 (A.D. 397).
[20] *Cod. Theod.* 13. 9. 3 (A.D. 380); cf. Tengström, *Bread*, p. 40.

goods confiscated, if they did not force him on his way immediately.[21]

On arrival at Portus the shippers passed under the control of the *praefectus annonae* and the urban prefect. They were given a receipt for the safe transport of their cargoes, which had to be delivered back to the governor of Africa, or they would have all their goods confiscated. But they were given two years in which to return with the receipt, and during that time were free to carry on private business exempt from demands by the state. Consequently the shippers were expected to ship fiscal cargoes once every two years.[22]

If the *praefectus annonae* discovered that more than the legally permitted amount was missing from the cargo, he had to set up an inquiry within five days together with the urban prefect and three senators according to a law of A.D. 414. But if the case against the shipper was established, he was returned to Africa for judgement by the *praefectus annonae Africae*.[23] The last word therefore lay with the authorities in Africa and the same was true in cases of shipwreck. The court of inquiry was held before the governor of whatever province was nearest to the scene of the shipwreck, or if at the Tiber mouth or on the high sea, before the *praefectus annonae* and the representative of the urban prefect at Porto. But the final judgement was given either by the *praefectus annonae Africae* or by the *praefectus praetorio*.[24] In A.D. 391 the shipper was held responsible for the lost cargo, but in A.D. 397 the more equitable decision was made that the loss should be to the *fiscus* if the shipwreck were caused by the elements.[25]

The superintendence of the shippers and their journey from Africa was therefore double; the *praefectus praetorio* and *praefectus annonae Africae* on the one hand and the *praefectus urbi* and the *praefectus annonae* at Rome on the other. Although the former were ultimately the more powerful, the rescripts concerning the rules about heredity and property of the shippers were sent to the latter as well.[26] It seems that by the early fourth century

[21] *Cod. Theod.* 13. 5. 33 (A.D. 409) and 34 (A.D. 410).
[22] *Cod. Theod.* 13. 5. 21 (A.D. 392) and 26 (A.D. 396); cf. Tengström, *Bread*, p. 45.
[23] *Cod. Theod.* 13. 5. 38; cf. Tengström, *Bread*, p. 51.
[24] *Cod. Theod.* 13. 9. 1 (A.D. 372) and 5 (A.D. 397).
[25] *Cod. Theod.* 13. 9. 4 and 5.
[26] *Cod. Theod.* 13. 5. 1 (A.D. 314) and 11 (A.D. 365).

A.D. some of the African shippers also worked some of the great African estates which were bound to provide contributions to the *canon frumentarius*.[27] If that is so, the special role of the African authorities is not surprising.

2

The operations of unloading the grain at Ostia or Portus, storing it, reloading it onto river boats, towing them upstream, unloading and storing in the capital itself are fairly well known, and not least from the rescripts of the late Empire.[28] Although supervised by the *praefectus annonae* and *praefectus urbi* and their staffs, the actual work involved was carried out by a multiplicity of different workmen. *Saccarii* acted as dockers, manhandling the grain, in sacks on their shoulders. *Mensores* examined and measured the cargoes on the boats before the officials of the *annona* office would give the receipt to set the shippers free; they worked as well in the granaries of the harbours and of Rome, assessing stores held, and measuring out grain assigned to the Tiber boatmen and to the bakers. They were to prevent fraud, and their own frauds were the subject of constant concern to the *praefectus annonae* himself. Above all they must see to it that the new *canon frumentarius* was not issued for public consumption until the old had been completely cleared from the granaries. The orders which streamed from the Emperors to the two prefects and presumably from them to the thousands of workers involved would have us believe that a perfectly organized system was being rigidly enforced at every point from the arrival in Portus to the issue of supplies in Rome. In fact this cannot have been so. Emergencies of all kinds demanded more flexible arrangements than those in the rescripts and the very repetition of many of the orders indicates that they were not being carried out. Even the very granaries themselves were being misused for other purposes or encroached upon by other buildings.[29]

All these workers had been important in the organization of

[27] Ch. Saumagne, 'Un tarif fiscal au IVe siècle de notre ère', *Karthago* i (1950), 159–79.

[28] Chastagnol, *Préfecture urbaine*, pp. 306–8; cf. Tengström, *Bread*, pp. 54–64.

[29] Rickman, *Roman Granaries*, pp. 190–2.

the supply and distribution system of Rome for many centuries, but the bakers of Rome take a pre-eminent position in the system only in the late Empire. It is true that the state had been interested in the bakers' corporation from the time of Trajan,[30] if not earlier, but it was replacement of grain by bread in the distributions, from the time of Aurelian, that really accentuated their importance to the state. The result is that the bakers are the best known of all the *collegia* which were associated with the *annona* in the late Empire, and they form the best example of the lengths to which the Roman state went in order to bind a group permanently to its will.[31]

In this case there was no obvious double control from the top. The city authorities, the *praefectus urbi* and the *praefectus annonae* together saw to it that the laws guaranteeing a plentiful supply of bakers were enforced. The main weapons of control were the inexorable grasp exerted by the state over the heredity and possessions of the bakers.[32] The sons of bakers were in theory at any rate destined to become bakers themselves and consequently the *praefectus urbi* and the *praefectus annonae* were as interested in the marriages of bakers and their offspring as in any other aspect of their life and work. All attempts to evade the role of baker were to be foiled by the bureaucracy, and punishment of crimes by civil servants themselves might well take the form of being forced to serve in a bakery. Official sanction of change of occupation was rarely given and often only on condition that the man's goods were left to the corporation and a replacement found. Even so it is clear that the numbers of bakers shrank and had to be topped up by strange means. In the reign of Theodosius I we are told that bakers had set up bars and brothels on the street fronts of their establishments and used them to kidnap extra labour.[33] A law of Constantine, which was reiterated in A.D. 370 and 380, laid down that the governors of the African provinces should send every five years qualified candidates to Rome to be enrolled in the bakers' guild. By the mid-fifth century there were many so-called bakers' estates (*praedia pistoria*) in the African provinces.[34]

[30] Frag. Vat. 233 (Ulpian).

[31] Chastagnol, *Préfecture urbaine*, pp. 308–11; Jones, *LRE*, pp. 699–701; cf. Tengström, *Bread*, pp. 71–88.

[32] *Cod. Theod.* 14. 3 *De Pistoribus et Catabolensibus*.

[33] Socrates, *Hist. Eccles.* 5. 18.

[34] Jones, *LRE*, p. 700.

The estates and goods of bakers were frozen and became part of the assets of the corporation as a whole. A baker had to be a man of property judged sufficient by the *praefectus urbi* no less than the *patroni* of the corporation. The *praefectus urbi* therefore kept a list not simply of the names of the college members but of their property as well, which they were not allowed to sell or alienate in any way. The same was true of the actual baking establishments themselves, some 254 or 274 in number according to the late regionary catalogues, between fifteen and twenty-four in each region of the city, and all their equipment, animate and inanimate. All were frozen and inalienable, part of the permanent and unchangeable machinery for supplying bread to the populace of Rome at the public expense. The only part of the machinery that did show signs of change towards the end of the fourth century A.D. was the process of milling. This had previously taken place within the bakeries themselves and the millstones had been worked by men or animals. But in A.D. 398 we have the first mention of water-powered mills on the slopes of the Janiculum fed by an offshoot of the *Aqua Traiana* and under the control of the *praefectus annonae*.[35] This led to the formation of a group of millers, *molendinarii*, distinct from the *pistores*, the bakers themselves. Their misdemeanours no less than those of the bakers were the subject of concern to the *praefectus urbi*.[36]

3

The distributions of the late Empire were many.[37] Bread distributions were substituted for grain distributions, and in addition there were distributions of oil, wine, and meat. All these were of interest to the *praefectus urbi*, but just as in the past the *praefectus annonae* was responsible only for the procurement of grain and oil, so now his interest was limited to distributions of bread and oil. Oil seems to have been organized along much the same lines as grain and there was a *canon olearius* no less than the *canon frumentarius*, derived mainly from Africa again, as well as

[35] *Cod. Theod.* 14. 15. 4, cf. Prud., *Contra Symm.* 2. 950; cf. Tengström, *Bread*, p. 76.

[36] *CIL* 6. 1711.

[37] Chastagnol, *Préfecture urbaine*, pp. 312–30.

Spain.[38] The outlets for oil, the *mensae oleariae*, some 2,300 of them in the city, were in hereditary possession like the bakeries and under the eye of the *praefectus annonae*.[39]

The bread distributions were the vital object of concern, and varied in size and organization after their institution. Aurelian when he substituted bread for grain made no charge to the recipients but seems, if we can trust a passage in the *Historia Augusta*, to have halved the previous ration. The daily ration of top-quality bread, *panes siliginei*, was to be 2 Roman lb. (654 g).[40] At some time before A.D. 364, perhaps under Constantine, the bread ration was doubled.[41] The daily ration was 20 *panes sordidi*, weighing in all some 50 Roman oz. (1,360 g). This was a return in size to the grain rations prior to Aurelian, but the bread was less good in quality, and payment for the ration is attested at least in 364 and 369.[42] Valentinian I in 369 reduced the ration by about one quarter, but increased the quality and removed the payment.[43] The ration consisted of 6 *bucellae* 'biscuits' weighing in all 36 Roman oz., 3 Roman lb. (980 g). What happened to the size of the ration after this we do not know, but it seems from a rescript of A.D. 398 that payment for the bread ration returned by the end of the fourth century A.D.[44]

Whatever the size of the ration, the bakers were obviously of crucial importance in the whole operation. It was the bakers who went themselves to the granaries to receive from the *mensores* the measured amounts of grain, and paid money for what they received, which went to the *arca frumentaria*. When the recipients paid for their bread ration, that too went to the *arca frumentaria* to help swell the accounts which reimbursed the bakers for the money spent at the granaries.[45] After the milling of the grain either in their own establishments or at the mills on the Janiculum, the bakers baked the bread in their bakeries, which were always liable to an inspection by the *praefectus annonae*.[46] But they were on no account to distribute or sell it

[38] H. Camps-Fabrier, *L'Olivier et l'huile dans l'Afrique romaine* (Algiers, 1953).

[39] *Cod. Theod.* 14. 24. 1 (A.D. 328).

[40] SHA *Aurel.* 35.

[41] *Cod. Theod.* 14. 17. 5.

[42] *Cod. Theod.* 14. 15. 1 and 14. 17. 5.

[43] *Cod. Theod.* 14. 17. 5.

[44] *Cod. Theod.* 14. 19. 1.

[45] *Cod. Theod.* 14. 15. 1 (A.D. 364); 16. 3 (A.D. 434), but see Tengström, *Bread*, p. 63.

[46] Cassiod. *Variae* 6. 18. 1.

from the bakeries themselves, which would seem to be, and had perhaps been, the natural outlet. Instead they were to distribute it at *gradus*, steps, located throughout the city and more than one to each region.[47] These stepped distributing centres helped to give the bread its alternative name, *panis gradilis*, which was simply another way of referring to *panis popularis*.[48] The distributions had to be daily since the bread would not keep for very long, and each bakery was due to deliver its quota each day to one or more of the *gradus* in its area. At the *gradus* the baker was assisted by a scribe, a *tabularius* of the *officium urbanum*.[49] The recipients were enrolled at the *gradus* nearest to their place of domicile. Each had a *tessera* with an official number and at each *gradus* was a list on a bronze tablet giving the names of the authorized recipients and the amounts of their rations according to the number in the family listed.[50]

4

Ultimately all had come to hinge upon the Emperor himself in the most directly personal way. Just as it was he who fixed the *canon* required for the feeding of Rome, so he also adjusted the amounts of the daily rations and the prices to be charged at the distributions to fit the changing circumstances of the state. As the head of a chain of command and responsibility which stretched in a series of specific links to the very agricultural labourers of the provinces he had to take decisions, and be seen to take them, about matters which in earlier periods would have been delegated. It was the final paradox that the more powerful the Emperor became and the more open his role in the state, the more trapped he was in the petty details of bureaucracy. The Emperor no less than the meanest baker had become a prisoner in the system that had been created. That system too was no more permanently successful than earlier efforts had been in guaranteeing a sense of security about its food supply among the population of Rome. Just as Seneca in the first century A.D. recorded the excitement and relief men

[47] *Cod. Theod.* 14. 17. 3 (A.D. 368).
[48] Van Berchem, *Distributions*, pp. 104–6.
[49] *Cod. Theod.* 14. 16. 3 (A.D. 434) and 17. 6 (A.D. 370).
[50] *Cod. Theod.* 14. 17. 5 (A.D. 369).

felt on the arrival of the Egyptian grain ships at Puteoli, so Symmachus in A.D. 384 dreamed longingly of the arrival of such ships at a time of want, and imagined the adoring welcome they would get from both people and senate.[51] Everything had changed, and yet nothing had changed.

[51] Sen. *Ep.* 77; Symm. *Rel.* 9. 7.

EPILOGUE

When in the Medieval period men visited the crumbling remains of ancient Rome, they were impressed not just by the spectacle of individual grand edifices, but by the sheer size of the former capital of the Roman Empire. It seems to modern scholars to be true that Rome outstripped in size by a large margin not only her predecessors but also the cities that were famous later in Medieval Europe. Perhaps we have come too easily to take that phenomenon for granted, to assume that because by the end of the Republic the resources of the whole Mediterranean were at Rome's call there was bound to be a successful large urban unit at the centre of it all. But the health and well being of large numbers of people living on top of one another in a sizeable city are not to be taken for granted, particularly in an age of limited technological and medical achievement.

The maintenance of so great a city as Rome demanded effort and organization of resources on the largest scale, and was not achieved without a price. The arrangements made by cities throughout the ancient Mediterranean to relieve the problems of their food supplies were often at the expense of others. Galen, writing of the difficulties of the mid-second century A.D., said:

> The city dwellers, as it was their custom to collect and store enough corn for all the next year immediately after the harvest, carried off all the wheat, barley, beans and lentils and left what remained to the country people, that is, pulses of various kinds, though they took a good deal of these too to the city. The country people finished the pulses during the winter, and so had to fall back on unhealthy foods during the spring; they ate twigs and shoots of trees and bushes and bulbs and roots of indigestible plants: they filled themselves with wild herbs and cooked fresh grass.

Many fell ill and died. Towns might be fed, while the countryside could starve. Even within the towns themselves the motives for sustaining a supply of food were often not humanitarian, as we understand the term, but political. In Rome it was not some altruistic theory of poor relief but the rights of citizenship, not shared by the whole community, which generated the effort to organize a proper food supply for the city. Later, in the Roman Empire, the supply and distributions were indissolubly associated with the boastful generosity of the Emperors on whose grace and favour all were to depend. But it helped to create the largest city the world had seen, or was to see for centuries.

The struggle to maintain such a city was long and precarious; there were many moments of failure to set against the overall pattern of success; there were many strands in the struggle to support a city of that size 15 miles (24 km) inland on the plain of Latium. But there was only one strand that was equal in importance to the supply of corn to the capital, and that was the supply of water. The Roman efforts to cope with that problem, spectacularly preserved in the ruins of the aqueducts, are justly world famous; the Roman efforts to ensure an adequate supply of corn, which were even greater but for which we have no similar single archaeological reminder, deserve to be so.

APPENDIX I

THE SENATE, THE EMPEROR, AND THE DISTRIBUTIONS

The traditional view that the cost of the corn supply and in particular of the distributions was transferred from the *aerarium* to the *fiscus*, from the senate to the Emperor, by the Emperor Claudius rests on inference from six pieces of indirect evidence which need careful scrutiny.

First Seneca in the *De Brevitate Vitae* written to urge the retirement of his father-in-law, Pompeius Paulinus, from his post which is likely to have been that of *praefectus annonae*, made no mention of the distributions of free corn at Rome as coming within the powers of the imperial *praefectus*.

Nevertheless Statius in the *Silvae* (3.3.85 and 90), alluding to the immense duties and power of Claudius Etruscus, the imperial *a rationibus* under Nero, indicated that the accounting for the corn distributions at Rome lay in his care and that the corn harvests of even senatorial provinces featured in his accounts.

Thirdly, Tacitus in the *Annals* (15.18) made the Emperor Nero boast in A.D. 62 about the size of his annual financial subvention of the state.

Fourthly, in the inscriptions giving the careers of men who held public office between the reign of Claudius and that of Trajan at the end of the first century A.D. there is no mention of the office *praefecti frumenti dandi ex s.c.* There is therefore a gap in the list of *praefecti frumenti dandi*, as if that office were, temporarily at any rate, abolished.[1]

Fifth, we 'know' that from the time of Claudius or Nero the corn distributions were concentrated at the Porticus Minucia with its own imperial official.[2]

Finally, there is a coin of Nerva, issued in A.D. 97, with the

[1] Lists given by H. G. Pflaum in *Historia* 2 (1953/4), 444–5, and revised and corrected in *Bonner Jahrbücher*, 163 (1963), 234–7.

[2] Momigliano, *Claudius*, p. 50.

legend 'PLEBEI URBANAE FRUMENTO CONSTITUTO—S.C.'[3]

The argument therefore runs: Seneca in A.D. 49 (the date suggested by Hirschfeld for the *De Brevitate Vitae*)[4] recognized the corn distributions as lying outside the sphere of an imperial official, the equestrian *praefectus annonae*, and therefore within the sphere of the senate. But Statius included both them and the revenues in corn of senatorial provinces within the sphere of an imperial official, the freedman *a rationibus*, under Nero. Nero's boast in the *Annals* of Tacitus must therefore relate to the cost of subsidizing the corn supply. A transfer of costs and responsibility for the corn supply must have taken place. This, together with the concentration of the corn distributions at the Porticus Minucia, explains the disappearance of the senatorial *praefecti frumenti dandi* at this time. Their reappearance later in the century was marked by the Nervan coin issue, when Nerva as an act of appeasement transferred the distributions back to the senate.[5]

There are loopholes in almost all the pieces of evidence which make one uneasy about this line of argument.

We do not know whether the *De Brevitate Vitae* was written in A.D. 49 or, as has recently been argued, in 55 after Claudius' death.[6] We do not know whether the omission of any reference to the distributions is significant or not.[7]

The allusion in Statius is to the work of a very different imperial official, a finance officer who by the very nature of the development of the financial accounting in the early Empire might be expected to keep a cost of the corn distributions, without implying total imperial control or exclusion of the senate.[8] The fact that a freedman *a rationibus* could be in account with revenues from senatorial provinces may prove nothing about the activities of the equestrian *praefectus annonae* and his officials. Indeed whether a poetic reference to the harvests of Africa can be pressed to mean senatorial revenues rather than

[3] Mattingly and Sydenham, *RIC* ii. 229 ff.

[4] O. Hirschfeld, 'Die Getreideverwaltung in der römischen Kaiserzeit', *Philologus* 29 (1870), 95–6.

[5] Van Berchem, *Distributions*, p. 77.

[6] M. T. Griffin, '*De Brevitate Vitae*', *JRS* 52 (1962), 104–13.

[7] Van Berchem, *Distributions*, p. 73.

[8] See above, p. 78.

produce of private estates greatly increased by new confiscations by the Emperor is perhaps doubtful.

Similarly Nero's proud boast of regularly subsidizing the state from private generosity has no necessary or obvious reference to the corn supply or corn distributions alone, and would be odd if all that he was referring to was something that had been part of a regular system from the time of Claudius.

The gap in the list of *praefecti frumenti dandi* may be there, or it may not. It may be pure chance that inscriptions recording the office have not been preserved for this period.[9] There has been a determined attempt by different scholars to show that M. Julius Romulus was a *praefectus frumenti dandi* after the death of Claudius and it has seemed to others that L. Caesennius Sospes might have held the office under Domitian.[10] There is certainly no statement in the literary authorities that the office, established by *senatus consultum*, was now abolished.

The reorganization of the distributing machinery of the *frumentationes* at the Porticus Minucia is only indirectly attested for this period. Despite Momigliano there is no evidence of a handover of power by the senatorial *praefecti frumenti dandi* to an imperial *procurator de Minucia.*[11] No post entitled *procurator de Minucia* ever existed, so far as I can discover. What we do have is an inscription from the time of either Claudius or Nero, to judge from the man's name which reads 'Ti. Claudius Aug. lib. Ianuarius curator de Minucia die XIIII ostio XLII'.[12] It was once thought that this freedman was a new imperial official working at the Porticus Minucia, the ludicrous fact that he only worked for one day in a month being largely ignored. It is certain however that the word 'curator' is not to be taken closely with 'de Minucia'. Ianuarius was simply a freedman who received public corn from the Porticus Minucia on a certain day at a certain entrance. The inscription is very important because of what it implies about the concentration

[9] Cardinali, *Frumentatio*, p. 248.

[10] G. E. F. Chilver, '*Princeps* and *Frumentationes*', *AJP* 70 (1949), 7–21; G. Vitucci, 'Note al cursus honorum di M. Iulius Romulus praefectus frumenti dandi ex s.c.', *RivFC* 25 (1947), 252 ff.; R. K. Sherk, 'The Legates of Galatia from Augustus to Diocletian' (Johns Hopkins Studies 69. 2) (1953), 87–9; also, decisively, R. Syme, 'The Enigmatic Sospes', *JRS* 67 (1977), 38–49.

[11] Momigliano, *Claudius*, p. 50.

[12] *CIL* 6. 10223 = *ILS* 6071.

of the corn distributions at the Porticus Minucia from the mid-first century A.D. but not for the officials working there. There may of course have been imperial officials working at and even in control of the Porticus Minucia, although we do not know their title and have no evidence for them. The earliest evidence for an imperial official working at the Porticus Minucia is dated about A.D. 110.[13] The equestrian M. Camurius Clemens is called on the inscription 'proc. Aug. ad Minuciam' but whatever he did he was not a replacement for the *praefecti frumenti dandi* since they were certainly in existence under Trajan. The equestrian post *procurator Minuciae* with a salary of 60,000 sesterces a year is only clearly attested on inscriptions of the third century A.D., when the role of the Porticus Minucia may have been different.[14] I suspect that even if there were imperial officials at the Porticus Minucia there was co-operation between them and the senatorial *praefecti* just as in the water administration there was co-operation between the *publica familia* paid from the *aerarium*, and the *familia Caesaris* created by Claudius, and paid from the *fiscus*.[15]

The coin type of Nerva, although of considerable interest and importance, is very unspecific in its reference—'the fixing of the corn supplies of the Roman plebs'.[16] The 'S.C.' on the coin is not to be read closely with the legend, being simply of general significance concerning the authority for coining.[17] Some reference, which we cannot now understand, is being made by Nerva to the special care he exerted on behalf of the urban plebs and their corn. It is unlikely that they would have cared much about the restoration of the senatorial *praefecti frumenti dandi*.

More worrying than individual difficulties in the evidence, however, are the underlying assumptions. The problem seems to be approached with the idea that there was some clear-cut dyarchy between Emperor and senate. But all the work that has been done recently, not just on the constitution, but also on

[13] *CIL* 11. 5669 = *ILS* 2728 (Pflaum, no. 87).

[14] *CIL* 3. 249 = *ILS* 1396; *CIL* 6. 1648; see below, p. 256.

[15] Frontinus, *De Aqu.* 116 and 118.

[16] G. Vitucci, 'PLEBEI URBANAE FRUMENTO CONSTITUTO', *ArchCl* 10 (1958), 310–14; A. Garzetti, *Nerva* (Rome, 1950), p. 69; cf. Chilver, *AJP* 70 (1949), 11.

[17] Aase Bay, 'The letters SC on Augustan *aes* coinage', *JRS* 62 (1972), 111–22.

the finances of the Empire, suggests that there was co-operation between senate and Emperor over a wide range of business.[18] I believe it to be true also in relation to the corn supply and the distributions.

[18] See above, p. 77; cf. Pavis D'Escurac, *Préfecture*, pp. 14–17, 21–6, 36–9.

APPENDIX 2

THE *PRAEFECTUS ANNONAE* AND *ANNONA* OFFICIALS UNDER THE EMPIRE

I

We have a number of inscriptions giving the careers of men who held the post of *praefectus annonae*. What do they tell us about the career structure of the *praefecti*?

We know virtually nothing of the earlier careers of the earliest *praefecti annonae* C. Turranius, Pompeius Paulinus, Faenius Rufus or Claudius Athenodorus, and of L. Laberius Maximus who was *praefectus annonae* in A.D. 80 only the fact that he had been procurator of Judaea in 71.[1] But C. Minicius Italus, who rose to be *praefectus annonae* by A.D. 101–2, had performed the usual equestrian triple military service with distinction under Vespasian, after which he became financial procurator of the province of the Hellespont in Vespasian's financial reorganization of that area of Asia, and even procurator extraordinary of the province of Asia itself *vice defuncti proconsulis*. The final post before his prefectship was the procuratorship of Gallia Lugdunensis.[2] Similarly M. Petronius Honoratus, who was prefect of the *annona* from A.D. 144 to 147, started with the triple military service, but then in a brilliantly rapid career became in succession *procurator monetae* (with a salary of 100,000 sesterces), *procurator XX hereditatum* and procurator of the province of Belgica and the two Germanies (both with a salary of 200,000 sesterces) and then *a rationibus* at Rome.[3]

[1] Seneca, *De Brevit. Vit.* (Paulinus); *CIL* 6. 8470 = *ILS* 1535 (Athenodorus). Pflaum, *Carrières*, no. 43 (Maximus). Cf. H. Pavis D'Escurac, *La Préfecture de l'annone: service administratif impérial d'Auguste à Constantin* (Rome, 1976), see especially Appendice: 'Étude Prosopographique'.

[2] Pflaum, no. 59, Pavis D'Escurac, p. 331.

[3] Pflaum, no. 117, Pavis D'Escurac, p. 343.

Whatever variations there may be in the preliminary parts of the careers of other prefects of the *annona* in the second and early third centuries A.D., in the higher reaches of their careers the Lugdunum procuratorship often features, as in the cases of C. Iunius Flavianus (*praefectus annonae* about A.D. 138), Ti. Claudius Secundinus Macedo (*praefectus annonae* some time after A.D. 147) and Q. Baienus Blassianus (*praefectus annonae* some time before A.D. 168). It was clearly a launching pad in a man's career for the great equestrian secretariats and prefectures in Rome. Perhaps more significant still is the way in which the post *a rationibus* precedes the prefectship of the *annona* also in the careers of L. Valerius Proculus (*praefectus annonae* A.D. 142–4), Ti. Claudius Secundinus Macedo, C. Iunius Flavianus, and L. Iulius Vehilius Gratus Iulianus (*praefectus annonae* about A.D. 186).[4] It presumably might well have featured also in the career of Minicius Italus if the post *a rationibus* had been clearly of equestrian status in his day—but it was still essentially a post held by freedmen in the first century A.D. In none of the careers that we know of is there an example of a man on his way to the prefectship of the *annona* holding a regular junior post in the corn supply, such as the *procurator annonae* at Ostia. Only L. Valerius Proculus, who at a very early stage in his career was prefect of the Roman fleet at Alexandria and the river guard on the Nile, could be said to have picked up any directly practical experience, and that may have been minimal.[5] It may also be that the experience gained by L. Iulius Vehilius Gratus Iulianus as commander of the fleets of Ravenna and Misenum in the early 180s A.D. stood him in good stead as *praefectus annonae* in the middle 180s A.D., since it may have been he that was called on by Commodus to organize the African corn fleet, attested by coins minted late in A.D. 186.[6] Indeed it may have been the reason why he was made *praefectus annonae*. On the other hand for a man to have been *a rationibus*, that is, to have held the major financial post in the Empire, to have superintended the accounts, the book-keeping, the figures of a great

[4] Pflaum, no. 109, Pavis D'Escurac, p. 345 (Macedo); Pflaum, no. 126, Pavis D'Escurac, p. 358 (Blassianus), but for date see P. A. Brunt, *JRS* 65 (1975), 145; Pflaum, no. 134, Pavis D'Escurac, p. 340 (Flavianus); Pflaum, no. 113, Pavis D.Escurac, p. 342 (Proculus); Pflaum, no. 180, Pavis D'Escurac, p. 350 (Iulianus).

[5] Pflaum, no. 113, Pavis D'Escurac, p. 342.

[6] Mattingly and Sydenham, *RIC* iii. 422, nos. 486–7.

treasury office was apparently thought a very relevant qualification for the *annona* job. This fact is revealing about the actual work done by the prefect and his subordinates for most of the first two centuries A.D.

Originally the *praefectus* as a deputy of the Emperor was merely trying to exercise a *cura* over the corn supply[7] and in no sense did he have monopolistic powers. But the earmarking of the corn production of certain areas such as Egypt and Sicily for the Roman market, together with the granting of privileges of various kinds to private merchants who helped the corn supply from the time of Claudius had the result that among the records of the prefect were not just abstract figures but lists of men together with their obligations and privileges. He could, and on an ever greater scale did, hear civil cases of great variety and from many types of complainants, including even women and slaves, providing they were 'propter utilitatem ad annonam pertinentem'.[8]

It is not surprising therefore that this important aspect of the prefect's work should be reflected more and more in the career structure of the *praefecti*. The first clear example comes in the reign of Antoninus Pius when L. Volusius Maecianus (*praefectus annonae* a little after A.D. 152) after a career of a mainly secretarial kind personally associated with Antoninus before as well as after the latter's elevation to the purple, was promoted from the post of *a libellis et censibus* to the *annona* job.[9] Normally the *a libellis* might have been promoted to the post of *praefectus vigilum* because of his legal knowledge gained from dealing with petitions, so the promotion of Volusius Maecianus, friend or pupil of Salvius Julianus the great jurist, to be *praefectus annonae* is a real sign of the increasing legal emphasis in the functions of that office. M. Aurelius Papirius Dionysius was similarly *a libellis et cognitionibus* at the start of Commodus' reign and learned in the law before elevation to the *annona* office in A.D. 189–90, while one of the most famous of all jurists, Domitius Ulpianus, was perhaps *praefectus annonae* in A.D. 222 before his promotion to be *praefectus praetorio*.[10]

[7] Tac. *Ann.* 3. 54. 6–8.

[8] *Dig.* 48. 2. 13 (Marcianus).

[9] Pflaum, no. 141; Pavis D'Escurac, p. 346.

[10] Pflaum, no. 181, Pavis D'Escurac, p. 352 (Dionysius); Pflaum, no. 294, Pavis D'Escurac, p. 361 (Ulpian).

But by the end of the second century A.D. it may be that the heyday of the *praefectus annonae* as a major equestrian office was over. We certainly possess far fewer inscriptions of the subordinates of the prefect of the *annona* and this may be related to the fact that the *praefectus praetorio* gives orders concerning the provincial supplies if not from the beginning of the third century then certainly from the time of the military crisis.[11] The *praefectus annonae* during the military crises of the third century A.D. seems to be well on the way to be becoming almost the local municipal official of Rome that he was in the later Roman Empire.

2

The prefect's immediate subordinate, at least in the first century A.D., seems to have had the title *adiutor*. Sex Attius Suburanus Aemilianus held this post in A.D. 81–2 as *adiutor* to Iulius Ursus and then followed him to Egypt to be his *adiutor* there, after which he became procurator in his own right *ad Mercurium*, one of the districts of Alexandria associated with the storage of grain, and was launched on a successful procuratorial career.[12] Another man of unknown name held the post in the 80s A.D. as *adiutor* to the *praefectus annonae* Mettius Rufus. But we also know of a freedman in the 90s A.D. as *adiutor* to Claudius Athenodorus.[13] Either the post, as personal aide, was open indiscriminately to equestrians and freedmen, or there was a bureau of freedmen parallel to the equestrian office, which is not impossible.

But at some point in the second century A.D. the title *subpraefectus annonae* came to be the official name of the regular second-in-command, nominated directly by the Emperor, and with a salary of 100,000 sesterces. The first holder that we know of is P. Cominius Clemens about A.D. 172 and it is likely that the post was created by M. Aurelius.[14] Although he went on to

[11] O. Hirschfeld, *Die kaiserlichen Verwaltungsbeamten*[2] (Berlin, 1905), p. 244; cf. SHA *Pesc. Nig.* 7. 4; but cf. Pavis D'Escurac, *Préfecture*, p. 282.

[12] *Æpigr.* (1939), 60, cf. Pflaum, no. 56, Pavis D'Escurac, p. 381.

[13] *CIL* 12. 671, cf. Pflaum, no. 52, Pavis D'Escurac, p. 383; *CIL* 6. 8470 = *ILS* 1535, Pavis D'Escurac, pp. 387 and 389.

[14] *CIL* 5. 8659 = *ILS* 1412, cf. Pflaum, no. 184, Pavis D'Escurac, p. 391.

have a successful procuratorial career he did not in fact become the *praefectus annonae* himself. The same is true of Ti. Claudius Xenophon at the time of the accession of Septimius Severus, Q. Cosconius Fronto just a little later, and Ulpius Victor under Caracalla.[15] But by this time, as has been stressed earlier, the post of *praefectus annonae* was increasingly held by legal experts.

3

The details of the minor officials in the *annona* office are rather lacking, and Hirschfeld has guessed that some of the many officials who have the title *a frumento* must have worked there.[16] We know of *dispensatores*, *actores*, and *procuratores*.

A rather clearer picture of the work of the lower organization emerges from Ostia.[17] Under Claudius the old *quaestor Ostiensis*, who had among his other duties dealt with corn passing through the river harbour, was replaced by a special *procurator annonae*,[18] who seems to have held his specialized post alongside the new *procurator portus* who looked after the running of the harbour generally. The *procurator annonae* at Ostia, belonging to the lowest grade of equestrian procurators, with an annual salary of 60,000 sesterces[19] was responsible to his superior the *praefectus annonae* at Rome but he himself had a small staff at Ostia. Like the *praefectus* in Rome he had both a *cornicularius* and a number of *beneficiarii* under him, that is, an adjutant, often of ex-centurion status and a few privileged soldiers.[20] There was a departmental chest of the procurator at Ostia, the *mensa nummularia fisci frumentarii Ostiensis*,[21] from which were presumably made the payments to shipmasters and to labourers

[15] *CIL* 3. 7127 = *ILS* 1421; cf. Pflaum, no. 222 (Xenophon), Pavis D'Escurac, p. 392. *CIL* 10. 7584 = *ILS* 1359; cf. Pflaum, no. 264 (Fronto), Pavis D'Escurac, p. 393. *CIL* 3. 1464 = *ILS* 1370; cf. Pflaum, no. 257 (Ulpius Victor), Pavis D'Escurac, p. 394.

[16] Hirschfeld, *KVB*², p. 244 n. 1; Pavis D'Escurac, *Préfecture*, pp. 97–102.

[17] Meiggs, *Roman Ostia*², pp. 299 ff.

[18] Suet. *Claud.* 24. 2; Dio 60. 24. 3 (A.D. 44).

[19] *CIL* 10. 7580.

[20] 'Cornicularius' *CIL* 14. 160 = *ILS* 1428 at Ostia, cf. *CIL* 11. 20 = *ILS* 2082 at Rome; 'beneficiarii' at Ostia *CIL* 14. 409 = *ILS* 6146.

[21] *CIL* 14. 2045.

at the docks and in the warehouses. The head of this departmental chest was an imperial freedman, and below him both at Ostia and at Portus worked a number of *dispensatores*, pay clerks, all imperial slaves of whom one at least worked at Puteoli as well as at Ostia.[22] Clearly there were *annona* officials at Puteoli even in the second century A.D., not only the *Aug(usti) disp(ensator) a frumento Puteolis et Ostis* under Antoninus Pius already mentioned, but also a *proximus commentariorum annonae*, deputy head of corn-supply records, perhaps early in Hadrian's reign.[23] Puteoli still handled some of Rome's corn reserves. There may even have been at Ostia an imperial freedman who investigated the claims of those shippers who said that they had put a ship with a capacity of 10,000 *modii* into the corn supply.[24] Whether there were similar officials of the *annona* office all over the Mediterranean in areas which exported corn to Rome, we do not know. It might seem desirable but the evidence is almost completely lacking.

We know of the existence in the second century A.D. at Arles of a man who was 'procurator Augusti ad annonam provinciae Narbonensis et Liguriae'.[25] The traditional view is that he was a representative of the central *annona* office who was stationed at Arles.[26] But there has always been a challenge to that view, most recently reiterated by Pflaum, who sees his job as dealing with local provisioning problems of the areas named, not those of Rome.[27] However in view of the fact that the shippers of Narbo and probably Arles had offices at Ostia,[28] and the inscription in this man's honour was set up by the *navicularii marini* of Arles, it seems to me still probable that he dealt in some way with export to Rome perhaps at a moment of crisis. We know from a remarkable bronze inscription that the *navicularii marini* of Arles were in the late second century A.D. regarded as serving the *annona* of Rome.[29]

[22] *CIL* 10. 1562 = *ILS* 344 'Aug. disp(ensator) a fruminto Puteolis et Ostis'.
[23] *CIL* 10. 1729, cf. P. Weaver, *Antichthon* 5 (1971), 77 ff.
[24] *CIL* 14. Suppl. 4319, 'Traiano Aug. lib. a Xm'—the meaning is doubtful but Meiggs's guess is ingenious and may well be right.
[25] *CIL* 12. 672 = *ILS* 1432.
[26] Hirschfeld, *KVB*², p. 243 n. 1.
[27] Pflaum, no. 186, p. 508; but cf. Pavis D'Escurac, *Préfecture*, pp. 129–34.
[28] Meiggs, *Roman Ostia*², p. 286.
[29] *CIL* 3. 14165/8 = *ILS* 6987; see above, p. 91.

What has often been regarded as the best evidence for agents of the *praefectus annonae* being stationed in the provinces proves not to be very compelling when scrutinized. It is the inscription set up at Hispalis (Seville) in Baetica in honour of Sextus Julius Possessor late in the second century A.D.[30] He was at one point in his career 'adiutor Ulpii Saturnini praef(ecti) annon(ae) ad oleum Afrum et Hispanum recensendum item solamina transferenda item vecturas naviculariis exsolvendas', 'aide to the *praefectus annonae* for keeping account of Spanish and African oil, for transporting supplies and paying the shippers'. Hirschfeld believed that he was stationed at Hispalis while performing these duties. It is difficult to see how Julius Possessor could have dealt with African as well as Spanish oil when stationed at Hispalis, and the reason why the *scapharii Hispalenses*, boatmen of Hispalis, put up the inscription in his honour there may have been because he went on to become *procurator ad ripam Baetis*. Moreover a new inscription discovered at Mactar, erected by Julius Possessor, reveals that he was an African and not a Spaniard by origin, as had previously been thought.[31] It also shows that after his duty on the river Baetis he was promoted first to be *procurator Augusti ad annonam* at Ostia and then to be *procurator ad Mercurium*, one of the districts at Alexandria associated with the storage of grain. Throughout his career he was therefore involved with supply problems in one way or another. He was of provincial origin and his career took him backwards and forwards to the provinces, but as *adiutor praefecti annonae* he may have been based in Rome, like others with this title. If this was so then he is not an example of an agent of the *praefectus annonae* stationed at Hispalis but part of the *annona* office in Rome with the special responsibility of keeping accounts of Spanish and African oil, smoothing the forward path of supplies and paying freightage to the shippers. Even if he was sent from Rome to deal with this problem in the provinces named, it was probably only a special mission at a time of special difficulty.

The evidence for permanent agents of the *praefectus annonae* in the provinces is therefore as slender as it has ever been. It seems

[30] *CIL* 2. 1180 = *ILS* 1403; cf. Hirschfeld, *KVB*², p. 242 n. 5; Pavis D'Escurac, p. 384.

[31] G.-Ch. Picard, *RA* 2 (1963), 90–2, cf. Pflaum, no. 185, p. 506.

to have been the governor and the local cities that were responsible for organizing the collection of grain in provincial areas in normal times.

APPENDIX 3

CORPORA NAVICULARIORUM

At Ostia the Piazzale delle Corporazioni, a large double colonnade behind the theatre, was built at the same time as the original construction of the theatre under Augustus.[1] In the form which has survived for us, sixty-one small rooms open off the colonnade and mosaics on the pavement of most of them illustrate the occupations of the owners. A large proportion of them illustrate the corn trade, and Africa is the most conspicuous of the overseas provinces represented, but these mosaics are not at the original level, and below them lay others of which it has been possible to examine only four, none of which seems to have any direct allusion to the corn trade.

Nevertheless Calza put forward the view that the merchants and shippers who were most important for the supplies of Rome were concentrated here by imperial authority under Augustus and that this was one of the main centres of imperial control with its function unchanged into the third century A.D. Rostovtzeff accepted this view and saw in it an example of close imperial control. He was convinced by the Ostian evidence, by his interpretation of the sherds from Monte Testaccio in Rome and from legal texts that 'from the very beginning the corporations of merchants and shipowners who dealt in some of the necessities of life, and especially the latter, were recognized by the state because they were agents of the state—more or less concessionaries of the Roman government'.[2]

So far as the Piazzale at Ostia is concerned, Tenney Frank pointed out that there was no evidence for the concentration of shippers in the colonnade until the raising of the level, which

In general see now L. C. Ruggini, 'Le associazioni professionali nel mondo romano-bizantino', *Settimane di studi nel centro italiano di studi sull' alto medioevo* 18. 1 (Spoleto, 1971), 59–193; G. Clemente, 'Il patronato nei collegia dell' impero romano', *SCO* 21 (1972), 142–229.

[1] Meiggs, *Roman Ostia*², pp. 283–7.

[2] G. Calza, 'Il piazzale delle corporazioni e la funzione commerciale di Ostia', *BullComm* 43 (1915), 178–206; Rostovtzeff, *SEHRE*², p. 607 n. 22.

Calza had dated to the end of the second century A.D. when the theatre was rebuilt.[3] He concluded that only then were the offices designed as centres of control by the government. Van Berchem[4] reacted even more strongly and argued that the colonnade had no commercial significance at all, but that was to go too far. Meiggs has since made clear both that there were overseas shippers represented in the colonnade long before the end of the second century A.D., and that its building history is more complicated than Calza supposed. But his conclusion is that the offices in the colonnade covered such a wide diversity of trades that it would be right to doubt whether it can be an illustration of bureaucracy. It is more probable that the colonnade was originally created for private traders from Ostia and elsewhere, who found it useful to have representatives there to take orders and see to business. It may have been that the *procurator annonae* at Ostia found it increasingly convenient to have so many representatives of the corn trade easily accessible in one place, but that was all. They did not set up office there either upon his orders, or just to receive them.[5]

The inscriptions on the jars in the Monte Testaccio at Rome have been so thoroughly examined by Grenier and Tenney Frank, that Rostovtzeff's belief that they 'speak of *navicularii* as working for the state under its control' can be firmly set aside.[6] The inscriptions if anything bear witness to the independent activity of Narbonensian and Spanish *navicularii* carrying goods from southern and eastern Spain to Rome on their own account and through their own commercial organizations.

So far as legal texts are concerned, the passage of Callistratus quoted by Rostovtzeff does not say, as he claims, that corporations of this kind were organized by the state, only that it was fair that *navicularii* should be freed from various obligations 'dum annonae urbis serviunt'.[7] Moreover there is no evidence to suggest that such groups were recognized, much less organized, earlier than such urban professional colleges as rag-men (*centonarii*) and builders (*fabri tignuarii*). In fact the earliest explicit

[3] Tenney Frank, 'Notes on Roman Commerce', *JRS* 27 (1937), 74 ff.

[4] Van Berchem, *Distributions*, p. 111.

[5] Meiggs, *Roman Ostia*², p. 287.

[6] A. Grenier, *Manuel d'archéologie gallo-romaine* ii. 2 (Paris, 1934), 609 ff.; Tenney Frank, 'Roman Commerce', *JRS* 27 (1937), 72–9.

[7] *Dig.* 50. 6. 6. 3 (Callistratus), cf. Rostovtzeff, *SEHRE*², p. 607 n. 22.

evidence for involvement by the state through colleges refers to that of the *pistores*, bakers of Rome, in the reign of Trajan.[8]

Although Rostovtzeff's thesis must be rejected, it must be admitted that the inscriptions and legal texts on which we have to rely are not easy to interpret. The difficulties are many. Just as the omission from an inscription or a document of the word *corpus* or *collegium* does not show that such a body did not exist, so a reference to a combination of members of the same trade or profession does not necessarily show that they were *corporati*. Moreover even where it can be shown that a person or persons were directly under contract with a public official, it does not follow that they were not also engaged in business on their own account. On the contrary, even in the fourth century A.D. *navicularii* enjoyed exemption from duties on articles of private commerce.[9] So even if it could be proved that *navicularii* were 'state-employed' at a certain time, it could be misleading to assume that wherever they were present they were necessarily engaged on public business.

It seems more profitable in general to follow the cautious approach of Waltzing and envisage a slow growth of free associations, which only in time came to be utilized by the state for its own purposes. But Waltzing does not explain in a detailed way how and why this development came about in the *annona*. He makes merely a broad division into three phases, largely differentiated by the type of evidence available;[10] the first, and least well known, period extending up to the Antonine Emperors; the second, not as clearly known as it might be from the classical jurists of the second and third centuries A.D.; the third and best known, illuminated by the regulations in the Theodosian Code for the fourth and fifth centuries A.D.

His reluctance to try to unravel the development in the first period in particular seems to be tied up with his two main theses about the *collegia*.

The first is that the legal conception of a *collegium*, as expounded by the third-century jurists, does not appear to include the capacity to make contracts.

The second is that, since a *collegium* might contain inactive members, or members active in other professions, to be a

[8] Frag. Vat. 233 (Ulpian); Gaius, *Inst.* i. 28, 34; Aurel. Vict. *De Caes.* 13. 5.
[9] *Cod. Theod.* 13. 5. 23 and 24 (A.D. 393). [10] Waltzing, *Corporations* ii. p. 42.

member of a *collegium* associated with the *annona* would not in itself constitute any claim to the privileges which were only enjoyed by those active in the service of the *annona*.

The first of these theses is clearly right. Although the conception of what a *collegium* was, and could do, was extensively developed and widened during the second century A.D.,[11] and there may have been no obvious reason why the state should not enter into contracts with the *collegia*, nevertheless the evidence is against the notion that the *collegium* as such negotiated with the state. Financial arrangements seem to have had no connection with the common chests of the *collegia*. *Navicularii* were not paid through the college but personally by an imperial procurator.[12] Individuals put their money directly into trading ventures, not through their colleges.[13] Liability was not corporate but, so far as we can see, always personal.[14] The *collegia* in short never bore the slightest resemblance to trading companies.

The second thesis however may not be so sound. If to be a member of a *collegium* associated with the *annona* did not constitute at least a prima-facie case for the enjoyment of certain privileges and immunities, there would have been no need for the rescripts of Trajan, Hadrian, and Marcus Aurelius and Lucius Verus confining these benefits to active members.[15] The very point made by Waltzing proves the opposite of his thesis. The jurists leave little doubt that in general it was through membership of certain colleges that immunity was obtained, for example: 'corpus mensorum frumenti . . . habet vacationem',[16] or 'quibusdam collegiis vel corporibus, quibus ius coeundi permissum est, immunitas tribuitur'.[17]

If this is correct, then we may have some clue as to the evolution of the *collegia* connected with the corn supply in terms of their usefulness both to their members and to the state. The

[11] *Dig.* 40. 3. 1 (Ulpian) (ability to manumit slaves); *Dig.* 34. 5. 20 (Paulus) (ability to receive legacies); cf. also *Dig.* 3. 4. 1 (Gaius), 10. 4. 7. 3 (Ulpian), 4. 2. 9. 1 (Ulpian).

[12] Cf. *CIL* 2. 1180 ('vecturas naviculariis exsolvendas').

[13] *Dig.* 50. 4. 5 (Scaevola), 50. 6. 6. 12 (Callistratus).

[14] *Dig.* 4. 9 (Ulpian); cf. 19. 2. 13. 1 (Ulpian).

[15] Frag. Vat. 233 (Ulpian); *Dig.* 50. 6. 6. 5 and 6 (Callistratus).

[16] *Dig.* 50. 5. 10. 1 (Paulus).

[17] *Dig.* 50. 6. 6. 12 (Callistratus).

state found in the lists kept by the *collegia* the quickest and most efficient method of keeping track of those eligible for privileges, and the shippers found membership of a *collegium* the easiest way of ensuring that their rights to privileges were brought to the notice of the state. It was an evolutionary process which seemed to be beneficial to both sides and not a revolution whereby the state imposed regimentation to suit its will.

APPENDIX 4

AFRICA AND EGYPT

There is no doubt that the two most important sources of corn for Rome in the early Empire were Africa and Egypt, and that by the latter part of the first century A.D. Africa was quantitatively the more important of the two. Can we say with any confidence exactly how much corn was sent to Rome from each country? It has traditionally been argued that we can.

We are informed by the *Epitome de Caesaribus*, a work of the fourth century A.D. whose author is unknown, that in the time of Augustus the annual shipments of grain from Egypt to Rome amounted to 20 million *modii*.[1] On the other hand the Jewish historian Flavius Josephus in his *Bellum Judaicum*, written in A.D. 75–9, put into the mouth of the Jewish prince Agrippa a speech enumerating the overwhelming resources of Rome in order to dissuade his fellow countrymen from revolt in A.D. 66.[2] It is alleged in this speech that African lands in the widest sense provided grain for the multitude (*plethos*) of Rome for eight months in the year. But clearly Egypt is not included in this generalization since it is dealt with separately later when Josephus states that Egypt provided food for Rome for four months in the year. It has been customary for scholars to combine the information about proportions from Josephus with the exact figure given by the *Epitome*, and to deduce that Rome imported 20 million *modii* annually from Egypt and 40 million *modii* annually from Africa.[3]

This seems to me now most unlikely, and to make nonsense of the recurring difficulties of the Roman corn supply during the

[1] *Epit. de Caesaribus* 1. 6.

[2] Josephus, *Bell. Iud.* 2. 383 and 386.

[3] The literature is vast, but see e.g.: Cardinali, *Frumentatio*, p. 305; Rostovtzeff, *Frumentum*, col. 132; R. Cagnat, 'L'annone d'Afrique', *MemAcInscr* 40 (1916), 253; S. L. Wallace, *Taxation in Egypt from Augustus to Diocletian* (Princeton, 1938), Ch. 18; G.-Ch. Picard, 'Néron et le blé d'Afrique', *Les Cahiers de Tunisie* 14 (1956), 163–73, cf. *CRAI* (1956), pp. 68–72; K. Hopkins, *Conquerors and Slaves*, pp. 97–8.

early Empire.[4] The *frumentationes*, at a ration of 5 *modii* for up to 200,000 people, would need only 12 million *modii*, and the total needs of Rome as a whole may not have exceeded some 40 million *modii*. If 60 million *modii* were arriving regularly from Egypt and Africa, whether from taxes or private traders, besides the imports from Sicily and other sources, there should have been a positive embarrassment of corn surpluses in Rome, and that was certainly not the case.

It hardly seems good historical method, either, simply to juxtapose two such disparate sources, and by a process of 'scissors and paste' produce a neat and schematic answer. We do not know with what authority so late a source as the *Epitome* could give a figure for Rome's import of Egyptian corn at the time of Augustus, and to use it as the cornerstone for the calculation seems unnecessarily hazardous. It seems better to concentrate on the passage in Josephus, to decide upon its meaning, and in quantifying the proportions given to make the best guesses that we can. Such guesses must then be tested against the few other pieces of evidence and against general probability.

The meaning of the Josephus' passage depends on the translation of the word 'plethos', which can mean either just the recipients of the *frumentationes*, that is up to 200,000 people, or the population of Rome as a whole, that is, in my view, nearer 1,000,000 people.[5] I believe that when read in context the intention of the passage is clearly in favour of the latter translation. Josephus was saying that North Africa fed the population of Rome as a whole for two-thirds of the year and was capable of rendering tribute as well in other forms; Egypt sent more tribute in one month than Judaea rendered in a whole year, and in addition to this money supplied corn as well sufficient for one-third of the year. If we assume that Rome may have needed about 40 million *modii* per annum,[6] it follows that at the time of Nero, according to this dramatic speech of the prince Agrippa, Rome received up to 13 million *modii* from Egypt and up to 27 million *modii* from Africa.

Are these figures even of the right order of magnitude? We need not doubt that Egypt could afford to export 13 million

[4] Rickman, *Roman Granaries*, Appendix 3 for a different approach.
[5] Z. Yavetz, *Plebs and Princeps*, pp. 141–55. [6] See above, p. 10.

modii a year. The figure given by the *Epitome* is higher than that and the only other, rather cryptic, piece of evidence for Egyptian grain export in the Late Empire appears to give nearly triple that amount. An edict of Justinian refers to the annual shipment of corn levied as tax from Egypt to Constantinople as amounting to 8 million of some unspecified unit.[7] The unit implied is the *artaba*, and if the *artaba* of the period was equivalent to 4½ *modii*, the corn tax from Egypt to Constantinople in the sixth century A.D. was 36 million *modii*.[8]

If there is a problem therefore about a notional figure of 13 million *modii* for Egyptian corn export to Rome at the time of Nero, it is why it is so low and whether the amount could have fallen from a higher figure at the time of Augustus. But explanations are not difficult to find. It is quite possible that under Augustus Rome took more Egyptian corn than was taken later in the first century A.D., when the great development of the African estates really got under way. The drop in the size of the Egyptian corn export to Rome is not likely to have been caused by any kind of economic recession in that country.[9] Despite some distress among the peasantry and natural fluctuations in the size of its harvests, Egyptian productivity probably remained high throughout the history of the Empire as the Edict of Justinian implies. There are two more compelling reasons to account for the drop. The first was the much greater proximity of Africa to Rome, which once there were expanding corn surpluses in that area, would count heavily in their favour in the Roman market. The journey of the corn freighters from Alexandria to Rome was by comparison long and difficult.[10] The second reason is that there were alternative demands on Egypt's corn throughout her history, particularly in the Eastern Mediterranean. The effect of the Roman capture of Egypt on the pattern of its corn exports has always puzzled scholars.[11] The change, in my view, may have been less profound

[7] Iust. *Ed.* 13. 8 (*Corpus Iuris Civilis*, pp. 780 ff.).

[8] Cf. Duncan-Jones, 'The Choenix, the Artaba and the Modius', *ZPE* 21 (1976), 43–52.

[9] Wallace, *Taxation*, p. 350 with reference to Milne, 'The ruin of Egypt by Roman mismanagement', *JRS* 17 (1927), 1–13.

[10] See above, p. 129.

[11] L. Casson, 'The Grain Trade of the Hellenistic World', *TAPA* 85 (1954), 168, suggested that Rome had taken an increasing amount of Egyptian corn during the

than we think; not because Rome had been taking an increasing amount of Egyptian corn during the late Republic, a hypothesis for which there is no evidence, but because even under Augustus Rome never took all Egypt's exportable surplus, and because with the development of Africa, Rome's claims on Egyptian corn rapidly lessened. Rome certainly controlled closely what happened to the corn revenues of Egypt, but never took them all for the support of the capital itself. Egypt's previous customers in the eastern Mediterranean could, and did, with permission, still buy from Egypt. There was a standard form of words to be used when asking for such permission which implies that it must have occurred more regularly than has been realized.[12]

So much for Egypt, but could Africa have supplied up to 27 million *modii* for the Roman market? I believe it could, not least because of two passages in the life of Septimius Severus in the *Historia Augusta*. In the first (§ 8.5) it is stated that although he found the grain supply at a very low ebb on his accession, the Emperor managed it so well that when he died he left the Roman people a surplus to the amount of seven years' tribute ('septem annorum canonem'). The second (§23.2) is more explicit: at his death he left a surplus of grain to the amount of seven years' tribute, or enough to distribute 75,000 *modii* a day. The *canon* of tribute implied is 27,375,000 *modii*. I believe, with A. H. M. Jones, that the author of the *Life* of Septimius Severus may well have taken his figure for average daily consumption not from a Severan source, but supplied it himself.[13] In that case what we have in this passage is an indication of the size of the *canon* of Rome not at the time of Severus but in the fourth century A.D. By that time a diminished Rome was totally dependent on the resources of the West, because all the Egyptian supplies had been diverted to Constantinople. In short, at a time when we know that Rome depended particularly on Africa, we have a figure of something more than 27 million *modii* for the *canon frumentarius*. I am

late Republic. This was refuted by Meiggs, *Roman Ostia*², p. 472, who stressed the lack of any reference by Cicero in his voluminous speeches about the work of Pompey and his letters and speeches about the affairs of Egypt in the 60s and 50s B.C.

[12] See above, p. 70.

[13] Jones, *LRE*, p. 698.

encouraged to believe therefore that such a figure may not be too out of scale as Africa's contribution from the late first century A.D. to the support of a bigger Roman population.

Whether these figures are accurate in any precise sense is of course to be doubted, but the evidence, if handled with care, yields a coherent, and not improbable, picture.

APPENDIX 5

WAREHOUSE LEASES IN PUTEOLI

The archive of wax tablets, at least 150 in number, discovered recently at Pompeii, are very important because of the varied nature of their contents, but unfortunately they are at times difficult to read and not easy to understand.[1]

A particular case in point is Tablet 7—a triptych which contains a record of the lease of part of a warehouse at Puteoli. After the names of Emperors Gaius and Claudius as consuls in A.D. 37, and the date, 2 July, the tablet records in the first person singular that Diognetus, slave of Gaius Novius Cypaerus, at the command of his master and in his presence, has leased to Hesicus, slave of a Euenus, a freedman of the Emperor Tiberius, in the middle part (?) of the public *Horrea Bassiana* in Puteoli *horreum* XII in which is stored Alexandrian wheat, which he received today as a security from a Gaius Novius Eunus. The tablet continues that likewise in these same *horrea* but in the lower part (?) *inter columnia* have been leased where there are stored 200 sacks of vegetables which he received as a security from the same man. It is then specified that there was to be a payment which was to run from 1 July and was to be 1 sesterce per month; the whole transaction being performed at Puteoli.

On other parts of the triptych there were, besides another complete version of the text above, some seals, and the signatures of, among others, C. Novius Cypaerus and also traces of a receipt for the corn stored in *horreum* XII by C. Novius Eunus.

The Italian scholar Bove has revealed that the explanation of the transaction and further details about the names are given in another, then unedited, diptych. Diognetus, slave of C. Novius Cypaerus has let part of the *horrea* to Hesicus, slave of an imperial freedman, whose full name is T. Iulius Augusti l. Eunus Primianus; Hesicus in his turn has loaned a certain sum

[1] Originally published by C. Giordano, 'Su alcune tavolette cerate dell' agro Murecine', *RendNap* 41 (1966), 107 ff.; cf. L. Bove, 'A proposito di nuove Tabulae Pompeianae', *RendNap* 44 (1969), 25–51; also in *Labeo* 17 (1971), 149–54.

of money to C. Novius Eunus who as a *pignus* for the debt has offered some goods deposited in the same *horrea*.

What Bove did not explain was whether the goods concerned were in the parts of the *horrea* now let to Hesicus, although the assumption is that they were, and if so, what the connection between the two transactions was.

Kunkel[2] has suggested that first Hesicus made his loan to Gaius Novius Eunus and accepted as *pignus* the goods mentioned, but he then decided, rather unusually, it had better be he who held the lease of the actual parts of the *horrea* in which these goods were stored. The reason for such an unusual action can be found in Kunkel's assumption from the origin of the goods that C. Novius Eunus was an Alexandrian merchant, who might easily disappear with the pledged goods, and the goods by their very nature would hardly be identifiable once they were moved from the storage place. All this made it imperative once Hesicus had made the loan against the security of some goods in store that he should take over the lease of the storage space as well.

This is the most helpful explanation of the transactions and how they are linked, but the money reference at the end of the tablet is still puzzling. The payment cannot be to do with the loan transaction which has already taken place in another document, and must be related to the renting of the *horrea* space. But 12 sesterces a year does seem very low, a mere peppercorn rent. Of course we do not know how big the storage space was, nor how much Alexandrian wheat there may have been, although 200 sacks of vegetables would have taken up some room. Nor do we know whether the rent to be charged to Hesicus was merely nominal, a sort of legal device so as to allow him greater control over the goods stored. If it is a realistic and accurate rent then it would indicate that storage no less than transport across the sea would add less than has sometimes been thought to the cost of marketing grain in Rome.

We must hope for more help on these problems. Recently another more fragmentary tablet[3] from the collection, dated

[2] W. Kunkel, 'Hypothesen zur Geschichte des römischen Pfandrechts', *ZSavignyStift* 90 (1973), 150–70, esp. p. 158.

[3] C. Giordano, 'Nuove tavolette cerate Pompeiane', *RendNap* 46 (1971), 195. Cf. J. Crook, 'Working Notes on some of the New Pompeii Tablets', *ZPE* 29 (1978), 229–39, esp. pp. 234–7.

A.D. 40, records another lease, this time by a slave Nardus at the command of his master P. Annius S. . . . He writes that a lease has been made to C. Sulpicius Faustus of *horreum* XXVI (?), which is in the *praedia* of Domitia Livia. After an unintelligible gap there is a reference to the fact that some 13 (?) thousand *modii* of Alexandrian wheat are in store. Unfortunately the rental payment at the end is too mutilated to be read. These tantalizing references to Alexandrian grain and the costs of warehouses leases are all that we have at present but we must hope that more tablets in better condition on the same themes will be published soon.

APPENDIX 6

PLINY *N.H.* 18.90: FLOUR PRICES AND THE PRICE OF GRAIN AT ROME

What looks at first sight to be our most explicit evidence for the average price of grain on the Roman market in the third quarter of the first century A.D. is given by Pliny the Elder. In a complicated passage dealing with different kinds of grain, different kinds of flour, and bread-making in his *Natural History*, Pliny says:[1] 'When the prices of grain are average, *farina* (meal) sells at 40 *asses* per *modius*, *similago* (ordinary flour from wheat) at 8 *asses* more, *siligo castrata* (best quality flour) at double' (*duplum*).

It sounds straightforward and it is certainly interesting that Pliny can think in terms of 'average' prices for grain, but unfortunately this passage raises more questions than it solves. We must ask not just what were the extraction rates for flour of varying qualities in the ancient world, but also whether the passage in Pliny shows signs of textual corruption, particularly in the numbers given, and whether Pliny himself seems to have had a good grasp and understanding of the information he has copied from his sources.

Rostovtzeff,[2] without going into the matter in any detail, argued that although the ratio of corn prices to flour prices in the modern world is about 1:1·5, the extraction rate in the ancient world was unlikely to have been so good and therefore the ratio would have been about 1:2. Therefore Pliny's price of 10 sesterces a *modius* and above for flour must have been the equivalent of a grain price of 5 sesterces a *modius*, from which must be deducted a further sum for the processing costs, which we have no means of calculating. Pliny's price for flour was therefore the equivalent of 5 sesterces or below for corn.

Jasny,[3] who was not really an ancient historian or classical

[1] Pliny, *N. H.* 18. 89–90.

[2] Rostovtzeff, *Frumentum*, col. 149.

[3] N. Jasny, *Wheat Prices and Milling Costs in Classical Rome* (Food Research Institute, Stanford University, 1944).

scholar, but who had the great advantage of 'five years as a flour mill manager, two years in a grain-export organization, and many more years spent on research pertaining to grain', made a detailed study of the Pliny passage and concluded that Pliny's flour prices implied a price of 8 sesterces for ordinary wheat and almost 10 for the best quality. This has been claimed as the only usable figure for a corn price in Rome.[4] I do not feel so confident.

Both Moritz and Duncan-Jones have shown that Jasny's calculations are not to be relied upon in their entirety.[5] Not enough attention was given to the actual text of Pliny and the collations with modern wheat prices which Jasny relied on for part of his argument are not reliable. The cost of milling and retailing charges in Rome can only be guessed at, but the wheat price corresponding to Pliny's flour prices is more likely to be about 6 sesterces and may even have been below that.[6]

There can be little doubt that the price of corn in Rome was in general distinctly higher than that in Italy. But that was true in general of large towns in the Empire.[7] Certainly if the average price of wheat in Rome in Pliny's day had been as high as Jasny believed, Nero's fixing of the price of corn in A.D. 64 at 3 sesterces a *modius* would have been an act of generosity of Herculean proportions.[8] It seems therefore unwise to rely too trustingly on the Pliny passage alone and the tortured mathematics needed to interpret it in order to deduce an average corn price at Rome.

[4] Brunt, *Italian Manpower*, p. 376.

[5] L. A. Moritz, *Grain-mills and Flour in Classical Antiquity* (Oxford, 1958), pp. 169, 184–90; Duncan-Jones, *ERE*, p. 346.

[6] Cf. also review of Jasny by T. R. S. Broughton, *Classical Weekly*, 88. 5 (1944), 39–40.

[7] Duncan-Jones, *ERE*, Appendix 8.

[8] Tac. *Ann.* 15. 39. 2.

APPENDIX 7

THE TABLE OF HERACLEA

The bronze tablet discovered in 1732 between Heraclea and Metapontum, on the western coast of the Gulf of Tarentum, contains three sections.[1] The first (lines 1–19) is incomplete and in the absence of its first part is difficult to understand. It lays down that certain individuals are to make a declaration ('profiteri) in person, or if they are absent from Rome, by proxy, or if they are minors or women under guardianship, through their guardians, before certain magistrates, namely a consul, or failing them, a praetor, or failing them, a tribune of the *plebs*. A list of these individuals is to be deposited in the public records; a duplicate is to be exhibited in the forum, and when corn is to be given to the people, at that place too. Any official who gives corn to anyone whose name appears in the list is to be fined 50,000 sesterces for every *modius* of corn so given.

The second section (20–82) lays down rules about the maintenance of the roads and footpaths, and the control of traffic in Rome.

The third section (83–163) deals with municipalities other than Rome and contains three parts; the first (83–141) has provisions relating to municipal councils, the second (142–58), regulations for a municipal census; while the third (159–63), rules that existing municipal charters are to be amended within a fixed time.

It was thought at first that the Tabula was the concluding part of a law of Caesar passed in 46 B.C., which laid down the basic principles of municipal constitutions—hence the name by which it is sometimes called, *lex Iulia municipalis.*[2] Later the commonly accepted theory was that of von Premerstein; that we had in the *tabula* drafts of some of Caesar's laws as they were put into force because of a special authorization, by the consuls

[1] *FIRA* i, no. 13 = *ILS* 6085.

[2] Cf. H. Rudolph, *Stadt und Staat im römischen Italien* (Leipzig, 1935), pp. 113–20.

Antony and Dolabella a few months after Caesar's death.[3] Now it seems more likely that the *tabula* contains a selection of provisions from different Roman laws, the only common factor being that they were of interest to the citizens of Heraclea, and that therefore it is not necessary to assume that all the laws are of the same date.[4]

Even so there are problems. It is perhaps understandable that legislation about the upkeep of roads at Rome should have been thought worth publishing at Heraclea as a pattern for local emulation. But why should legislation on corn distributions at Rome be published there? It has been stressed that Heraclea had her own *sitagertai* for supply and transport of grain, and that they might well be interested in corn distributions at Rome.[5] Even if this is true I think we may question whether the mutilated first section has anything directly to do with the organization of corn distributions at Rome and the Caesarian process of *subsortitio* at all. There is no mention of the corn distributions until line 16 of the total of nineteen lines in this section. There is no mention of the use of the lot, nor of the filling of places in a list vacated by death. The list that is to be made appears to include women and minors, and, unlike the lists of recipients under the Empire, is specifically of those to whom no corn is to be issued, on pain of a large fine. An official who gave just one month's ration, 5 *modii*, to even one such person could be fined a quarter of 1,000,000 sesterces. The officials who are to preside over the making of the list range from the consul down to the *tribunus plebis*, but do not include the aediles, who were traditionally associated with the corn supply.

The case is not proven but I suspect strongly that the list of individuals was to be constructed for some purpose which was stated in the missing first part of the inscription, and which was relevant to both Rome and Heraclea, but that it was something other than the routine administration of the corn distributions at Rome. It just so happened that one of the disabilities to be

[3] A. von Premerstein, 'Die Tafel von Heraclea und die Acta Caesaris', *ZSavigny-Stift* 3. 43 (1922), 45 ff.; cf. M. Gelzer, *Caesar* (trans. P. Needham, Oxford, 1968), p. 290 n. 2.

[4] M. W. Frederiksen, 'The Republican Municipal Laws: Errors and Drafts', *JRS* 55 (1965), 183–98. Cf. Brunt, *Italian Manpower*, Appendix 2.

[5] Frederiksen, *JRS* 55 (1965), 197.

suffered by the people on the list was that they were to be ineligible for public corn rations. The penalty for giving corn to these people seems peculiarly excessive, if they were merely on a regular waiting list of possible candidates for the process of *subsortitio*. And what women would be doing on such a list anyway rather defies explanation.

APPENDIX 8

TESSERAE FRUMENTARIAE

It seems that control of the distributions during the Republic was managed solely by means of lists, but from the time of Augustus we hear of *tesserae* which play an important role in the administration. Unfortunately the evidence about them and their use is confusing. We know of them from references in literature, in documents from Egypt, and from the legal sources. The passages are worth quoting in full:

Suetonius, writing at the turn of the first and second centuries A.D., says in his life of Augustus (40):

> He revised the lists of the people *vicus* by *vicus*, and to prevent the *plebs* being called away from their occupations too often because of the distributions of grain he determined to give out *tesserae* for four months' supply three times a year; but at their urgent request he allowed a return to the old custom of receiving a share each month.

In the next chapter of the life of Augustus (41) there is a more cryptic reference after a series of allusions to Augustus' generosity in distributions of money. The final sentence reads: 'In times of scarcity too (*in annonae difficultatibus*) he often distributed grain to each man at a very low figure, sometimes for nothing, and he doubled the *tesserae nummariae*.'

In the life of Nero (11) Suetonius says: 'Every day all kinds of presents were thrown to the people; these included a thousand birds of every kind each day, various kinds of food, *tesserae frumentariae*, clothing, gold, silver . . . ships, blocks of houses, and farms.' Clearly tokens for these presents are meant.

Persius, writing in the mid-first century A.D., deals at one point in Satire v (74) with his conception of freedom. He says: 'What we want is true liberty; not by that kind is it that any Publius enrolled in the Veline tribe becomes the possessor of a *tesserula* for a ration of mangy corn.' The scholiast on the passage comments that it had been the custom at Rome that all manumitted slaves become eligible for public corn.

Juvenal, writing at the end of the first century A.D., in Satire vii. 171 ff. gives his views of the unhappy and poverty-stricken life of teachers of rhetoric, and how they have to involve themselves in real lawsuits to recover the fees for their teaching. He says: 'So, if my advice goes for anything, I would recommend the man who comes down from his rhetorical shade in order to fight for a sum that would buy a trumpery *tessera*—for that's the most handsome fee he will every get—to discharge himself, and enter upon some other walk of life.'

These are the only references to *tesserae* in the literature of the early Empire but there are three references to them in legal sources of the third century A.D.

In the *Digest* 31.49.1 the jurist Paul says: 'If a *frumentaria tessera* is bequeathed to Titius and he dies, some people think that the legacy is extinguished, but this is not true, for if anyone is left a *tessera* or a post in the public service (*militia*) it is as if he were left the monetary value of it.'

In the *Digest* 31.87 pr.:

Titia wished that a *tessera frumentaria* should be bought for Seius after 30 days from her own death. I put the question whether in the event that he begins to hold a *tessera* during the lifetime of the testatrix as the result of some gift, an action is available to him, since he cannot claim that which he already holds. The response of Paul was that the cost of the *tessera* should be given to the person concerned in the question because the substance of such a trust lies more in the value than in the nature of it.

In the *Digest* 5.1.52.1 the jurist Ulpian says: 'If a man wills that *tesserae frumentariae* be bought for his freedmen even if the greater part of his estate lies in the provinces, still it must be stated that the trust is to be executed at Rome, since it is apparent from the nature of the provision that that was the testator's intention.'

The fundamental question raised by these passages is whether the literary and legal sources are talking about the same thing.

Rostovtzeff argued that whereas the *tesserae* of the early literary sources were individual small tokens issued for each distribution (and he identified them with some of the lead tokens with corn symbols that he was studying at the time), the *tesserae* of the legal sources were different. They were documents of legitimation for life, a sort of identity card, which specified the holder and the day and arcade at which he was to receive corn in the detailed way we know of from inscriptions.[1]

Cardinali espoused this theory and believed with Rostovtzeff that the *tessera* of the jurists was a later development than the earlier small tokens, and to be dated to the time of the centralization of corn distribution at the Porticus Minucia, but that both kinds of *tesserae* existed side by side, aiding each other in the system of control.[2]

Van Berchem also accepted Rostovtzeff's theory but believed that the identity-card *tessera* simply replaced the earlier tokens of exchange. He tried to back up his belief by arguing that this was the reason why Suetonius once used the phrase *tesserae nummariae* with reference to Augustus. During the reign of the first *princeps* tokens had been given up 'as if they were money' but that was no longer true at the time Suetonius was writing, when the *tesserae* were in the form of tablets which were retained by the holder.[3]

Rea has recently rejected Rostovtzeff's theory altogether. In the Oxyrhynchus archive he found references to *tablai*, tokens of exchange, which seem to have remained valid only so long as the officers who issued them remained in power. Building on a hint thrown out by Cardinali he argued that the reference to the *tessera* in the legal sources should be interpreted as a metaphor, as a symbol of the right to public corn, just as *tribus* can stand as a symbol of the right to citizenship.[4]

Any attempt to try to resolve the conflict by invoking outside aid, for example from archaeology, is useless at present. We do not know for certain whether the lead pieces studied by Rostovtzeff were *tesserae frumentariae* or not. Van Berchem's suggestion, now reinforced by Nicolet, that *tesserae frumentariae* were in the form of wooden rectangles, later diptychs, and can be seen on certain coins and works of art has not been substantiated by any actual finds.

Consequently we are left only with the passages themselves, what they mean and what they imply.

[1] Rostovtzeff, *Frumentum*, col. 178; cf. 'Römische Bleitesserae', *Klio* Beiheft 3 (1905).

[2] Cardinali, *Frumentatio*, pp. 271 ff.

[3] *Distributions*, pp. 85–8.

[4] *Oxy. Pap.* xl. 101 ff; cf. *Dig.* 32. 35 pr.

The first passage in Suetonius, *Augustus* (40), establishes beyond doubt the existence of tokens of exchange issued regularly throughout the year. Such tokens are also implied by Suetonius, *Nero* (11), and the passages in Persius and Juvenal.

The reference in the second passage in Suetonius, *Augustus* (41), to *tesserae nummariae* seems to me irrelevant to the problem of the corn *tesserae*, their shape or their function.

The real problem lies in what the legal passages mean. There is unfortunately no description of the physical shape of the *tesserae* either stated or implied in them. Rostovtzeff's notion of an identity card is not demanded by the actual words in the passages, only by the implication that the lawyers, when they use the term *tessera frumentaria*, are not referring to just one distribution, and by our knowledge, drawn from inscriptional evidence, that specific days and arcades were assigned to individuals, and these might be expected to be recorded on some document in their hands. It may be that we should not allow that knowledge to influence us.

But even if *tesserae* were not in the form of identity cards, clearly something has changed, since not only does the term *tessera frumentaria* have a long-term validity, but also there is talk of buying (which implies selling) and even of bequeathing, which seems to go against what we know of the qualifications for the corn doles.

Van Berchem believed that it was the state which sold *tesserae frumentariae*, and only to citizens not born in Rome, but newly settled there.[5] That idea was bound up with his thesis, which has been criticized earlier, that it was only citizens with Roman *origo*, who qualified naturally for *frumentum publicum*. There is no solid evidence for his idea, and it would be surprising if it were only for this category of persons that sale of *tesserae* had been created.

Rea argued that the fixed number on the list at Rome was managed by a lottery but that freedmen were exempt from this process (cf. Persius *Sat.* v. 73). One of the *Digest* passages specifically refers to freedmen (*Digest* 5.1.52.1) and there is no reason, in his opinion, why the legatees of the two other passages should not have been freedmen also. He believed

[5] *Distributions*, pp. 49–53.

therefore that a patron by freeing a slave in his will automatically gave him the right to *frumentum publicum* and in that sense 'bequeathed' a *tessera frumentaria*. The question of buying the right arose only in the case of those with Latin status. It was by performing public services and in that sense expending money or 'buying' that the man, either by himself or with aid from others, achieved full citizen status and the right to *frumentum publicum*.[6]

But this argument by Rea seems contrived. It is based on the assumptions that there was a lottery at Rome, for which we have no evidence during the Empire, and that new freedmen automatically got rights that other full citizens might have to wait a chance for, which seems improbable. Only one of the passages deals with freedmen, the others need not. Moreover the notion that the freeing of a slave by will could be described as the bequeathing of a *tessera frumentaria*, and that the buying of a *tessera frumentaria* contains a hidden allusion to the performance of public service seems a perverse understanding of the Latin. 'Ex causa lucrativa' ('as the result of a gift') in *Dig*. 31.87. pr. is the proper term in legal Latin for receiving something by bequest, or as a gift, precisely when one did not pay for it oneself whether by public service or any other way. Rea has perhaps been overinfluenced, in interpreting these passages, by the documents from Oxyrhynchus, where freedmen could gain a place in the corn distributions by public service.

From the legal passages alone it is necessary to assume that at some unknown date the right to *frumentum publicum* became a real right of property owned by those on the list, alienable by sale or by gift, and transferable by legacy. If the total number of recipients was fixed, there would be no disadvantage in principle to the state in the new system. There would however be severe practical problems for the state in such an open market in *tesserae*. There would be the possibility of constant changes in the holders of the right, of men buying up more than one such right, of a 'black market' developing, in short of complete chaos in the lists. That apparently did not happen, which means there must have been some control.

There seem to be two possibilities. First, as Cardinali argued,

[6] *Oxy. Pap.* xl. 103 ff.

there may have developed a limited right of sale by the state, and by the state alone, of *tesserae*, which for one reason or another had fallen forfeit to the state.[7] Therefore *tesserae* had not in any indiscriminate sense become alienable. In support of this theory Cardinali quoted *Cod. Theod.* 14.24.1 when in relation to the oil distributions of the late Empire rights which fell vacant or forfeit to the state were sold by the state. One difficulty with this theory is that there is no mention of sale by the state in the legal passages; another is that legacy of *tesserae* between private individuals would hardly have been possible. Such legacies could not have been executed. Cardinali tries to get round this by pointing to passages in the *Digest* where there are legacies of *res alienae* difficult to execute (e.g. *Dig.* 5.30.39.7) where the value was given instead. But in our case in *Dig.* 31.49.1 the value of the legacy of a *tessera* had to be given only because the named legatee had himself died.

The second and more likely possibility is that the *tesserae* really had become alienable and heritable by the early third century A.D., but under the supervision of the state. In other words the transfer by sale, or legacy, of a right to public corn had to be registered with officials who would scrutinize the transaction and adjust the list accordingly. I believe that, whatever the exact nature of the *tesserae*, the right to public corn came to be owned in some way that was nevertheless compatible with overall control of the situation by public officials.[8]

[7] Cardinali, *Frumentatio*, pp. 257–60.

[8] See now C. Nicolet, 'Tessères frumentaires et tessères de vote', *Mel. J. Heurgon* (Rome, École Franç. de Rome, 1976), pp. 695–716.

APPENDIX 9

PORTICUS MINUCIA

It is natural that we should wish to confirm the evidence about the Porticus Minucia actually on the ground, but the nature and location of this *porticus* is one of the most disputed questions in the topography of Rome.[1] It is by no means certain that there was only one *porticus* with this name. We have two documents from the late Empire, cataloguing in some detail the buildings of each of the regions of Rome, the *Notitia*, probably dating from A.D. 354, and the *Curiosum* from A.D. 375. In Region IX (Circus Flaminius) the *Notitia* lists, between 'Porticum Philippi and 'Cryptam Balbi', 'Minucias II, veterem et frumentariam', while the *Curiosum* lists in the same place 'Minuciam veterem et frumentariam'.[2] We also know from Velleius Paterculus that M. Minucius Rufus, cos. 110 B.C., celebrated his triumph over the Scordisci by building 'porticus quae hodieque celebres sunt'.[3]

The area concerned is the south-eastern part of the Campus Martius which began to be developed with monumental structures during the second century B.C. The building of a Porticus Minucia somewhere in this area at the end of the second century B.C. would therefore not be surprising. The plural used by Velleius is however not to be pressed since he uses the plural form for other porticoes, which we know were single buildings. There is nothing therefore to prevent us from supposing that this building is the 'Minucia vetus' of the late Regionary Catalogues. It apparently had some repairs carried out on it by

[1] Platner–Ashby, *A Topographical Dictionary of Ancient Rome* (London, 1929), p. 424; G. Lugli, *I monumenti antichi di Roma e suburbio*, Supplemento, Vol. i (Rome, 1940), p. 145; for a judicious discussion of the whole problem, F. Castagnoli, 'Il Campo Marzio nell' antichità: Cap. VII Porticus Minuciae', *MemLinc*[8] 1 (1948), 175–80.

[2] A. Nordh, *Libellus de Regionibus Urbis Romae* (Gleerup, 1949), p. 86.

[3] Velleius 2. 8. 3.

Domitian, since a 'Minucia vetus' is listed by another late source among his buildings.[4]

What is in doubt is whether it was this building which was in some way adapted, and put to new use for the distribution of corn from the middle of the first century A.D., or whether in addition to it another building was constructed or adapted, and for some reason also called 'Minucia' and which therefore had to be distinguished from the old *porticus* by being called 'frumentaria'. In my view it is much more likely that there were two buildings not far from one another in the same region. Momigliano long ago suggested a plausible reason for the re-use of the name 'Minucia' for a corn-distribution centre;[5] the learned and antiquarian Emperor Claudius might be expected to recall the story of the Minucius who featured in the famous story of the grain distribution in the mid-fifth century B.C. Certainly the distinction between 'Minucia vetus' and 'Minucia frumentaria' preserved in the late Regionary catalogues is best explained by assuming that there were two buildings.

If this is true then the new coupling of fragments of the Severan Marble Plan of Rome which fixes the location of the Porticus Minucia immediately to the east of the theatre and *porticus* of Pompey[6] may not have settled definitively the location and layout of the corn distribution centre as some have thought.[7] The traces of the plan of this building suggest an elegant and monumental structure surrounding a temple off-centre within it. This does not seem to be a functional porticus such as the porticus, previously thought to be the Porticus Aemilia, down in the Emporium district near the Tiber was and such as the 'Minucia frumentaria' must have been.[8] This therefore is likely to have been the 'Minucia vetus' originally built at the end of the second century B.C.

Where 'Minucia frumentaria' was and what it looked like

[4] *Chron. Ann.* 354, p. 189 (Mommsen).

[5] A. Momigliano, 'Due punti di storia Romana arcaica', *SDHI*² 2. (1936) = *Quarto contributo*, p. 332; see above, p. 31.

[6] L. Cozza, 'Pianta Marmorea Severiana, nuove recomposizioni di frammenti', *Studi di topografia romana* (Rome, 1968), pp. 9–16; cf. F. Castagnoli, *Topografia e urbanistica di Roma antica*² (Bologna, 1969), p. 189.

[7] e.g. H. Kloft, *Liberalitas Principis* (Cologne, 1970), p. 96 n. 55.

[8] W. L. MacDonald, *The Architecture of the Roman Empire* (New Haven, 1965), pp. 5–6; cf. L. Richardson, Jnr., 'The Evolution of the Porticus Octaviae', *AJA* 80 (1976), 57–64.

we still have no idea. There are remains of a building very similar to the Emporium *porticus* in plan and structure lying under the Church of S. Maria in Via Lata.[9] The date of the original open arcaded building in travertine is believed to have been Claudian, and it stretched along the old Via Flaminia leading north from the centre of Rome on the eastern edge of the Campus Martius. Castagnoli has put forward the theory that this was the 'Porticus Minucia Frumentaria'.[10] Certainly the building had a long history, and some commercial and storage function; in association with it grew up the *diaconia* of S. Maria in Via Lata when the Christian church took over the job of distributing food to the poor. Proof is impossible in the present state of the evidence, but the theory remains a possibility, not disproved yet by the work on the Marble Plan.[11]

[9] E. Sjöqvist, 'Gli avanzi antichi sotto la chiesa di S. Maria in Via Lata', *Opuscula Archaeologica* 4 (1946), 48.

[10] Castagnoli, *MemLinc*[8] 1 (1948) 180.

[11] For a different view see C. Nicolet, 'Le temple des Nymphes et les distributions frumentaires à Rome', *CRAI* (1976), pp. 29–51, esp. pp. 30–7.

APPENDIX 10

CURATORES AQUARUM ET MINICIAE

When Van Berchem wrote his important study of the imperial corn distributions it was believed that it was under Septimius Severus that the old *curator aquarum* became *curator aquarum et Miniciae* (which became the normal spelling for Minucia from this period of the Empire).[1] Some scholars had supposed that this meant that the Porticus Minucia had ceased to be concerned with corn distributions and was now caught up in the water administration. Van Berchem was not convinced and argued strongly that the Porticus Minucia was so bound up with the corn distributions that the *praefecti frumenti dandi* were often called *praefecti Miniciae*, which was a mere 'incorrect title' but one in current use. A few years after Severus in place of the *praefectus Miniciae* of praetorian rank appeared a consular *curator Miniciae* followed later by *curatores aquarum et Miniciae*. It was a simple linear development of a single office.

Van Berchem argued that what all this meant was that under Septimius Severus two different public services were unified under one head of consular rank. It was true, he granted, that *praefecti frumenti dandi* existed again during the third century A.D., but not under Septimius Severus, Caracalla or Elagabalus. They only reappeared under Severus Alexander or his successor. This was to be explained by the fact that whereas in the second century A.D. the *frumentationes* were run jointly by *princeps* and senate as a result of a compromise, officials nominated by the senate but supported by the resources of the *princeps*, Septimius Severus was hostile towards the senate and deprived them of the right of feeding the people. The new consular *curator* was just an agent of the Emperor. Severus Alexander reversed this process but the reaction was shortlived, because the *praefecti frumenti dandi* are not heard of again after Maximinus.

[1] *Distributions*, pp. 97 ff. and 178.

Since Van Berchem's book, both Chastagnol and Pflaum have written on these problems and a more careful scrutiny has been made of a greater number of inscriptions. In 1954 Pflaum accepting the whole of Van Berchem's thesis simply published a list of senators responsible for the grain distributions to the end of the third century A.D.[2] Chastagnol[3] in his study of the urban prefecture published in 1960 tacitly corrected certain errors, such as the incorrect expansion of the title *cur. Min.* in the career of L. Fabius Cilo Septimius Catinius Acilianus Lepidus; it is now known to stand for *cur(atori) min(ori)*, not *cur(atori) Min(iciae)*, so that mythical official can be struck off the list.

According to Chastagnol, Septimius Severus combined the grain distribution organization with that of the aqueducts under the command of a consular who from that time was entitled *curator aquarum et Miniciae*. But there remained alongside this imperial *curator* a *praefectus frumenti dandi* or *praefectus Minuciae* of praetorian rank, who was a senatorial official, at least until the reign of Gordian III or Philip the Arab. At that time the junior office disappeared and the consular *curator* remained in sole charge of the grain distributions until the change-over to distributions of bread under Aurelian.

Pflaum returned to the problem in 1963 with an amended list of office holders and much more exact dating of the point in the career when a particular title was held.[4] Pflaum's position now was that the whole evolution was more complex than anyone, Chastagnol and himself included, had realized. It was not a single linear development as Van Berchem had supposed, nor an overlapping development as in Chastagnol's theory, but a double development and it started not with Septimius Severus but with Commodus. On the one hand the senator of praetorian rank responsible for the distributions had had set above him an imperial official of consular standing. On the other hand the praetorian director of the distributions, responsible to the imperial *curator*, was now himself also nominated by the Emperor and this explains the change in title from *praefectus*

[2] H. G. Pflaum, *Historia* 2 (1953–4), between pp. 444 and 445.

[3] A. Chastagnol, *La Préfecture urbaine à Rome sous le bas-empire* (Paris, 1960), pp. 56–7.

[4] H. G. Pflaum, 'Les *praefecti Miniciae*', *Bonner Jahrbücher* 163 (1963), 232–3 and list, pp. 234–7.

frumenti dandi ex s.c. to *praefectus Minuciae*. As such it was a double imperial takeover and all part of the anti-senatorial policy of Commodus, which was continued by Septimius Severus, Caracalla, and Elagabalus from A.D. 193 to 222. On the other hand Severus Alexander and Gordian III, who were pro-senatorial in outlook, restored the distributions to the senatorial *praefecti frumenti dandi*, back, in short, to the system of the Antonine Emperors, although their actions were separated by those of the anti-senatorial Maximin who followed the policy of the Severans. The *praefecti frumenti dandi* and *praefecti Miniciae* were not interchangeable, as Chastagnol implied, but were distinctly different; although both of praetorian rank, the former were senatorial officials and solely responsible for grain distributions, while the latter were imperial officials and shared the responsibility with their superior *curatores*. It is Pflaum's belief that during the reigns of the pro-senatorial Severus Alexander and Gordian III these consular *curatores aquarum* lost the part of their title *et Miniciae*, and the *praefecti frumenti dandi* were left in glorious but short-lived independence; but he admits that since we know of no holder of the post of *curator aquarum* at these crucial moments the final coping stone of his theory is missing.

It is difficult to accept this argument. The dating of the tenure of the various offices is done with all the sensitivity and magisterial authority that Pflaum has built up over a lifetime's study of inscriptions of careers, but it is necessarily not absolutely precise. Moreover there is no proof of imperial nomination of the *praefecti Miniciae* any more than there is any proof that the *praefecti frumenti dandi ex s.c.* were nominated by the senate. Moreover the pro-senatorial feelings of Emperors such as Severus Alexander may be exaggerated. It is difficult to tell how much goodwill there was towards the senate in the young Emperor, and it is more than possible that the SHA *Life of Severus Alexander* has exaggerated it.[5] Even if we grant that there was a struggle going on between senate and Emperor over the titles of the officials involved, we have to ask seriously what all this meant in real terms. Combining the administration of the

[5] F. Millar, *A Study of Cassius Dio* (Oxford, 1964), p. 103; R. Syme, *Emperors and Biography* (Oxford, 1971), Ch. 9, particularly p. 159; A. Jardé, *Études critiques sur la vie et le règne de Sévère Alexandre* (Paris, 1925), Ch. II.

grain and water supply of the city might well seem to be a good idea. The increase in the amount of good-quality water brought into the city was an achievement of Agrippa and of Augustus that was equal in importance to the improvement of the supplies of grain.[6] Both senate and Emperor had co-operated in the administration of each of the two supply systems from almost the beginning of the Empire.[7] The amalgamation of both under a single *curator aquarum et Minuciae* might make good administrative sense, but it was not something which really could be done, and undone, at will every few years. Whatever the titles of the officials, the work they did was real and could not afford to be disrupted. It is interesting that what little evidence we have for the existence of an equestrian *procurator Minuciae* or *Miniciae* seems to come from the early third century A.D.,[8] and how this official fitted into the real work of running the *porticus* and related to the senatorial officials has been omitted from this controversy.

[6] *Res Gestae Divi Augusti*, ed. P. A. Brunt and J. Moore (Oxford, 1967), pp. 61–2.
[7] Frontinus, *De Aqu.*, *passim.*
[8] *CIL* 3. 249 = *ILS* 1396; *CIL* 6. 1648.

APPENDIX II

CORN AND COINS

The legends and types of ancient coins could be used in two ways, to indicate the authority responsible for the coins and to convey a message put out by that authority. The first piece of information must be given for a coin to be a coin at all, the second may be regarded as an optional extra.[1]

On the whole the Greeks chose not to take up the second option. Their coins are marked by the minimal use of lettering and by the repetition of often very beautiful but conventional types. The Romans, as is well known, took up the option with a vengeance and filled their coins with information, which would be seen and read by ordinary people. Given the importance of the feeding of the populace of the capital it is not surprising to find allusions to the corn supply in both legends and types. What is surprising is that the allusions do not become regular and complex until the time of Claudius and, more especially, of Nero in the first century A.D.

When the Roman Republic in the third century B.C. took up the idea of coinage it first adopted the attitude of the Greeks towards coin types. For virtually a century the public coins had little or no lettering and referred only to Rome or her gods. It is true that one of the pieces of early cast-bronze coinage had an ear of barley depicted on it, but nothing more than perhaps a general reference to the importance of that crop can be deduced.[2] From early in the second century B.C., however, the magistrates responsible for the production of the coinage came to make the coins more private and less public in their reference. Their names, alongside that of Rome, and then alone, were on the coins and they chose the types to suit themselves. Since they were often members of Rome's highest classes, by the first century B.C. the coin types increasingly were related to the competition among the Roman *nobilitas* that was to culminate in the civil wars.

[1] M. H. Crawford, *Roman Republican Coinage* (Cambridge, 1974), ii. 712.
[2] *RRC* i. 132, no. 6.

Even so the number of direct allusions to the corn supply are surprisingly few. Very often the type chosen had almost as much to do with family prestige and 'ancestor worship' as to the problems of the corn supply at the moment of minting. The most famous example is the *denarius* of 135 B.C. produced by C. Minucius Augurinus which depicted the monument erected to one of his Minucian ancestors outside the Porta Trigemina for some supposed beneficent action in relation to the corn supply.[3] But there are other examples where the moneyer pays a graceful compliment to an earlier member of his own family. A certain M. Marcius Mn. f., otherwise unknown, produced a *denarius* in 134 B.C. with a helmeted head of Roma and a *modius* on the obverse, while the reverse was Victory in a biga with two corn ears. This seems to be a reference to his ancestor who as plebeian aedile was supposed in the mid-fifth century B.C. to have been the first to distribute corn to the people at the price of 1 *as* per *modius*.[4]

There are, of course, coins during the late Republic which do have a specific and contemporary allusion to the corn supply. The *denarii* issued in 100 B.C. by the two quaestors L. Calpurnius Piso and Q. Servilius Caepio perhaps as *quaestor Ostiensis* and *quaestor urbanus* are a case in point.[5] On the obverse is a head of Saturn and on the reverse two male figures are seated on a bench, side by side, framed by two corn ears and with the legend 'Ad. Fru. Emu. Ex S.C.'. The issue was clearly related to the corn crisis associated with the name of tribune Saturninus from 104 to 100 B.C. Similarly in 86 B.C. the two aediles L. Critonius and M. Fannius advertised their functions in relation to corn distribution by producing *denarii* with a bust of Ceres on the obverse, while on the reverse two male figures sit on a bench flanked by a corn ear.[6] The designs are similar but quite distinct. But perhaps the most obvious reference to work done for the corn supply was on the *denarius* produced in 56 B.C. by Faustus Cornelius Sulla.[7] On the obverse was the head of Hercules, wearing a lionskin; on the reverse a globe surrounded by wreaths, the curved stern of a ship, and a corn

[3] *RRC* i. 273–5, no. 242; cf. above, p. 31.
[4] *RRC* i. 277, no. 245; cf. above, p. 35 and n. 34.
[5] *RRC* i. 330, no. 330; cf. above, p. 163.
[6] *RRC* i. 367, no. 351.
[7] *RRC* i. 450, no. 426 (4b); cf. above, p. 55.

ear. As the son-in-law of Pompey he was paying a compliment not to a remote ancestor but to his wife's father who at that moment was exercising a *cura annonae* which was empire-wide.

Family reference could also be self-advertisement and it seems that in the late second century B.C. the moneyers often held their office within ten years of their consulates. The suggestion has been made that in the case of such men it was a substitute for the aedileship. They seem to have placed on their coins an indication of what they would have provided in the way of games or corn distributions if they had been elected aediles.[8]

All this means that there was a personal quality about the types which made the consistent projection of a developing state policy concerning the corn supply, even if there had been one, an impossibility. The senate was indeed responsible for the annual volume of emission of coins and it is possible to plot the decreases and the increases, some of which seem to be related to the needs of the corn supply of the capital.[9] But despite the number of corn ears sprinkled around individually on some coin types and the relative popularity of a goddess such as Ceres with a wreath of corn ears in her hair, there seems to be no consistent attempt by the senate to depict state concern for the corn supply. Instead there is the more and more strident personality cult of the late Republic culminating in the introduction of individual portraiture of Caesar, Antony, Lepidus, and Octavian.

After the death of Pompey the Pompeian remnants gathered in Africa. There, before the final confrontation with Julius Caesar at Thapsus, the Pompeian commanders like Q. Metellus Scipio struck their own coins and even Cato abandoned his principles and struck in his own name. The corn ears which appear on some of their coins along with the head of Africa reflect little more than the traditional attributes of Africa, and are only indirectly relevant to the corn supply of the city.[10]

In this respect, despite his use of coins for propaganda purposes in general, and despite his actual work on problems concerning the corn supply of Rome, Augustus was curiously Republican and Tiberius followed his lead. The coin types

[8] *RRC* ii. 729 n. 3.
[9] *RRC* ii. Ch. VII with Table LVIII is important.
[10] *RRC* i. 472–3, nos. 460, 461, 462.

which refer specifically to the feeding of Rome are virtually non-existent. The only development which is marked is the identification between Ceres and the Empress Livia which starts under Augustus and is continued by her son Tiberius.[11] A seated female figure with a bunch of corn ears in one hand and sometimes a sceptre in the other is both a traditional Ceres type and yet has the features of Livia. By the end of the first century A.D. Ceres had become the standard allegorical type of the empress and the identification had been made explicit in the legends.[12]

Under the Emperor Claudius references to the feeding of the capital became less ambiguous on the coins. Claudius was faced with a crisis on his accession and was interested in improving the supply of the city.[13] From the start of his reign on the brass and copper coins of the smaller denominations circulating in the pockets of the humblest people were depicted two types. The first was of Ceres seated veiled holding two corn ears in her right hand, but there was a specific legend 'CERES AUGUSTA S.C.'.[14] The second showed a corn *modius* standing on three legs.[15] It was a simple and effective motif, used in the past in odd corners of a composite picture, but now promoted for its own sake. The message was clear, the new Emperor cared.

Even so Claudius' importance in relation to the corn supply should not be exaggerated numismatically any more than in the history of administration. It was Nero, who in the famous *sestertius* of A.D. 64–6, created not only one of the most beautiful Roman coin types but the most explicit for the provisioning of Rome.[16] The beauty was worthy of an Emperor with aesthetic interests and is perhaps not unexpected; the explicit iconography and legend may help to reinforce the idea that Nero was more important in the history of the corn supply than is sometimes admitted. On the obverse was the head of Nero laureate; on the reverse, a draped female figure representing *Annona* stands with a cornucopia in her left hand, while her

[11] H. Mattingly and E. A. Sydenham, and others, *Roman Imperial Coinage* (London, 1923–), i. 90, no. 352; 103, no. 3.

[12] See below, p. 262.

[13] See above, p. 74.

[14] *RIC* i. 129, no. 67.

[15] *RIC* i. 130, no. 72.

[16] *RIC* i. 150, nos. 73–87.

right hand is on her hip, facing towards Ceres, who is veiled and seated, holding corn ears in her right hand and a torch in her left. Between them is a garlanded altar on which stands a *modius* with corn ears, while in the background at the right is the garlanded stern of a ship. The legend reads 'ANNONA AUGUSTI CERES S.C.'. The composition is elaborate and beautiful, the symbolism simple. The ship suggests sea-borne corn. Ceres with corn ears and torch has the position of honour as a presiding deity of great antiquity while the corn harvest, *Annona*, personified, stands before her as an attendant, and between them the corn measure is placed on an altar. It was so beautiful and effective as a coin type that it was repeated in whole or in part by later Emperors such as Galba, Domitian, Nerva, and Septimius Severus.

With the fall of Nero and the struggle for power between four contenders for the imperial throne there was an added impetus to the use of propaganda and reassurance about the corn supply of the capital on the coinage. Galba simply repeated the Ceres part of the Neronian design on his copper coinage with the legend 'CERES AUGUSTA S.C.'.[17] Otho also featured Ceres on *denarii*, but standing holding two corn ears and cornucopiae and with the legend 'CERES AUGUSTA'.[18] It was Vitellius, however, faced with Vespasian in control of Egypt and threatening to invade Africa, who naturally went to most pains to try to reassure the population of Rome that all was well with the corn supply. Besides repeating the Ceres part of the Neronian design like Galba with the legend 'CERES AUGUSTA S.C.'[19] he introduced two new types between July and December A.D. 69. *Dupondii* and *asses* were issued with *Annona* standing, holding Victory and cornucopiae, between a basket and ship with the legend 'ANNONA AUGUSTI S.C.',[20] while *sestertii*, even more remarkably, depicted Vitellius himself bareheaded in military dress standing, holding a spear in his right hand facing Ceres seated, holding a patera in her right hand, a torch in her left, while between them was a lighted altar and in the background was the prow of a ship. The legend read 'ANNONA AUG S.C.'.[21] The whole scene deliberately recalled the Neronian

[17] *RIC* i. 204, no. 52; 216, no. 162.
[18] *RIC* i. 219, no. 1.
[19] *RIC* i. 226, no. 2.
[20] *RIC* i. 227, no. 18.
[21] *RIC* i. 226, no. 1.

sestertius without precisely copying it and significantly substituting for the standing figure of *Annona* the Emperor himself in arms, safeguarding the corn supply. In such a period of discord it was also true that Concordia was a favourite coin type and with her were often associated corn ears and cornucopiae.

Vespasian as the real controller of Rome's corn supply had less need to advertise the safe guarding of sea-borne provisions. Certainly it seems to be only towards the end of his reign in the 70s A.D. that we find a series of coins in gold, silver, and copper with *Annona*, Ceres, and *Modii* as the main themes of the types. Not only are the types quite new but they seem perhaps to have less to do with the importation of corn from abroad than with a revival of Roman and Italian agricultural prosperity. On gold and silver coins *Annona* is seated on a throne, her feet on a stool, holding on her lap an open sack of corn ears, the ties in her hands, with the legend 'ANNONA AUG.'.[22] The same type is repeated on the copper coinage but with the legend 'ANNONA AUGUST. S.C.'. On all denominations the head on the obverse is not always that of Vespasian himself but of his son Titus and even of Domitian. The build up of the sons of the new royal house was obvious even here. On gold and silver coins also Ceres was depicted in a new way.[23] She stands facing left with two corn ears and a poppy in her extended right hand and a long vertical sceptre in her left, with the legend 'CERES AUGUST'. On *denarii* is depicted a *modius* standing on three legs as on the coins of Claudius, but this time with five corn ears upright in it and two hanging over at the sides.[24] Finally, there is a type with Mars helmeted and naked with a corn ear sprouting from the ground.[25] The absence of any allusion to shipping may, or may not, be significant, but given that these coins were issued alongside others depicting sows and their young, a goatherd milking a goat, they may be connected with a programme of restoration of agricultural prosperity after civil war.

Titus repeated the types with the seated *Annona* with corn ears on her lap[26] and the standing Ceres with her long vertical sceptre, but the equation of the Empress with Ceres was made

[22] *RIC* ii. 29, no. 131; cf. ii. 94, no. 680. [23] *RIC* ii. 43, no. 248.
[24] *RIC* ii. 27, no. 110. [25] *RIC* ii. 18, no. 33. [26] *RIC* ii. 127, no. 87.

explicit since some of the coins had the bust of Julia, Titus' wife, on the obverse.[27] Titus, however, also introduced a new and interesting type.[28] *Annona* stands facing left holding a statuette of *Aequitas* with scales and rod in her right hand, and a cornucopia in her left. At her feet stands a *modius* filled with corn ears while behind her on the right is the stern of a ship. The legend reads simply 'ANNONA AUG.'. The introduction of the little figure of *Aequitas* carries with it notions of fair dealing in relation to the corn supply. A very similar coin type was to reappear under Commodus, an emperor whose reign was of importance in the corn supply, but Titus did not live long enough to be put to the test.

Domitian's coinage is basically rather conservative in its reference to the corn supply. He revived the beautiful Neronian sestertius with its whole scene of *Annona* and Ceres but with the simplified legend 'ANNONA AUGUST S.C.'.[29] He also revived the standing Ceres with her sceptre used first by his father Vespasian and then by his brother Titus, but this time there were versions with the bust of Domitia on the obverse and the legend 'DIVI CAES. MATER S.C.'.[30] He did, however, introduce one completely new type, the interpretation of which is difficult. *Dupondii* from A.D. 84 show *Annona* seated facing right, holding open on her lap by the two ends a bag full of corn ears and confronted by a small figure who holds the other two ends of the bag. In the background is the stern of a ship and the legend is 'ANNONA AUG S.C.'.[31] Given the presence of the ship it is difficult to interpret the small figure as an Italian farmer facing the goddess, and see in the type some allusion to Domitian's encouragement of grain growing in Italy.[32] The same type reappears under the Emperor Hadrian and a version of it under Septimius Severus. Whether the small figure is to be thought of as representing farmers in general, or shippers in general, or simply humans in general is not clear.

During Nerva's brief reign, as one would expect, there is little novelty concerning corn on the coins. The Neronian

[27] *RIC* ii. 139, no. 177.
[28] *RIC* ii. 126, no. 86.
[29] *RIC* ii. 189, no. 277.
[30] *RIC* ii. 209, no. 443.
[31] *RIC* ii. 187, no. 262.
[32] Suet. *Domit.* 7. 2; cf. M. I. Finley, *The Ancient Economy*, p. 212, n. 47.

sestertius of Annona and Ceres, revived by Domitian, is continued[33] and small bronze coins with a *modius* and corn ears, a type started by Vespasian, are revived.[34] The most dramatic variant on this theme is the *sestertius* of A.D. 89 which depicts a three-legged *modius* full of corn ears and a poppy but has the elaborate legend 'PLEBEI FRUMENTO CONSTITUTO—S.C.', the meaning of which is not clear.[35]

Trajan's coins are remarkable not least for the lack of any legends referring to the corn supply. Neither 'ANNONA' nor 'CERES' find any mention on the coins. Most often the legend reads 'S.P.Q.R. OPTIMO PRINCIPI'. Yet the type with standing Ceres and her long sceptre, started by Vespasian and a characteristic coin type of all the Flavian Emperors is revived,[36] and two new *Annona* types are introduced. On the first of these *Annona* draped and wearing a wreath of corn ears stands facing left holding corn ears downwards in her right hand over a *modius* containing corn ears, while in her left hand is a cornucopia, to the right behind her is the prow of a ship garlanded.[37] On the second of these *Annona* stands in a frontal pose facing to her right, holding corn ears down by her side in her right hand, and a cornucopia in her left; by her right side stands a child facing front.[38] The legend, 'S.P.Q.R. OPTIMO PRINCIPI ALIM ITAL.', reveals the nature of this new and special type.

There had already been indications under previous emperors that the corn attributes usually associated with *Annona* or *Ceres* could be associated with other figures, for example with *Fides* under Domitian.[39] During the reign of Hadrian the old association of corn ears and baskets with certain provinces or areas of the Roman Empire was revived in a dramatic way. *Africa* and *Alexandria* appear on the coins of this much travelled man with their traditional corn references.[40] But many of the same *Ceres* and *Annona* types continue as well, a flood of issues starting in A.D. 118, just before Hadrian's arrival in Rome. Of particular interest is a new variant of the standing *Annona* with *modius* and prow of ship introduced by Trajan. Under Hadrian she has a

[33] *RIC* ii. 226, no. 52.
[34] *RIC* ii. 230, nos. 109–14.
[35] *RIC* ii. 229, no. 89; cf. above, pp. 214 and 216.
[36] *RIC* ii. 255, no. 151.
[37] *RIC* ii. 255, no. 165.
[38] *RIC* ii. 261, no. 243.
[39] *RIC* ii. 185, no. 244.
[40] *RIC* ii. 374, no. 298; ii. 446, no. 843.

rudder in her left hand.[41] Most of these coins have the legend 'ANNONA AUG. S.C.'. But there is a new type of *Annona* without a legend. *Annona* draped and standing has her right foot placed on an inverted *modius*. While in her left hand she holds her usual cornucopia, in her right she holds a hook or sickle upwards.[42]

During the second century A.D. the practice of associating normal corn attributes with an ever-widening group of imperial concepts continued apace—*Tranquillitas*, *Felicitas*, *Bonus Eventus*;[43] peace and happiness implied plenty. Ceres continues but is by no means so prominent as *Annona* during this century. Most often *Ceres* is associated with the Empress on the obverse.[44] *Annona* has been emancipated from her inferiority and it is *Annona* who is pushed insistently among the types on the coins of Antoninus Pius, mainly variants of the draped standing figure holding corn ears down over a *modius* with the prow of a ship in the background introduced by Trajan. The most interesting of all the *Annona* types of Antoninus Pius is an entirely new one dated between A.D. 145 and 161 which is never repeated by later Emperors.[45] *Annona* draped stands looking to her right holding up a tablet (?) in her right hand and a rudder upright in her left. Below her right arm appear parts of two ships, one carrying a *modius* with corn ears and poppy. From behind her left side appears a lighthouse in three storeys with beacon light. The legend reads 'ANNONA AUG FELIX S.C.'. Clearly the allusion is to some improvement in the corn supply situation and perhaps involved a lighthouse. We know from SHA *Antoninus* 8.2 that among his building works was *Phari restitutio*, restoration of the lighthouse, but which is not known—perhaps the famous one at Alexandria.

Under Marcus Aurelius the *Ceres* coins have Faustina II on the obverse and are minted throughout almost the whole reign,[46] but the most notable spate of coins comes in the period A.D. 174–5, and they are a reaction to the revolt of Avidius Cassius in the East. Besides coin types common to times of revolt and uncertain loyalty such as *Fides Exercituum* and *Concordia Exercituum* the figure of *Annona* holding her corn ears

[41] *RIC* ii. 441, nos. 796–8. [42] *RIC* ii. 360, no. 169.
[43] *RIC* iii. 37, no. 100; iii. 134, no. 860; iii. 102, no. 555.
[44] *RIC* iii. 70, no. 356. [45] *RIC* iii. 123, no. 757. [46] *RIC* iii. 268, no. 668.

down over a *modius* is prominent although there is no legend on the coins.[47] Anxiety may have been felt about Egypt's adhesion to Cassius and the need for reassurance of the populace.

Commodus, or the administration during his reign, has an important role in the history of the corn supply of Rome. It is only to be expected therefore that in addition to the usual *Ceres* coin types with a bust of Crispina on the obverse,[48] there should be some marked emphasis in the *Annona* series. Certainly an unusually rich new type appeared in A.D. 181–2.[49] *Annona* stands looking to her right, holding on her right hand a statuette of *Concordia* (with *patera* and sceptre), and in her left hand a cornucopia; at her right side on the ground stands a *modius* with corn ears in it, while behind her on her left appears part of a ship with two figures in it, and with *Victory* on its side. The legend reads 'ANN AUG S.C.'. The type seems to be almost a fusion of the types first put out by Titus and by Trajan. Despite its complexity the design seems elegant and concise with an emphasis on shipping and the men involved in it, proper to an Emperor who organized the African corn fleet for the first time. It was not for nothing that *modius* and corn ears were given as attributes on the coins to *Felicitas*.

With the emergence of Septimius Severus as the victor in the civil war which followed Commodus' death, there were revived two famous *annona* types. One was the *sestertius* of Nero with the standing *Annona* facing the seated Ceres and the legend 'ANNONA AUG CERES S.C.'.[50] The other was the Domitianic type with the seated *Annona* holding out a lapful of corn ears to a small figure in front of her.[51]

As the third century advanced it was significant that Ceres as a reverse type ceased to be of importance even for identification with the reigning empress. The *annona* types continue throughout most of the century, prominently displayed under the Emperor Severus Alexander, completely absent under the anti-senatorial and anti-Roman Maximinus.[52] But the undermining of the *annona* type itself had begun. With Elagabalus came the introduction of a new type *Abundantia Aug.* with many of the corn attributes previously associated with the *annona*

[47] *RIC* iii. 302, no. 1128.

[48] *RIC* iii. 442, no. 674.

[49] *RIC* iii. 405, no. 325.

[50] *RIC* iv. 1. 193, no. 756.

[51] *RIC* iv. 1. 199, no. 794.

[52] *RIC* iv. 2. 64; cf. iv. 2. 135.

coins.[53] The *annona* coins continue in diminishing numbers however throughout the crises of the third century and even survive into the beginning of the reign of Diocletian.[54] What swept them away seems to have been the reform of the coinage by Diocletian in A.D. 294. *Ceres*, *Annona*, and *Abundantia* disappeared from the coinage at that point.[55]

Annona had emerged during the first century A.D. from under the shadow of Ceres and had been established as a potent theme in imperial propaganda. The changing conditions of the later Roman Empire, the spread of citizenship, diminution of the status of the city of Rome itself, military confusion, and monetary collapse meant that the word 'annona' acquired new shades of meaning. Instead of alluding only to the corn supply it meant also a salary in kind. The fact was that the Emperors of the late third century and early fourth century A.D. were struggling with even more pressing problems than the feeding of one privileged capital city. The reassuring message of the *annona* type had had its day, but for more than 200 years it had conveyed imperial policy to the Roman public with ingenuity and elegance.

[53] *RIC* iv. 2. 32, no. 56. [54] *RIC* v. 2. 236, no. 155. [55] *RIC* vi. 698.

BIBLIOGRAPHY

ALBERTINI, E. F. (1923). *La Composition dans les ouvrages philosophiques de Seneque* (Paris).
ANDRÉ, J. (1961). *L'Alimentation et la cuisine à Rome* (Paris).
AUSTIN, M., and VIDAL-NAQUET, P. (1972, Eng. Trans. London, 1977). *Économies et sociétés en Grèce ancienne* (Paris).
BADIAN, E. (1973). *Publicans and Sinners* (Blackwell).
—— (1968). *Roman Imperialism in the Late Republic*[2] (Oxford).
BARBOUR, N. (ed.). (1962). *A Survey of North-West Africa*, 2nd edn. (London).
BAY, A. (1972). 'The letters SC on Augustan *aes* coinage', *JRS* 62, 111.
BECATTI, G. (1965). *Scavi di Ostia IV: I Mosaici e pavimenti marmorei* (Rome).
BELOCH, K. J. (1886). *Die Bevölkerung der griechisch-römischen Welt* (Leipzig).
BERCHEM, D. VAN. (1939). *Les Distributions de blé et d'argent à la plèbe romaine sous l'empire* (Geneva).
BINDER, O. (1905). *Die Abfassungszeit von Senekas Briefen*, Diss. (Tübingen).
BLOCH, H. (1953). 'Ostia: Iscrizioni rinvenute tra il 1930 e il 1939', *NSc*, 239.
BLOCH, M. (1939). 'L'histoire des prix', *Annales* 1, 141.
BOETHIUS, A., and WARD-PERKINS, J. B. (1970). *Etruscan and Roman Architecture* (Harmondsworth).
BONNEAU, D. (1972). *Le Fisc et le Nil. Incidences des irregularités de la crue du Nil sur la fiscalité foncière dans l'Égypte grecque et romaine* (Paris).
BOREN, A. H. (1957–8). 'The urban side of the Gracchan economic crisis', *AHR* 63, 890.
—— (1968). *The Gracchi* (New York).
BÖRNER, E. (1939). *Der staatliche Korntransport im griechisch-römischen Aegypten* (Hamburg).
BOUCHIER, E. S. (1917). *Sardinia in Ancient Times* (Oxford).
BOVE, L. (1969, also in *Labeo* 17 (1971), 149). 'A proposito di nuove Tabulae Pompeianae', *RendNap* 44, 24.
BRAUDEL, F. (1972). *The Mediterranean and the Mediterranean World in the Age of Philip II* (London).
BROGAN, O. (1953). *Roman Gaul* (London).
BROTHWELL, D. and P. (1969). *Food in Antiquity* (London).
BROUGHTON, T. R. S. (1929). *The Romanization of Africa Proconsularis* (Baltimore).
—— (1951–2). *The Magistrates of the Roman Republic*, American Philological Association Monographs No. 15 (Lancaster, Pa.: Oxford).
BRUNT, P. A. (1966). 'The Fiscus and its development', *JRS* 56, 75.
—— (1966). 'The Roman Mob', *Past and Present* 35, 1.
—— (1971). *Italian Manpower* (Oxford).
—— (1975). 'The administrators of Roman Egypt', *JRS* 65, 124.
—— (1976). 'The Equites in the Late Republic', reprinted in *The Crisis of the Roman Republic*, ed. R. Seager, p. 83 (authorized and revised German

text in H. Schneider (ed.), *Zur Sozial- und Wirtschaftsgeschichte der späten römischen Republik* (Darmstadt), p. 175).
—— and Moore, J. (eds.). (1967). *Res Gestae Divi Augusti* (Oxford).
Burford, A. M. (1960). 'Heavy Transport in Classical Antiquity', *EcHR*², 13, 1.
Cagnat, R. (1916). 'L'annone d'Afrique', *MemAcInscr* 40, 253.
Calderone, S. (1960). 'Il problema delle città censorie e la storia agraria della Sicilia romana', *Kokalos* 6, 3.
Calza, G. (1915). 'Il piazzale delle corporazioni e la funzione commerciale di Ostia', *BullComm* 43, 178.
Camps-Fabrier, H. (1953). *L'Olivier et l'huile dans l'Afrique romaine* (Algiers).
Carcopino, J. (1914). *La Loi de Hieron et les romains* (Paris).
—— (1936). *Histoire romaine* Vol. ii, Part 2 (Paris).
Cardinali, G. '*Frumentatio*', *Dizionario epigrafico di antichità romane* (de Ruggiero).
Carney, T. F. (1971). 'The Emperor Claudius and the Grain Trade', *Pro Munere Grates*, Studies presented to H. L. Gonin (Pretoria), p. 39.
Carrié, J.-M. (1975). 'Les distributions alimentaires dans les cités de l'Empire romain tardif', *MEFR*, 2. 995.
Cary, M. (1949). *Geographic Background of Greek and Roman History* (Oxford).
Casson, L. (1950). 'The Isis and her voyage', *TAPA* 81, 43.
—— (1954). 'The grain trade of the Hellenistic World', *TAPA* 85, 168.
—— (1965). 'Harbour and river boats of ancient Rome', *JRS* 55, 31.
—— (1971). *Ships and Seamanship in the Ancient World* (Princeton).
—— (1978). 'Unemployment: the Building Trade and Suetonius *Vesp.* 18', *BASP* 15, 43.
Castagnoli, F. (1948). 'Il Campo Marzio nell' antichità: Cap. VII Porticus Minuciae', *MemLinc*⁸, i, 175.
—— (1969). *Topografia e Urbanistica di Roma Antica*² (Bologna).
Chastagnol, A. (1960). *La Préfecture urbaine à Rome sous le bas-empire* (Paris).
Chilver, G. E. F. (1949). '*Princeps* and *Frumentationes*', *AJP* 70, 7.
Clemente, G. (1972). 'Il patronato nei collegia dell' impero romano', *SCO* 21, 142.
Coarelli, P. (1977). 'Public building in Rome between the Second Punic War and Sulla', *PBSR* 45, 1.
Cozza, L. (1968). 'Pianta Marmorea Severiana, nuove recomposizioni di frammenti', *Studi di topografia romana* (Rome).
Crawford, D. (1971). *Kerkeosiris* (Cambridge).
—— (1973). 'The Opium Poppy: a study in Ptolemaic Agriculture', *Problèmes de la terre en Grèce ancienne, sous la direction de M. I. Finley* (Paris), p. 223.
—— (1976). 'Imperial Estates', M. I. Finley (ed.), *Studies in Roman Property* (Cambridge), p. 35.
Crawford, M. H. (1974). *Roman Republican Coinage* (Cambridge).
Crook, J. (1967). *Law and Life of Rome* (London).
—— (1978). 'Working Notes on some of the New Pompeii Tablets', *ZPE* 29, 229.

D'ARMS, J. (1974). 'Puteoli in the second century of the Roman Empire: A social and economic study', *JRS* 64, 104.

—— (1972). 'CIL X. 1792: A municipal notable of the Augustan Age', *HSCP* 76, 207.

D'ESCURAC, H. PAVIS (1976). *La Préfecture de l'annone: service administratif impérial d'Auguste à Constantin* Bib. des écoles françaises d'Athènes et de Rome, p. 226 (Rome).

DITTENBERGER, W. (1915–24). *Sylloge inscriptionum Graecarum*³ (Leipzig).

DOUGLAS, A. E. (1966). 'Oratorum Aetates', *AJP* 87, 298.

DUDLEY, D. (1970). *The Romans* (London).

DUNCAN-JONES, R. P. (1965). 'An Epigraphic Survey of Costs in Roman Italy', *PBSR* N.S. 20, 221.

—— (1974). *The Economy of the Roman Empire* (Cambridge).

—— (1976). 'The size of the modius castrensis', *ZPE* 21, 53.

—— (1976). 'The Choenix, the Artaba and the Modius', *ZPE* 21, 43.

—— (1976). 'The price of wheat in Roman Egypt under the Principate', *Chiron* 6, 241.

ENSSLIN, W. (1954). '*Praefectus*', *RE* 22, 2, col. 1268.

FINLEY, M. I. (1968). *Ancient Sicily* (London).

—— (1973). *The Ancient Economy* (London).

FRANK, TENNEY (1937). 'Notes on Roman Commerce', *JRS* 27, 72.

—— (1962). *An Economic History of Rome*² (New York).

—— (ed.) (1933–40). *An Economic Survey of Ancient Rome*, 5 vols. (Baltimore).

FREDERIKSEN, M. W. (1965). 'The Republican Municipal Laws: Errors and Drafts', *JRS* 55, 183.

GAPP, K. S. (1935). 'The Universal Famine under Claudius', *HThR* 28, 258.

CARNSEY, P. D. A. and WHITTAKER, C. R. (eds.) (1978). *Imperialism in the Ancient World* (Cambridge).

GARZETTI, A. (1950). *Nerva* (Rome).

GELZER, M. (1968). *Caesar* (trans. P. Needham) (Oxford).

GENTRY, A. P. (1976). *Roman Military Stone-built Granaries in Britain* (British Archaeological Reports 32).

GEREMEK, H. (1969). *Karanis communauté rurale de l'Égypte Romaine au IIᵉ–IIIᵉ siècle de notre ère* (Warsaw).

GERNET, L. (1909). 'L'approvisionnement d'Athènes en blé au Vᵉ et IVᵉ siècle', in G. Bloch, *Mélanges d'histoire ancienne* (Paris).

GILLIAM, J. F. (1961). 'The plague under Marcus Aurelius', *AJP* 82, 225.

GIORDANO, C. (1966). 'Su alcune tavolette cerate dell' agro Murecine', *RendNap* 41, 107.

—— (1971). 'Nuove tavolette cerate Pompeiane', *RendNap* 46, 195.

GJERSTAD, E. (1960–1). 'Legends and facts of early Roman history', *Scripta Minora*, (Lund), 2. 33.

GRASER, E. R. (1940). 'Two new fragments of the Edict of Diocletian', *TAPA* 71, 161.

GREENIDGE, A. H. J., and CLAY, A. M. (1960). *Sources for Roman History 133–70 B.C.*, second edn., revised by E. W. Gray (Oxford).

GRENIER, A. (1934). *Manuel d'archéologie gallo-romaine* ii (Paris).

GRIFFIN, M. T. (1962). '*De Brevitate Vitae*', *JRS* 52, 104.
GROSSO, F. (1964). *La lotta politica al tempo di Commodo* (Turin).
GRUEN, E. S. (1974). *The Last Generation of the Roman Republic* (California).
HANDS, A. R. (1968). *Charities and Social Aid in Greece and Rome* (London).
—— (1972). 'The Date of Saturninus' Corn Bill', *CR* 22, 12.
HASEBROEK, J. (1933). *Trade and Politics in Ancient Greece* (London).
HASSALL, M., CRAWFORD, M., and REYNOLDS, J. (1974). 'Rome and the Eastern Provinces at the end of the second century B.C.', *JRS* 64, 195.
HEICHELHEIM, F. (1930). *Wirtschaftliche Schwankungen* (Jena).
—— (1935). 'Sitos', *RE* Sup. 6, 819.
HIRSCHFELD, O. (1870). 'Die Getreideverwaltung in der römischen Kaiserzeit', *Philologus* 29, 1.
—— (1905). *Die kaiserlichen Verwaltungsbeamten*[2] (Berlin).
HOHLWEIN, N. (1938). 'Le blé d'Égypte', *EtPap* 4, 33.
HOPKINS, K. (1978). *Conquerors and Slaves* (Cambridge).
HUNT, A. S., and EDGAR, C. C. (1932, 1934). *Select Papyri* (Loeb), 2 vols. (New York: London, Vol. i, Vol. ii).
HUSSON, G. (ed.) (1970). *Lucien: Le Navire ou les souhaits* (Paris).
JARDÉ, A. (1925). *Études critiques sur la vie et le règne de Sévère Alexandre* (Paris).
JASNY, N. (1941–2). 'Competition among grains in classical antiquity', *AHR* 47, 747.
—— (1944). *The Wheats of Classical Antiquity*, Johns Hopkins Univ. Studies lxii (Baltimore).
—— (1944). *Wheat Prices and Milling Costs in Classical Rome* (Stanford University).
JONES, A. H. M. (1952–3). 'Inflation under the Roman Empire', *EcHR*[2] 5, 295.
—— (1957). *Athenian Democracy* (Oxford).
—— (1964). *The Later Roman Empire* (Oxford).
KLOFT, H. (1970). *Liberalitas Principis*, Kölner Historische Abhandlungen Bd. 18 (Cologne).
KOLENDO, J. (1968). 'La hiérarchie des procurateurs dans l'inscription d'Aïn-el-Djemala (*CIL* viii. 25943)', *REL* 46, 319.
KORNEMANN, E. (1904). 'Nochmals das Monumentum Ancyranum', *Klio* 4, 90.
KUNKEL, W. (1973). 'Hypothesen zur Geschichte des römischen Pfandrechts', *ZSavignyStift* 90, 150.
LAET, S. J. DE (1949). *Portorium* (Bruges).
LANDELS, J. G. (1978). *Engineering in the Ancient World* (London).
LE GALL, J. (1953). *Le Tibre, fleuve de Rome, dans l'antiquité* (Paris).
LOANE, H. J. (1938). *Industry and Commerce of the City of Rome, 50 B.C.–200 A.D.* (Baltimore).
LUGLI, G. (1931–8, Supplemento 1940). *I monumenti antichi di Roma e suburbio*, 3 vols. (Rome).
MACDONALD, W. L. (1965). *The Architecture of the Roman Empire* (New Haven).
MACGEACHY, J. A. (1942). *Quintus Aurelius Symmachus* (private edn., Chicago).

MacMullen, R. (1967). *Enemies of the Roman Order* (Cambridge, Mass.).
—— (1974). *Roman Social Relations* (New Haven).
Magie, D. (1950). *Roman Rule in Asia Minor* (Princeton).
Maier, F. G. (1953–4). 'Römische Bevölkerungsgeschichte und Inscriftenstatistik', *Historia* 2, 318.
Mattingly, H. (1923–50). *Coins of the Roman Empire in the British Museum* (London).
Mattingly, H., Sydenham, E. A., and others. (1923—). *Roman Imperial Coinage* (London).
Mattingly, H. B. (1969). 'Saturninus' corn bill and the circumstances of his fall', *CR* 19, 267.
Mazzarino, S. (1951). *Aspetti sociali del quarto secolo. Ricerche di storia tardoromana* (Problemi e ricerche di storia antica, i) (Rome).
Meiggs, R. (1973). *Roman Ostia*[2] (Oxford).
Millar, F. G. B. (1964). *A Study of Cassius Dio* (Oxford).
—— (1977). *The Emperor in the Roman World* (London).
Milne, J. G. (1924). *A History of Egypt under Roman Rule*[3] (London).
—— (1927). 'The ruin of Egypt by Roman mismanagement', *JRS* 17, 1.
Momigliano, A. (1936). 'Due punti di storia romana arcaica', *SDHI*[2], 2, 373.
—— (1961). *Claudius: the Emperor and his achievement* (repr. Cambridge).
Mommsen, T. (1887). *Römisches Staatsrecht*[3] (Leipzig).
Moritz, L. (1958). *Grain Mills and Flour in Classical Antiquity* (Oxford).
Mottram, V. H., and Graham, G. (1956). *Hutchison's Food and the Principles of Dietetics*, 11th edn. (London).
Nash, E. (1961, 1962). *A Pictorial Dictionary of Ancient Rome*, 2 vols. (London).
Niccolini, G. (1934). *I fasti dei tribuni della plebe* (Milan).
Nicolet, C. (1976). 'Tessères frumentaires et tessères de vote', *Mélanges J. Heurgon* (Rome, École Franç. de Rome), 695.
—— (1976). 'Le Temple des Nymphes et les distributions frumentaires à Rome', *CRAI*, 29.
—— (1977). *Rome et la conquête du monde méditerranéen, I Les structures de l'Italie romaine* (Paris).
Nordh, A. (1949). *Libellus de Regionibus Urbis Romae* (Gleerup).
Ogilvie, R. M. (1965). *Commentary on Livy I–V* (Oxford).
Oost, S. I. (1955). 'Cato Uticensis and the Annexation of Cyprus', *CP* 50, 98.
Palanque, J.-R. (1931). 'Famines à Rome à la fin du IVe siècle', *REA* 33, 346.
Pflaum, H. G. (1950). *Les Procurateurs équestres sous le haut-empire romain* (Paris).
—— (1953–4). 'La chronologie de la carrière de L. Caesennius Sospes', *Historia* 2, 444.
—— (1960). *Les Carrières procuratoriennes équestres sous le haut-empire romain* (Paris).
—— (1963). 'Les *praefecti Miniciae*', *Bonner Jahrbücher* 163, 232.
Picard, G.-Ch. (1956). 'Néron et le blé d'Afrique', *Les Cahiers de Tunisie* 14, 163.

PIGANIOL, A. (1947). *L'Empire chrétien* (Paris).

PIGGOTT, S. (1939). 'Timber circles: a re-examination', *AJ* 96, 220.

PLATNER, S. B., and ASHBY, T. (1929). *A Topographical Dictionary of Ancient Rome* (London).

PRÉAUX, C. (1973). Review of *Ox. Pap.* xl, *Chronique d'Égypte* 48, 382.

PREMERSTEIN, A. VON. (1922). 'Die Tafel von Heraclea und die Acta Caesaris', *ZSavignyStift* 3. 43, 45.

PRITCHARD, R. T. (1970). 'Cicero and the *Lex Hieronica*', *Historia* 19, 352.

—— (1971). 'Gaius Verres and the Sicilian Farmers', *Historia* 20, 224.

—— (1972). 'Some aspects of first century Sicilian agriculture', *Historia* 21, 651.

RAWSON, B. (1966). 'Family life among the lower classes at Rome in the first two centuries of the Empire', *CP*, 71.

REA, J. (1972). *Oxyrhynchus Papyri* xl (London).

RENFREW, J. M. (1973). *Palaeoethnobotany. The prehistoric food plants of the Near East and Europe* (London).

RICHARDSON, L. (JR.) (1976). 'The evolution of the Porticus Octaviae', *AJA* 80, 57.

RICKMAN, G. E. (1971). *Roman Granaries and Store Buildings* (Cambridge).

ROSTOVTZEFF (ROSTOWZEW), M. (1905). 'Römische Bleitesserae', *Klio* Beiheft 3.

—— (1957). *The Social and Economic History of the Roman Empire*, 2nd edn. (by P. M. Fraser), 2 vols. (Oxford).

—— *Frumentum*, PAULY–WISSOWA, *Real-Encyclopädie der Classischen Altertumswissenschaft*.

—— (1906). 'Kornerheburg und transport im griechisch-römischen Ägypten', *APF* 3, 201.

ROUGÉ, J. (1952). 'La navigation hivernale sous l'Empire romain', *REA* 54, 316.

—— (1966). *Recherches sur l'organisation du commerce maritime en Méditerranée sous l'empire romain* (Paris).

—— (1966). *Expositio totius mundi et gentium*, ed. Rougé (Paris).

ROWLAND, R. J. (JNR.) (1965). 'The Number of Grain Recipients in the late Republic', *Act. Antiq. Acad. Scient. Hung.* 13, 81.

RUDOLPH, H. (1935). *Stadt und Staat im römischen Italien* (Leipzig).

RUGGINI, L. C. (1971). 'Le associazioni professionali nel mondo romano-bizantino', *Settimane di Studi nel Centro italiano di Studi sull' alto Medioevo* 18. 1 (Spoleto), 59.

SAUMAGNE, C. (1950). 'Un tarif fiscal au IVe siècle de notre ère', *Karthago* 1, 159.

SCHNEIDER, H. (1974). *Wirtschaft und Politik* (Erlangen).

SCHOVÁNEK, J. G. (1972). 'The date of M. Octavius and his *Lex Frumentaria*', *Historia* 21, 235.

—— (1977). 'The provisions of the *Lex Octavia Frumentaria*', *Historia* 26, 378.

SCHWARTZ, J. (1948). 'Le Nil et le ravitaillement de Rome', *BIFAO* 47, 179.

—— (1961). *Les Archives de Sarapion* (Cairo).

SEGRÈ, A. (1934). 'Note sull' economia dell' Egitto ellenistico nell' età tolemaica', *BSAA* 29, 257.

Semple, E. C. (1932). *The Geography of the Mediterranean Region in relation to Ancient History* (London).
Sherk, R. K. (1953). 'The Legates of Galatia from Augustus to Diocletian', Johns Hopkins Studies 69. 2, 87.
Sherwin White, A. N. (1973). *The Roman Citizenship*² (Oxford).
Sjöqvist, E. (1946). 'Gli avanzi antichi sotto la chiesa di S. Maria in Via Lata', *Opuscula Archaeologica* 4, 48.
Slicher Van Bath, B. H. (1963). *The Agrarian History of Western Europe A.D. 500–1850* (London).
Smithson, E. L. (1969). 'The Grave of an Early Athenian Aristocrat', *Archaeology* 22, 18.
Sperber, D. (1974). *Roman Palestine: Money and Prices* (Jerusalem).
Ste. Croix, G. E. M. de (1974). 'Ancient Greek and Roman Maritime Loans', *Debits, Credits, Finance and Profits*, Essays in honour of W. T. Baxter, ed. Harold Edey and B. S. Yamey (London).
Stevens, C. E. (1966). 'Agriculture and rural life in the later Roman Empire', *CEHE*² 1, 92.
Stockton, D. L. (1979). *The Gracchi* (Oxford).
Sumner, G. V. (1973). *Orators in Cicero's Brutus: Prosopography and Chronology* (Toronto).
Sutherland, C. H. V. (1951). *Coinage in Roman Imperial Policy, 31 B.C.–A.D. 68* (London).
Syme, R. (1971). *Emperors and Biography* (Oxford).
—— (1977). 'The Enigmatic Sospes', *JRS* 67, 38.
Tengström, E. (1974). *Bread for the People: Studies of the Corn Supply of Rome during the late Empire* (Stockholm).
Testaguzza, O. (1970). *Portus* (Rome).
Toubert, P. (1973). *Les Structures du Latium médiéval*, Bib. des Écoles Franç. d'Ath. et de Rome, 221 (Rome).
Toynbee, A. J. (1965). *Hannibal's Legacy* (Oxford).
Verbrugghe, G. P. (1972). 'Sicily 210–70 B.C.: Livy, Cicero, and Diodorus', *TAPA* 103, 535.
—— (1976). *Itinera Romana 2, Sicilia* (Berne).
Viereck, H. D. L. (1975). *Die römische Flotte* (Herford).
Vita-Finzi, C. (1969). *The Mediterranean Valleys, Geological Changes in Historical Times* (Cambridge).
Vitucci, G. (1947). 'Note al cursus honorum di M. Julius Romulus praefectus frumenti dandi ex s.c.', *RivFC* 25, 252.
—— (1958). 'PLEBEI URBANAE FRUMENTO CONSTITUTO', *ArchCl* 10, 310.
Wallace, S. L. (1938). *Taxation in Egypt from Augustus to Diocletian* (Princeton).
Walsh, P. G. (1965). 'Massinissa', *JRS* 55, 151.
Waltzing, J. P. (1895–1900). *Étude historique sur les corporations professionnelles chez les romains*, 4 vols. (Louvain).
Warmington, B. H. (1954). *The North African Provinces from Diocletian to the Vandal Conquest* (Cambridge).
Weaver, P. (1971). 'Cognomina, Supernomina and *CIL* X. 1729', *Antichthon* 5, 77.

WESTERMANN, W. L. (1955). *The Slave Systems of Greek and Roman Antiquity* (Philadelphia).

WESTERMANN, W. L., and KEYES, C. W. (1932). *Tax Lists and Transportation Receipts from Theadelphia* (New York).

WHITE, K. D. (1963). 'Wheat farming in Roman times', *Antiquity* 37, 207.

—— (1970), *Roman Farming* (London).

WHITE, L. (1962). *Mediaeval Technology and Social Change* (Oxford).

WHITTAKER, C. R. (1964). 'The revolt of Papirius Dionysius A.D. 190', *Historia* 13, 348.

WÖRRLE, M. (1971). 'Ägyptisches Getreide für Ephesos', *Chiron* 1, 325.

YAVETZ, Z. (1969). *Plebs and Princeps* (Oxford).

YEO, C. (1946). 'Land and Sea Transportation in Imperial Italy', *TAPA* 77, 242.

INDEX OF CLASSICAL AUTHORS

Acts of the Apostles 27: *119, 131*
Ambrose, *De Off. Minist.* 3. 7. 45: *201*
Appian, *B.C.* 1. 21: *49, 158, 159*; 1. 24: *44*; 1. 111: *167*; 2. 54: *58, 59*; 2. 61: *58*; 2. 66: *58*; 2. 120: *160, 174*; 5. 4: *60*; 5. 18: *61*; 5. 66–72: *61*; *Mithr.* 63: *50*; 94: *51*; *Pun.* 136: *44*
Aelius Aristides, *To Rome* 12: *106*
Asconius (ed. Clark), p. 8: *49, 151, 172*; p. 59: *180*
Augustus, *Res Gestae* 5: *48, 62*; 15. 1. 10–12: *62, 179*; 15. 2: *8, 176, 181*; 15. 4: *63*; 18: *62*
Caesar, *B.C.* 1. 30: *58*
Cassiodorus, *Var.* 4. 5: *104*; 6. 18. 1: *207*; 12. 9: *93*
Cato, *De Agri cult.* 56–8: *10*
Cicero, *Pro Archia* 4. 9: *182*; *Ad Att.* 4. 1. 6–7: *55*; 9. 9: *58*; 14. 3: *61*; 15. 9: *61*; *Pro Balbo* 41: *107*; *Brut.* 62. 222: *161*; *De Domo* 11: *53, 105, 143*; 25: *52, 174*; *Ad Fam.* 13. 75: *56, 126*; 13. 79: *57*; *De Fin.* 2. 84: *126, 139*; *De har. resp.* 43: *47, 162*; *Ad Herenn.* 1. 21: *163*; 2. 17: *163*; 4. 35: *163*; *De Imp. Gn. Pomp.* 33: *51*; 34 (*Pro Lege Manilia* 12. 9): *37, 45, 67, 107*; *leg. agr.* 1. 5: *108*; 2. 50: *50*; 2. 80: *45*; 2. 83: *162*; *De Leg.* 3. 3. 7: *35*; *Pro Murena* 18: *47*; *De Off.* 2. 17. 58: *35, 169*; 2. 21. 72: *161*; *Phil.* 2. 31: *61*; *Ad Q.F.* 2. 1–6: *56*; 2. 5. 1: *55*; *Pro Scauro* 43: *57, 107*; *Pro Sestio* 39: *47, 162*; 55: *151, 170*; *Tusc. Disp.* 3. 20. 48: *49, 159*; *In Verr.* 2. 1. 12: *51*; 2. 1. 56: *50*; 2. 3. 12: *107*; 2. 3. 18: *40*; 2.3 36: *40, 120*; 2. 3. 72: *166, 168*; 2. 3. 84: *147*; 2. 3. 90: *40, 147*; 2. 3. 112: *103*; 2. 3. 163: *45, 105, 166*; 2. 3. 172: *40*; 2. 3. 173: *147*; 2. 3. 189: *146*; 2. 3. 192: *146*; 2. 3. 214–15: *146*; 2. 3. 216: *146*; 2. 3. 227: *146*; 2. 4. 144: *51*; 2. 5: *51*; 2. 5. 21. 52: *166*
Claudian, *De Bell. Gild.* 62: *69*; *In Eutrop.* 1. 405–7: *107, 201*
Cod. Theod. 1. 6. 7: *201*; 7. 4: *112*; 7. 4. 11: *73*; 8. 5: *120*; 11. 1. 2: *112*; 11. 14. 1: *93, 200*; 11. 30. 4: *112*; 13. 5: *73*; 13. 5. 1: *203*; 13. 5. 6: *130*; 13. 5. 11: *203*; 13. 5. 21: *203*; 13. 5. 23: *228*; 13. 5. 24: *228*; 13. 5. 26: *203*; 13. 5. 27: *202*; 13. 5. 33: *203*; 13. 5. 34: *203*; 13. 5. 38: *203*; 13. 9. 1: *203*; 13. 9. 3: *15, 202*; 13. 9. 4: *203*; 13. 9. 5: *203*; 14. 3: *205*; 14. 4. 9: *93, 122*; 14. 4. 10: *198*; 14. 15. 1: *207*; 14. 15. 4: *206*; 14. 16. 1: *201*; 14. 16. 3: *208*; 14. 17. 3: *208*; 14. 17. 5: *207, 208*; 14. 17. 6: *208*; 14. 19. 1: *207*; 14. 23. 1: *93*; 14. 24. 1: *200, 207, 249*
Columella, *De Re Rust.* 1 praef. 20: *126*; 3. 3. 4: *103*
Demosthenes 20. 30–7: *27*; 25. 50–4: *27*; 34. 36–9: *27*
Digest 1. 2. 33: *92*; 3. 4. 1: *229*; 4. 2. 9. 1: *229*; 4. 9: *229*; 5. 1. 52. 1: *191, 245, 247*; 5. 30. 39. 7: *249*; 10. 4. 7. 3: *229*; 14. 1. 1. 3: *125*; 14. 1. 1. 15: *124*; 14. 1. 1. 18: *126*; 14. 2. 2. 1: *125*; 19. 2. 13. 1: *229*; 19. 2. 13. 2: *124*; 19. 2. 31: *133*; 19. 5. 1. 1: *125*; 27. 1. 17. 6: *90*; 31. 49. 1: *191, 245, 249*; 31. 87 pr.: *191, 245, 248*; 32. 35 pr.: *182, 246*; 34. 5. 20: *229*; 40. 3. 1: *229*; 45. 1. 122. 1: *127*; 47. 11. 6 pr.: *154*; 48. 2. 13: *48, 220*; 48. 19. 37: *154*; 50. 4. 3 pr.: *183*; 50. 4. 5: *229*; 50. 5. 3: *17, 123*; 50. 5. 10. 1: *229*; 50. 6. 6. 3: *90, 227*; 50. 6. 6. 6: *91, 229*; 50. 6. 6. 12: *229*
Dio 36. 22: *51*; 39. 9. 2: *53*; 39. 9. 3: *55*; 39. 24. 1: *49, 58, 160, 169, 174*; 41. 18: *58*; 42. 6. 3: *60*; 43. 21. 4: *59, 176*; 43. 51. 3: *59*; 46. 39. 3: *61*; 52. 24. 6: *79, 81*; 54. 1. 4: *62, 180*; 54. 17: *62, 180*; 55. 22. 3: *63*; 55. 26. 1–3: *63, 179, 185*; 55. 28. 1: *63*; 55. 31. 4: *63*; 60. 11. 3: *75*; 60. 24. 3: *48, 76, 222*; 62. 18. 5: *187*; 76. 1. 1: *181*
Diodorus 16. 69. 1: *32*; 36. 12: *47, 162*; 54. 1: *62*; 55. 10. 1: *181*; 57. 14. 2: *181*; 60. 24. 5: *107*
Dion. Halic. 4. 24. 4–5: *49, 160, 169, 174*; 5. 26: *29*; 12. 1–4: *30*
Epictetus 1. 10. 2–5: *79*; 1. 10. 10: *70*

Epit. de Caesaribus 1. 6: *61, 118, 231*; 35. 6: *197*
Expositio totius mundi (Rougé) 65: *106*
Festus p. 392L: *22, 159*; p. 437L: *28*
Frag Vat. 233 (Ulpian): *90, 205, 228, 229*
Frontinus, *De Aqu.* 100: *62, 180, 189*; 108: *190*; 116–18: *195, 216*
Fronto (Naber) p. 210: *185*
Gaius, *Inst.* 1. 28: *90, 228*; 1. 32c: *17, 28, 57, 76, 107, 123*; 1. 34: *90, 228*
Horace, *Odes* 4. 5. 19: *71*
Josephus, *Ant. Iud.* 15. 304–16: *70*; 20. 51: *70*; 20. 101: *70*; *Bell. Iud.* 2. 383–5: *61, 68, 112, 118, 231*; *Vita* 15: *124*
Justinian, *Ed.* 13. 8: *233*
Juvenal, *Sat.* 7. 171: *245*
Licinianus (Flemisch) p. 34: *166*
Livy 2. 9. 6: *29, 31*; 2. 34. 2–5: *29, 31*; 4. 12. 9: *29*; 4. 13–16: *30*; 5. 28. 2: *51*; 6. 6. 1: *36*; 7. 27. 2: *32*; 8. 14: *32*; 9. 30. 4: *32*; 10. 11. 9: *35*; 10. 13: *35*; 22. 11: *33*; 23. 41. 7: *35*; 23. 48–49: *33, 75*; 26. 39. 1: *37*; 26. 40. 15–16: *37*; 27. 5: *37*; 30. 26. 5–6: *35, 67, 150*; 30. 38. 5: *150*; 31. 50: *67*; 33. 42. 8: *44, 67, 150*; 35. 10. 12: *46*; 35. 41. 10: *46*; 36. 2. 12: *44*; 36. 3: *67*; 36. 4. 5: *44*; 37. 2. 12: *44*; 38. 35. 5: *35, 44*; 40. 51. 4–6: *46*; 41. 27. 8: *46*; 43. 2. 12: *107*; *Per.* 55: *164*; 60: *151, 158*; 71: *164*; 104: *55*
Lucian, *Navig.* 5: *17, 123*; 9: *129*
Lydus, *De Mag.* 1. 27: *32*
Orosius 5. 23: *50*
Persius, *Sat.* 5. 73: *247*; 5. 74: *244*
Philo, *In Flaccum* 26: *124*; *Leg. ad Gaium* 23: *185*
Philostratus, *Vit. Apoll. Tyan.* 7. 16: *19*
Plautus, *Rud.* 1014: *124*
Pliny, *N.H.* 3. 59: *36, 102*; 3. 88–91: *64*; 5. 58: *116*; 15. 75: *128*; 18. 15: *35*; 18. 35: *86, 111*; 18. 66: *83, 106, 107, 112, 113*; 18. 87: *45, 102*; 18. 89–90: *153, 239*; 18. 306: *135*; 19. 3–4: *128*; 31. 89: *28*
Pliny, *Ep.* 5. 6. 1: *102*; 10. 27, 28: *85*; *Paneg.* 26–8: *184, 189*; 29. 4–5: *86*; 31: *115*
Plutarch, *Caes.* 8. 6: *52, 170*; 48: *60*; 55: *108, 176*; 58. 10: *59*; *Cat. Min.* 26: *52, 168, 170*; 27. 1: *128*; *C. Gracchus* 2: *160*; 6: *22, 47, 49, 158, 159*; *T. Gracchus* 8. 4–5: *156*; 8. 9: *36*; *Marius* 4: *161*; *Pomp.* 25: *51*; 45: *170*; 49–50: *56, 67, 107*
Polybius 2. 15: *147*; 3. 22: *32*; 3. 24. 9: *32*; 9. 44: *150*; 28. 2: *105*; 34. 8. 7: *147*
Procopius, *Bell. Goth.* 3. 16: *106*
Prudentius, *Contra Symm.* 2. 939–44: *106, 201*; 2. 950: *206*
Sallust, *Cat.* 37: *160, 169, 174*; *Hist.* 1. 55. 11 (Maurenbrecher) (*Oratio Lepidi* 11): *165, 166*; 1. 62 M: *163*; 2. 43 M: *167*; 2. 45 M (Fr. 3 Kurfess): *1, 167*; 2. 47. 6–7 M: *167*; 3. 48. 17–19 M (*Oratio Macri* 17–19): *30, 166*
Salvian 6. 68: *106*
Schol. Bobb. (Stangl) p. 132: *49, 172*
SHA, *Aurelian* 35: *187, 197, 207*; 47: *187*; 48: *197*; *Commodus* 17. 7: *68, 112, 118, 130, 196*; *Marc.* 7. 8: *184, 189*; 26. 6: *184, 189*; *Pesc. Nig.* 7. 4: *221*; *Pius* 8. 1: *184, 189*; 8. 2: *265*; *Alex. Sev.* 22: *197*; 33: *91*; 39. 3: *139*; *Sept. Sev.* 8: *68, 234*; 18: *197*; 23: *198, 234*
Seneca, *De Benef.* 4. 28. 2: *182*; *De Brevit. Vitae* 18. 3: *81, 82, 92*; 18. 5: *74*; 19. 1: *81, 86*; 20. 3: *80*; *Ep.* 77: *71, 72, 75, 118, 129, 209*
Sulpicius Severus, *Dial.* 1. 1. 3: *129*
Sidonius Apollinaris, *Ep.* 1. 10: *199, 201*
Socrates, *Hist. Eccles.* 5. 18: *205*
Statius, *Silvae* 3. 3. 85, 90: *213*; 4. 3. 11–12: *12*
Strabo 3. 144: *107*; 6. 265c: *64*; 6. 273: *106*; 17. 788: *116*; 17. 817: *116*
Suetonius, *Aug.* 16. 1: *61*; 18. 2: *61*; 37: *62, 180*; 40. 2: *63, 181, 185, 186, 244*; 41: *8, 184, 244*; 42. 2–3: *63, 143, 150, 169, 174, 181*; 49. 1: *33*; 98. 2: *71*; 101: *181*; *Caes.* 41. 3: *59, 176, 177, 180*; 42. 1: *59, 176*; *Calig.* 19: *74*; *Claud.* 18–19: *2, 28, 33, 57, 72, 75, 127, 139, 143, 152, 155*; 20. 1: *59*; 24. 2: *48, 222*; *Dom.* 7. 2: *12*; 14. 2: *12*; *Nero* 11: *244*; 16. 1: *76*; 31. 3: *59*; 57: *187*; *Tib.* 8: *48*; 34: *152*; 76: *181, 190*
Symmachus, *Ep.* 3. 5: *201*; 3. 82: *69*; 4. 54: *69*; 7. 63: *69*; *Rel.* 9. 7: *209*; 37. 2: *201*; 40. 4: *201*

Tacitus, *Agric.* 19: *83*; *Ann.* 1. 7: *64*, *80*; 1. 8: *181*; 2. 59: *70*; 2. 87: *72*, *74*, *143*, *152*; 3. 54. 4: *63*; 3. 54. 6–8: *2*, *62*, *74*, *92*, *220*; 4. 5: *71*; 4. 6: *84*; 6. 13: *152*; 11. 31: *80*; 12. 43: *68*, *76*; 12. 45. 6: *194*; 13. 14. 1: *78*; 13. 22: *80*; 13. 51: *76*; 14. 57: *80*; 15. 8. 3: *18*; 15. 18: *213*; 15. 36: *74*; 15. 39. 2: *152*, *187*, *240*; 15. 42: *76*; *Hist.* 1. 4: *187*; 1. 73: *68*; 2. 82: *67*; 3. 8: *67*; 3. 48: *68*; 4. 38: *68*
Theophrastus, *Plants* 8. 7. 6: *97*
Ulpian (Schulz) 3. 6: *76*
Valerius Maximus 3. 7. 3: *164*; 7. 6. 1: *107*
Varro, *R.R.* 1. 2. 6: *102*; 1. 9. 6: *102*, *103*; 1. 44: *103*; 2. 3: *107*, *174*
Vegetius 4. 39: *15*
Velleius Paterculus 1. 15. 4: *108*; 2. 8. 3: *250*; 2. 31: *51*; 2. 77. 1: *61*; 2. 94. 3: *48*
Aurelius Victor, *De Caes.* 13. 5: *90*, *228*; 35. 7: *197*; 41. 19–20: *197*
Xenophon, *Ec.* 20. 27–8: *27*
Zosimus 1. 61: *187*

INDEX OF PAPYRI

BGU 31: 117
104: 117
105: 117
160: 117
172: 117
P. Bouriant 42: 117
P. Lond. 948: 121
P. Oxy. 708: 122
1259: 121
1451: 72
2892: 177
2894: 178
2898: 178
2899: 178
2958: 115, 149

INDEX OF INSCRIPTIONS

Corpus No.	*ILS No.*	*Page*
CIL 1		
206 (FIRA i no. 13)	6085	177, 185, 241
CIL 2		
1180	1403	89, 224, 229
1197	—	85
1970	1341	72
CIL 3		
249	1396	216, 256
1458	—	194
1464	1370	222
6813	1038	194
7127	1421	222
14165/8	6987	91, 223
14195/9	7193–5	65, 84
CIL 5		
8659	1412	221
CIL 6		
85	3399	87
220	2163	188, 189
544	1540	78
634	1540^{a}	78
814	—	143
943	6045	188
1151/31248	707	200
1408	1141	195
1460	887	180
1480	907	180
1648	—	216, 256
1711	—	206
2584	2049	189
8470	1535	218, 221
8473	1705	81
8474–7	1541–4	78
8853	1536	85
9626	7267	87
9683	7488	142
10217	6060	183
10220	6064	189
10221	6063	189
10222	6065	184
10223	6071	192, 215
10224	6069	192
10225	6070	192
10227	6067	184
10228	6066	183, 189
31713	901	85
33747	5914	140
33860	5913	140
33883	7268	87
CIL 8		
5348	1228	200
5351	1435	85
10570/14464	6870	111
12442	1110	195
17891	1055	194
18909	9017	85
25902	—	111
25943	—	111
26416	—	111
CIL 9		
3306	932	195
CIL 10		
1562	344	223
1700	1231	200
1729	—	223
4752	1223	197
5182	972	194
7344	—	194
7580	1358	222
7584	1359	222
8291	1041	194
CIL 11		
20	2082	222
5669	2728	194, 216
6117	—	148
CIL 12		
671	—	221
672	1432	113, 223
4393	7259	125
CIL 14		
131	687	200
160	1428	200, 222
409	6146	222
2045	1534	78, 222
2852	3696	91
3603	6171	48
3608	986	83
4142	6140	91
4234	3417	142
4449	—	200
4620	—	142
Suppl. 4319	—	223
Suppl. 4702	—	47

Corpus No.	*ILS No.*	*Page*
CIL 16		
32	—	72
AEpigr		
(1925) 126b		148
(1939) 60		221
(1940) 99		194
(1942) 105		85
(1952) 225		85
(1971) 23		200
CIG		
5889=*IG Italiae* (Kaibel) 918		72, 129

Corpus No.	*Page*
5973=*IG Italiae* (Kaibel) 919	72, 82, 129
Dittenberger	
Sylloge[3] 976	156
IG	
12 Suppl. no. 348 (*SEG* 17. 417)	123
ILS	
6045	185
9275	183
Tod	
GHI 2. 167	27
200	27

GENERAL INDEX

Abudia Megiste, 142
Actores a frumento, 222
Aediles, 34–6, 81, 150, 157, 258, 259
Aediles Cereales, 59, 62, 180, 186
L. Aelius Seianus, 80
M. Aemilius Lepidus (*cos.* 78 B.C.), 166
M. Aemilius Lepidus, triumvir, 259
M. Aemilius Scaurus (*cos.* 115 B.C.), 47, 162
M. Aemilius Scaurus (*pr.* 56 B.C.), 56
Aerarium, 73, 77, 78, 213, 216
Africa, 13, 33, 64, 83, 91, 96, 154, 168, 264; Italian settlers at Carthage, 44–5, 108–9; Pompey, 52, 56, 58, 259; private corn merchants, 65, 110; relative importance of African and Egyptian corn for Rome, 67–71, 231–5; corn revenues from *ager publicus* and imperial estates, 84, 86, 92, 110–12, 214; overland transport system for grain, 120–1; shippers at Ostia, 69, 126, 226; sea-journey to Italy, 128–30; corn storage pits, 135; *alimenta*, 148; Jugurtha, 162; importance in late Empire, 198, 201, 202–4, 205, 206; personified, 264; *see also* Corn lands, Corn fleets
Ager publicus, 84
Agoranomoi, 35
Agrippa II, 124, 231, 232
Alaric, 199
Alexandria, sea journey to Rome, 14, 15, 124, 128, 129, 131–2, 233; freightage rate to Rome, 14, 150; size of corn ships, 17, 123–4; Neapolis district and its *procurator*, 69, 82, 121–2; Mercurium district and its *procurator*, 82, 121, 221, 224; Germanicus, 70; naval fleet, 71–2, 219; commercial fleet, 19, 72, 75, 82, 129–31; link with Puteoli, 15, 19, 75, 124, 128, 129, 132, 236–8; personified, 264; lighthouse, 265
A libellis, 220
Alimenta, 189
Annona, personified, 77, 260–7
Antinoopolis, 178
Antioch in Pisidia, 148
Antium, 12, 32, 36, 102
Antoninus Pius, Emperor, 184, 189, 220, 223, 265
M. Antonius (*cos.* 99 B.C.), 50
M. Antonius Creticus (*pr.* 74 B.C.), 146, 167, 169
M. Antonius, triumvir, 50, 61, 242, 259
Apothecae, 140
L. Appuleius Saturninus (*tr.* 103 and 100 B.C.), 47, 50, 162, 163, 164, 258
A rationibus, 78, 80, 213, 214, 218, 219
Arca frumentaria, 199, 207
Aristodemus of Cumae, 31
Arles, 91, 92, 113, 223
Armaria, 140
Arno, River, 102
Asia, farming of tithes to *publicani*, 39, 42–4, 45, 49, 160, 172; tax system reformed by Caesar, 60, 72; corn commission of Brutus and Cassius, 60–1, 119; journey, Italy to Asia Minor, 128–9; corn prices, 148, 153; *see also* Corn Lands (h) Eastern Provinces
Athens, 2, 26, 27, 28, 118
Attalids, 43
Sex. Attius Suburanus Aemilianus, 221
P. Aufidius Fortis, 142
Augustus, Emperor, distributions, 8, 10, 60–6, 157, 176, 179–85, 186, 188, 190, 193, 194, 195, 244, 246; manumission laws, 9, 184; naval fleets, 33, 71; *cura annonae*, 48, 62; rise to power, 50; procurement of corn, 10, 60–6; Sicilian tithes abolished, 64, 67; Egypt, 70, 116, 118, 149, 231–5; creates *praefectus annonae*, 63–4, 73, 74, 79; coinage, 75, 259, 260; *collegia*, 88; corn market and prices, 151; water supply, 11, 256
Aurelian, Emperor, 177, 187, 197, 199, 205, 207, 254
Marcus Aurelius, Emperor, 10, 80, 184, 189, 221, 229, 265
Aurelius Agathus Daemon, 177
C. Aurelius Cotta (*cos.* 75 B.C.), 1
M. Aurelius Papirius Dionysius, 220
Aurelius Victorianus, 200
C. Avianius Flaccus, 56–7

Avianius Symmachus, 200
Avidius Cassius, 265, 266

Baiae, 74
Q. Baienus Blassianus, 219
Bakers, 90, 142, 204, 205–6, 207, 208, 228
Barley, 5, 257
Britain, 83

Q. Caecilius Metellus Creticus (*cos.* 69 B.C.), 51, 169
Q. Caecilius Metellus Nepos (*cos.* 57 B.C.), 55
Q. Caecilius Metellus Scipio (*cos.* 52 B.C.), 259
M. Caerellius Iazymis, 142
L. Caesennius Sospes, 215
T. Caesius Primus, 91
L. Calpurnius Piso (*qu.* 100 B.C.), 163, 258
L. Calpurnius Piso Frugi (*cos.* 133 B.C.), 159
Campania, 5, 12, 28, 29, 30, 31, 32, 45, 96, 201; *see also* Corn lands, Italy
M. Camurius Clemens, 216
C. Caninius, 23, 47
Canon frumentarius, 198, 201, 202, 204, 206, 208, 234
Canon olearius, 206
Caracalla, Emperor, 222, 253, 255
Carales, 83, 106, 107
Carthage, 32, 33, 44, 49, 67, 108, 110, 112, 128, 202
C. Cassius Longinus (*cos.* 73 B.C.), 166
C. Cassius Longinus (*pr.* 44 B.C.), 60, 119
P. Cassius Longinus (*pr.* 66 B.C.), 180
Cato, *see* Porcius
Caupones, 141, 142
Centonarii, 227
Cereal crops, 4, 96, 100–1; *see also* Barley, Wheat
Ceres, 34, 74, 77, 81, 258–67
Cilicia, 50, 167
Cimbri, 162
Cincinnatus, Dictator, 30
Classis Augusta Alexandrina, 72, 129
Claudius, Emperor, 90, 143, 152, 236; assaulted in Forum, 1, 76, 155; water supply, 11, 195; harbour at Ostia, 18, 48, 59, 75; privileges for corn merchants, 33, 57, 72, 75, 89, 123, 127, 220; reorganization of corn supply? 73–9, 193, 213–17, 251; coinage, 74, 257, 260, 262
Claudius II, Emperor, 177
Claudius Athenodorus, 218, 221
Claudius Etruscus, 213
Tiberius Claudius Ianuarius, 192, 215
Claudius Julianus, 91
Ti. Claudius Secundinus Macedo, 219
Ti. Claudius Xenophon, 222
Cleander, 80, 196
Cleopatra, 70
Climate, Mediterranean, 96–100
P. Clodius Pulcher (*tr.* 58 B.C.), 49, 52, 58, 157, 158, 169, 170, 171, 172, 173, 174, 186
Sextus Cloelius, 52, 173, 174, 175
P. Cluvius Maximus Paullinus, 194
Codicarii, 87
Coin types, 31, 74, 75, 77, 163, 164, 213, 216, 257–67
Collegia, 87–92, 126, 142, 202, 205–6, 226–30
P. Cominius Clemens, 221
Commodus, Emperor, 68, 71, 80, 112, 118, 129, 195, 196, 219, 220, 254, 255, 263, 266
Compendiaria, 140
Constantine, Emperor, 199, 205
Constantinople, 69, 118, 198, 201, 233, 234
Corn fleets, African, 19, 68, 71, 129–30, 196, 219, 266; Alexandrine, 19, 71, 72, 75, 82, 129–32
Corn lands, Italy, 101–4; Sicily, 104–6; Sardinia, 106–7; Spain, 107–108; Africa, 108–12; Gaul, 112–13; Egypt, 113–18; Eastern Provinces, 118–19
Corn merchants, Greek, 27; in early Republican Rome, 31–4; fined by *aediles*, 35; used by Pompey, 56–7, 173; granted privileges, 57, 72, 76, 88, 220; in Sicily, Africa, Egypt and Spain, 65, 72–3, 108; under the Empire, 86, 87–92, 152; development of *collegia*, 87–92, 226–30; and shippers, 124–7, 150; retail trade, 140–3
L. Cornelius Cinna (*cos.* 87–84 B.C.), 164
P. Cornelius Dolabella (*cos.* 44 B.C.), 242
Faustus Cornelius Sulla (*qu.* 54 B.C.), 258

L. Cornelius Sulla (*cos.* 88 and 80 B.C.), 161, 164, 165, 166
Corpora, see *Collegia*
Q. Cosconius Fronto, 222
Crete, 50, 51, 167
Crispina, 266
L. Critonius (*aed.* 86 B.C.), 258
Cura annonae, Emperor Tiberius' complaint, 2; duty of aediles, 35; Augustus, 48, 62, 179, 180, 186; Pompey, 55–8, 157, 173, 174, 179, 180, 186, 259; *praefectus annonae*, 64, 74, 92, 186, 220; praetors, 180
Curator aquarum et Miniciae, 195, 197, 200, 253–6
C. Curiatius (*tr.* 138 B.C.), 164
Cursus clabularius, 120
C. Curtius Justus, 194
Cyprus, 118, 172
Cyrene, 118, 129, 167, 172

Dardanarii, 154
Decumani, 38–41
Diet, 3–7, 173
Digmata, 122
Dimissoria, 130
Diocletian, Emperor, 14, 199, 267
Diognetus, 236
Dispensatores a frumento, 222, 223
Distributions, of corn, 2, 24, 43, 47, 48, 49, 58, 61, 62, 63, 65, 89, 143, 151, 156–97, 198–208, 213–17, 232, 244–9, 253–6, 258; ration, size of, 10, 49, 159, 166, 173, 232, 242; price of, 151, 159, 160, 163, 164, 166; lists of recipients, 58, 175, 176, 180, 181, 186, 189–91, 244; numbers of recipients, 59, 61, 62, 159, 165, 166, 168, 169–72, 176, 181, 198, 232, 247, 248; admission of Praetorian guard, 181, 183, 188; of Vigiles, 181, 188; of urban cohorts, 181, 188; of children, 183–4, 189; of *tibicines*, 188; of *aeneatores*, 188; see also *Leges frumentariae*
Distributions, of bread, 187, 197, 199, 205, 206–8; of oil, 197, 199, 206; of pork, 197, 199, 206; of wine, 197, 199, 206
Domicilium, 182
Domitian, Emperor, 12, 148, 215, 251, 261, 262, 263, 264, 266
A. Domitius Sincaius, 57
Domitius Ulpianus, 220
'Dry-farming', 100–1
Duumviri navales, 32

Egypt, 26, 64, 89, 150, 154, 209, 220; Praefect of, 61, 70, 80, 82, 116, 221; land and water transport, 13, 116, 120–2; captured by Octavian, 61, 114; private corn trade, 65; relative importance of Egyptian and African corn for Rome, 67–71, 231–5; corn taxes and rents, 72, 117; corn administration, 82, 116–18; imperial estates, 92, 117; *digmata*, 122; corn stores, 135; corn prices, 148–9; corn for Constantinople, 198, 201; *tablai*, 244, 246; *see also* Alexandria, Corn fleets, Corn lands, Nile
Eirenaios, 130
Elagabalus, Emperor, 253, 255, 266
Emporoi, *see* Corn merchants
Ephesus, 43
Estates, imperial, 84, 86, 110, 111–12
Etruria, 5, 11, 28, 29, 30, 33, 36, 45; *see also* Corn lands, Italy

L. Fabius Cilo Septimius Catinius Acilianus Lepidus, 254
Q. Fabius Maximus (*aed.* 299 B.C.), 35
Fabri tignuarii, 227
Sextus Fadius Musa, 125
L. Faenius Rufus, 80, 218
Famine, 1, 29, 44, 45, 49, 50, 51, 53, 55, 62, 63, 74, 115, 144, 150, 167, 198, 199, 201
M. Fannius (*aed.* 86 B.C.), 258
Far, 6
Faustina, 184
Faustina II, 265
Festus, *tabellarius*, 81
Fiscus, 73, 77, 78, 85, 203, 213, 216
Fiscus frumentarius, 78, 199
Fiscus frumentarius Ostiensis, 222
C. Flaminius (*cos.* 187 B.C.), 44
T. Flavius Macer, 85
Flour, prices of, 153, 239–40
Forum Sempronii, 148
Frumentationes, *see* Distributions
Frumentatores, *see* Corn merchants
Frumentum mancipale, 65, 84–5
Frumentum publicum, 182–5, 187, 188, 191, 192, 247, 248; *see also* Distributions

Q. Fulvius Flaccus (*pr.* 215 B.C.), 35
M. Fulvius Nobilior (*cos.* 189 B.C.), 46

A. Gabinius (*cos.* 58 B.C.), 51
Gaius, Emperor, 74, 75, 124, 236
Galba, Emperor, 187, 188, 261
Gaul, 112–13, 201, 223; *see also* Corn lands
Geography, Mediterranean, 94–100
Germanicus Julius Caesar, 70
Germany, 201
Gildo, 199
Gordian III, Emperor, 193, 195, 254, 255
Gracchus, *see* Sempronius
Gradus, 208
Grammateus siteresiou, 177
Granaries, see *Horrea*
Gratian, Emperor, 201
Greece, 26–8, 59, 135, 156–7

Hadrian, Emperor, 119, 229, 263, 264
Hannibal, 32, 33, 36, 37, 67, 150
Hanseatic traders, 56
Helena of Adiabene, 70
Heraclea, 241, 242
Herod Agrippa, 124
Herod the Great, 70
Hesicus, 236
Hiero II of Syracuse, 37, 105
Hispalis, 85, 224
Horrea, 159, 185, 204; types, 136–8; raised floors, 137–8; military, 138; ownership, 139–40; leases (see also *locatio-conductio*), 139–40, 236–8; *see also* under Rome, Ostia, Portus, Puteoli
Horrearii, 87, 139, 141
Hypomnematographus, 178

Incisi, 184, 189
Intercolumnia, 140, 236
Isis Giminiana, 133

Judaea, 218, 231, 232
Jugurtha, 162
Julia, wife of Titus, 263
C. Julius Caesar, 54, 157; planned harbour at Ostia, 18, 75; civil war with Pompey, 50, 58; corn supply and distributions reorganized, 59–60, 175–9, 180, 181, 182, 185, 186, 190, 192 (see also *Recensus*, *Subsortitio*); Numidia, 108; Gaul, 112; Table of Heraclea, 241–2; coinage, 259
T. Iulius Eunus Primianus, 236
Sextus Julius Possessor, 224
M. Julius Romulus, 215
Iulius Ursus, 221
L. Julius Vehilius Gratus Julianus, 80, 219
M. Junius Brutus (*pr.* 44 B.C.), 60, 119
M. Junius Faustus, 91
C. Iunius Flavianus, 219
Ius gladii, 200
Justinian, Emperor, 127, 233

Kapeloi, 141

L. Laberius Maximus, 218
Laodicea, 43
Latium, 1, 5, 11, 102, 103, 150, 201, 211; *see also* Corn Lands, Italy
Leges frumentariae, 157–86; *Aemilia*, 166, 168; *Appuleia*, 162–4; *Clodia*, 172, 174, 186; *Livia*, 164–5; *Octavia*, 161–5; *Porcia*, 168–72; *Sempronia*, 48, 49, 156, 158–61, 162, 163, 164, 165, 172; *Terentia-Cassia*, 45, 166–8, 171
P. Cornelius Lentulus Spinther (*cos.* 57 B.C.), 55
Leontini, 103, 104
Lex Fufia Caninia, 184
Lex Gabinia, 169
Lex Hieronica, 38
Lex horreorum, 140
Lex Papia Poppaea, 76
C. Licinius Macer (*tr.* 73 B.C.), 166
C. Licinius Sacerdos (*pr.* 75 B.C.), 146
Livia, Empress, 260
M. Livius Drusus (*tr.* 91 B.C.), 164, 165
Loca armaris, 140
Locatio-conductio, 139–40; see also *Horrea*, leases
Lollii, 22
Lucilla, 184
Lucius Verus, 184, 229
Lugdunum, 218, 219

Macedonia, 119, 201
Mactar, 224
Maecenas, 79
Spurius Maelius (*tr.* 436 B.C.), 30, 31
Mallia Aemiliana, 183
Malta, 51, 129, 132, 167
Mancipes, 41, 84

T. Manlius Torquatus (*cos.* 235 B.C.), 35
Manumission of slaves, 160, 168–9, 174, 176, 184, 186, 248
M. Marcius, *monetalis*, 258
C. Marius (*cos.* 107, 104–100, 86 B.C.), 109, 161, 162, 164
Masinissa, 44
Maximinus, Emperor, 253, 255, 266
Mensae oleariae, 207
Mensores frumentarii, 20, 86, 204, 207, 229; *mensores machinarii frumenti publici*, 86
Mercatores frumentarii, *see* Corn merchants
Messina, 128, 129, 167
C. Messius (*aed.* 55 B.C.), 55
Metelli, 162; *see also* Caecilius
M. Mettius Rufus, 221
C. Minicius Italus, 218, 219
L. Minucius Esquilinus Augurinus (*cos.* 458 B.C.), 30–1, 251
C. Minucius Augurinus, *monetalis*, 258
M. Minucius Rufus (*cos.* 110 B.C.), 250
Misenum, 71, 219
Mithridates VI, 50, 167
Modius castrensis, 14
Moesia, 83, 183, 194
Molendarii, 206
Myra, 119, 129, 131

Naeratius Cerealis, 200
Narbo, 223
Nardus, 238
Naukleroi, *see* Shippers
Naves codicariae, 19, 46, 142, 204
Naves tabellariae, 71, 130
Navicularii, *see* Shippers
Navy, Roman, 32–3, 71–2
Negotiatores frumentarii, *see* Corn merchants
Nero, Emperor, 68, 75, 143, 233, 244; canal from Lake Avernus to Ostia, 59, 76; coinage, 77, 257, 260–1, 263, 266; African estates, 86, 111; privileges for corn merchants, 89; fire of Rome A.D. 64, and suspension of distributions, 152, 187–8, 240; corn for Praetorian guard, 181; annual financial subvention of state, 213, 214, 215
Nerva, Emperor, 74, 213, 214, 216, 261, 263
Nile, River, 69, 82, 83, 96, 113, 114–16, 121, 122, 133, 149, 219; nilometers, 116
Gaius Novius Cypaerus, 236
Gaius Novius Eunus, 236, 237
Numidia, 44, 85, 108, 110

L. Octavius (*cos.* 75 B.C.), 1
M. Octavius Cn. f. (*tr.* 90s B.C.?), 161, 162, 163, 164, 165
Olbia, 56, 106
Origo, 182–4, 247
Ostia, 17, 28, 88, 93, 106, 110, 128, 129, 187, 204, 224; Piazzale delle Corporazioni, 69, 83, 107, 109, 113, 126, 226–7; *horrea*, 21, 23, 136–8, 139, 196; river harbour, 23, 33, 45, 47; *quaestor*, 48, 76, 222; plundered by pirates, 51, 169; *annona* office, 78, 222–3; *mensores frumentarii*, 86; retail trade, 142; controlled by *praefectus annonae* in late Empire, 200; Claudian harbour (*see also* Portus), 18, 19, 20, 23, 59, 75, 76, 77, 89, 199; Trajanic Harbour (*see also* Portus), 18, 19, 23, 75, 137, 199
Otho, Emperor, 261
Oxyrhynchus, corn dole, 177–8, 190, 246, 248

Pacceius, *quaestor Ostiensis*, 48
Palestine, 148, 153
Pallas, freedman, 78
Panis gradilis, 208
Panis popularis, 208
Paphlagonia, 85
Patara, 119
Paul, St., 119, 131–2
Sextus Peducaeus (*pr.* 77 B.C.), 146
Pergamum, 42, 119
Pescennius Niger, Emperor, 68
M. Petronius Honoratus, 218
Philip the Arab, Emperor, 193, 254
Piracy, 17, 33, 50–3, 71, 162, 167, 169
Pistores, *see* Bakers
Furius Placidus, 200
Ti. Plautius Silvanus Aelianus, 83
Plebs frumentaria, 62, 63, 185 (*see also* Distributions)
Po, River, 101, 103, 147, 153 (*see also* Corn lands, Italy)
Polenta, 5
Pompeii, 140, 236

Cn. Pompeius Magnus (*cos.* 70, 55 and 52 B.C.), 54, 67, 170, 185, 251; civil war with Caesar, 50; pirate command, 51–2, 169; *cura annonae*, 53, 55–8, 66, 107, 126, 157, 173–5, 179, 186, 259
Sextus Pompeius, 50, 61
Pompeius Paulinus, 82, 213, 218
Pomptine marshes, 12, 29, 102
Pontifical annals, 29
M. Porcius Cato 'Censorius' (*cos.* 195 B.C.), 128
M. Porcius Cato Uticensis (*pr.* 54 B.C.), 52, 168, 169, 170, 171, 172, 259
Portoria, 40, 42, 84
Portus, 19, 23, 93, 122, 137, 139, 200, 203, 204, 223 (*see also* Ostia, Claudian harbour and Trajanic harbour)
Posidonius (Triadelphus), 121
Praedia pistoria, 205
Praefectus annonae, office created by Augustus, 48, 63–4, 66, 74, 180, 186; relations with shippers and merchants, 73, 89, 90, 91, 93, 126; subordinate officials, 48, 76, 221–5; *fiscus frumentarius*, 78; role and duties, 79–93, 112, 152, 194, 213, 214; subordinate to *praefectus urbi* in late Empire, 199–208; career structure, 79–81, 218–21; *adiutor*, 221, 224; *subpraefectus*, 199, 221, 222
Praefectus annonae Africae, 93, 112, 202, 203
Praefectus annonae Alexandrinae, 93
Praefecti frumenti dandi, 62, 180, 189, 193–5, 213–17, 253–6; *scribae*, 189; *librarii*, 189; *accensi*, 189
Praefecti Miniciae, 195, 253–6
Praefectus praetorio, 79, 80, 93, 112, 202, 203, 220, 221
Praefectus urbi, 23, 93, 199–208
Praefectus vigilum, 220
Praepositi horreorum, 202
Prices, corn, 35, 44, 47, 49, 52, 53, 54, 64, 72, 74, 143–55, 169–72, 187, 258
Privileges, granted to corn merchants and shippers, 57, 76, 88–91, 107, 220, 230
Procurator Augusti ad annonam provinciae Narbonensis et Liguriae, 223
Procurator ad Mercurium, 82, 121, 221, 224
Procurator Augusti ad Minuciam, 194, 216
Procuratores a frumento, 222
Procurator annonae Ostis, 48, 76, 200n., 219, 222, 224, 227
Procurator Minuciae, 216, 256
Procurator Neaspoleos, 69, 82, 83, 121
Procurator portus Ostiensis, 48, 76, 222
Procurator tractus Numidiae a frumentis, 85
Procurement, of corn, importance of, 2–3, 24; under Republic, 26–54; Pompey, Caesar and Augustus, 55–66; under early Empire, 67–93; under late Empire, 198–209; areas with corn surpluses, 94–119, 231–5; transport, storage and prices, 120–55
Proximus commentariorum annonae, 223
Ptolemies, 69, 113, 114, 116
Publicani, 39, 40, 42, 43, 60, 84
Puls, 5
Puteoli, traffic with East, 15, 23, 71, 75, 76, 86, 89, 124, 128, 129, 130, 132, 136, 142, 209, 223; natural harbour, 18, 47; warehouses to let, 22, 126, 139, 140, 236–8; shippers' offices, 126; *Horrea Bassiana*, 236–7

Quaestores classici, 32, 47
Quaestor Ostiensis, 47, 48, 62, 76, 162, 222, 258

Rainfall, Mediterranean, 98–9, 109, 114
Ravenna, 71, 219
Receipts, shippers', 121–2, 127, 139, 203, 204
Recensus, 175, 176, 181, 184
Rhodes, 105, 119, 129
Rhodian Sea Law, 127
Rome, position of, 1, 28–9; size of population of, 8–11, 166, 232; Marble Plan of, 21, 136, 137, 141, 251, 252; Fire of (A.D. 64), 76, 84, 152, 187, 188; retail trade, 140–3, 237; corn prices, 149–55, 237, 239–40; water supply, 3, 11, 158, 189, 190, 195, 196, 197, 211, 216, 253–6; water-mills, 206, 207; Emporium district, 19, 46, 138, 139, 140, 143, 199, 251, 252; Forum Boarium, 45, 81, 141; Forum Holitorium, 45, 141; *Horrea Galbana*, 22, 23, 137, 139, 140, 141, 199; *Horrea Lolliana*, 22; *Horrea Agrippiana*, 136, 141; (*Horrea*) *Aemiliana*, 139n.; *macella*, 141; Porticus Aemilia, 46,

138, 251, 252; Porticus Minucia, 77, 143, 158, 159, 192–7, 213–17, 246, 250–2, 253–6; *Statio Annonae*, 81; *Vicus Frumentarius*, 143
Russia, southern, 26, 96

Saburarii, 20
Saccarii, 20, 87, 133, 138, 204
Sailing season, 15, 128, 202
Salvius Julianus, 220
Samos, 156
Sardinia, 33, 64, 128, 150, 154, 168, 201; tithe system, 13, 37, 44; T. Manlius Torquatus (*propraetor* 215 B.C.), 35; Pompey, 52, 56, 57, 67; Caesar, 58, 59; shippers at Ostia, 83, 91; *see also* Corn lands
Scriptura, 40, 42
Sejanus, *see* Aelius
C. Sempronius Gracchus (*tr.* 123, 122 B.C.), state granaries, 22, 47, 53, 138; tax contracts in Asia, 42; corn distributions, 2, 30, 43, 47, 48, 151, 156–65, 172; settlers at Carthage, 44, 108
Tiberius Sempronius Gracchus (*tr.* 133 B.C.), 12, 30, 36
Seneca, the younger, 117
L. Sergius Catilina (*pr.* 68 B.C.), 169
C. Servilius Ahala (*mag. equ.* 439 B.C.), 30, 31
Q. Servilius Caepio (*qu.* 100 B.C.), 163, 164, 258
P. Servilius Vatia Isauricus (*cos.* 79 B.C.), 50, 167
Servius Tullius, 192
Septimius Severus, Emperor, 68, 79, 82, 88, 129, 136, 158, 181, 197, 222, 234, 253, 255, 261, 263, 266
Alexander Severus, Emperor, 91, 139, 195, 253, 255, 266
Sextia Saturnina, 184
Shippers, 25, 72–3, 83, 87–93, 107, 124–7, 129–32, 141–3, 202–4, 223, 224, 226–30, 263, 266
Ships, ownership of, 17, 124–5; sizes of, 17, 19, 123–4, 223
Sicily, 33, 44, 51, 52, 53, 67, 83, 150, 154, 220, 232; source of corn in early Republic, 12, 29; source of corn for Greeks, 26; Roman province, 12, 32, 37; corn tithe system, 37–42, 45, 120, 126, 143, 160, 166, 167, 168; reformed, 60, 64–5, 72, 84; Pompey, 56–8; Caesar, 59–61; Sextus Pompeius, 61; Augustus, 64–5; fertility, 96, 99; corn prices, 145–7, 153; Second Slave War, 162; in late Empire, 201; *see also* Corn lands
Siligo, 7, 102, 239
Sitagertai, 242
Sitologoi, 121
Soranus of Ephesus, 7
Spain, 12, 35, 36, 54, 67, 201; freightage rate from Syria, 14; *frumentum mancipale*, 84, 85; *vicesima*, 107; oil trade, 125, 207, 227; storage pits, 135; corn prices, 147; *see also* Corn lands
Spartacus, 45, 50, 168
State, intervention in supply of corn, 2, 28, 34, 37, 48, 51, 53, 55, 61–4, 66, 67–92, 122, 143, 152, 218–25, 226–30 (*see also* Procurement of corn); intervention in distribution of corn, 2, 48, 52, 59, 62, 156–97, 213–17, 244–9, 250–6 (*see also* Distributions); control of whole corn supply system, 87, 198–209 (see also *Collegia*); propaganda about corn supply on coins, 257–67 (*see also* Coin types)
Storage, corn, 21–4, 47, 53, 134–43, 150, 159; in ships, 132–4; in pits, 135 (see also *Horrea*)
Subsortitio, 177–9, 180, 190, 241–3, 247, 248
Sulpicii Galbae, 22, 139
C. Sulpicius Faustus, 238
Syria, 14, 119, 128

Tabellarius ex officio annonae, 81
Tablai, 246
Table of Heraclea, 177, 185, 241–3
Taxes, 84, 156, 201–4, 208; Corn taxes: Sardinia, Sicily (*decumae*), 37–42, 43, 44, 45, 53, 67, 105, 106, 160, 166–8 (reformed by Caesar or Augustus, 60, 64–5, 72, 84); Asia (*decumae*) 42–5, 49, 160 (reformed by Caesar, 60, 72); Egypt, 61, 116–18; Africa, 44, 111–112, 201, 214–15, 234 (*frumentum mancipale*, 84); Spain (*vicesima*), 107 (*frumentum mancipale*, 84); Oil tax, 197, 206–7
Q. Terentius Priscianus, 184
M. Terentius Varro Lucullus (*cos.* 73 B.C.), 166

Terracina, 59
Tesserae frumentariae, 62, 186, 191, 208, 244–9
Teutones, 162
Thasos, 123
Theodosius I, Emperor, 205
Thracian Chersonese, 119
Tiber, River, 1, 17–20, 23, 45, 46, 81, 102, 133, 141, 203, 251
Tiberius, Emperor, 2, 48, 62, 63, 70, 72, 75, 80, 84, 151, 152, 181, 187, 236, 259, 260
Titus, Emperor, 143, 188, 262, 263, 266
Titus Titius, 56
Trajan, Emperor, 89, 193, 213, 216; harbour at Ostia, 18, 75; corn buying for *annona*, 85; privileges for bakers, 90, 205, 228; *collegia*, 89–91, 205, 228, 229; Trajan's Market, 141; *alimenta*, 148; generosity in distributions, 181, to boys, 184, 189; coinage, 264, 265, 266
Transhumance, 95–6
Transport, land, 13–20, 103, 120–1; water, 14–20, 70–1, 116, 119, 120–34, 149–50
Tripolitania, 197
M. Tullius Cicero (*cos.* 63 B.C.), 61, 64, 125; prosecution of Verres, 38–42, 105, 145–7, 166, 167, 168; Pompey's *cura annonae*, 53, 55–7; *Pro lege Manilia*, 67; *lex Octavia* approved of, 161; cost and effect of the *lex Clodia*, 169–73
Quintus Tullius Cicero (*pr.* 62 B.C.), 55, 56
C. Turranius, 63, 80, 218
Turris, 107
Tyre, 126

Ulpius Saturninus, 224
Ulpius Victor, 222
C. Ummidius Quadratus, 194
Urinatores, 20

Valentinian I, Emperor, 200, 202, 207
L. Valerius Proculus, 219
Q. Varius Geminus, 195
Veneria Sicca, 110, 148
C. Verres (*pr.* 74 B.C.), 38–42, 51, 105, 145–7, 166, 167
Vespasian, Emperor, 67, 68, 112, 218, 261, 262, 263, 264
C. Vibius Salutaris, 84
Vicarius urbis Romae, 202
Vilicus, 139
M. Vipsanius Agrippa, 256
Vitellius, Emperor, 261
L. Volusius Maecianus, 220

Wheat, 5; varieties of, 6–7, 102, 112; yields, 102–4